# The Greek Way

---

# The Roman Way

# THE GREEK WAY

# THE ROMAN WAY

*Two Volumes in One*

## Edith Hamilton

BONANZA BOOKS
*New York*

This 1986 edition is published by Bonanza Books, distributed by Crown Publishers, Inc., 225 Park Avenue South, New York, New York 10003, by arrangement with W. W. Norton & Company, Inc.

Printed and Bound in the United States of America

Library of Congress Cataloging in Publication Data

Hamilton, Edith, 1867-1963.
    The Greek way/The Roman way.

    Reprint (1st work). Originally published: New York : Norton, c1930.
    Reprint (2nd work). Originally published: New York : Norton, c1932.
    1. Greece—Civilization—To 146 B.C.   2. Greek literature—History and criticism.   3. Rome—Civilization.   4. Latin literature—History and criticism.
I. Hamilton, Edith, 1867-1963.   Roman way.   1986.
II. Title.
DF77.H34   1986        938        86-9695
ISBN 0-517-61809-5

h g f e d c b a

# CONTENTS

# Volume One

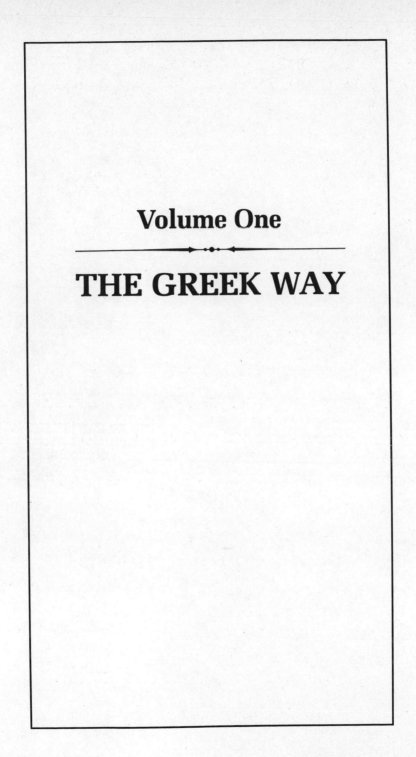

# THE GREEK WAY

TO

DORIS FIELDING REID

Κοινὰ τὰ τῶν φίλων

# CONTENTS

# PREFACE

THE FIRST edition of *The Greek Way* was an incomplete work. A number of the writers of the great age of Greece were discussed in it, but others quite as notable and important were omitted. The result was a picture of Greek thought and art at the time of their highest achievement with some of the very greatest thought and art left out; the poet Pindar, for instance, put by the Greeks themselves in the same class with Æschylus; the two historians, Herodotus and Thucydides, still foremost among the historians of the world. There cannot, indeed, be any real perception of the breadth and depth and splendor of the intellectual life in fifth-century Athens without some knowledge of Herodotus with his keen curiosity and warm humanity, and the profundity of thought and somber magnificence of Thucydides.

The present volume has made good the former omissions. All the writers of the Periclean age are considered.

I have felt while writing these new chapters a fresh realization of the refuge and strength the past can be to us in the troubled present. "Let us keep our silent sanctuaries," Sénancour wrote, "for in them the eternal perspectives are preserved." Religion is the great stronghold for the untroubled vision of the eternal; but there are others too. We have many silent sanctuaries in which we can find a breathing space to free ourselves from the personal, to rise above our harassed and perplexed minds and catch sight of values that are stable, which no selfish and timorous preoccupations can make waver, because they are the hard-won and permanent possession of humanity. "Excellence," said Aristotle, "much labored for by the race of men."

When the world is storm-driven and the bad that happens and the worse that threatens are so urgent as to shut out everything else from view, then we need to know all the strong fortresses of the spirit which men have built through the ages. The eternal perspectives are being blotted out, and our judgment of immediate issues will go wrong unless we bring them back. We can do so only, Socrates said in the last talk before his death, "when we seek the region of purity and eternity and unchangeableness, where when the spirit enters, it is not hampered or hindered, but ceases to wander in error, beholding the true and divine (which is not matter of opinion.)"

A great French scholar of the last century said to his class at the Collège de France shortly after Sedan and the triumphant occupation of Paris by the German army:

> Gentlemen, as we meet here today we are in a free country, the republic of letters, a country which has no national boundaries, where there is neither Frenchman nor German, which knows prejudice nor intolerance, where one thing alone is value, truth in all her manifold aspects. I propose to study with you this year the works of the great poet and thinker, Goethe.

How noble and how tranquilizing. The eternal perspectives open out, clear and calm. Intolerance, hatred—how false they look and how petty.

"Beyond the last peaks and all seas of the world" stands the serene republic of what Plato calls "the fair and immortal children of the mind." We need to seek that silent sanctuary to-day. In it there is one place distinguished even above the others for sanity and balance of thought—the literature of ancient Greece.

> Greece and her foundations are
> Built below the tide of war,
> Based on the crystalline sea
> Of thought and its eternity.

# *Chapter* I

## EAST AND WEST

FIVE hundred years before Christ in a little town on the far western border of the settled and civilized world, a strange new power was at work. Something had awakened in the minds and spirits of the men there which was so to influence the world that the slow passage of long time, of century upon century and the shattering changes they brought, would be powerless to wear away that deep impress. Athens had entered upon her brief and magnificent flowering of genius which so molded the world of mind and of spirit that our mind and spirit to-day are different. We think and feel differently because of what a little Greek town did during a century or two, twenty-four hundred years ago. What was then produced of art and of thought has never been surpassed and very rarely equalled, and the stamp of it is upon all the art and all the thought of the Western world. And yet this full stature of greatness came to pass at a time when the mighty cilivilzations of the ancient world had perished and the shadow of "effortless barbarism" was dark upon the earth. In that black and fierce world a little centre of white-hot spiritual energy was at work. A new civilization had arisen in Athens, unlike all that had gone before.

What brought this new development to pass, how the Greeks were able to achieve all they did, has significance for us to-day. It is not merely that Greece has a claim upon our attention because we are by our spiritual and mental inheritance partly Greek and cannot escape if we would that deep influence which worked with power through the centuries, touching with light of reason and grace of beauty the wild Northern savages. She has a direct contribution for us as well. The actual Greek remains are so few and so far away, so separated from us by space and a strange, difficult language, they are felt to be matters for the travellers and the scholars and no more. But in truth what the Greeks discovered, or rather how they made their discoveries and how they brought a new world to birth out of the dark confusions of an old world that had crumbled away, is full of meaning for us to-day who have seen an old world swept away in the space of a decade or two. It is worth our while in the confusions and bewilderments of the present to consider the way by which the Greeks arrived at the clarity of their thought and the affirmation of their art. Very different conditions of life confronted them from those we face, but it is ever to be borne in mind that though the outside of human life changes much, the inside changes little, and the lesson-book we cannot graduate from is human experience. Great literature, past or present, is the expression of great knowledge of the human heart; great art is the expression of a solution of the conflict between the demands of the world without and that within; and in the wisdom of either there would seem to be small progress.

Of all that the Greeks did only a very small part has come down to us and we have no means of knowing if we have their best. It would be strange if we had. In the convulsions of that world of long ago there was no law that guaranteed to art the survival of the fittest. But this little remnant preserved by the haphazard of chance shows the high-water mark reached in every region of thought and beauty the Greeks entered. No sculpture comparable to theirs; no buildings ever more beautiful; no writings superior. Prose, always late of development, they had time only to touch upon, but they left masterpieces. History has yet to find a greater exponent than Thucydides; outside of the Bible there is no poetical prose that can touch Plato. In poetry they are all but supreme; no epic is to be mentioned with Homer; no odes to be set beside Pindar; of the four masters of the tragic stage three are Greek. Little is left of all this wealth of great art: the sculptures, defaced and broken into bits, have crumbled away; the buildings are fallen; the paintings gone forever; of the writings, all lost but a very few. We have only the ruin of what was; the world has had no more than that for well on to two thousand years; yet these few remains of the mighty structure have been a challenge and an incitement to men ever since and they are among our possessions to-day which we value as most precious. There is no danger now that the world will not give the Greek genius full recognition. Greek achievement is a fact universally acknowledged.

The causes responsible for this achievement, however, are not so generally understood. Rather is it the fashion nowadays to speak of the Greek miracle, to consider the radiant bloom of Greek genius as having no root in any soil that we can give an account of. The anthropologists are busy, indeed, and ready to transport us back into the savage forest where all human things, the Greek things, too, had their beginnings; but the seed never explains the flower. Between those strange rites they point us to through the dim vistas of far-away ages, and a Greek tragedy, there lies a gap they cannot help us over. The easy way out is to refuse to bridge it and dismiss the need to explain by calling the tragedy a miracle, but in truth the way across is not impassable; some reasons appear for the mental and spiritual activity which made those few years in Athens productive as no other age in history has been.

By universal consent the Greeks belong to the ancient world. Wherever the line is drawn by this or that historian between the old and the new the Greeks' unquestioned position is in the old. But they are in it as a matter of centuries only; they have not the hall-marks that give title to a place there. The ancient world, in so far as we can reconstruct it, bears everywhere the same stamp. In Egypt, in Crete, in Mesopotamia, wherever we can read bits of the story, we find the same conditions: a despot enthroned, whose whims and passions are the determining factor in the state; a wretched, subjugated populace; a great priestly organization to which is handed over the domain of the intellect. This is what we know as the Oriental state to-day. It has persisted down from the ancient world through thousands of years, never changing in any essential. Only

in the last hundred years—less than that—it has shown a
semblance of change, made a gesture of outward conformity with the demands of the modern world. But the
spirit that informs it is the spirit of the East that never
changes. It has remained the same through all the ages
down from the antique world, forever aloof from all that
is modern. This state and this spirit were alien to the
Greeks. None of the great civilizations that preceded them
and surrounded them served them as model. With them
something completely new came into the world. They were
the first Westerners; the spirit of the West, the modern
spirit, is a Greek discovery and the place of the Greeks is
in the modern world.

The same cannot be said of Rome. Many things there
pointed back to the old world and away to the East, and
with the emperors who were gods and fed a brutalized
people full of horrors as their dearest form of amusement,
the ancient and the Oriental state had a true revival. Not
that the spirit of Rome was of the Eastern stamp. Common-
sense men of affairs were its product to whom the cogita-
tions of Eastern sages ever seemed the idlest nonsense.
"What is truth?" said Pilate scornfully. But it was equally
far removed from the Greek spirit. Greek thought, science,
mathematics, philosophy, the eager investigation into the
nature of the world and the ways of the world which was
the distinguishing mark of Greece, came to an end for
many a century when the leadership passed from Greece
to Rome. The classical world is a myth in so far as it is
conceived of as marked by the same characteristics. Athens
and Rome had little in common. That which distinguishes
the modern world from the ancient, and that which divides
the West from the East, is the supremacy of mind in the
affairs of men, and this came to birth in Greece and lived
in Greece alone of all the ancient world. The Greeks were
the first intellectualists. In a world where the irrational had
played the chief role, they came forward as the protagonists
of the mind.

The novelty and the importance of this position are
difficult for us to realize. The world we live in seems to us
a reasonable and comprehensible place. It is a world of

definite facts which we know a good deal about. We have
found out a number of rules by which the dark and tremendous forces of nature can be made to move so as to
further our own purposes, and our main effort is devoted
to increasing our power over the outside material of the
world. We do not dream of questioning the importance of
what acts, on the whole, in ways we can explain and turn
to our advantage. What brings about this attitude is the
fact that, of all the powers we are endowed with, we are
making use pre-eminently of the reason. We are not soaring
above the world on the wings of the imagination or searching into the depths of the world within each one of us by
the illumination of the spirit. We are observing what goes
on in the world around us and we are reasoning upon our
observations. Our chief and characteristic activity is that
of the mind. The society we are born into is built upon the
idea of the reasonable, and emotional experience and intuitive perception are accorded a place in it only if some
rational account can be given of them.

When we find that the Greeks, too, lived in a reasonable
world as a result of using their reason upon it, we accept
the achievement as the natural thing that needs no comment. But the truth is that even to-day our point of view
obtains only within strict limits. It does not belong to the
immense expanse and the multitudinous populations of the
East. There what goes on outside of a man is comparatively
unimportant and completely undeserving of the attention of
the truly wise. The observing reason which works on what
we of the West call the facts of the real world, is not
esteemed in the East. This conception of human values has
come down from antiquity. The world in which Greece
came to life was one in which the reason had played the
smallest role; all that was important in it belonged to the
realm of the unseen, known only to the spirit.

That is a realm in which outside fact, everything that
makes up this visible, sensible, audible world, plays only
an indirect part. The facts of the spirit are not seen or felt
or heard; they are experienced; they are peculiarly a man's
own, something that he can share with no one else. An
artist can express them in some sort, partially at best. The

saint and the hero who are most at home in them can put them into words—or pictures or music—only if they are artists, too. The greatest intellect cannot do that through the intellect. And yet every human being has a share in the experiences of the spirit.

Mind and spirit together make up that which separates us from the rest of the animal world, that which enables a man to know the truth and that which enables him to die for the truth. A hard and fast distinction between the two can hardly be made; both belong to the part of us which, in Platonic phraseology, draws us up from that which is ever dragging down or, in the figure Plato is fondest of, that which gives form to the formless. But yet they are distinct. When St. Paul in his great definition says that the things that are seen are temporal and the things that are not seen are eternal, he is defining the realm of the mind, the reason that works from the visible world, and the realm of the spirit that lives by the invisible.

In the ancient world before Greece the things that are not seen had become more and more the only things of great importance. The new power of mind that marked Greece arose in a world facing toward the way of the spirit. For a brief period in Greece East and West met; the bias toward the rational that was to distinguish the West, and the deep spiritual inheritance of the East, were united. The full effect of this meeting, the immense stimulus to creative activity given when clarity of mind is added to spiritual power, can be best realized by considering what had happened before Greece, what happens, that is, when there is great spiritual force with the mind held in abeyance. This is to be seen most clearly in Egypt where the records are fullest and far more is known than about any other nation of antiquity. It is materially to the point, therefore, to leave Greece for a moment and look at the country which had had the greatest civilization of all the ancient world.

In Egypt the centre of interest was the dead. The ruling world-power, a splendid empire—and death a foremost preoccupation. Countless numbers of human beings for countless numbers of centuries thought of death as that which was nearest and most familiar to them. It is an

extraordinary circumstance which could be made credible
by nothing less considerable than the immense mass of
Egyptian art centred in the dead. To the Egyptian the
enduring world of reality was not the one he walked in
along the paths of every-day life but the one he should
presently go to by the way of death.

There were two causes working in Egypt to bring about
this condition. The first was human misery. The state of
the common man in the ancient world must have been
wretched in the extreme. Those tremendous works that
have survived through thousands of years were achieved
at a cost in human suffering and death which was never
conceived of as a cost in anything of value. Nothing so
cheap as human life in Egypt and in Nineveh, as nothing
more cheap in India and China to-day. Even the well-to-do,
the nobles and the men of affairs, lived with a very narrow
margin of safety. An epitaph extant of a great Egyptian
noble holds him up to admiration in that he was never
beaten with whips before the magistrate. The lives and
fortunes of all were completely dependent upon the whims
of a monarch whose only law was his own wish. One has
but to read the account Tacitus gives of what happened
under the irresponsible despotism of the early Roman
emperors to realize that in the ancient world security must
have been the rarest of goods.

In such conditions men, seeing little hope for happiness
in this world, turned instinctively to find comfort in another. Only in the world of the dead could there be found
security and peace and pleasure which a man, by taking
thought all his life for, might attain. No concern of earthly
living could count to him in comparison or be esteemed
as real in comparison. Little profit for him there to use his
mind, his reasoning powers. They could do nothing for
him in the one matter of overwhelming importance, his
status in the world to come. They could not give him hope
when life was hopeless or strength to endure the unen-
durable. People who are terrified and hard pressed by
misery do not turn to the mind for their help. This instinctive recoil from the world of outside fact was enormously reinforced by the other great influence at work

upon the side of death and against the use of the mind, the Egyptian priesthood.

Before Greece the domain of the intellect belonged to the priests. They were the intellectual class of Egypt. Their power was tremendous. Kings were subject to it. Great men must have built up that mighty organization, great minds, keen intellects, but what they learned of old truth and what they discovered of new truth was valued as it increased the prestige of the organization. And since Truth is a jealous mistress and will reveal herself not a whit to any but a disinterested seeker, as the power of the priesthood grew and any idea that tended to weaken it met with a cold reception, the priests must fairly soon have become sorry intellectualists, guardians only of what seekers of old had found, never using their own minds with freedom.

There was another result no less inevitable: all they knew must be kept jealously within the organization. To teach the people so that they would begin to think for themselves, would be to destroy the surest prop of their power. No one except themselves must have knowledge, for to be ignorant is to be afraid, and in the dark mystery of the unknown a man cannot find his way alone. He must have guides to speak to him with authority. Ignorance was the foundation upon which the priest-power rested. In truth, the two, the mystery and those who dealt in it, reinforced each other in such sort that each appears both the cause and the effect of the other. The power of the priest depended upon the darkness of the mystery; his effort must ever be directed toward increasing it and opposing any attempt to throw light upon it. The humble role played by the reason in the ancient world was assigned by an authority there was no appeal against. It determined the scope of thought and the scope of art as well, with an absolutism never questioned.

We know of one man, to be sure, who set himself against it. For a few years the power of the Pharaoh was pitted against the power of the priests and the Pharaoh won out. The familiar story of Akhenaton, who dared to think for himself and who built a city to enshrine and propagate the worship of the one and only God, might appear to point to a weakness in the great priestly body, but the proof is, in point of fact, rather the other way about. The priests were men deeply learned and experienced in human nature. They waited. The man of independent thought had only a very brief reign—did his contests with the priests wear him out, one wonders?—and after his death nothing of what he had stood for was allowed to remain. The priests took possession of his successor. They erased his very name from the monuments. He had never really touched their power.

But whatever their attitude to this autocrat or that, autocratic government never failed to command the priests' allegiance. They were ever the support of the throne as well as the power above it. Their instinct was sure: the misery of the people was the opportunity of the priest. Not only an ignorant populace but one subjugated and wretched was their guarantee. With men's thoughts directed more and more toward the unseen world, and with the keys to it firmly in their own grasp, their terrific power was assured.

When Egypt ended, the East went on ever farther in the direction Egypt had pointed. The miseries of Asia are a fearful page of history. Her people found strength to endure by denying any meaning and any importance to what they could not escape. The Egyptian world where dead men walked and slept and feasted was transmuted into what had always been implicit in its symbolism, the world of the spirit. In India, for centuries the leader of thought to the East, ages long since, the world of the reason and the world of the spirit were divorced and the universe handed over to the latter. Reality—that which we have heard, which we have seen with our eyes and our hands have handled, of the Word of life—was dismissed as a fiction that had no bearing upon the Word. All that was seen and heard and handled was vague and unsubstantial and forever passing, the shadow of a dream; only that was real which was of the spirit. This is always man's way out when the facts of life are too bitter and too black to be borne. When conditions are such that life offers no earthly hope, somewhere, somehow, men must find a refuge. Then they fly from the terror without to the citadel within, which famine and pestilence and fire and sword cannot shake. What Goethe calls the inner universe, can live by its own laws, create its own security, be sufficient unto itself, when once reality is denied to the turmoil of the world without.

So the East found a way to endure the intolerable, and she pursued it undeviatingly through the centuries, following it to its farthest implications. In India the idea of truth became completely separated from outside fact; all outside was illusion; truth was an inner disposition. In such a world there is little scope for the observing reason or the seeing eye. Where all except the spirit is unreal, it is manifest folly to be concerned with an exterior that is less than a shadow.

It is easy to understand how in these conditions the one department of the intellect that flourished was mathematics. Nothing is less likely to react practically upon life or to intrude into the domain of theology than the world of the idea revealed to the mathematical imagination. Pure mathematics soars into a region far removed from human wretchedness and no priest ever troubled himself about the effects of free inquiry along mathematical lines. There the mind could go where it pleased. "Compared with the Egyptians we are childish mathematicians," observes Plato. India, too, made notable contributions in this field. But, sooner or later, if the activity of the mind is restricted anywhere it will cease to function even where it is allowed to be free. To-day in India the triumph of the spirit over the mind is complete, and wherever Buddhism, the great product of the Indian spirit, has prevailed, the illusoriness of all that is of this earth and the vanity of all research into its nature is the centre of the faith.

As in Egypt, the priests saw their opportunity. The power of the Brahmans, the priestly caste, and of the great Buddhist hierarchy, is nothing less than stupendous. The circle is complete: a wretched populace with no hope save in the invisible, and a priesthood whose power is bound up with the belief in the unimportance of the visible so that they must forever strive to keep it an article of faith. The

circle is complete in another sense as well: the wayfarer
sheltering for the night in an abandoned house does not
care to mend the roof the rain drips through, and a people
living in such wretchedness that their one comfort is to
deny the importance of the facts of earthly life, will not try
to better them. India has gone the way of the things that are
not seen until the things that are seen have become invisible.

That is what happens when one course is followed undeviatingly for ages. We are composite creatures, made up
of soul and body, mind and spirit. When men's attention
is fixed upon one to the disregard of the others, human
beings result who are only partially developed, their eyes
blinded to half of what life offers and the great world holds.
But in that antique world of Egypt and the early Asiatic
civilizations, that world where the pendulum was swinging
ever farther and farther away from all fact, something
completely new happened. The Greeks came into being and
the world, as we know it, began.

# Chapter II

## MIND AND SPIRIT

EGYPT is a fertile valley of rich river soil, low-lying, warm, monotonous, a slow-flowing river, and beyond, the limitless desert. Greece is a country of sparse fertility and keen, cold winters, all hills and mountains sharp cut in stone, where strong men must work hard to get their bread. And while Egypt submitted and suffered and turned her face toward death, Greece resisted and rejoiced and turned full-face to life. For somewhere among those steep stone mountains, in little sheltered valleys where the great hills were ramparts to defend and men could have security for peace and happy living, something quite new came into the world; the joy of life found expression. Perhaps it was born there, among the shepherds pasturing their flocks where the wild flowers made a glory on the hillside; among the sailors on a sapphire sea washing enchanted islands purple in a luminous air. At any rate it has left no trace anywhere else in the world of antiquity. In Greece nothing is more in evidence. The Greeks were the first people in the world to play, and they played on a great scale. All over Greece there were games, all sort of games; athletic contests of every description: races—horse-, boat-, foot-, torch-races; contests in music, where one side outsung the other; in dancing—on greased skins sometimes to display a nice skill of foot and balance of body; games where men leaped in and out of flying chariots; games so many one grows weary with the list of them. They are embodied in the statues familiar to all, the disc thrower, the charioteer, the wrestling boys, the dancing flute players. The great games—there were four that came at stated seasons—were so important, when one was held, a truce of God was proclaimed so that all Greece might come in safety without fear. There "glorious-limbed youth"—the phrase is Pindar's, the athlete's poet—strove for an honor so coveted as hardly anything else in Greece. An Olympic victor—triumphing generals would give place to him. His crown of wild olives was set beside the prize of the tragedian. Splendor attended him, processions, sacrifices, banquets, songs the greatest poets were glad to write. Thucydides, the brief, the severe, the historian of that bitter time, the fall of Athens, pauses, when one of his personages has conquered in the games, to give the fact full place of honor. If we had no other knowledge of what the Greeks were like, if nothing were left of Greek art and literature, the fact that they were in love with play and played magnificently would be proof enough of how they lived and how they looked at life. Wretched people, toiling people, do not play. Nothing like the Greek games is conceivable in Egypt or Mesopotamia. The life of the Egyptian lies spread out in the mural paintings down to the minutest detail. If fun and sport had played any real part they would be there in some form for us to see. But the Egyptian did not play. "Solon, Solon, you Greeks are all children," said the Egyptian priest to the great Athenian. At any rate, children or not, they enjoyed themselves. They had physical vigor and high spirits and time, too, for fun. The witness of the games is conclusive. And when Greece died and her reading of the great enigma was buried with her statues, play, too, died out of the world. The brutal, bloody Roman games had nothing to do with the spirit of play. They were fathered by the Orient, not by Greece. Play died when Greece died and many and many a century passed before it was resurrected.

To rejoice in life, to find the world beautiful and delightful to live in, was a mark of the Greek spirit which distinguished it from all that had gone before. It is a vital distinction. The joy of life is written upon everything the Greeks left behind and they who leave it out of account fail to reckon with something that is of first importance in understanding how the Greek achievement came to pass in the world of antiquity. It is not a fact that jumps to the eye for the reason that their literature is marked as strongly by sorrow. The Greeks knew to the full how bitter life is as well as how sweet. Joy and sorrow, exultation and tragedy, stand hand in hand in Greek literature, but there is no contradiction involved thereby. Those who do not know the one do not really know the other either. It is the depressed, the gray-minded people, who cannot rejoice just as they cannot agonize. The Greeks were not the victims of depression. Greek literature is not done in gray or with a low palette. It is all black and shining white or black and scarlet and gold. The Greeks were keenly aware, terribly aware, of life's uncertainty and the imminence of death. Over and over again they emphasize the brevity and the failure of all human endeavor, the swift passing of all that is beautiful and joyful. To Pindar, even as he glorifies the victor in the games, life is "a shadow's dream." But never, not in their darkest moments, do they lose their taste for life. It is always a wonder and a delight, the world a place of beauty, and they themselves rejoicing to be alive in it.

Quotations to illustrate this attitude are so numerous, it is hard to make a choice. One might quote all the Greek poems there are, even when they are tragedies. Every one of them shows the fire of life burning high. Never a Greek poet that did not warm both hands at that flame. Often in the midst of a tragedy a choral song of joy breaks forth. So Sophocles, of the three tragedians the soberest, the most severe, sings in the *Antigone* of the wine-god, "with whom the stars rejoice as they move, the stars whose breath is fire." Or in the *Ajax* where "thrilling with rapture, soaring on wings of sudden joy," he calls to "Pan, O Pan, come, sea-rover, down from the snow-beaten mountain crag. Lord of the dance the gods delight in, come, for now I, too, would dance. O joy!" Or in the *Œdipus Coloneus,* where tragedy is suddenly put aside by the poet's love of the out-of-door world, of the nightingale's clear thrilling note and the stainless tide of pure waters and the glory of the narcissus and the bright-shining crocus, "which the quire of the muses love and Aphrodite of the golden rein." Passages like these come again and again, lifting the black curtain of tragedy to the full joy of life. They are no artifice or trick to heighten by contrast. They are the natural expression of men who were tragedians indeed but Greeks first, and so thrillingly aware of the wonder and beauty of life, they could not but give it place.

The little pleasures, too, that daily living holds, were felt as such keen enjoyment: "Dear to us ever," says Homer, "is the banquet and the harp and the dance and changes of raiment and the warm bath and love and sleep." Eating and drinking have never again seemed so delightful as in the early Greek lyrics, nor a meeting with friends, nor a warm fire of a winter's night—"the stormy season of winter, a soft couch after dinner by the fire, honey-sweet wine in your glass and nuts and beans at your elbow"— nor a run in the springtime "amid a fragrance of woodbine and leisure and white poplar, when the plane-tree and the elm whisper together," nor a banqueting hour, "moving among feasting and giving up the soul to be young, carrying a bright harp and touching it in peace among the wise of the citizens." It is a matter of course that comedy should be their invention, the mad, rollicking, irresponsible fun of the Old Comedy, its verve and vitality and exuberant, overflowing energy of life. A tomb in Egypt and a theatre in Greece. The one comes to the mind as naturally as the other. So was the world changing by the time the fifth century before Christ began in Athens.

"The exercise of vital powers along lines of excellence in a life affording them scope" is an old Greek definition of happiness. It is a conception permeated with energy of life. Through all Greek history that spirit of life abounding moves. It led along many an untried way. Authoritarianism and submissiveness were not the direction it pointed to. A high-spirited people full of physical vigor do not obey easily, and indeed the strong air of the mountains has never been wholesome for despots. The absolute monarch-submissive slave theory of life flourishes best where there are no hills to give a rebel refuge and no mountain heights to summon a man to live dangerously. When history begins in Greece there is no trace of the ancient state. The awful, unapproachable sacred potentate, Pharaoh of Egypt, priest-

king of Mesopotamia, whose absolute power none had
questioned for thousands of years, is nowhere in the scene.
There is nothing that remotely resembles him in Greece.
Something we know of the Age of the Tyrants in Greek
history but what we know most clearly is that it was put a
stop to. Abject submission to the power on the throne
which had been the rule of life in the ancient world since
kings began, and was to be the rule of life in Asia for
centuries to come, was cast off by the Greeks so easily, so
lightly, hardly more than an echo of the contest has come
down to us.

In the *Persians* of Æschylus, a play written to celebrate
the defeat of the Persians at Salamis, there is many an
allusion to the difference between the Greek way and the
Oriental way. The Greeks, the Persian queen is told, fight
as free men to defend what is precious to them. Have they
no master? she asks. No, she is told. No man calls Greeks
slaves or vassals. Herodotus in his account adds, "They
obey only the law." Something completely new is here. The
idea of freedom has been born. The conception of the
entire unimportance of the individual to the state, which
had persisted down from earliest tribal days and was universally accepted in all the ancient world, has given place
in Greece to the conception of the liberty of the individual
in a state which he defends of his own free will. That is
a change not worked by high spirit and abounding vigor
alone. Something more was at work in Greece. Men were
thinking for themselves.

One of the earlier Greek philosophic sayings is that of
Anaxagoras: "All things were in chaos when Mind arose
and made order." In the ancient world ruled by the irrational, by dreadful unknown powers, where a man was
utterly at the mercy of what he must not try to understand,
the Greeks arose and the rule of reason began. The fundamental fact about the Greek was that he had to use his
mind. The ancient priests had said, "Thus far and no
farther. We set the limits to thought." The Greeks said,
"All things are to be examined and called into question.
There are no limits set to thought." It is an extraordinary

fact that by the time we have actual, documentary knowledge of the Greeks there is not a trace to be found of that domination over the mind by the priests which played such a decisive part in the ancient world. The priest plays no real part in either the history or the literature of Greece. In the *Iliad* he orders a captive taken back to appease an angry god and stop a pestilence, and is given a grudging obedience—with the backing of the pestilence, but that is his sole appearance on the scene. The Trojan War is fought out by gods and men with no intermediaries. A prophet or two appears in the tragedies but for evil oftener than for good. In the *Agamemnon* of Æschylus, a hundred years before Plato, there is a criticism of the dark powers exercised by the ministers of religion which goes with precision to the heart of the matter:

> And, truly, what of good
> ever have prophets brought to men?
> Craft of many words,
>     only through
> evil your message speaks.
>     Seers bring aye
> terror, so to keep
>     men afraid.

The conclusion might be drawn from the words that something of that sort of power was in fact wielded then by priest and prophet, but what is certainly true is that the poet who spoke them to a great audience, with the most important priests sitting in the front-row seats, won for himself not disapproval but the highest mark of favor the people could give. There is nothing clearer and nothing more astonishing than the strict limits the Greeks set to the power of the priests. Priests in numbers there were and altars and temples, and at a time of public danger, disrespect shown to the forms of religion would arouse even in Athens superstition and popular fury, but the place of the priest in Greece was in the background. The temple was his and the temple rites, and nothing else.

The Greek kept his formal religion in one compartment

and everything that really mattered to him in another. He never went to a priest for guidance or advice. Did he want to know how to bring up his children or what Truth was, he went to Socrates, or to the great sophist Protagoras, or to a learned grammarian. The idea of consulting a priest would never have occurred to him. The priests could tell him the proper times and the proper forms for sacrifices. That was their business and only that. In the *Laws*, written in Plato's old age and on the whole in a spirit of reaction against his earlier revolts, the entire subject of religion is discussed without a single reference to a priest. The *Laws*, it should perhaps be pointed out, is not written for the ideal state, the heavenly pattern of the *Republic*, but is addressed to the ideas and feelings of the Greeks of that day. The Athenian, who is the chief speaker, often meets with criticism from the two other personages of the dialogue when he proposes an innovation, but they accept without a word of surprise or dissent a statement that those who talk loosely about the gods and sacrifices and oracles, should be admonished by—members of the governing Council! These are to "converse with them touching the improvement of their soul's health." There is not a suggestion from any of the three that a priest might be of use here. Furthermore, "Before a man is prosecuted for impiety the guardians of the law shall determine if the deed has been done in earnest or only from childish levity." It was clearly not the idea that in matters touching the life and liberty of a Greek citizen the priest should have a voice. At the end of the argument the priest's proper domain is briefly indicated: "When a man is disposed to sacrifice, let him place his offerings in the hands of the priests and priestesses who have under their care the holy rite." That is the sum total of what the speakers hold to be the priest's part in religion, and he has no part in anything except religion. Even more noteworthy as illustrating the Greek point of view is the Athenian's characterization as "monstrous natures" of those "who say they can conjure the dead and bribe the gods with sacrifices and prayers"— in other words, those who used magic and tried to obtain favors from heaven by practices not unknown in the most civilized lands to-day.

No doubt the oracles, at Delphi notably, played a prominent role in Greece, but none of the oracular sayings that have come down to us bear the familiar priestly stamp. Athens seeking guidance from the Delphic priestess at the time of the Persian invasion is not told to sacrifice hecatombs to the god and offer precious treasure to the oracle, but merely to defend herself with wooden walls, a piece of acute worldly wisdom, at least as interpreted by Themistocles. When Crœsus the rich, the king of Lydia, sent to Delphi to find out if he would succeed in a war against Persia and paved his way by magnificent gifts, any priests in the world except the Greeks would have made their profit for their church by an intimation that the costlier the offering the surer his success, but the only answer the Greek holy of holies gave him was that by going to war he would destroy a great empire. It happened to be his own, but, as the priestess pointed out, she was not responsible for his lack of wit, and certainly there was no intimation that if he had given more, things would have turned out better. The sentences which Plato says were inscribed in the shrine at Delphi are singularly unlike those to be found in holy places outside of Greece. *Know thyself* was the first, and *Nothing in excess* the second, both marked by a total absence of the idiom of priestly formulas all the world over.

Something new was moving in the world, the most disturbing force there is. "All things are at odds when God lets a thinker loose on this planet." They were let loose in Greece. The Greeks were intellectualists; they had a passion for using their minds. The fact shines through even their use of language. Our word for school comes from the Greek word for leisure. Of course, reasoned the Greek, given leisure a man will employ it in thinking and finding out about things. Leisure and the pursuit of knowledge, the connection was inevitable—to a Greek. In our ears Philosophy has an austere if not a dreary sound. The word is Greek but it had not that sound in the original. The

Greeks meant by it the endeavor to understand everything there is, and they called it what they felt it to be, the *love of knowledge:*

How charming is divine philosophy—

In the world of antiquity those who practiced the healing art were magicians, priests versed in special magic rites. The Greeks called their healers physicians, which means those versed in the ways of nature. Here in brief is an exemplification of the whole trend of the Greek mind, its swing away from antiquity and toward modernity. To be versed in the ways of nature means that a man has observed outside facts and reasoned about them. He has used his powers not to escape from the world but to think himself more deeply into it. To the Greeks the outside world was real and something more, it was interesting. They looked at it attentively and their minds worked upon what they saw. This is essentially the scientific method. The Greeks were the first scientists and all science goes back to them.

In nearly every field of thought "they took the first indispensable steps." The statement means more than is apparent on the surface. The reason that antiquity did not give birth to science was not only because fact tended to grow more and more unreal and unimportant. There was an even more cogent cause: the ancient world was a place of fear. Magical forces ruled it and magic is absolutely terrifying because it is absolutely incalculable. The minds of those who might have been scientists had been held fastbound in the prison of that terror. Nothing of all the Greeks did is more astonishing than their daring to look it in the face and use their minds about it. They dared nothing less than to throw the light of reason upon dreadful powers taken completely on trust everywhere else, and by the exercise of the intelligence to banish them. Galileo, the humanists of the Renaissance, are glorified for their courage in venturing beyond the limits set by a power that could damn their souls eternally, and in demanding to know for themselves what the universe was like. No doubt it was high courage, great and admirable, but it was altogether beneath that shown by the Greeks. The humanists ventured upon the fearful ocean of free thought under guidance. The Greeks had preceded them there. They chanced that great adventure all alone.

High spirit and the energy of great vital powers had worked in them to assert themselves against despotic rule and to refuse to submit to priestly rule. They would have no man to dictate to them and being free from masters they used their freedom to think. For the first time in the world the mind was free, free as it hardly is to-day. Both the state and religion left the Athenian free to think as he pleased.

During the last war a play would have had short shrift here which showed up General Pershing for a coward; ridiculed the Allies' cause; brought in Uncle Sam as a blustering bully; glorified the peace party. But when Athens was fighting for her life, Aristophanes did the exact equivalent of all these things many times over and the Athenians, pro- and anti-war alike, flocked to the theatre. The right of a man to say what he pleased was fundamental in Athens. "A slave is he who cannot speak his thought," said Euripides. Socrates drinking the hemlock in his prison on the charge of introducing new gods and corrupting the youth is but the exception that proves the rule. He was an old man and all his life he had said what he would. Athens had just gone through a bitter time of crushing defeat, of rapid changes of government, of gross mismanagement. It is a reasonable conjecture that he was condemned in one of those sudden panics all nations know, when the people's fears for their own safety have been worked upon and they turn cruel. Even so, he was condemned by a small majority and his pupil Plato went straight on teaching in his name, never molested but honored and sought after. Socrates was the only man in Athens who suffered death for his opinions. Three others were forced to leave the country. That is the entire list-and to compare it with the endless list of those tortured and killed in Europe during even the last five hundred years is to see clearly what Athenian liberty was.

The Greek mind was free to think about the world as it

pleased, to reject all traditional explanations, to disregard all the priests taught, to search unhampered by any outside authority for the truth. The Greeks had free scope for their scientific genius and they laid the foundations of our science to-day.

Homer's hero who cried for more light even if it were but light to die in, was a true Greek. They could never leave anything obscure. Neither could they leave anything unrelated. System, order, connection, they were impelled to seek for. An unanalyzed whole was an impossible conception for them. Their very poetry is built on clarity of ideas, with plan and logical sequence. Great artists though they were, they would never give over trying to understand beauty as well as to express it. Plato is speaking as a typical Greek when he says that there are men who have an intuitive insight, an inspiration, which causes them to do good and beautiful things. They themselves do not know why they do as they do and therefore they are unable to explain to others. It is so with poets and, in a sense, with all good men. But if one could be found who was able to add to his instinct for the right or the beautiful, a clear idea of the reason for its rightness or beauty, he would be among men what a living man would be in the dead world of flitting shades. That statement is completely Greek in its conception of values. There never were people farther from the idea of the contemplation of beauty as a rest to the mind. They were not in the world to find rest for their mind in anything. They must analyze and reflect upon everything. Any general term they found themselves using must be precisely realized and the language of all philosophy is their creation.

But to leave the intellectuality of the Greeks here would be to give only half of the picture. Even in Greece Science and Philosophy wore a sober look, but the Greeks did not think soberly about the exercise of the intellect. "Thoughts and ideas, the fair and immortal children of the mind," as a Greek writer calls them, were a delight to them. Never, not in the brightest days of the Renaissance, has learning appeared in such a radiant light as it did to the gay young men of imperial Athens. Listen to one of them talking to

Socrates, just waked up in the early dawn by a persistent hammering at his door: "What's here?" he cries out, still half asleep. "O Socrates," and the voice is that of a lad he knows well, "Good news, good news!" "It ought to be at this unearthly hour. Well, out with it." The young fellow is in the house now. "O Socrates, Protagoras has come. I heard it yesterday evening. And I was going to you at once but it was so late—" "What's it all about—Protagoras? Has he stolen something of yours?" The boy bursts out laughing. "Yes, yes, that's just it. He's robbing me of wisdom. He has it—wisdom, and he can give it to me. Oh, come and go with me to him. Start now." That eager, delightful boy in love with learning can be duplicated in nearly every dialogue of Plato. Socrates has but to enter a gymnasium; exercise, games, are forgotten. A crowd of ardent young men surround him. Tell us this. Teach us that, they clamor. What is Friendship? What is Justice? We will not let you off, Socrates. The truth—we want the truth. "What delight," they say to each other, "to hear wise men talk!" "Egypt and Phœnicia love money," Plato remarks in a discussion on how nations differ. "The special characteristic of our part of the world is the love of knowledge." "The Athenians," said St. Luke, "and the strangers sojourning there spend their time in nothing else but to tell or to hear some new thing." Even the foreigners caught the flame. That intense desire to know, that burning curiosity about everything in the world—they could not come into daily contact with it and not be fired. Up and down the coast of Asia Minor St. Paul was mobbed and imprisoned and beaten. In Athens "they brought him unto the Areopagus, saying, 'May we know what this new teaching is?'"

Aristotle, the model scientist, the man of cool head and detached observation, unbiased, impersonal, does not display any dispassionate aloofness in his consideration of reason. He so loves it and delights in it that when it is the theme of discourse he cannot be held within the sober bounds of the scientific spirit. His words must be quoted, they are so characteristically Greek:

Since then reason is divine in comparison with man's whole nature, the life according to reason must be divine in comparison with (usual) human life. Nor ought we to pay regard to those who exhort us that as men we ought to think human things and keep our eyes upon mortality: nay, as far as may be, we should endeavor to rise to that which is immortal, and live in conformity with that which is best, in us. Now, what is characteristic of any nature is that which is best for it and gives most joy. Such to man is the life according to reason, since it is this that makes him man.

Love of reason and of life, delight in the use of the mind and the body, distinguished the Greek way. The Egyptian way and the way of the East had led through suffering and by the abnegation of the intellect to the supremacy of the spirit. That goal the Greeks could never come within sight of. Their own nature and the conditions of their life alike, shut them off from it, but they knew the way of the spirit no less. The all-sufficing proof that the world of the spirit was where the flame of their genius burned highest is their art. Indeed their intellectuality has been obscured to us precisely by virtue of that transcendent achievement. Greece means Greek art to us and that is a field in which the reason does not rule. The extraordinary flowering of the human spirit which resulted in Greek art shows the spiritual power there was in Greece. What marked the Greeks off from Egypt and India was not an inferior degree of spirituality but a superior degree of mentality. Great mind and great spirit combined in them. The spiritual world was not to them another world from the natural world. It was the same world as that known to the mind. Beauty and rationality were both manifested in it. They did not see the conclusions reached by the spirit and those reached by the mind as opposed to each other. Reason and feeling were not antagonistic. The truth of poetry and the truth of science were both true.

It is difficult to illustrate this conception of reality by isolated quotations, but the attitude of the greatest of Greek scientists may serve as an example. Aristotle was in one sense the typical scientist, a man endowed with extraordinary powers of observation and of reasoning upon his data, preoccupied with what he could see and what he could know. Anywhere else and at any other time he would have been the man of pure reason, viewing with condescension if not contempt conclusions reached in any way except that of the mind. But to Aristotle the Greek the way of the spirit was also important, and the scientific method sometimes to be abandoned in favor of the poetic method. In his well-known statement in the *Poetics* that poetry has a higher truth than history since it expresses truth of general application whereas that of history is partial and limited, he is not speaking as a scientist nor would the statement commend itself to the scientific mind outside of Greece. There is no evidence, again, of the scientist's point of view in the great passage where he sets forth the reason for the work of his life, his search into the nature of all living things:

> The glory, doubtless, of the heavenly bodies fills us with more delight than the contemplation of these lowly things, but the heavens are high and far off, and the knowledge of celestial things that our senses give us, is scanty and dim. Living creatures, on the contrary, are at our door, and if we so desire we may gain full and certain knowledge of each and all. We take pleasure in a statue's beauty; should not then the living fill us with delight? And all the more if in the spirit of the love of knowledge we search for causes and bring to light evidences of meaning. Then will nature's purpose and her deep-seated laws be revealed in all things, all tending in her multitudinous work to one form or another of the beautiful.

Did ever scientist outside of Greece so state the object of scientific research? To Aristotle, being a Greek, it was apparent that the full purpose of that high enterprise could not be expressed in any way except the way of poetry, and, being a Greek, he was able so to express it.

Spirituality inevitably brings to our mind religion. Greek religion is known to us chiefly or only as a collection of fairy tales, by no means always edifying. This is to belie the immense hold the Greeks had on things spiritual. It

would have been impossible for the nation that produced
the art and the poetry of Greece to have a permanently
superficial view of religion, just as it would have been
impossible for them not to use their minds on Homer's
gods and goddesses. Those charming stories which came
down from a time when men had a first-hand knowledge
of nature now forever lost, were never, it is true, anathe-
matized with book and bell and public recantation. That
was not the Greek way. They loved them and their fancy
played with them, but they found their way through them
to what underlies all religion, East or West. Æschylus will
speak like a prophet of Israel, and the Zeus he praises
Isaiah would have understood:

> Father, Creator, mighty God,
> great craftsman, with his hand he fashioned man.
> Ancient in wisdom, working through all things,
> into safe harbor guiding all at last. . . .
> With whom the deed and word are one,
> to execute with swiftness all the ends
> conceived in the deep counsels of his mind.

"Ye men of Athens," said St. Paul on the Areopagus, "I
perceive that in all things ye are too superstitious"—so the
Bible version runs, but the last word could quite as accurately be translated "in dread of the divine power," a
meaning borne out by the reason St. Paul gives for his use
of it: "For as I passed by and beheld your devotions I
found an altar with this inscription, *To the Unknown
God*." The words carry us far away from the gay company
of the Olympians. They go back to the poet who had
written, "Through thick and shadowed forests stretch the
pathways of his purpose, beyond our power to search out."
That altar to the Unknown God who is past our power
to search out, could have been raised only by men who
had gone beneath the pleasant surface of comfortable
orthodoxies and easy certainties. A single sentence of
Socrates, spoken when he was condemned to death, shows
how the Greek could use his mind upon religion, and by
means of human wisdom joined to spiritual insight could
sweep aside all the superficialities and see through to the

thing that is ultimate in religion: "Think this certain, that to a good man no evil can happen, either in life or in death." These words are the final expression of faith.

There is a passage in Socrates' last talk with his friends before his death, which exemplifies with perfect fidelity that control of the feelings by the reason, and that balance between the spirit and the mind, which belonged to the Greek. It is the last hour of his life and his friends who have come to be with him to the end have turned the talk upon the immortality of the soul. In such a moment it would be natural to seek only for comfort and support and let calm judgment and cool reason loosen their hold. The Greek in Socrates could not do that. His words are:

At this moment I am sensible that I have not the temper of a seeker after knowledge; like the vulgar, I am only a partisan. For the partisan, when he is engaged in a dispute, cares nothing about the rights of the question, but is anxious only to convince his hearers. And the difference between him and me at the present moment is only this— that while he seeks to convince his hearers that what he says is true, I am seeking to convince myself; to convince my hearers is a secondary matter with me. And do but see how much I have to gain by this. For if what I say is true, then I do well to believe it; and if there be nothing after death, still, I shall save my friends from grief during the short time that is left me, and my ignorance will do me no harm. This is the state of mind in which I approach the argument. And I would ask you to be thinking of the truth and not of Socrates. Agree with me if I seem to you to speak the truth; or, if not, withstand me might and main that I may not deceive you as well as myself in my desire, and like the bee leave my sting in you before I die. And now let us proceed.

Thus in Greece the mind and the spirit met on equal terms.

# *Chapter* III

## THE WAY OF THE EAST
## AND THE WEST IN ART

THE WAY a nation goes, whether that of the mind or that of the spirit, is decisive in its effect upon art. A brief consideration will show that it must be so. The spirit has not essentially anything to do with what is outside of itself. It is the mind that keeps hold of reality. The way of the spirit is by withdrawal from the world of objects to contemplation of the world within and there is no need of any correspondence between what goes on without and what goes on within. Not the mind but the spirit is its own place, and can make a Hell of Heaven, a Heaven of Hell. When the mind withdraws into itself and dispenses with facts it makes only chaos.

In the early days of the Restoration a great discussion was held by the learned men in the presence of the king on why, if a live fish were put into a brimming pail, the water would not overflow, while if the fish were dead, it would. Many elevating reasons that had to do with the inner significance of life and death were adduced for this spiritually suggestive property of water—or fish, until the king asked that two such pails be brought in and the fish added to them before his eyes. When it turned out that the water reacted in the same way to the fish alive or dead, the scientists received a lesson that had far-reaching results on the advisability of the mind's not going the way of the spirit and withdrawing into itself to exercise the pure reason free and unhampered, but of remaining strictly within the limits of the outside world. Abide by the facts, is the dictum of the mind; a sense for fact is its salient characteristic.

In proportion as the spirit predominates, this sense disappears. So in the Middle Ages when the West was turning more and more to the way of the spirit, the foremost intellects could employ their great powers in questioning how many angels could stand on a needle's point, and the like. Carry this attitude toward the world of fact a few steps farther and the result is the Buddhist devotee swaying before the altar and repeating *Amida* a thousand, thousand times until he loses all consciousness of altar, *Amida,* and himself as well. The activity of the mind has been lulled to rest and the spirit, absorbed, is seeking the truth within itself. "Let a man," say the Upanishads, the great Brahman document, "meditate on the syllable Om. This is the imperishable syllable and he who knowing this, loudly repeats that syllable, enters into it and becomes immortal." "God offers to everyone," says Emerson, "his choice between truth and repose. Take which you please—you can never have both." That is the West speaking and the way of the mind. Truth means, from this point of view, finding out about things—very active exercise.

The practical effect of the divergence is of course immediately apparent in the intellectual realm. Those whose aim is to be completely independent of "this muddy vesture of decay" do not become scientists or archæologists or anything that has to do with actualities past or present. In art the result, though less immediately apparent, is no less decisive. In proportion as the spirit predominates, the real shapes and looks of things become unimportant and when the spirit is supreme, they are of no importance at all.

In Egypt, as has been said, the reality of the unseen world slowly overshadowed that of the seen, but invisible though it was, it remained substantial. The dead bodies must be preserved from returning to dust; they must be placed in tombs that were underground fortresses safe from disturbance; they must be surrounded by all the furnishings they had made use of in life. The body was enormously important and there was no idea that the abundance of the things a man possessed was not eternally important too. The art of such a people would keep a firm hold on reality. The pyramids are as real as the hills. They look to be nothing made by hands but a part of the basic structure of the earth. Where the wind lifts the sand into shapes of a gigantic geometry—triangles which, as one watches, pass into curves and break again into sharp-pointed outlines, a cycle of endless change as fixed as the movement of the stars, against the immensity of the desert which never changes—the pyramids, immutable, immovable, are the spirit of the desert incased in granite. All the tremendous art of Egyptian sculpture has something of this unity with the physical world. The colossal statues have only just emerged from the rocks of the hills. They keep the marks of their origin as securely as the marks of the artist's tools that shaped them from their background.

This hold on reality is something completely different from that grasped by the mind. It has nothing to do with the action of the mind; it is a profound intuition on the part of people whose consciousness has not yet divided them from the ways of nature. This intuitive feeling is as different from the conception of reality which the mind attains to as an Egyptian tomb, where life and death are hardly differentiated, is from that prison in which Socrates sat, trying to think out what was true in the hope of immortality.

What Egyptian art would have resulted in if it had been allowed a free development, is one of those questions that forever engage the attention through the realization of an immense loss to the world. But the priests stepped in, and that direct experience of nature which was being illumined more and more by the experience of the spirit was arrested at a certain point and held fast. The priests set a fixed pattern for art all must conform to. Art can work in chains for a long time as the mind cannot, and it was centuries before the full effect appeared of the control of the artist's spirit by the priest's dogma; but by the time it was apparent, Egyptian art was ended. Plato's comment is to all intents and purposes its funeral oration:

In Egypt the forms of excellence were long since fixed and patterns of them displayed in the temples. No painter or artist is allowed to innovate on the traditional forms or invent new ones. To this day, no alteration is allowed—

none at all. Their works of art are painted or molded in the same forms which they had 10,000 years ago.

But in the East there was no arrested development. There the spirit was free—it alone was free—to work unhampered. Hindoo art was produced by men who had been trained from earliest youth to look at all outside them as illusion. The belief in a solid, durable stuff which the senses induce, was the fundamental falsehood men must clear themselves from. That which appears solid and durable is only a perpetually shifting appearance, a kaleidoscope always moving, where each pattern is forever dissolving into another and all are no more significant than a spectacle for a child. Reality, permanence, importance, belong alone to the world within where truth is absolutely known because it is experienced and where the man who wills can achieve complete mastery. This is the fundamental dogma of the Upanishads:

> The infinite is the Self. He who perceives this, is lord and master of all the world. Air, fire, water, food, appearances, disappearances—all spring from the Self. He who sees this sees everything and obtains everything.

It is difficult for us to associate this idea with the production of art. Art is to us of the West the unifier of what is without and what is within. It is as firmly rooted in the one as in the other. And it is quite true that the complete mystic, if such a one could be, would never even desire to put into any concrete form the beatific vision. He would remain in utter quiescence, desiring nothing:

> When to a man who understands, the Self has become all things, what sorrow, what seeking, can there be, to him who once beholds that unity?

But mystical rapture even in the East is for the few. To all the rest, reality, however illusory it is conceived of as being, remains to be reckoned with. The great Hindoo artists were not prevented from expressing themselves through it as all artists will forever, but their conception of it shaped the mold of their art. The procedure laid down for a Buddhist artist before beginning his work is applicable in what it aims at to all Hindoo art. He was to proceed to a place of solitude. There he must prepare himself, first, by performing "the Sevenfold Office" and offering to the hosts of Buddhas "real or imaginary flowers." (It is clear that the first had no superiority over the second.) Next, he must realize "the four infinite moods" and meditate upon the emptiness and non-existence of all things, until "by the fire of the idea of the abyss" he lost all consciousness of self and was able to identify himself with the divinity he desired to portray. Then, at last, calling upon him he would behold him. There would come to him visibly the very image of the god, "like a bright reflection," to serve him for his model. It would appear in no human shape, we may be sure. The whole procedure was designed to make that impossible. The conviction had been bred within the artist that the truth of his art was above and apart from all reality. In his solitary watch he had sought to purify it from all that had to do with the flesh, to banish earthly memories and through the spirit undefiled find the manifestation of the eternal. The prerequisite of the statue would be its non-humanity. Scrolls of bright blue hair must mark it off from a mere man, or many heads or arms; or an impression of inhuman force, given by a woman brandishing a human head torn from a mangled body underfoot.

It is said of Polygnotus that when he wished to paint Helen of Troy, he went to Crotona, famed for the beauty of its women, and asked to see all those who were thought to be the most beautiful. These he studied long before painting his picture, and yet when it was done it was not a representation of any one of those lovely faces he had seen but fairer by far than the fairest of them all. The Greek artist, the story would tell us, was not a photographer, any more than his Buddhist confrère; he too in the end withdrew from the visible forms of the women before him and created within himself his own form of beauty; but the story points the difference between the two as well. The studio of the Greek was not a lonely cave of meditation, but the world of moving life. His picture was based on the women he had studied; it was conditioned by their actual bodily shapes; it was super-individual but not supernatural.

The Hindoo artist was subject to no conditions; of all artists he was the freest. The Egyptian was submissive to the ways of nature and the dogma of the priest; the Greek was limited by his mind that would not let him lose sight of the things that are seen; the Hindoo was unhampered by anything outside of himself except the material he worked in, and even there he often refused to recognize a limitation. The art of India and of all the nations of the East she influenced shows again and again sculpture that seems to struggle to be free of the marble. No artists have ever made bronze and stone move as these did. There was nothing fixed and rigid for them; nothing in the world of the spirit is fixed and rigid. Hindoo art is the result of unchecked spiritual force, a flood held back by no restraints save those the artist chose to impose upon himself.

But, even though the visible world had no hold upon his conscious attention, he could not, of course—no human being can—create purely within the depths of the spirit what had no connection with facts, no semblance of anything he had seen. His artistic vision was conditioned by actualities, but only indirectly since his aim was to detach himself from them. Reality and probability appeal to the mind alone and to that appeal he was completely indifferent; he was concentrated upon spiritual significance. To him the multitudinous hands and arms of the god who appeared to him in his trance were symbolic; they stood for a truth of the spirit and expressed the only kind of reality worth an artist's while.

Presuppose a complete lack of significance in the visible world and there is only one way out for the artist, the way of symbolism. He of all men is least capable of complete abstraction. The mathematician and the philosopher can deal with pure concepts; to the artist the world of abstract ideas offers nothing at all. In symbolism he can hold to something solid and concrete even while affirming that the real has nothing to do with that which the senses perceive. Symbols are always real things invested with unreality.

They are the reflection in the mirror through which we in the flesh can see, if darkly. In symbolism realities are important, even if their only importance is that they stand for something other than what they are. The mystical artist is free to make use of reality and to dispense with it as he pleases. He is at liberty also to improvise his own symbolism which can be of the simplest: many arms to express multiform power; many breasts to show spiritual nourishment; a sublimated pictorial writing. His only restraint comes from within his own self, but, despising as he does the outside world, predisposed against seeing real things as beautiful, the artist within him, who must find spiritual significance somewhere, is irresistibly impelled toward the pattern which he can make symbolic and, so, significant.

The mystical artist always sees patterns. The symbol, never quite real, tends to be expressed less and less realistically, and as the reality becomes abstracted the pattern comes forward.

The wings on Blake's angels do not look like real wings, nor are they there because wings belong to angels. They have been flattened, stylized, to provide a curving pointed frame, the setting required by the pattern of the composition. In Hindoo art and its branches, stylization reaches its height. Human figures are stylized far beyond the point of becoming a type; they too are made into patterns, schematic designs of the human body, an abstraction of humanity. In the case of an Eastern rug all desire to express any semblance of reality has gone. Such a work of art is pure decoration. It is the expression of the artist's final withdrawal from the visible world, essentially his denial of the intellect.

Dismiss the real world, see it as hateful and hopeless, and the effect upon art is fundamentally the same whether the result is a Fra Angelico angel or a monster-god. Winged angels radiant against a golden background, a many-handed god, both belong to the same conception of the world. The artist has turned his back upon the things that are seen. He has shut the eyes of his mind. The art of the West, after Rome fell and the influence of Greece was lost, went the way of the East as all else did. Pictures grew more and more decorative. The flat unreality of the primitive developed into the flat unreality of the stylized, until at the Renaissance the visible world was re-discovered with the re-discovery of Greece.

Two thousand years after the golden days of Phidias and Praxiteles, of Zeuxis and Apelles, when their statues were defaced and broken and all but irretrievably lost, and their paintings were completely gone forever, men's minds were suddenly directed to what was left of the literature of Greece and Rome. A passion for learning like that of Plato's time swept Italy. To study the literature of Greece was to discover the idea of the freedom of the mind and to use the mind as it had not been used since the days of Greece. Once again there was a fusion of rational and spiritual power. In the Italian Renaissance a great artistic development coincided with a great intellectual awakening and the art that resulted is in its essence more like that of Greece than any other before or since. In Florence, where great painters had great minds, the beauty of the real world was discovered and men painted what they saw with their eyes. Italian painters found the laws of perspective—of course. Not because Signorelli was greater than Simone Martini but only because he and his like were looking at real things and desiring to paint realities, not heavenly visions.

Whether the Greek artists used perspective or not can never be known; not a trace is left of their work; but what they felt about painting things as they are can be known without the possibility of a doubt. Their attitude is revealed in many an allusion.

A famous Greek painter exhibited a picture of a boy holding a bunch of grapes so lifelike, the birds flew down to peck at them, and the people acclaimed him as the master-artist. "If I were," he answered, "the boy would have kept the birds away." The little tale with its delightful assumption of intelligent birds is completely Greek in its fundamental assumption. Grapes were to be painted to look like grapes and boys to look like boys, and the reason was that nothing could be imagined so beautiful and so significant as the real. "Say not, who shall ascend unto Heaven or who shall descend into Hell: for lo, the Word is very nigh thee, in thy mouth and in thy heart." The Greek artist thought neither of Heaven nor of Hell; the word was very nigh unto him; he felt the real world completely sufficient for the demands of the spirit. He had no wish to mark the images of his gods with strange, unearthly attributes to lift them away from earth. He had no wish to alter them at all from what he saw as most beautiful, the shapes of the human beings around him.

A Brahman bronze of Shiva stands poised in the dance, arrested for a moment in an irresistible movement. Many arms and hands curving outward from his body add to the sense of an endless rhythmic motion. The shape, light, slim-waisted, is refined away from the human. Strange symbolic things surround him, deck him, a weaving cobra, a skull, a mermaid creature, long pendants waving from hair and ears, a writhing monster beneath his feet. His beauty is like nothing beautiful ever seen upon the earth.

The Olympic Hermes is a perfectly beautiful human being, no more, no less. Every detail of his body was shaped from a consummate knowledge of actual bodies. Nothing is added to mark his deity, no aureole around his head, no mystic staff, no hint that here is he who guides the soul to death. The significance of the statue to the Greek artist, the mark of the divinity, was its beauty, only that. His art had taken form within him as he walked the streets, watched the games, noted perpetually the people he lived among. To him what he saw in those human beings was enough for all his art; he had never an impulse to fashion something different, something truer than this truth of nature. In his eyes the Word had become flesh; he made his image of the eternal what men could be. The Winged Victory is later Greek; the temple on the Acropolis was built to the Wingless Victory.

The endless struggle between the flesh and the spirit found an end in Greek art. The Greek artists were unaware of it. They were spiritual materialists, never denying the importance of the body and ever seeing in the body a spiritual significance. Mysticism on the whole was alien to the Greeks, thinkers as they were. Thought and mysticism never go well together and there is little symbolism in Greek art. Athena was not a symbol of wisdom but an embodiment of it and her statues were beautiful grave women, whose seriousness might mark them as wise, but who were marked in no other way. The Apollo Belvedere is not a symbol of the sun, nor the Versailles Artemis of the moon. There could be nothing less akin to the ways of symbolism than their beautiful, normal humanity. Nor did decoration really interest the Greeks. In all their art they were preoccupied with what they wanted to express, not with ways of expressing it, and lovely expression, merely as lovely expression, did not appeal to them at all.

Greek art is intellectual art, the art of men who were clear and lucid thinkers, and it is therefore plain art. Artists than whom the world has never seen greater, men endowed with the spirit's best gift, found their natural method of expression in the simplicity and clarity which are the endowment of the unclouded reason. "Nothing in excess," the Greek axiom of art, is the dictum of men who would brush aside all obscuring, entangling superfluity, and see clearly, plainly, unadorned, what they wished to express. Structure belongs in an especial degree to the province of the mind in art, and architectonics were preeminently a mark of the Greek. The power that made a unified whole of the trilogy of a Greek tragedy, that envisioned the sure, precise, decisive scheme of the Greek statue, found its most conspicuous expression in Greek architecture. The Greek temple is the creation, *par excellence,* of mind and spirit in equilibrium.

A Hindoo temple is a conglomeration of adornment. The lines of the building are completely hidden by the decorations. Sculptured figures and ornaments crowd its surface, stand out from it in thick masses, break it up into a bewildering series of irregular tiers. It is not a unity but a collection, rich, confused. It looks like something not planned but built this way and that as the ornament required. The conviction underlying it can be perceived: each bit of the exquisitely wrought detail had a mystical meaning and the temple's exterior was important only as a means for the artist to inscribe thereon the symbols of the truth. It is decoration, not architecture.

Again, the gigantic temples of Egypt, those massive immensities of granite which look as if only the power that moves in the earthquake were mighty enough to bring them into existence, are something other than the creation of geometry balanced by beauty. The science and the spirit are there, but what is there most of all is force, unhuman force, calm but tremendous, overwhelming. It reduces to nothingness all that belongs to man. He is annihilated. The Egyptian architects were possessed by the consciousness of the awful, irresistible domination of the ways of nature; they had no thought to give to the insignificant atom that was man.

Greek architecture of the great age is the expression of men who were, first of all, intellectual artists, kept firmly within the visible world by their mind, but, only second to that, lovers of the human world. The Greek temple is the perfect expression of the pure intellect illumined by the spirit. No other great buildings anywhere approach its simplicity. In the Parthenon straight columns rise to plain capitals; a pediment is sculptured in bold relief; there is nothing more. And yet—here is the Greek miracle—this absolute simplicity of structure is alone in majesty of beauty among all the temples and cathedrals and palaces of the world. Majestic but human, truly Greek. No superhuman force as in Egypt; no strange supernatural shapes as in India; the Parthenon is the home of humanity at ease, calm, ordered, sure of itself and the world. The Greeks flung a challenge to nature in the fullness of their joyous strength. They set their temples on the summit of a hill overlooking the wide sea, outlined against the circle of the sky. They would build what was more beautiful than hill and sky and greater than all these. It matters not at all if the temple is large or small; one never thinks of the size. It matters not—really—how much it is in ruins. A few white columns dominate the lofty height at Sunion as securely as the great mass of the Parthenon dominates all the sweep of sea and land around Athens. To the Greek architect

man was master of the world. His mind could understand
its laws; his spirit could discover its beauty.

The Gothic cathedral was raised in awe and reverence
to Almighty God, the expression of the aspiration of the
lowly:

We praise thee, O God, we who are as nothing save in
our power to praise thee.

The Parthenon was raised in triumph, to express the
beauty and the power and the splendor of man:

Wonders are there many—none more wonderful than man.
His the might that crosses seas swept white by storm
winds . . .
He the master of the beast lurking in the wild hills . . .
His is speech and wind-swift thought—

Divinity was seen incarnate; through perfected mortality
man was immortal.

# *Chapter* **IV**

## THE GREEK WAY OF WRITING

THE ART of the Greek sculptors of the great age is known to us by long familiarity. None of the Greek statues upon first sight appear strange in any respect. There is no need to look long, to orient mind and eye, before we can understand them. We feel ourselves immediately at home. Our own sculptors learned their art from them, filled our galleries with reminiscences of them. Plaster casts more or less like them are our commonest form of inappropriate decoration. Our idea of a statue is a composite of Greek statues, and nothing speaks more for the vitality of the originals than their survival in spite of all we have done to them.

The same is true of the Greek temple. No architecture is more familiar to us. That pointed pediment supported by fluted columns—we are satiated with it. Endless replicas of it decorate the public buildings of all our cities and the sight of it anywhere is an assurance of something official within. Greece has been copied by sculptors and builders from the days of Rome on.

The art of the literature of Greece stands in singular contrast to these, isolated, apart. The thought of the Greeks has penetrated everywhere; their style, the way they write, has remained peculiar to them alone. In that one respect they have had no copyists and no followers. The fact is hardly surprising. One must know a foreign language very well to have one's way of writing actually altered by it; one must, in truth, have entered into the genius of that language to such a degree as is hardly possible to a foreigner. And Greek is a very subtle language, full of delicately modifying words, capable of the finest distinctions of meaning. Years of study are needed to read it even tolerably. Small wonder that the writers of other countries left it alone and, unlike their brother artists in stone, never imitated Greek methods. English poetry has gone an altogether different way from the Greek, as has all the art that is not copied but is native to Europe.

This art, the art natural to us, has always been an art of rich detail. In a Gothic cathedral not an inch is left unelaborated in a thousand marvellous patterns of delicate tracery worked in the stone. In a great Renaissance portrait minutest distinctions of form and color are dwelt upon with loving care, frost-work of lace, patterned brocade, the finely wrought links of a chain, a jewelled ring, wreathed pearls in the hair, the sheen of silk and satin and fur-bordered velvet, beauty of detail both sumptuous and exquisite. It is eminently probably that if the temples and the statues of Greece had only just been discovered, we would look at them dismayed at the lack of any of the elaboration of beauty we are used to. To turn from St. Mark's or Chartres to the Parthenon for the first time, or from a Titian to the Venus of Milo never seen before, would undoubtedly be a chilling experience. The statue in her straight, plain folds, her hair caught back simply in a knot, no ornament of any description to set her off, placed beside the lady of the Renaissance or the European lady of any period, is a contrast so great, only our long familiarity with her enables us not to feel her too austere to enjoy. She shows us how unlike what the Greeks wanted in beauty was from what the world after them has wanted.

So the lover of great literature when he is confronted all unprepared with the Greek way of writing, feels chilled at first, almost estranged. The Greeks wrote on the same lines as they did everything else. Greek writing depends no more on ornament than the Greek statue does. It is plain writing, direct, matter-of-fact. It often seems, when translated with any degree of literalness, bare, so unlike what we are used to as even to repel. All the scholars who have essayed translation have felt this difficulty and have tried to win an audience for what they loved and knew as so great by rewriting, not translating, when the Greek way

seemed too different from the English. The most distinguished of them, Professor Gilbert Murray, has expressly
stated this to be his method:

> I have often used a more elaborate diction than
> Euripides did because I found that, Greek being a very
> simple and austere language and English an ornate one, a
> direct translation produced an effect of baldness which was
> quite unlike the original.

The difficulty is there, no doubt, and yet if we are
unable to get enjoyment from a direct translation, we shall
never know what Greek writing is like, for the Greek and
the English ways are so different, when the Greek is
dressed in English fashion, it is no longer Greek. Familiarity has made their statues and their temples beautiful to
us as none are more. It is possible that even through the
poor medium of translation we might acquire a taste for
their writings as well, if, in addition to the easily perceived
beauty of such translations as Professor Murray's Euripides, we were willing to accustom ourselves to translations
as brief and little adorned as the original, and try to discover what the art that resulted in the Parthenon and the
Venus has produced in literature. To be willing to learn
from the Greeks in this matter also and to be enabled not
only to feel the simple majesty of the Greek temple along
with the splendor of St. Mark's and the soaring immensity
of Bourges, but to love the truth stated with simplicity as
well as the truth set off by every adornment the imagination can devise, to care for the Greek way of writing as
well as the English way, is to be immensely the richer; it
is to have our entire conception of poetry widened and
purified.

Plain writing is not the English genius. English poetry is
the Gothic cathedral, the Renaissance portrait. It is adorned
by all that beautiful elaboration of detail can do. The
words are like rich embroideries. Our poets may draw upon
what they will to deck their poems. They are not held
down to facts. Greek poets were. "The Greeks soar but
keep their feet on the ground," said Landor. Our poets
leave earth far behind them, freed by what the Greeks had

small use and no name for, poetic license. Our minds are full of pictures of "caverns measureless to man, down to a sunless sea," of "flowers so sweet the sense faints picturing them," of "sermons in stones, books in the running brooks," of "magic casements opening on the foam of perilous seas," of "the floor of heaven thick inlaid with patines of bright gold . . . still quiring to the young ey'd cherubins." When Homer says, "The stars about the bright moon shine clear to see, for no wind stirs the air and all the mountain peaks appear and the high headlands," when Sophocles describes "White Colonus where the nightingale sings her clear note deep in green glades ivy-grown, sheltered alike from sunshine and from wind," when Euripides writes, "At high-tide the sea, they say, leaves a deep pool below the rockshelf; in that clear place where the women dip their water jars—" the words so literal, so grave, so unemphatic, hardly arrest our attention to see the beauty in them. Our imagery would have left the Greeks as cold. Clarity and simplicity of statement, the watchwords of the thinker, were the Greek poets' watchwords too. Never to them would the humblest flower that blows have brought thoughts that do often lie too deep for tears. A primrose by the river's brim was always a simple primrose and nothing more. That a skylark was like a glow-worm golden in a dell of dew or like a poet hidden in a light of thought, would have been straight nonsense to them. A skylark was just a skylark. Birds were birds and nothing else, but how beautiful a thing was a bird, "that flies over the foam of the wave with careless heart, sea-purple bird of spring"!

The Greeks were realists, but not as we use the word. They saw the beauty of common things and were content with it:

Bring white milk good to drink, from a cow without blemish; bright honey, too, the drops the bee in her flowery work distils, with water that purifies, drawn from a virgin spring—

The strange glory of the narcissus . . . a wonder to all, immortal gods and mortal men. A hundred blossoms grew from the roots of it and very sweet was the fragrance, and all the wide sky above and all the land laughed and the salt wave of the sea.

As flakes of snow fall thick of a winter's day, and the crests of the high hills are covered, and the farthest head-lands and the meadow grass and the rich tillage of men. Over the inlets and the shore of the gray sea fast it falls and only the on-sweeping wave can ward it off.

These three instances, from Æschylus, the *Hymn to Demeter,* and the *Iliad* are selected almost at random. There is hardly a Greek poem from which such examples could not be taken. The Greeks liked facts. They had no real taste for embroidery, and they detested exaggeration.

Sometimes, if rarely, the Greek idea of beauty is found in English poetry. Curiously, Keats, than whom no poet delights more in rich 'detail, has in the *Ode to Autumn* written a poem more like the Greek than any other in English; the concluding lines are pure Greek:

> Then in a wailful choir the small gnats mourn
> Among the river sallows, borne aloft
> Or sinking as the light wind lives or dies;
> And full-grown lambs loud bleat from hilly bourn;
> Hedge-crickets sing; and now with treble soft
> The red-breast whistles from a garden croft,
> And gathering swallows twitter in the skies.

The things men live with, noted as men of reason note them, not slurred over or evaded, not idealized away from actuality, and then perceived as beautiful—that is the way Greek poets saw the world.

It follows that the fancy which must ever roam very far from home, played a humble role in Greek poetry. They never wanted to "splash at a ten-league canvas with brushes of comet's hair." What have not our lover-poets said of their beloved! Earth in her springtime, the starry heavens, sun and moon and dawn and sunset, have not sufficed for them:

> Oh, thou art fairer than the evening air
> Clad in the beauty of a thousand stars.

> She seemed a splendid angel, newly dressed,
> Save wings, for heaven—

Everyone can supply quotations for himself.

The Greek lover-poet kept his Greek sense for fact. Occasionally he would allow himself a brief flight of fancy: "Flower among the flowers, Zenophile is blooming. My girl is better than garlands sweet to smell." But as a rule he was chary of imagery and of adjectives as well. One epithet or two, at most, contented him: "Golden Telesila," "Heliodora, delicate darling," "Demo with the lovely hair," "Wide-eyed Anticleia," "A forehead white as ivory above dark-lashed eyes." Such modest tributes were all that the girls whose beauty inspired the Greek sculptors could win from lovers who had been trained in the Greek way.

Everywhere fancy travels with a tight rein in the poetry of Greece, as everywhere in English poetry it is given free course. Byron uses no curb when he wants to describe a high mountain:

> —the monarch of mountains.
> They crowned him long ago
> On a throne of rocks, in a robe of clouds,
> With a diadem of snow.

When Æschylus has the same thing in mind, he will allow himself a single touch, but no more:

> the mighty summit, neighbor to the stars.

Coleridge is not using his eyes when he perceives Mont Blanc

> like some sweet beguiling melody,
> So sweet, we know not we are listening to it—

Pindar is observing Ætna with accurate care:

> Frost-white Ætna, nurse all year long of the
> sharp-biting snow.

Coleridge was letting his fancy wander where it pleased. He was occupied with what he happened to feel when he stood before the mountain. Obviously he might have felt almost anything else; there is no logical connection between the spectacle and his reaction. The Greek poet was a precise observer giving a truthful account of a great snow mountain. His attitude was that the mountain is the important thing, not this or that fanciful idea it might suggest to him. He felt limited by the facts; the English poet was completely independent of them.

Meleager prays for night to come as a Greek lover would do: "Morning star, herald of dawn, swiftly come as the evening star and bring again in secret her whom thou takest from me." Juliet's prayer is after the model of English poetry:

> Come, gentle night; come, loving black-brow'd night.
> Give me my Romeo: and when he shall die,
> Take him and cut him out in little stars,
> And he will make the face of heaven so fine,
> That all the world will be in love with night—

"Gray dawn," says the Greek lover, "hater of those who love, why risest thou so swift around my bed where but now I nestled close to Demo? Would thou wouldst turn thy fleet steeds backward and be evening, O bearer of the sweet light that is so bitter to me." Not in that direct and literal fashion does the English lover cry out upon the dawn:

> What envious streaks
> Do lace the severing clouds in yonder east.
> Night's candles are burnt out, and jocund day
> Stands tiptoe on the misty morning tops—

The influence of the English Bible has had its share in making the Greek way hard for us. The language and the style of it have become to us those appropriate to religious expression, and Greek religious poetry which makes up much of the lyrical part of the tragedies, perhaps the greatest of all Greek poetry, is completely un-

Hebraic. Hebrew and Greek are poles apart. Hebrew poetry is directed to the emotions; it is designed to make the hearer feel, not think. Therefore it is a poetry based on reiteration. Everyone knows the emotional effect that repetition produces, from the tom-tom in the African forest to the rolling sound of "Dearly beloved brethren, the Scripture moveth us—to acknowledge and confess our manifold sins and wickedness; and that we should not dissemble nor cloak them—when we assemble and meet together—to ask those things which are requisite and necessary—" Nothing is gained for the idea by these repetitions; the words are synonyms; but the beat upon the ear dulls the critical reason and opens the way to gathering emotion. The method is basic in Hebrew poetry:

> To cause it to rain on the earth where no man is, on the wilderness wherein there is no man.
> Sing, O barren, thou that didst not bear; break forth into singing, thou that didst not travail with child—

The complete contrast this way of writing offers to the Greek can be seen most clearly in passages where the idea expressed is the same. In the Sermon on the Mount—the style of the New Testament is, of course, formed on that of the Old—occurs the passage:

> Ask and it shall be given you; seek and ye shall find; knock and it shall be opened unto you: For every one that asketh receiveth; and he that seeketh findeth; and to him that knocketh it shall be opened.

This thought is expressed in the Greek way by Æschylus:

> Men search out God and searching find him.

Not a word more is added. The poet felt the statement as it stood adequate for the idea and he had no desire to elaborate or ornament it.

The chorus in the *Agamemnon*, to which this sentence belongs, is a good instance of Greek brevity and straightforwardness:

He wills and it is done. One spoke, saying, God cares not when men tread underfoot holy things inviolate. But who spoke thus knew not God. We have seen with our eyes the price they pay whose breath is pride, who dare beyond man's daring, whose dwellings overflow with riches. The greatest good is not there, wealth enough to keep misery away and a heart wise to use it. Gold is no bulwark to the arrogant, to him who spurns out of sight the great altar of God's justice. Temptation that persuades to evil, offspring intolerable of far-seeing destruction—when these constrain, there is no remedy. No hiding place can cover sin. It ever blazes forth, a light of death.

All these ideas are found repeatedly in the Bible and are familiar through many a well-known verse from psalm or prophet, but written as the Hebrew writes they are so long that quotation here is impossible.

One parallel, however, must be given in full. A familiar and completely characteristic example of the Hebrew way is the description of wisdom in Job:

But where shall wisdom be found? and where is the place of understanding? The depth saith, It is not in me: and the sea saith, It is not with me. It cannot be gotten for gold, neither shall silver be weighed for the price thereof. It cannot be valued with the gold of Ophir, with the precious onyx, or the sapphire. The gold and the crystal cannot equal it: and the exchange of it shall not be for jewels of fine gold. No mention shall be made of coral, or of pearls: for the price of wisdom is above rubies. The topaz of Ethiopia shall not equal it, neither shall it be valued with pure gold. Whence then cometh wisdom? and where is the place of understanding?—Behold, the fear of the Lord, that is wisdom; and to depart from evil is understanding.

The thought behind these sonorous sentences is simple: wisdom cannot be bought; it is the reward of righteousness. The effectiveness of the statement consists entirely in the repetition. The idea is repeated again and again with only slight variations in the imagery, and the cumulative effect is in the end great and impressive. It happens that a direct comparison with the Greek way is possible, for Æschylus too had his conception of the price of wisdom:

> God, whose law it is that he who learns must suffer. And even in our sleep pain that cannot forget, falls drop by drop upon the heart, and in our own despite, against our will, comes wisdom to us by the awful grace of God.

This passage is as characteristically Greek as the quotation from Job is Hebrew. There is little repetition, little enhancement, in the statement. The thought that wisdom's price is suffering and that it is always paid unwillingly although sent in truth as a gift from God, is stated almost as briefly and almost as plainly as is possible to language. The poet is preoccupied with his thought. He is concerned to get his idea across, not to emotionalize it. His sense for beauty is as unerring as the Hebrew poet's, but it is a different sense for beauty.

The same difference between the two methods is marked in another parallel where the wicked man is shown praying to deaf ears. In the Bible it runs:

> When distress and anguish cometh then shall they call upon me but I will not answer; then they shall seek me but they shall not find me.

The Greek expresses the bare idea, not a word more:

> And does he pray, no one hears.

Socrates and Phædrus once were discussing a certain piece of writing for which the younger man had a great admiration. He insisted that Socrates should feel the same. "Well," said the latter, "as to the sentiments, I submit to your judgment but as to the style, I doubt whether the author himself would be able to defend it. I speak under correction, but I thought he repeated himself two or three times, either from want of words or want of pains. And he seemed to me ambitious to show that he could say the same thing over in two or three ways—"

We are lovers of beauty *with economy*, said Pericles. Words were to be used sparingly like everything else.

Thucydides gives in a single sentence the fate of those brilliant youths who, pledging the sea in wine from golden goblets, sailed away to conquer Sicily and slowly died in the quarries of Syracuse: "Having done what men could, they suffered what men must." One sentence only for their glory and their anguish. When Clytemnestra is told that her son is searching for her to kill her, all she says of all she feels, is: "I stand here on the height of misery."

Macbeth at the crisis of his fate strikes the authentic note of English poetry. He is neither brief nor simple:

> —all our yesterdays have lighted fools
> The way to dusty death. Out, out, brief candle!
> Life's but a walking shadow; a poor player
> That struts and frets his hour upon the stage—

The English poet puts before his audience the full tragedy as they would never see it but for him. He does it all for them in words so splendid, in images so poignant, they are lifted to a vision that completely transcends themselves. The Greek poet lifts one corner of the curtain only. A glimpse is given, no more, but by it the mind is fired to see for itself what lies behind. The writer will do no more than suggest the way to go, but he does it in such a fashion that the imagination is quickened to create for itself. Pindar takes two lovers to the door of their chamber and dismisses them: "Secret are wise persuasion's keys unto love's sanctities." This is not Shakespeare's way with Romeo and Juliet. The English method is to fill the mind with beauty; the Greek method was to set the mind to work.

# Chapter V

## PINDAR

### THE LAST GREEK ARISTOCRAT

"PINDAR ASTOUNDS," says Dr. Middleton in *The Egoist*, "but Homer brings the more sustaining cup. One is a fountain of prodigious ascent; the other, the unsounded purple sea of marching billows."

The problem anyone faces who would write about Pindar is how to put a fountain of prodigious ascent into words. Homer's unsounded purple sea is in comparison easy to describe. Homer tells a great story simply and splendidly. Something of his greatness and simplicity and splendor is bound to come through in any truthful account of him; the difficult thing would be to obscure it completely. The same is true of the tragedians. The loftiness and majesty of their thoughts break through our stumbling attempts at description no matter how little is left of the beauty of their expression. Even translation does not necessarily destroy thoughts and stories. Shelley's poet

> hidden
> In the light of thought,
> Singing hymns unbidden
> Till the world is wrought
> To sympathy with hopes and fears it heeded not—

could be turned into another tongue without a total loss.

But this kind of poetry is at the opposite pole to Pindar's. Hopes and fears unheeded by the world he lived in were never his. The light of thought shed no glory of new illumination upon his mind. Such thinking as he did went along conventional, ready-made channels and could have moved no one to sympathy except the most stationary

minds of his day. Nevertheless he was a very great poet.
He is securely seated among the immortals. And yet only
a few people know him. The band of his veritable admirers
is and always has been small. Of all the Greek poets he
is the most difficult to read, and of all the poets there ever
were he is the most impossible to translate. George Meredith with his fountain of prodigious ascent gives half of
the reason why. So, too, does Horace, who paints essentially the same picture of him:

> Like to a mountain stream rushing down in fury,
> Overflowing the banks with its rain-fed current,
> Pindar's torrent of song sweeps on resistless,
> 　　Deep-voiced, tremendous.
> Or by a mighty wind he is borne skyward,
> 　　Where great clouds gather.

Pindar is all that. One feels "life abundantly" within him,
inexhaustible spontaneity, an effortless mastery over trea-
sures of rich and incomparably vivid expression, the fountain shooting upward, irresistible, unforced—and beyond
description. But in spite of this sense he gives of ease and
freedom and power, he is in an equal degree a consummate
craftsman, an artist in fullest command of the technique
of his art, and that fact is the other half of the reason why
he is untranslatable. His poetry is of all poetry the most
like music, not the music that wells up from the bird's
throat, but the music that is based on structure, on fundamental laws of balance and symmetry, on carefully calculated effects, a Bach fugue, a Beethoven sonata or symphony. One might almost as well try to put a symphony
into words as try to give any impression of Pindar's odes
by an English transcription.

We ourselves know little about that kind of writing. It
is impossible to illustrate Pindar's poetry from English
poetry. Metre was far more important to the Greeks than
it is to us. That may seem a strange assertion. The rhythmic
beauty and lovely sound of the verse of countless English
poets is one of the characteristics we think most of in them.
Even so, it is true that the Greeks thought more of metrical
perfections. They would have in their poetry balanced

measure answering measure, cunningly sought correspondence of meaning and rhythm; they loved a great sweep of varied movement, swift and powerful, yet at the same time absolutely controlled. The sound is beautiful in

Bare ruined choirs where late the sweet birds sang

and in

Under the glassy, cool, translucent wave

Nevertheless Shakespeare and Milton are painters with words more than they are master craftsmen in metrical effects. "A poem is the very image of life," Shelley said. No Greek poet would have thought about his art like that, hardly more than Bach would about his. The English-speaking race is not eminently musical. The Greek was, and the sound of words meant to them something beyond anything we perceive. Pindar's consummate craftsmanship, which produces the effect upon the ear of a great sweep of song, cannot be matched in English literature.

But Kipling has something akin to him. The swift movement and the strong beat of the measure in some of his poems come nearer than anything else we have—if not to Pindar himself, at any rate to what an English reader unversed in the intricacies of musical composition can get from him. Compare

That night we stormed Valhalla, a million years ago—

with the two lines just quoted from Shakespeare and Milton, and Kipling's characteristic speed of movement and strength of stress become evident. Pindar could be as stately as Shakespeare and Milton on occasion; he could do anything he chose with words, but the measures he preferred have the sweep and lift Kipling shows so often:

Follow the Romany patteran
Sheer to the Austral Light,
Where the besom of God is the wild South wind,
Sweeping the sea-floors white.

The Lord knows what we may find, dear lass,
And the Deuce knows what we may do—
But we're back once more on the old trail, our own trail,
    the out trail,
We're down, hull-down, on the long trail, the trail that is
    always new.

In such lines the rhythm is of first importance. What they say is not of any especial consequence; the great movement holds the attention. The lines stay in the mind as music, not thoughts, and that is even truer of Pindar's poetry. His resources of vivid and beautiful metrical expression are immensely greater than Kipling's, and the compass of his music, too. The mirror Kipling holds up to him is a tiny thing; nevertheless we shall not find a better. It is worthy of note that Kipling himself declared that he was one of the little band of Pindar's lovers:

> Me, in whose breast no flame hath burned
> Life-long, save that by Pindar lit.

If Pindar's poetry is, when all is said and done, indescribable and his thoughts merely conventional, it would seem superfluous to write about him. It is anything but that to one who wants to understand Greece. Pindar is the last spokesman for the Greek aristocracy and the greatest after Homer. The aristocratic ideal, so powerful in shaping the Greek genius, is shown best of all in his poetry.

He was an aristocrat by race and by conviction, born in the late sixth century when aristocracy in Greece was nearing its end. The first democracy in the world was coming to birth in Athens. Pindar was the figure upon which much romantic pity and sympathy have been expended—the champion of a dying cause. The man who fights for a new cause does not receive that tribute. He is up against the immense force of stubborn resistance the new always arouses. He must give battle without trumpets and drums and with the probability that he will not live to see the victory. Indeed he cannot be sure that there will ever be a victory. Nevertheless he is far more to be envied

than the man who tries to turn the tide back; and that is
what Pindar did.

To judge him fairly one must consider what the ideal
was that produced the aristocratic creed. It was founded
upon a conception altogether different from the one behind
tyranny, of all power in the hands of a single man. The
tyrants departed from Greece unlamented, and never to
be revived again even in wishful thinking, except for Plato's
rulers who were to be given absolute power only upon the
condition that they did not want it, a curious parallel to
the attitude prescribed by the early Church. A man appointed to the episcopacy was required to say—perhaps
still must say, forms live so long after the spirit once in
them is dead—"I do not want to be a bishop. *Nolo
episcopari.*" To the Fathers of the Church as to Plato, no
one who desired power was fit to wield it.

But the case for the aristocracy was different. In the
aristocratic creed, power was to be held by men who alone
were immune to the temptations that beset, on the one
hand, those struggling to be powerful and, on the other,
those struggling to survive. The proper leaders of the world,
the only ones who could be trusted to guide it disinterestedly, were a class from generation to generation raised
above the common level, not by self-seeking ambition, but
by birth; a class which a great tradition and a careful
training made superior to the selfish greed and the servile
meanness other men were subject to. As a class they were
men of property, but position was not dependent upon
wealth. The blood ran as blue in the veins of the poor
noble as in the rich, and precedence was never a mere
matter of money. Thus, absolutely sure and secure, free
from the anxious personal preoccupations which distract
men at large, they could see clearly on the lofty eminence
they were born to, what those lower down could not catch
a glimpse of, and they could direct mankind along the way
it should go.

Nor was their own way, the aristocratic way, by any
means a path of ease. They had standards not accessible
to ordinary men, standards well-nigh impossible to men
obliged to fight for their daily bread. An aristocrat must

not tell a lie (except in love and war); he must keep his word, never take advantage of another, be cheated in a bargain rather than cheat by so much as a hair's breadth. He must show perfect courage, perfect courtesy, even to an enemy; a certain magnificence in the conduct of his life, a generous liberality as far as his means could be stretched, and he must take pride in living up to this severe code. Aristocrats subjected themselves as proudly and willingly to the exacting discipline of the gentleman as they did to the rigid discipline of the warrior. High privilege was theirs, but it was weighted by great responsibility. The burden of leadership lay upon them; they must direct and protect the unprivileged. Nobility of birth must be matched by nobility of conduct.

This was the creed of the aristocracy. Theoretically it is impeccable. Men placed by birth in a position where disinterestedness was easy were trained from childhood to rule other men for their greater welfare. Purely as a theory there is not another that can compete with it, except the one that all men are to be enabled to be disinterested, trained to be rulers, not of others, but each of his own self, and all interdependent, equally bound to give help and to accept it. This utopia, the merest dream so far, is the only conception that surpasses or even matches the conception of authority in the hands of the disciplined best. But most unfortunately for the world it did not work. There was no fault with the idea, only with its supporters. It was never allowed to work by those who upheld it. That is beyond dispute to us to-day. From the first moment that we catch sight of it in history it is a failure. Class privilege has become class prejudice, if it had ever been anything else; inherited power creates a thirst for acquiring more power; nobility of birth has no connection with spiritual nobility. The aristocrats always failed every time they had their chance. Their latest embodiment, the English House of Lords, endowed by birth with all the best the world could give—power, riches, reverential respect—fought throughout the nineteenth century with almost religious resolution every attempt to raise the condition, the wages or education, of the agricultural laborer.

We all know that by now; but Pindar did not. He believed that the great had and would use their power for the benefit of others. His poems express to perfection and for the last time in Greek literature the class consciousness of the old Greek aristocracy, their conviction of their own lofty moral and religious value. It has often been pointed out that the perfect expression of anything means that that thing has reached its culmination and is on the point of declining. *La clarté parfaite, n'est elle pas le signe de la lassitude des idées?* The statue of the man throwing the discus, the charioteer at Delphi, the stern young horsemen of the Parthenon frieze, and the poetry of Pindar—all show the culmination of the great ideal Greek aristocracy inspired just before it came to an end: physical perfection which evokes mysteriously the sense of spiritual perfection. Every poem Pindar wrote is a tribute to that union.

The games, the great games, had belonged time out of mind to the aristocrats. Only they had money enough and leisure enough to undergo the strenuous discipline of the athlete for the reward of a crown of wild olives. When Pindar lived, the bourgeois were beginning to take part in them, but professionalism had not yet come into being. Almost all his poems that we have are songs in honor of a noble victor at one of the four chief games—the Pythian near Delphi, the Isthmian at Corinth, the Nemean in Argolis, and, most glorious of all, the Olympic at Olympia. These triumphal odes are written in a way peculiar to Pindar. No other poems that praise physical achievement, poems of battle and adventure and the like, bear the least resemblance to them, and it is Pindar's creed as an aristocrat that marks them out. Anyone who has not read him would expect his songs to centre in the encounter he celebrates, to describe the thrilling scene when the chariots went whirling down the race course, or the light flashing feet of the runners carried them past the breathless crowd, or two splendid young bodies locked together in the tension of the wrestling match. Nothing light was at stake. A victory meant the glory of a lifetime. The soul-stirring excitement together with the extreme beauty of the spectacle would seem to give a theme fitted to the heart's desire

of a poet. But Pindar dismisses all of it. He hardly alludes
to the contest. He describes nothing that happened. A good
case could be made out for his never having been present
at a game. He sings praises to a victor and he disdains to
mention a detail of the victory. His attention is fixed upon
the young hero, not upon his achievement. He sees him as
the noble representative of the noble, showing in himself
the true ideal for humanity. He sees him as a religious
figure, bringing to the god in whose honor the game was
held the homage of a victory won by the utmost effort of
body and spirit. What did this or that outside event matter
—the way a horse ran or a man, or the way they looked,
or the way they struggled? Pindar was glorifying one who
had upheld the traditions of the great past upon which all
the hope of the world depended.

In all his odes there is a story of some hero of old told
with solemnity. The hero of the present, the victor, is
pointed back to what men in other ages did and so shown
what men in future ages could do. Pindar gives him a
model upon which to form himself and make himself fit
to join the august company of the noble dead. Pindar in
his own eyes had a mission to the world lofty enough to
employ worthily the great endowments of genius and noble
blood he had been born to. He was the preacher and the
teacher divinely appointed to proclaim the glory of the
golden past and to summon all the nobly born and the
highly placed to live their own lives in the light of that
glory. This was his great charge, and no man on earth,
however powerful, could make him think himself inferior.
He felt not the slightest degree of subserviency. He spoke
to his patron invariably as one equal to another. So they
were in his eyes. In point of birth, they were both aristocrats; in point of achievement, the glory of an Olympic
victory did not surpass the glory of his poetry. When sum-
moned to Sicily to make an ode in honor of one or another
of the mighty tyrants there who often competed in the
games, he would admonish him and exhort him exactly as
he would any lesser noble. Indeed, in the many poems he
wrote to Hieron the Magnificent, the tyrant of Syracuse,
he speaks more plainly even than elsewhere. "Become what

you really are," he bids the great ruler. Pindar will show
him his true self and spur him not to sink below it. "Be
straight-tongued"—in the old aristocratic tradition, which
is ever "in harmony with God, and shoulder the yoke
which God has laid upon you."

There is nothing quite so unique in literature as these
solemn admonitory poems dedicated to the praise of a
powerful ruler and a popular hero crowned in an athletic
victory, and written in a way that is the very reverse of
the popular, never condescending to one word of flattery.
"Wherefore seeing we are compassed about with so great a
cloud of witnesses, let us run with patience the race that is
set before us." Something like that Pindar said to his
victorious athletes, and no other poems written to praise
an exploit, athletic or military or of any sort, ever said
anything in the least like that—as witness all the poets
laureate.

He is different from them all. His subjects were chosen
for him just as theirs were, and no doubt he too was paid
for his poems; but these were matters of no importance
to him. The thing that mattered was that he always would
and could write exactly as he pleased. His odes were
written at command, but how they were written was his
affair alone. He was loftily sure of his own position. There
never was a writer more proudly conscious of superiority.
He is "an eagle soaring sunward," he declares, while below
him the other poets "vainly croak like ravens," or "feed
low like chattering crows." His odes are "radiant blossoms
of song"; "an arrow of praise that will not miss the mark";
they are "a torch, a flame, a fiery dart"; "a golden goblet
full of foaming wine."

"I will set ablaze the beloved city with my burning song.
To every quarter of the earth my word shall go, swifter
than noble horse or winged ship." "Within Apollo's golden
vale I build a treasure-house of song. No rain of winter
sweeping to the uttermost parts of the sea upon the wings
of the wind, no storm-lashed hurricane, shall lay it low,
but in pure light the glorious portal shall proclaim the
victory."

Such poetry proves its sublime descent. The power to

write it, Pindar says in many an ode, comes from God alone. It is no more to be acquired than noble blood by the baseborn. Can excellence be learned? Socrates was to ask the Athenians that question again and again in a later day, but Pindar first propounded it and his answer was, No. "Through inborn glory a man is mighty indeed, but he who learns from teaching is a twilight man, wavering in spirit." That is the *ne plus ultra* of the aristocratic creed, and so stated it cannot be refuted. To us to-day the theory of the aristocracy has almost ceased to be. The fact that there are aristocrats remains. Power, of poetry or anything else, comes to a man by birth; it cannot be taught in the public schools.

The Greeks put Pindar with Æschylus and Thucydides, in the "austere" school of writing, the severe and unadorned. It seems a curious judgment in view of his power of rich and vivid expression, which is one of his most marked characteristics, but there is much truth in it. Pindar is austere. Splendor can be cold, and Pindar glitters but never warms. He is hard, severe, passionless, remote, with a kind of haughty magnificence. He never steps down from his frigid eminence. Aristocrats did not stoop to lies, and his pen would never deviate from the strict truth in praising any triumph. He would glorify a victor so far as he was really glorious, but no further. As he himself puts it, he would not tell "a tale decked out with dazzling lies against the word of truth." Only what was in actual fact nobly praiseworthy would be praised by him. "Now do I believe," he says, "that the sweet words of Homer make great beyond the fact the story of Odysseus, and upon these falsities through Homer's winged skill there broods a mysterious spell. His art deceives us. . . . But as for me, whoever has examined can declare if I speak crooked words." Again, "In ways of single-heartedness may I walk through life, not holding up a glory fair-seeming but false." And in another ode:

> Forge thy tongue on an anvil of truth
> And what flies up, though it be but a spark,
> Shall have weight.

Nevertheless, also strictly in the aristocratic tradition, he would leave the truth unsaid if it was ugly or unpleasant, offensive to delicate feeling. "Believe me," he writes, "not every truth is the better for showing its face unveiled." He adds:

> That which has not the grace of God is better far in silence.

The reserve which has always been held to characterize gentlefolk is stamped on everything he wrote. "It is fitting," he writes, "for a man to utter what is seemly and good," and in one way and another the idea is repeated throughout the odes. Essentially the same feeling makes him unwilling to touch with his pen the torments of the damned in hell which so many great writers have loved to linger on. The joys of the saved, yes:

> Their boon is life forever free from toil.
> No more to trouble earth or the sea waters
> With their strong hands,
> Laboring for the food that does not satisfy.
> But with the favored of the gods they live
> A life where there are no more tears.
> Around those blessed isles soft sea winds breathe,
> And golden flowers blaze upon the trees,
> Upon the waters, too.

But as for the others, "those bear anguish too great for eye to look upon." A gentleman will not join the staring crowd. Neither Virgil nor Dante would have tempted Pindar to journey in their company.

If Pindar had lived where he belonged by all his convictions and ideas—in the sixth century, or the seventh, instead of the fifth, he would be that not uncommon figure among men of exceptional gifts, a man of genius moving with the tide and not great enough to perceive that the flow is feeble and the ebb is near. But Pindar's life was lived when the tide of Greek achievement was at fullest flow, and he withstood it. Marathon, Thermopylæ, Salamis —he had no part in them nor in the exultant and solemn triumph the land felt when the Persian power was broken. Not an echo of these heroic events is in his poetry. His city, Thebes, did not join in the glorious struggle. She refused to help, and her poet took his stand with her. He acted as the aristocrats always act in the face of whatever threatens to disturb things as they are. He did concede praise to the chief defender of Greece, Athens, in two famous lines,

> O shining white and famed in song and violet-wreathed,
> Fortress of Hellas, glorious Athens, city of God,

but that was the utmost he could do for the new cause. What was dawning in Greece would give light to the world for all ages to come, but Pindar would not look at it. He kept his eyes fixed on the past. He used his genius, his grave and lofty spirit, his moral fervor, to defend a cause that was dying through the unworthiness of its own supporters. And that, not the difficulty of understanding his poetry, is at bottom the reason why he has not meant more and has become to the world a name without a content. What has the man who is bent wholly on the past to say to those who come after him? Æschylus, also an aristocrat, was able to discard the idea of being set apart by noble birth and become the spokesman for the new freedom which after Salamis leveled old barriers. His poetry is permeated with aspiration toward a good never known before, and with insight into loftier possibilities for humanity than had ever yet been discerned. He saw Athens no longer divided into ruler and ruled, but the common possession of a united people. To compare this spirit with Pindar's is to see why with all his great gifts Pindar essentially failed. Æschylus is greatly daring as the leader to new heights must be; Pindar is cautious and careful, as the defensive always must be. Stay within safe limits, he constantly urges. The aristocrats must attempt nothing further if they are to keep what they have. He warns them solemnly not only against ambition, but against aspiration as well. It is dangerous; it tempts a man to stray from the old roads to the unknown. Be content, he tells the victor in the games. Seek nothing further. Man's powers are bounded by his mortality; it is sheer folly to think that that can ever be transcended. "Strive not thou to become a god. The things of mortals best befit mortality." And again, "Desire not the life of the immortals, but drink thy fill of what thou hast and what thou canst." "May God give me," he prays, "to aim at that which is within my power." An Olympic victory is the height of human achievement, as is also in a different sense the splendor and dignity and remoteness from all things vulgar of a great prince's court, as Hieron's in Syracuse. That height once gained, all that remains is to defend it and keep it inviolate for nobles and tyrants forever.

As a result, Pindar is often sad. The brilliant odes of victory have an undercurrent of dejection. It is a discouraging task to defend in perpetuity. Hieron's festal board is spread; the wine sparkles in the golden cups; the highborn gather to celebrate; they chant the praise of driver and steeds that won the glorious race—and the mournfulness of all things human weighs down the poet's heart. That terrifying page has been reached in the book of man's destiny which Flaubert says is entitled "Accomplished Desires." There is nothing to look forward to. The best has been achieved, with the result that hope and endeavor are ended. Then turn your eyes away from the future. It can bring nothing that is better; it may bring much that is worse. The past alone is safe, and the brief moment of the present. This point of view has no especial distinction; it is not profound, neither deeply melancholy nor poignantly pathetic. It is hardly more than dissatisfaction, a verdict of "Vanity of vanities; all is vanity." "Brief is the growing time of joy for mortals and brief the flower's bloom that falls to earth shaken by grim fate. Things of a day! What are we and what are we not. Man is a shadow's dream." That is Pindar's highest contribution toward solving the enigma of human life.

Only in a very minor capacity does he still speak to the world as the greatest interpreter of the Greek aristocracy at its greatest moment. In his true and sovereign capacity as a mighty poet he has almost ceased to speak. It is our irreparable loss that his peculiar beauties of language and rhythm cannot ever be transferred in any degree into English. It is our still more irreparable loss that this man of genius used his great gifts to shed light only upon the past and turned away from the present which was so full of promise for the future of all the world to come.

# Chapter VI

## THE ATHENIANS AS PLATO SAW THEM

ONCE upon a time—the exact date cannot be given but it was not far from 450 B.C.—an Athenian fleet cast anchor near an island in the Ægean as the sun was setting. Athens was making herself mistress of the sea and the attack on the island was to be begun the next morning. That evening the commander-in-chief, no less a one, the story goes, than Pericles himself, sent an invitation to his second in command to sup with him on the flag-ship. So there you may see them sitting on the ship's high poop, a canopy over their heads to keep off the dew. One of the attendants is a beautiful boy and as he fills the cups Pericles bethinks him of the poets and quotes a line about the "purple light" upon a fair young cheek. The younger general is critical: it had never seemed to him that the color-adjective was well chosen. He preferred another poet's use of rosy to describe the bloom of youth. Pericles on his side objects: that very poet had elsewhere used purple in the same way when speaking of the radiance of young loveliness. So the conversation went on, each man capping the other's quotation with one as apt. The entire talk at the supper table turned on delicate and fanciful points of literary criticism. But, nonetheless, when the battle began the next morning, these same men, fighting fiercely and directing wisely, carried the attack on the island.

The literal truth of the charming anecdote I cannot vouch for, but it is to be noted that no such story has come down to us about the generals of any other country except Greece. No flight of fancy has ever conceived of a discussion on color-adjectives between Cæsar and the trusty Labienus on the eve of crossing the Rhine, nor, we may feel reasonably assured, will any soaring imagination in the future depict General Grant thus diverting himself with General Sherman. That higher truth which Aristotle claimed for poetry over history is here perfectly exemplified. The little story, however apocryphal, gives a picture true to life of what the Athenians of the great age of Athens were like. Two cultivated gentlemen are shown to us, of a great fastidiousness, the poets their familiar companions, able the evening before a battle to absorb themselves in the lesser niceties of literary criticism, but, with all this, mighty men of action, soldiers, sailors, generals, statesmen, any age would be hard put to it to excel. The combination is rarely found in the annals of history. It is to be completely civilized without having lost in the process anything of value.

Civilization, a much abused word, stands for a high matter quite apart from telephones and electric lights. It is a matter of imponderables, of delight in the things of the mind, of love of beauty, of honor, grace, courtesy, delicate feeling. Where imponderables are the things of first importance, there is the height of civilization, and if, at the same time, the power to act exists unimpaired, human life has reached a level seldom attained and very seldom surpassed. Few individuals are capable of the achievement; periods of history which have produced such men in sufficient numbers to stamp their age are rare indeed.

Pericles, according to Thucydides, held the Athens of his day to be one of them. The most famous of his sayings gives, in brief but to perfection, the height of civilization attained with undiminished power to act. The Athenians, he says, are "lovers of beauty without having lost the taste for simplicity, and lovers of wisdom without loss of manly vigor."

We need no proof that the Greeks of the fifth century B.C. had not lost their manly vigor. Marathon, Thermopylæ, Salamis, are names that will forever be immortal for valor matched against overwhelming numbers, and the grandsons of those same great warriors whom Pericles was addressing were themselves engaged in a stern and bitter war. But it is difficult for us to-day to realize how important the imponderables were in Greece. The poet Sophocles, so the story is told, in his extreme old age was brought into court by his son who charged him with being incompetent to manage his own affairs. The aged tragedian's sole defense was to recite to the jurors passages from a play he had recently written. Those great words did not fall on deaf ears. Judge a man who could write such poetry not competent in any way? Who that called himself Greek could do that? Nay: dismiss the case; fine the complainant; let the defendant depart honored and triumphant.

Again, when Athens had fallen and her Spartan conquerors held high festival on the eve of destroying the city altogether, razing to the ground the buildings, not a pillar to be left standing on the Acropolis, one of the men charged with the poetical part of the entertainment—even Spartans must have poetry to their banquet—gave a recitation from Euripides, and the banqueters, stern soldiers in the great moment of their hard-won triumph, listening to the beautiful, poignant words, forgot victory and vengeance, and declared as one man that the city such a poet had sprung from should never be destroyed. So important were imponderables to the Greeks. Poetry, all the arts, were matters of high seriousness, which it appeared perfectly reasonable that the freedom of a man and a city's life might hang upon.

It is clear that in Greece the values were different from our own to-day. Indeed we are not able really to bring into one consistent whole their outlook upon life; from our point of view it seems to involve a self-contradiction. People so devoted to poetry as to make it a matter of practical importance must have been, we feel, deficient in the sense for what is practically important, dreamers, not alive to life's hard facts. Nothing could be further from the truth. The Greeks were pre-eminently realists. The temper of mind that made them carve their statues and paint their pictures from the living human beings around them, that kept their poetry within the sober limits of the possible, made them hard-headed men in the world of every-day affairs. They were not tempted to evade facts.

It is we ourselves who are the sentimentalists. We, to whom poetry, all art, is only a superficial decoration of life, made a refuge from a world that is too hard for us to face by sentimentalizing it. The Greeks looked straight at it. They were completely unsentimental. It was a Roman who said it was sweet to die for one's country. The Greeks never said it was sweet to die for anything. They had no vital lies.

The great funeral oration of Pericles, delivered over those fallen in the war, stands out as unlike all other commemoration speeches ever spoken. There is not a trace of exaltation in it, not a word of heroic declamation. It is a piece of clear thinking and straight talking. The orator tells his audience to pray that they may never have to die in battle as these did. He does not suggest or imply to the mourning parents before him that they are to be accounted happy because their sons died for Athens. He knows they are not and it does not occur to him to say anything but the truth. His words to them are:

> Some of you are of an age at which they may hope to have other children, and they ought to bear their sorrow better. To those of you who have passed their prime, I say: Congratulate yourselves that you have been happy during the greater part of your days; remember that your life of sorrow will not last long, and take comfort in the glory of those who are gone.

Cold comfort, we say. Yes, but people so stricken cannot be comforted, and Pericles knew his audience. They had faced the facts as well as he had. To read the quiet, grave, matter-of-fact words is to be reminded by the force of opposites of all the speeches everywhere over the tombs of the Unknown Soldier.

Completely in line with this spirit is the often quoted epitaph on the Lacedæmonians who fell at Thermopylæ. Every one of them fell, as they knew beforehand they would. They fought their battle to the death with no hope to help them and by so dying they saved Greece, but all the great poet who wrote their epitaph found it fitting to say for them was:

O passer-by, tell the Lacedæmonians that we lie here in obedience to their laws.

We rebel; something more than that, we feel, is due such heroism. But the Greeks did not. Facts were facts and deeds spoke for themselves. They did not need ornament.

Often we are repelled by words that seem to us wanting in common human sympathy. When Œdipus appears for the last time before his exile and speaks his misery, all that his friends say is:

These things were even as thou sayest.

And to his wish that he had died in infancy they answer:

I also would have had it thus.

The attitude seems hard but it is always to be borne in mind that the Greeks did not only face facts, they had not even a desire to escape from them. When Iphigenia says that Orestes must die but Pylades may go free, he refuses to take his life on such terms, but he refuses like a Greek and not a modern. It is not love of his friend alone that constrains him but also fear of what people would say, and he knows it and speaks it straight: "Men will whisper how I left my friend to die. Nay—I love you and I dread men's scorn." That is honest but we cannot any more be honest like that. It shocks us. The combination that resulted in the Athenian is baffling to us, lovers of beauty who held poetry and music and art to be of first importance—in their schools the two principal subjects the boys learned were music and mathematics—and at the same time, lovers of fact, who held fast to reality. Pindar prays: "With God's help may I still love what is beautiful and strive for what is attainable." "What I aspire to be and am not, comforts me," would never have appealed to a Greek.

The society these men made up whose sense of values is so strange to us, can be in some sort reconstructed, an idea of what their ways and their manner of life was like is to be had, even though the historical records, as usual, say nothing about the things we most want to know. Stories like those given above were not told of the Greeks because one man or two, a Pericles, a Socrates, had such notions. The golden deeds of a nation, however mythical, throw a clear light upon its standards and ideals. They are the revelation that cannot be mistaken of the people's conscience, of what they think men should be like. Their stories and their plays tell more about them than all their histories. To understand the mid-Victorians one must go not to the history writers but to Dickens and Anthony Trollope. For the Athenians of the great age we turn not to Thucydides, the historian, interested in Athens rather than her citizens, but to two writers unlike in every respect but one, their power to understand and depict the men they lived with: to Aristophanes, who made fun of them and scolded them and abused them and held them up for themselves to see in every play he wrote, and to Plato, who, for all that his business lay with lofty speculations on the nature of the ideal, was a student and lover of human nature too, and has left us in the personages of his dialogues characters so admirably drawn, they still live in his pages.

Many of the men met there are known to us from other writers. Some of the most famous persons of the day take part in the discussions. Whether all of them were real people or not there is no means of knowing, but there can be no doubt that they all are true to life, and that they seemed to Plato's hearers perfectly natural men, such as any upper-class Athenian was used to. Nothing else is credible. To suppose that Plato's idealism extended to his dramatis personæ, and that he put his doctrines in the mouths of personages who would appear unreal and absurd to his pupils, is to insult their intelligence and his. It is true that he does not give a cross-section of Athens, any more than Trollope does of England. A few people "not in society" make their appearance—a man who earns his living by giving recitations from Homer; a soothsayer, to Plato on the same social level as a clergyman to Sir Roger de Coverley—but the people he really knows are the gentlemen of Athens and he knows them as Trollope knows his parsons and his M.P.'s.

This society he introduces us to is eminently civilized, of men delighting to use their minds, loving beauty and

elegance, as Pericles says in the funeral oration, keenly
alive to all the amenities of life, and, above all, ever ready
for a talk on no matter how abstract and abstruse a subject: "When we entered the house"—the speaker is Socrates
—"we found Protagoras walking in the cloister; a train of
listeners accompanied him; he, like Orpheus, attracting
them by his voice and they following. Then, as Homer says,
'I lifted up my eyes and saw' Hippias the Elean sitting in
the opposite cloister and many seated on benches around
him. They were putting to him questions on physics and
astronomy and he was discoursing of them. Also Prodicus
the Cean was there, still in bed—the day, be it noted, was
just dawning—and beside him on the couches near, a
number of young men. His fine deep voice re-echoed
through the room." Socrates begs Protagoras to talk to
them of his teaching and when the great man agrees, "As
I suspected that he would like a little display and glorifica-
tion in the presence of Prodicus and Hippias, I said, 'But
why should we not summon the rest to hear?' 'Suppose,'
said Callias, the host, 'we hold a council in which you may
sit and discuss?' This was agreed upon and great delight
was felt at the prospect of hearing wise men talk." And
so they all settle down happily to argue about the identity
of virtue and knowledge and whether virtue can be taught.

It is, one perceives, a leisured society. Socrates speaks
to the young Theætetus of "the ease which free men can
always command. They can have their talk out in peace,
wandering at will from one subject to another, their only
aim to attain the truth." But the direct witness is hardly
needed; an atmosphere of perfect leisure is the setting of
all the dialogues and to immerse oneself in them is to be
carried into a world where no one is ever hurried and
where there is always time and to spare. "I went down
yesterday to the Piræus with Glaucon," so the *Republic*
begins, "to offer up my prayers to the goddess and also
to see how they would celebrate the festival. When we had
finished and were turned toward the city, Polemarchus
appeared and several others who had been at the procession. 'You are on your way to the city?' he said, 'But do
you see how many we are? And are you stronger than all

these? If not, you will have to stay.' 'But,' said I, 'may there not be an alternative? May we not persuade you to let us go?' 'Can you, if we refuse to listen? And you may be sure we shall. Stay and see the torch race on horseback this evening. And there will be a gathering of young men and we will have a good talk.' "

After some such fashion nearly every dialogue begins. The most charmingly leisured of them is, perhaps, the *Phædrus*. "Where are you bound?" Socrates asks Phædrus, to which the young man answers that he is going for a walk outside the wall to refresh himself after a morning spent in talk with a great rhetorician: "You shall hear about it if you can spare time to accompany me." Well, Socrates says, he so longs to hear it that he would go all the way to Megara and back rather than miss it. With this, Phædrus begins to be doubtful if he can do justice to the great man: "Believe me, Socrates, I did not learn his very words—oh, no. Still, I have a general notion of what he said and can give you a summary." "Yes, dear lad," replies Socrates, "but you must first of all show what you have under your cloak—for that roll I suspect is the actual discourse, and much as I love you, I am not going to have you exercise your memory at my expense." Phædrus gives in—he will read the whole essay; but where shall they sit? Oh, yes, under "that tallest plane-tree, where there is shade and gentle breezes and grass on which to sit or lie." "Yes," Socrates answers, "a fair resting place, full of summer sounds and scents, the stream deliciously cool to the feet, and the grass like a pillow gently sloping to the head. I shall lie down and do you choose the position you can best read in. Begin." A number of hours are spent under that plane-tree, discussing "the nature of the soul—though her true form be ever a theme of large and more than mortal discourse"; and "beauty shining in company with celestial forms"; and "the soul of the lover that follows the beloved in modesty and holy fear"; and "the heavenly blessings of friendship"; and "all the great arts, which require high speculation about the truths of nature"; and men who "are worthy of a proud name befitting their serious pursuit of life. Wise, I may not call them, for that

is a great name which belongs to God alone—lovers of
wisdom is their fitting title." That is the way two gentlemen would while away a summer morning in the Athens
of Plato.

It is a society marked also by an exquisite urbanity, of
men gently bred, easy, suave, polished. The most famous
dinner-party that was ever given was held at the house of
Agathon the Elegant, who declared to his guests as they
took their places that he never gave orders to his servants
on such occasions: "I say to them: Imagine that you are
our hosts and I and the company your guests; treat us well
and we shall commend you." Into this atmosphere of ease
and the informality past masters in the social art permit
themselves, an acquaintance is introduced by mistake who
had not been invited, a mishap with awkward possibilities
for people less skilled in the amenities than our banqueters.
Instantly he is made to feel at home, greeted in the most
charming fashion: " 'Oh, welcome, Aristodemus,' and
Agathon, 'you are just in time to sup with us. If you come
on any other matter put it off and make one of us. I was
looking for you yesterday to invite you if I could have
found you.' "

Socrates is late. It appears that he has fallen into a meditation under a portico on the way. When he enters,
"Agathon begged that he would take the place next to him
'that I may touch you and have the benefit of that wise
thought which came into your mind in the portico.' 'How
I wish,' said Socrates, taking his place as he was desired,
'that wisdom could be infused by touch. If that were so
how greatly should I value the privilege of reclining at
your side, for you would fill me with a stream of wisdom
plenteous and fair, whereas my own is of a very questionable sort.' " An argument is started and Agathon gives way:
"I cannot refute you, Socrates." "Ah no," is the answer.
"Say rather, dear Agathon, that you cannot refute the
truth, for Socrates is easily refuted." It is social intercourse
at its perfection, to be accounted for only by a process of
long training. Good breeding of that stamp was never
evolved in one generation nor two, and yet these men were
the grandsons of those that fought at Marathon and

Salamis. Heroic daring and the imponderables of high civilization were the inheritance they were born to.

Through the dialogues moves the figure of Socrates, a unique philosoper, unlike all philosophers that ever were outside of Greece. They are, these others, very generally strange and taciturn beings, or so we conceive them, aloof, remote, absorbed in abstruse speculations, only partly human. The completest embodiment of our idea of a philosopher is Kant, the little stoop-shouldered, absent-minded man, who moved only between his house and the university, and by whom all the housewives in Königsberg set their clocks when they saw him pass on his way to the lecture-room of a morning. Such was not Socrates. He could not be, being a Greek. A great many different things were expected of him and he had to be able to meet a great many different situations. We ourselves belong to an age of specialists, the result, really, of our belonging to an age that loves comfort. It is obvious that one man doing only one thing can work faster, and the reasonable conclusion in a world that wants a great many things, is to arrange to have him do it. Twenty men making each a minute bit of a shoe, turn out far more than twenty times the number of shoes that the cobbler working alone did, and in consequence no one must go barefoot. We have our reward in an ever-increasing multiplication of the things everyone needs but we pay our price in the limit set to the possibilities of development for each individual worker.

In Greece it was just the other way about. The things they needed were by comparison few, but every man had to act in a number of different capacities. An Athenian citizen in his time played many parts. Æschylus was not only a writer of plays; he was an entire theatrical staff, actor, scenic artist, costumer, designer, mechanician, producer. He was also a soldier who fought in the ranks, and had probably held a civic office; most Athenians did. No doubt if we knew more about his life we should find that he had still other avocations. His brother-dramatist, Sophocles, was a general and a diplomat and a priest as well; a practical man of the theatre too, who made at least one important innovation. There was no artist class in Greece, withdrawn from active life, no literary class, no learned class. Their soldiers and their sailors and their politicians and their men of affairs wrote their poetry and carved their statues and though out their philosophy. "To sum up"—the speaker is Pericles—"I say that Athens is the school of Greece and that the individual Athenian in his own person seems to have the power of adapting himself to the most varied forms of action with the utmost versatility and grace"—that last word a touch so peculiarly Greek.

So Socrates was everything rather than what we expect a learned man and a philosopher to be. To begin with, he was extremely social; he delighted above all in company. "I am a lover of knowledge," he says of himself, "and men are my teachers." He would have them gentlemen, however. He liked a man who had been brought up to do things properly. "A narrow, keen, little legal mind—one who knows not how to wear his cloak like a gentleman," is his dismissal of an objectionable person.

He takes us sometimes into very illustrious company indeed. Just before a great public funeral he meets an acquaintance on his way from the Agora who tells him the Council are about to choose the orator for the occasion, and asks: "Do you think you could speak yourself if they were to choose you?" "It would be no great wonder if I could," Socrates answers, "considering the admirable mistress I have in the art of speaking—she who has made so many good speakers, one of whom was the best among all the Greeks—Pericles." "I suppose you mean Aspasia," says the other. "Yes, I do," replies Socrates. "Only yesterday I heard her composing an oration about these very dead. She had been told, as you were saying, that the Athenians were going to choose a speaker and she repeated to me the sort of speech he should deliver, partly improvising and partly putting together fragments of the funeral oration which Pericles spoke, but which, as I believe, she composed." "Can you remember what Aspasia said?" the friend asks, and is told, "I ought to be able, for she taught me and she was ready to strike me because I kept forgetting." The oration is then rehearsed and at its close Socrates, who has declared that he is afraid Aspasia will be angry with him for giving publicity to her speech, warns his hearer, "Take care not to tell on me to her and I will repeat to you many other excellent political speeches of hers."

At that famous supper table in Agathon's house where a company of young men was gathered not easily matched for brilliancy by any other age; Agathon himself, who had just been awarded the first prize for a play, Aristophanes, greatest of comedians, that gilded youth, Alcibiades, among the brilliant always the most brilliant—by these and their like, Socrates, when he enters, is treated as a boon companion, beloved, admired, and the best of company. They joke with him and make fun of him with an undertone of loving delight in him, all of which Socrates receives with amused tolerance and the complete assurance of the man of the world. "Don't answer him, dear Agathon," calls out Phædrus, the young man who took that walk to the tall plane-tree, "for if he can only get a companion to whom he can talk, especially a good-looking one, he will be of no use for anything else."

In the conversation that follows, it appears that he can do all the things young men admire most, the world over. "He can drink any quantity of wine," says Alcibiades, "and not get drunk." This declaration is made in humorous despair, after he has insisted on Socrates' draining a two-quart wine jar, which Socrates does with entire composure. Alcibiades himself, when he first appeared at the door, "crowned with a garland of ivy and violets," had asked, "Will you have a very drunken man as companion?" And all the rest of the company had already echoed Aristophanes' suggestion that they avoid deep drinking because they had all drunk too much the day before—"except Socrates, who can always drink or not, and will not care which we do."

So, too, he is the typical young man's hero in his power to endure hardship. Alcibiades and he had messed together in one campaign and the young man says, "I had an opportunity of seeing his extraordinary power of sustaining fatigue. And his endurance was simply marvellous when we were cut off from supplies—there was no one to be compared with him." It was winter and very cold, and everybody else "had on an amazing quantity of clothes and their feet done up in felt and fleeces," but Socrates, "in ordinary dress and with bare feet, marched on the ice better than the others." Yet with all this, "if we had a feast he was the only person who had real powers of enjoyment."

*The Symposium* ends with the narrator's confession that they all did finally drink too much, and he himself fell asleep until the dawn, when, on waking up, he found everybody else asleep except Socrates, Aristophanes and Agathon. The two latter were still drinking while Socrates discoursed to them. He was arguing "that the true artist in tragedy would be an artist in comedy also. To which the others had to assent, being drowsy and not quite up to the argument. And first Aristophanes dropped off, then Agathon. Socrates having laid both to sleep, departed. At the Lyceum he took a bath and passed the day as usual."

He could make schoolboys feel equally at home with him: "His friend, Menexenus, came and sat down by us and Lysis followed. I asked, 'Which of you two boys is the older?' He answered that it was a matter of dispute between them. 'Which is the better looking?' The two lads laughed. 'I shan't ask you which is the richer,' I said, 'for you two are friends, are you not?' 'Certainly,' they replied. 'And friends have all things in common,' I said, 'so that one of you cannot be richer than the other.' 'No, indeed,' they agreed."

Follows a talk on friendship, broken off by the boys' tutors who bid them go home as it is getting late. "I said, however, a few words to the lads at parting: 'O Menexenus and Lysis, here is a joke: you two boys and I, an old boy who would fain be one of you, think we are friends and yet we have not been able to discover what is a friend!' "

Such a conclusion or rather absence of conclusion, illustrates the attitude peculiar to Socrates among all the great teachers of the world. He will not do their thinking for the men who come to him, neither in matters small nor great. In the *Cratylus* where that young man and his friend approach him with a question about language and how names are formed, all the satisfaction they get is: "If I had not been a poor man I might have heard the fifty-drachma course of the great Prodicus, which is a complete education in grammar and language—these are his own words—and then I should have been able at once to answer your question. But, indeed, I have only heard the single-drachma course, and therefore I do not know the truth about such matters. Still, I will gladly assist you in the investigation of them." The investigation, however, ends with: "This may be true, Cratylus, but is also very likely to be untrue; and therefore I would not have you be too easily persuaded of it. Reflect well, for you are young and of an age to learn. And when you have found the truth, come and tell me." To which the young man answers—he must have been very young—"I will do as you say, Socrates."

This ironic inconclusiveness is his most distinctive characteristic. Always when he is convicting his world of that dark crime in Greece, ignorance, as always when he is—so unobtrusively—leading them on to great thoughts and the conception of their high calling, he assumes that he is in the same case with his hearers, or worse. His habitual manner is a charming diffidence. "I know it may all be quite wrong," he seems to say. He suggests merely—with a question mark. It is the way of the most sophisticated people in the *ne plus ultra* of civilized society.

One other illustration must be given to show the deep seriousness which underlay that attitude so whimsical and deprecatory. It is taken from the talk during the summer stroll with Phædrus—"Is not the road to Athens made for conversation?" The younger man asks if they are not near the place where Boreas is said to have carried off Orithya: "The little stream is delightfully clear and bright. I can fancy there might be maidens playing near. Tell me, Socrates, do you believe the tale?" "The wise are doubtful," Socrates answers, "and I should not be singular if, like them, I too, doubted. I might have a rational explanation that Orithya was playing when a northerly gust carried her over the rocks, and therefore she was said to have been carried off by Boreas. Now I quite acknowledge that these allegorical explanations are very nice, but he is not to be envied who has to make them up: much labor and in-

genuity will be required of him; he will have to go on and
rehabilitate Hippo-centaurs and chimæras dire. Gorgons
and winged steeds flow in apace, and numberless inconceivable and portentous natures. And if he would fain
reduce them to the rules of probability it will take up a
deal of time. Now I have no leisure for such enquiries;
shall I tell you why? I must first know myself, as the
Delphic inscription says; to be curious about things not my
concern while I am still in ignorance of my own self, would
be absurd. And therefore I bid farewell to all that sort of
thing. I want to know about myself: am I a monster more
complicated and swollen with passion than the serpent
Typho, or a creature of a gentler and simpler sort, to
whom Nature has given a lowlier and a diviner destiny?"

The complete lack of dogmatism in an avowed teacher
is startling, not to say repellent, to most of us to-day,
accustomed as we are and devoted as we are to ex cathedra
utterances and ipse dixits. But in Athens, in Platonic
Athens, at least, the idea that each man must himself be a
research worker in the truth if he were ever to attain to
any share in it, seemed rather to attract than to repel.
Plato, it may be fairly admitted, knew something about the
Greek way in such respects. For years and years after
Socrates' death he taught the men of Athens in the world's
first Academy, and there is no suggestion anywhere that
he paid for his kind of teaching by unpopularity. If the
Platonic dialogues point to any one conclusion beyond
another, it is that the Athenian did not want someone else
to do his thinking for him.

In a sense, therefore, extraordinary man though he was,
Socrates yet holds up the mirror to his own age. A civilized
age, where the really important matters were not those
touched, tasted, or handled, an age whose leaders were
marked by a devotion to learning and finding out the truth,
and an age able to do and dare and endure, still capable
of an approach to the heroic deeds of a past only a few
years distant. Mind and spirit in equal balance was the
peculiar characteristic of Greek art. Intellectuality and
exquisite taste balanced by an immense vitality was the
distinctive mark of the people—as Plato saw them.

# Chapter VII

## ARISTOPHANES AND THE
## OLD COMEDY

"TRUE COMEDY," said Voltaire, "is the speaking picture of the Follies and Foibles of a Nation." He had Aristophanes in mind, and no better description could be given of the Old Comedy of Athens. To read Aristophanes is in some sort like reading an Athenian comic paper. All the life of Athens is there: the politics of the day and the politicians; the war party and the anti-war party; pacifism, votes for women, free trade, fiscal reform, complaining taxpayers, educational theories, the current religious and literary talk —everything, in short, that interested the average citizen. All was food for his mockery. He was the speaking picture of the follies and foibles of his day.

The mirror he holds up to the age is a different one from that held up by Socrates. To turn to the Old Comedy from Plato is a singular experience. What has become of that company of courteous gentlemen with their pleasant ways and sensitive feelings and fastidious tastes? Not a trace of them is to be found in these boisterous plays, each coarser and more riotous than the last. To place them in the audience is much more difficult than to imagine Spenser or Sir Philip Sidney listening to Pistol and Doll Tearsheet, just to the degree that Elizabeth's court was on a lower level of civilization than the circle around Pericles, and Aristophanes capable of more kinds of vulgarity and indency than Shakespeare ever dreamed of.

None the less there is a close relationship between the comedy of Athens and the comedy of sixteenth-century England. The *Zeitgeist* of those periods of splendor and magnificent vigor was in many points, the most important points, alike. The resemblance between Aristophanes and certain of the comedy parts of Shakespeare jumps to the eye. The spirit of their times is in them. There is the same tremendous energy and verve and vitality; the same swinging, swashbuckling spirit; the same exuberant, effervescing flow of language; the same rollicking, uproarious fun. Falstaff is a character out of Aristophanes raised to the *n*th power; Poins, Ancient Pistol, Mistress Quickly, might have come straight out of any of his plays.

The resemblance is not on the surface only. The two men were alike in the essential genius of their comedy. In those supreme ages of the drama, Elizabethan England and the Athens of Pericles, the step from the sublime to the ridiculous was easily taken. Uproarious comedy flourished side by side with gorgeous tragedy, and when one passed away the other passed away too. There is a connection between the sublime and the ridiculous. Aristophanes' comedy and, pre-eminently, Shakespeare's comedy, and theirs alone, has a kinship with tragedy. "The drama's laws the drama's patrons give." The audiences to whose capacity for heightened emotion *Lear* and the *Œdipus Rex* were addressed, were the same that delighted in Falstaff and in Aristophanes' maddest nonsense, and when an age succeeded in no wise less keen intellectually, but of thinner emotions, great comedy as well as great tragedy departed.

Greek drama had reached its summit and was nearing its decline when Aristophanes began to write. Of the Old Comedy, as it is called, we have little; none of the plays of Aristophanes' often successful rivals, and only eleven of the many he himself wrote; but the genre is clearly to be seen in those eleven. There were but three actors. A chorus divided the action by song and dance (there was no curtain) and often took part in the dialogue. About halfway through, the plot, a very loose matter at best, came practically to an end, and the chorus made a long address to the audience, which aired the author's opinions and often had nothing to do with the play. After that would follow scenes more or less connected. A dull picture, this, of a brilliantly entertaining reality. Nobody and nothing escaped the ridicule of the Old Comedy. The gods came in

for their share; so did the institutions dearest to the
Athenians; so did the most popular and powerful individuals, often by name. The freedom of speech is staggering
to our ideas.

In the passages that follow the metres of the originals
have been reproduced, as they are an essential part of the
comic effect. When the *Acharnians* opens a man is explaining how the war started:

> For men of ours—I do not say the City,
> Remember that—I do not say the City,
> But worthless fellows, just bad money, coins
> No mint has ever seen, kept on denouncing
> The men of Megara. Trifles, I grant,
> —Our way here—but some tipsy youngsters then
> Go steal from Megara a hussy there.
> Then men of Megara come here and steal
> Two of Aspasia's minxes. And those three,
> No better than they should be, caused the war.
> For then in wrath Olympian Pericles
> Thundered and lightened and confounded Greece.
> Enacting laws against the Megarians
> That sounded just like drinking songs—

But it was not only the great who had cause to feel
uneasy. Any man might suddenly find himself mocked at
by name. The *Wasps* opens with two servants discussing
their master's father:

> FIRST SLAVE
>             He's got a strange disease
> Nobody knows—Or will you try a guess?
> [*Looking at audience.*]
> Amynias down there, Pronapes' son,
> Says it's a dice-disease, but he's quite off.
>
> SECOND SLAVE
> Ah—diagnosing from his own disease.
>
> FIRST SLAVE
> But Sosias here, in front declares he knows
> That it's a drink disease.

SECOND SLAVE
No—no—confound it!
That's the disease of honest gentlemen.

The names, of course, were changed as the audience changed. In a town that was small enough for everyone to know everyone else, the possibilities the method offered were endless.

The best known of Aristophanes' plays are the *Birds*, where Athens is shown up in contrast to the utopian city the birds build in the clouds; the *Frogs*, a parody of popular writers; the *Clouds*, which makes fun of the intelligentsia and Socrates who "walks on air and contemplates the sun"; and three plays about women, the *Thesmophoriazusæ*, the *Lysistrata*, and the *Ecclesiazusæ*, in which the women take hold of literature, the war, and the state, to the great betterment of all.

The characters have little in common with Plato's. The delightful host of the *Symposium*, the courteous, witty Agathon, is a different person as seen by Aristophanes. In the *Thesmophoriazusæ* Euripides and an elderly man, Mnesilochus, are walking along a street:

EURIPIDES
That house is where great Agathon is living,
The tragic poet.

MNESILOCHUS
Agathon? Don't know him.

EURIPIDES
Why, he's the Agathon—

MNESILOCHUS *interrupting*
A big dark fellow, eh?

EURIPIDES
Oh, no, by no means. Haven't you ever seen him?
But let us step aside. His servant's coming
He's got some myrtle and a pan of charcoal.
He's going to pray for help in composition.

**SERVANT**

Let sacred silence rule us here.
Ye people all, lock up your lips,
For the Muses are revelling there within,
The Queens of poetry-making.
Let the air be still and forget to blow,
And the gray sea wave make never a sound—

**MNESILOCHUS**

Stuff and *nonsense*—

**EURIPIDES**

                    *Will* you be quiet!

**SERVANT** *scandalized*

What's this that I hear?

**MNESILOCHUS**

                    Oh, just as you said.
It's the air that's forgetting to blow.

**SERVANT**

He's making a play.
First the keel he will lay
With neatly joined words all new,
Then the bottom he'll round,
And chisel the sound,
And fasten the verses with glue.
A maxim he'll take,
And an epithet make;
And call by new names what is old.
He'll form it like wax
And fill in the cracks,
And cast it at last in a mold.
[*Enter Agathon. He has on a silk dress and his hair is
    in a net.*]

**MNESILOCHUS**

Who are you? Were you born a man?
No, you're a woman surely.

**AGATHON**

Know, sir, I choose my dress to suit my writing.
A poet molds himself upon his poems,

And when he writes of women he assumes
A woman's dress and takes on woman's habits.
But when he sings of men a manly bearing
Is his therewith. What we are not by nature
We take unto ourselves through imitation.

Socrates fares no better. Aristophanes had noted well the homely imagery Socrates loved to illustrate high discourse with. In the *Clouds* a father goes to "The thinking-school" to enter his son, and there as he is being shown around, he sees a curious spectacle:

FATHER
Well now. Who's that—that man up in the basket?

STUDENT
Himself!

FATHER
Who *is* Himself?

STUDENT
Why, Socrates.

FATHER
Dear me. That Socrates? Oh, call him for me.

STUDENT
Really, I haven't time. Call him yourself.

FATHER
O Socrates! O—dear—sweet—Socrates!

SOCRATES
Mortal! Why call you on me?

FATHER
Tell me, please,
What are you doing up there in a basket?

SOCRATES
I walk on air and con-template the sun.
I could not search into celestial matters
Unless I mingled with the kindred air

My subtle spirit here on high. The ground
Is not the place for lofty speculations.
The earth would draw their essence to herself.
The same too is the case with watercress.


FATHER

Well, well. Thought draws the essence into watercress.


The two passages illustrate a further point: they presuppose an educated audience, perfectly at home in the best thought and literature of the day. It is the presupposition of all the plays. The intellectual side of the society Plato knew is constantly suggested. Much of the fun in the *Frogs* turns on parodies of Æschylus and Euripides which imply an exhaustive acquaintance with them on the part of the spectators, and as Æschylus is said to have written ninety plays and Euripides seventy-five, it meant something substantial in the way of culture to be well-read in them. Occasionally too we catch a faraway glimpse of people by whom the arts are taken seriously. In the *Clouds,* the father who entered his son in Socrates' thinking-school, finds him much the worse therefor. He pours out his complaints:


I told him to go and fetch his harp and help the supper
  along
By singing us good Simonides' Ram or another fine old song.
But he replied that to sing at meals was coarse and quite
  out of style,
And Simonides now was obsolete—had been for a good
  long while.
I really could hardly restrain myself at his finicking,
  poppycock ways,
But I did and I asked him to give us then a selection from
  Æschylus' plays.
But he answered, "Æschylus is to me an unmitigated bore,
A turgid, swollen-up, wind-bag thing that does nothing but
  ramp and roar."
When he talked like that my bosom began to heave extremely fast.
But I kept myself in and politely said, "Then give us one
  at the last,

Of the very newest you young men like." And he started a
  shameful thing
Euripides wrote, the sort of stuff no gentleman ever would
  sing,
Then, then, I could bear no more. I confess, I stormed and
  struck him too,
And he turned on me, his own father, he did, and beat me
  black and blue.

SON

And rightly too when you dared to blame that wisest of
  poets—he
Who is high over all, Euripides.

FATHER
The boy's just a fool, I see.

But these are only shadowy glimpses, and few and far
between, at that. Aristophanes' Athens is for the most part
inhabited by a most disreputable lot of people, as un-
platonic as possible. The *Plutus* begins with a scene where
a blind man is groping his way along a street, followed by
an elderly, respectable-appearing man and his slave. The
slave asks his master why they are following a blind man:

CHREMYLUS
I'll tell you why, straight out. Of all my slaves
I know you are the best, most constant—thief.
Well—I have been a good, religious man.
But always poor—no luck.

SLAVE
And so you have.

CHREMYLUS
While a church robber, and those thieves who live
On politics, get rich.

SLAVE
And so they do.

CHREMYLUS
So then I went to ask—not for myself,
I've pretty well shot all my arrows now—

But for my son, my only son. I prayed
That he might change his ways and turn into
A scoundrel, wicked, rotten through and through,
And so live happily forever after.
The god replied, the first man I fell in with
To follow.

SLAVE
   Yes—Quite good. Of course, a blind man
Can see it's better nowadays to be
A rotten scoundrel.

The man in front proves to be Wealth himself, not aware
of his power because he is blind. The two others proceed
to enlighten him:

CHREMYLUS
Why, everything there is, is just Wealth's slave.
The girls, now, if a poor man comes along,
Will they look at him? But just let a rich one,
And he can get a deal more than he wants.

SLAVE
Oh, not the sweet, good, modest girls. They never
Would ask a man for money.

CHREMYLUS
   No? What then?

SLAVE
Presents—the kind that cost a lot—that's all.

CHREMYLUS
Well, all the voting's done for Wealth of course.
You man our battleships. You own our army.
When you're an ally, that side's sure to win.
Nobody ever has enough of you.
While all things else a man can have too much of—
Of love.

SLAVE
  Of loaves.

CHREMYLUS
  Of literature.

SLAVE

Of candy.

CHREMYLUS

Of fame.

SLAVE

Of figs.

CHREMYLUS

Of manliness.

SLAVE

Of mutton.

This kind of invective has a certain familiar ring in our ears. Writers who hold their own country and their own times to be the worst possible ever, can, it appears, trace their descent back through a great many centuries.

The playwright most like Aristophanes, the man whose sense of humor was most akin to his, lived in an age as unlike his as Shakespeare's was like it. The turbulent democracy that gave birth to the Old Comedy, and the England over whose manners and customs Queen Victoria ruled supreme, had little in common, and yet the mid-Victorian Gilbert of *Pinafore* fame saw eye to eye with Aristophanes as no other writer has done. The differences between Aristophanes and Gilbert are superficial; they are due to the differences of their time. In their essential genius they are alike.

The unknown is always magnificent. Aristophanes wears the halo of Greece, and is at the same time softly dimmed by the dust of centuries of scholarly elucidation. A comparison, therefore, with an author familiar and beloved and never really thought about wears a look of irreverence— also of ignorance. Dear nonsensical Gilbert, and the magnificent Aristophanes, poet, political reformer, social uplifter, philosophical thinker, with a dozen titles to immortality—how is it possible to compare them? The only basis for true comparison, Plato says, is the excellence that is peculiar to each thing. Was Aristophanes really a great lyric poet? Was he really bent on reforming politics or

ending democracy? Such considerations are beside the
point. Shakespeare's glory would not be enhanced if Hamlet's soliloquy was understood as a warning against suicide,
or if it could be proved that in *Pericles* he was attacking the
social evil. The peculiar excellence of comedy is its excellent fooling, and Aristophanes' claim to immortality is
based upon one title only: he was a master maker of
comedy, he could fool excellently. Here Gilbert stands side
by side with him. He, too, could write the most admirable
nonsense. There has never been better fooling than his,
and a comparison with him carries nothing derogatory to
the great Athenian.

Striking resemblances, both general and particular,
emerge from such a comparison. The two men fooled in
the same way; they looked at life with the same eyes. In
Gilbert's pages Victorian England lives in miniature just
as Athens lives in Aristophanes' pages. Those sweet pretty
girls, those smart young dragoons, those matchmaking
mammas; those genial exponents of the value of a title, a
safe income, a political pull; that curious union of sentimental thinking and stoutly practical acting; that intimate
savor of England in the eighteen eighties—who has ever
given it so perfectly as he? He was one of the cleverest of
caricaturists, but the freedom Aristophanes enjoyed was
not his, and his deft, clear-cut pictures of dishonesty and
sham and ignorance in high places are very discreet and
always nameless. Essentially, however, he strikes with the
same weapon as his Greek predecessor. He, too, ridicules
the things dearest to his countrymen: the aristocracy in
*Iolanthe;* army training in the *Pirates;* the navy in *Pinafore;*
English society in *Utopia Limited;* and so on, through all
his thirteen librettos. It is never cruel, this ridicule, as
Aristophanes' sometimes is, but this difference is the inevitable result of the enormous difference between the two
men's environment. The Athenian was watching cold and
hunger and bitter defeat draw ever nearer to Athens. The
Englishman wrote in the safest and most comfortable world
mankind has ever known. But underneath that difference
their fundamental point of view was the same. They were
topical writers, both of them, given over to the matters of

the moment, and yet Aristophanes has been laughed with for two thousand years, and Gilbert has survived a half century of such shattering change, his England seems almost as far away from us. They saw beneath the surface of the passing show. They wrote of the purely ephemeral and in their hands it became a picture not of the "Follies and Foibles" of a day and a nation, but of those that exist in all nations and all ages and belong to the permanent stuff of human nature.

Of the two, Aristophanes has the bigger canvas, leagues to Gilbert's inches, but the yardstick is not a measure of art and the passages that follow will show how closely they resemble each other in the quality of their humor. It is true that Aristophanes wrote for an audience on a higher level intellectually than Gilbert's, made up of the keenest minds, the most discriminating critics, the theatre has ever known. It would be impossible to imagine the Victorians listening delightedly to hundreds of lines on end that were nothing except exquisitely skillful parodies of Browning and Tennyson. In the vital matter of an audience the Athenian was greatly more fortunate than the Englishman, and his plays have inevitably a far wider scope. None the less, it remains true that while the difference in their intellectual appeal may quite well have been due to the difference between the people each wrote for their resemblances are far more striking and are certainly due to a close kinship of spirit.

Even in matters of technique, which is wont to vary so greatly from age to age, there are many similarities. To both men the fooling is the point, not the plot. In that subtle, individual thing, the use of metre, they are strikingly alike. The metre of a comic song is as important as its matter. No one understood that more clearly than Gilbert:

All children who are up in dates and floor you with 'em
flat,
All persons who in shaking hands, shake hands with you
like THAT.

Aristophanes understood it too as none better:

Come listen now to the good old days when the children,
strange to tell,

Were seen not heard, led a simple life, in short were
brought up well.

This jolly line is a favorite with him but he uses an
endless variety. Examples will be found in the passages
translated, in all of which, as I have already said, except
the one indicated, I have reproduced the original metres.
The effect of them is essentially that of Gilbert's.

A device of pure nonsense in Gilbert, which seems
peculiarly his own, and which he uses, for example, in
the second act of *Patience*, is the appeal to something
utterly irrelevant that proves irresistible:

GROSVENOR *wildly*
But you would not do it—I am sure you would not.
[*Throwing himself at* BUNTHORNE's *knees, and clinging to
him.*] Oh, reflect, reflect! You had a mother once.

BUNTHORNE
Never!

GROSVENOR
Then you had an aunt! [BUNTHORNE *deeply affected.*]
Ah! I see you had! By the memory of that aunt, I implore
you.

Precisely the same nonsensical device is used by Aristophanes. In the *Acharnians* the magic appeal before which
all opposition melts is, not to an aunt, but to a scuttle of
coal, as it might have been a few years back in England.
Fuel was scarce in Athens just then; war was raging.

The scene is a street in Athens. A man, Dikæopolis by
name, has said something in favor of Sparta, Athens'
enemy. The crowd is furious:

DIKÆOPOLIS
This I know, the men of Sparta, whom we're cursing all
   day long,
Aren't the only ones to blame for everything that's going
   wrong.

CROWD

Spartans not to blame, you traitor? Do you dare tell such
a lie?
At him! At him, all good people. Stone him, burn him. He
shall die.

DIKÆOPOLIS

Won't you hear me, my dear fellows?

CROWD

Never, never. Not a word.

DIKÆOPOLIS

Then I'll turn on you, you villains. Would you kill a man
unheard?
I've a hostage for my safety, one that's very dear to you.
I will slaughter him before you. [*Goes into house at back
of stage.*]

CROWD

What is it he's gone to do?
How he threatens. You don't think he's got a child of ours
in there?

DIKÆOPOLIS [*from behind stage*]

I've got something. Now, you scoundrels, tremble, for I
will not spare.
Look well at my hostage. This will test your mettle, every
soul. [*He comes out lugging something behind him.*]
Which among you has true feeling for—a scuttle full of
coal?

CROWD

Heaven save us! Oh, don't touch it. We'll give in. Say what
you please.

In the *Lysistrata* occurs the following:

FIRST SPEAKER

For through man's heart there runs in flood
A natural and a noble taste for blood.

SECOND SPEAKER

To form a ring and fight—

THIRD SPEAKER
To cut off heads at sight—

ALL
It is our right.

Matter and manner are perfectly Gilbert's. Anyone not knowing the author would inevitably assign it to him, to the *Princess Ida*, perhaps, along with:

> We are warriors three,
>   Sons of Gama Rex,
> Like most sons are we,
>   Masculine in sex.
> Bold and fierce and strong, ha! ha!
>   For a war we burn,
> With its right or wrong, ha! ha!
>   We have no concern.

Aristophanes was amused by grand talk that covered empty content. In the first scene of the *Thesmophoriazusæ* two elderly men enter, one with the lofty air that befits a Poet and Philosopher, the other an ordinary, cheerful old fellow. He speaks first:

MNESILOCHUS
Might I, before I've lost my wind entirely,
Be told, where you are taking me, Euripides?

EURIPIDES *solemnly*
You may not hear the things which presently
  You are to see.

MNESILOCHUS
          What's that? Say it again.
I'm not to hear—?

EURIPIDES
          What you shall surely see.

MNESILOCHUS
And not to see—?

EURIPIDES
The things you must needs hear.

MNESILOCHUS
Oh, how you talk. Of course you're very clever.
You mean I must not either hear or see?

EURIPIDES
They two are twain and by their nature diverse,
Each one from other.

MNESILOCHUS
What's that—diverse?

EURIPIDES
Their elemental parts are separate.

MNESILOCHUS
Oh, what it is to talk to learned people!

Gilbert was amused by the same thing. In the second
act of the *Princess Ida* the first scene is the hall of the
Women's University. The principal has been addressing
the faculty and students, and as she finishes asks:

Who lectures in the Hall of Arts to-day?

LADY BLANCHE
I, madam, on Abstract Philosophy.
There I propose considering at length
Three points—the Is, the Might Be, and the Must.
Whether the Is, from being actual fact,
Is more important than the vague Might Be,
Or the Might Be, from taking wider scope,
Is for that reason greater than the Is:
And lastly, how the Is and Might Be stand
Compared with the inevitable Must!

PRINCESS
The subject's deep.

Every kind of sham is dear to Aristophanes but especially the literary sham. He is forever making fun of him.

In the *Birds* Peisthetærus, an Athenian, is helping the birds found their new city in the clouds, which is called Cloud-cuckoo-town. To it flock the quacks and the cranks. A priest has just been chased off the stage when enter a poet, singing:*

O Cloud-cuckoo-town!
Muse, do thou crown
With song her fair name,
Hymning her fame.

PEISTHETÆRUS
What sort of thing is this? I say,
Who in the world are you, now, pray?

POET
A warbler of a song,
Very sweet and very strong.
Slave of the Muse am I,
Eager and nimble and spry,
—As Homer says.

PEISTHETÆRUS
Does the Muse let her servants wear
That sort of long, untidy hair?

POET
Oh, we who teach the art
Of the drama, whole or part,
Servants of the Muse must try
To be eager and nimble and spry,
—As Homer says.

PEISTHETÆRUS
That nimbleness, no doubt is why
You're all in rags. You are too spry.

POET
Oh, I've been making lovely, lovely lays,
Old and new-fashioned too, in sweetest praise
Of your Cloud-cuckoo-town.

*Except the first four lines this quotation is not in the original metre, which varies from line to line as English metre does not.

... And won't you see
If you have something you can give to ME?

Gilbert enjoyed the sham artist quite as much. In
*Patience* the officers of the Dragoons are on the stage:

COLONEL
Yes, and here are the ladies.

DUKE
But who is the gentleman with the long hair?

BUNTHORNE *enters, followed by the ladies, two by two.*

BUNTHORNE *aside*
Though my book I seem to scan
In a rapt ecstatic way,
Like a literary man
Who despises female clay,
I hear plainly all they say.
Twenty love-sick maidens they!
*Exit ladies.*

BUNTHORNE *alone*
Am I alone
And unobserved? I am!
Then let me own
I'm an æsthetic sham!
This air severe
Is but a mere
    Veneer!
This costume chaste
Is but good taste
    Misplaced!

Both writers make the same kind of jokes about military
matters and the like. In the *Knights* the two generals introduced were among the most famous of their time:

DEMOSTHENES
How goes it, poor old chap?

NICIAS
    Badly. Like you.

DEMOSTHENES

Let's sing a doleful ditty and then weep.
[*Both sing, break down and sob.*]


DEMOSTHENES

No use in whimpering. We'd do better far
To dry our tears and find some good way out.


NICIAS

What way? You tell me.


DEMOSTHENES
                            No. Do you tell me.
If you won't speak I'll fight you.


NICIAS
                                    No, not I.
You say it first and then I'll say it after.


DEMOSTHENES

Oh, speak for me and say what's in my heart.


NICIAS

My courage fails. If only I could say it
Neatly and sweetly, like Euripides.
Well, then, say SERT, like that, and say it smartly.


DEMOSTHENES

All right. Here goes: SERT.


NICIAS
                            Good! Have courage now.
Say first SERT and then DE, repeating fast
The two words, very fast.


DEMOSTHENES
                            Ah, yes. I get you.
Sert de, sert de sert, DESERT!


NICIAS
                            You have it.
Well, doesn't it sound nice?

DEMOSTHENES
It's HEAVENLY.

But—but—

NICIAS
What's that?

DEMOSTHENES
They FLOG deserters.

Gilbert's jokes, of course, were in a lighter vein. War seemed remote to the mid-Victorian. The passage most like the one quoted from Aristophanes is the marching song of the Police in the *Pirates:*

MABEL
Go, ye heroes, go to glory,
Though ye die in combat gory,
Ye shall live in song and story,
    Go to immortality!

POLICE
Though to us it's evident,
    Tarantara! tarantara!
These intentions are well meant,
    Tarantara!
Such expressions don't appear,
    Tarantara, tarantara,
Calculated men to cheer,
    Tarantara!
Who are going to meet their fate
In a highly nervous state,
    Tarantara!

Politicians in Athens and in London seem very much the same. In the *Plutus* a slave, Carion, meets one. He asks:

You're a good man, a patriot?

POLITICIAN
            Oh, yes,
If ever there was one.

CARION
                    And, as I guess,
A farmer?

POLITICIAN
        I? Lord save us. I'm not mad.

CARION
A merchant then?

POLITICIAN
                    Ah, sometimes I have had
To take that trade up—as an alibi.

CARION
You've some profession surely.

POLITICIAN
                                No, not I.

CARION
How do you make a living?

POLITICIAN
                                Well, there're several
Answers to that. I'm Supervisor General
Of all things here, public and private too.

CARION
A great profession that. What did you do
To qualify for it?

POLITICIAN
        I WANTED it.

So Gilbert in the song of the duke and duchess in the *Gondoliers:*

To help unhappy commoners, and add to their enjoyment,
Affords a man of noble rank congenial employment;
Of our attempts we offer you examples illustrative:
The work is light, and, I may add, it's most remunerative.
Small titles and orders
For Mayors and Recorders
I get—and they're highly delighted.

M. P.'s baronetted,
Sham Colonels gazetted,
And second-rate Aldermen knighted.

In the *Knights* an oracle has just foretold that Athens
will be ruled some day by a sausage-seller. At that moment
one enters and is greeted with enthusiasm.

DEMOSTHENES
Dear Sausage-seller, rise, our Saviour and the State's.

SAUSAGE-SELLER
What's that you say?

DEMOSTHENES
                    O happy man and rich!
Nothing to-day, to-morrow everything.
O Lord of Athens, blest through you!

SAUSAGE-SELLER
                                    I see, sir,
That you must have your joke. But as for me,
I've got to wash the guts and sell my sausage.

DEMOSTHENES
But you are going to be our greatest man.

SAUSAGE-SELLER
Oh, I'm not fit for that.

DEMOSTHENES
                    What's that? Not fit?
Is some good action weighing on your conscience?
Don't tell me that you come of honest folk?

SAUSAGE-SELLER
Oh, dear me, no sir. Bad 'uns, out and out.

DEMOSTHENES
You lucky man. Oh, what a start you've got
For public life.

SAUSAGE-SELLER
                But I don't know a thing
Except my letters.

DEMOSTHENES
Ah, the pity is
That you know anything.

A parallel passage is Sir Joseph's song in *Pinafore:*

I grew so rich that I was sent
By a pocket borough into Parliament.
I always voted at my party's call,
And I never thought of thinking for myself at all.
I thought so little they rewarded me
By making me the Ruler of the Queen's Navee!

The woman joke, of course, is well to the fore with both men. It is ever with us. *Plus ça change, plus c'est la même chose.* Any number of passages might be selected.

The song of the duchess in the *Gondoliers* is completely in the customary style:

On the day when I was wedded
   To your admirable sire,
I acknowledge that I dreaded
   An explosion of his ire.

I was always very wary,
   For his fury was ecstatic—
His refined vocabulary
   Most unpleasantly emphatic.

Giving him the very best, and getting back the very worst—
That is how I tried to tame your great progenitor—at first!
But I found that a reliance on my threatening appearance,
And a resolute defiance of marital interference,
Was the only thing required for to make his temper supple,
And you couldn't have desired
A more reciprocating couple.
So with double-shotted guns and colours nailed unto the
   mast,
I tamed your insignificant progenitor—at last!

Aristophanes' ladies are of quite the same kind. They form the chorus of the *Thesmophoriazusæ*, and they begin their address to the audience as follows:

We now come forward and appeal to you to hear how the
  men all flout us,
And the foolish abuse and the scandals let loose the silly
  things tell about us.
They say all evil proceeds from us, war, battles, and
  murder even;
We're a tiresome, troublesome, quarrelsome lot, disturbers
  of earth and of heaven.
Now, we ask you to put your minds on this: if we're really
  the plague of your lives,
Then tell us, please, why you're all so keen to get us to be
  your wives?
Pray, why do you like us to be at home, all ready to smile
  and greet you,
And storm and sulk if your poor little wife isn't always
  there to meet you?
If we're such a nuisance and pest, then why—we venture
  to put the question—
Don't you rather rejoice when we're out of the way—a
  reasonable suggestion.
If we stay the night at the house of a friend—I mean, the
  house of a lady,
You hunt for us everywhere like mad and hint at some-
  thing shady.
Do you like to look at a plague and a pest? It seems you
  do, for you stare
And ogle and give us killing looks if you see us anywhere.
And if we think proper to blush and withdraw, as a lady,
  no doubt, should be doing,
You will try to follow us all the more, and never give over
  pursuing.
But we can show you up as well.
The ways of a man we all can tell.
Your heart's in your stomach, every one,
And you'll *do* any one if you're not first *done*.
We know what the jokes are you love to make,
And how you each fancy yourself a rake.

Parallels such as these could be given indefinitely. The
world moves slowly. Aristophanes in Athens, fifth century,
B.C., Gilbert in nineteenth-century England, saw the same
things and saw the same humor in them. Some things, however, were seen by the Athenian which the Englishman was

constrained not to see and this fact constitutes the chief point of difference between them. What a gulf divides the Old Comedy, so riotous and so Rabelaisian and the decorous operettas that would never raise a blush on the cheek of Anthony Trollope's most ladylike heroine. A gulf indeed, but it is the gulf between the two periods. England's awful arbiter of morals, the formidable Queen in her prime, was the audience that counted in Gilbert's day, and it may be stated with certainty that Aristophanes himself would have abjured indecency and obscenity in that presence. Equally certainly, if he had lived in the age, *par excellence,* of gentility, he would have tempered his vigor, checked his swiftness, moderated his exuberance. Gilbert is an Aristophanes plentifully watered down, a steady and stolid-y, jolly Bank-holiday, every-day Aristophanes, a mid-Victorian Aristophanes.

The question is irresistibly suggested, if Gilbert had lived in those free-thinking, free-acting, free-speaking days of Athens, "so different from the home life of our own dear Queen," would he too have needed a Lord High Chamberlain

> To purge his native stage beyond a question
> Of "risky" situation and indelicate suggestion.

There are indications that point to the possibility, had he not been held down by the laws the Victorian patrons of the drama gave. He could not but submit to these limitations, and only rarely, by a slip as it were, is a hint given of what he might have done if there had not always been before him the fear of that terrible pronunciamento: We are NOT amused!

But Aristophanes' audiences set no limits at all. Were Plato's characters found among them, the meditative Phædrus, the gentle-mannered Agathon, Socrates, the philosophic, himself? Beyond all question. They sat in the theatre for hours on end, applauding a kind of Billingsgate Falstaff at his worst never approached; listening to violent invectives against the men—and the women—of Athens as a drunken, greedy, venal, vicious lot; laughing at jokes that would have put Rabelais to the blush.

Such a theatre to our notions is not a place gentlemen of the Platonic stamp would frequent. A polite Molière comedy would be the kind of thing best suited to them, or if they must have improprieties to divert them, they should be suggested, not shouted. But our Athenians were not French seventeenth-century nobles, nor yet of Schnitzler's twentieth-century Vienna; they were vigorous, hardy, hearty men; lovers of good talk but talk with a body to it, and lovers quite as much of physical prowess; hard-headed men, too, who could drink all night and discuss matters for clear heads only; realists as well, who were not given to drawing a veil before any of life's facts. The body was of tremendous importance, acknowledged to be so, quite as much as the mind and the spirit.

Such were Plato's gentlemen and such were Aristophanes' audiences. The comic theatre was a means of working off the exuberant energy of abounding vitality. There were no limitations to the subjects it could treat or the way of treating them. The result is that the distinctive quality of the Old Comedy cannot be illustrated by quotation. The most characteristic passages are unprintable. Something completely indecent is caricatured, wildly exaggerated, repeated in a dozen different ways, all fantastically absurd and all incredibly vulgar. The truth is that the jokes are often very funny. To read Aristophanes through at a sitting is to have Victorian guide posts laid low. He is so frank, so fearless, so completely without shame, one ends by feeling that indecency is just a part of life and a part with specially humorous possibilities. There is nothing of Peeping Tom anywhere, no sly whispering from behind a hand. The plainest and clearest words speak everything out unabashed. Life looks a coarse and vulgar thing, lived at the level of nature's primitive needs, but it never looks a foul and rotten thing. Degeneracy plays no part. It is the way of a virile world, of robust men who can roar with laughter at any kind of slapstick, decent or indecent, but chiefly the last.

Look upon this picture and on this. It is impossible for

us to-day to make a coherent whole out of Aristophanes' Athens and Plato's. But if ever a day comes when our intelligentsia is made up of our star football players we shall be on the way to understanding the Athenians—as Aristophanes saw them.

# *Chapter* VIII

## HERODOTUS

### THE FIRST SIGHT-SEER

### *The Slave in Greece*

HERODOTUS is the historian of the glorious fight for liberty
in which the Greeks conquered the overwhelming power
of Persia. They won the victory because they were free
men defending their freedom against a tyrant and his army
of slaves. So Herodotus saw the contest. The watchword
was freedom; the stake was the independence or the en-
slavement of Greece; the issue made it sure that Greeks
never would be slaves.

The modern reader cannot accept the proud words without a wondering question. What of the slaves these free
Greeks owned? The Persian defeat did not set them free.
What real idea of freedom could the conquerors at Marathon and Salamis have had, slaveowners, all of them? The
question shows up, as no other question could, the difference between the mind of to-day and the mind of antiquity.
To all the ancient world the freeing of slaves would have
been sheer nonsense. There always had been slaves. In
every community the way of life depended on them; they
were a first necessity, accepted as such without a thought—
literally; nobody ever paid any attention to them. Life in
Greece as everywhere else was founded on slaves, but in
all Greek literature up to the age of Pericles they never
come into sight except as individuals here and there; the
old nurse in the Odyssey, or the good swineherd, whose
condition is accepted as naturally as any fact in nature.

That is true from Homer to Æschylus, who makes Clytemnestra say to Cassandra, the Trojan princess, now her slave:

> If one is a slave
> It is well to serve in an old family
> Long used to riches. Every man who reaps
> A sudden harvest, wealth past all his hopes,
> Is savage to his slaves beyond the common.
> From us expect such use as custom grants.

From time immemorial that was the attitude in all the
world. There was never anywhere a dreamer so rash or so
romantic as to imagine a life without slaves. The loftiest
thinkers, idealists, and moralists never had an idea that
slavery was evil. In the Old Testament it is accepted without comment exactly as in the records of Egypt and Mesopotamia. Even the prophets of Israel did not utter a word
against it, nor, for that matter, did St. Paul. What is
strange is not that the Greeks took slavery for granted
through hundreds of years, but that finally they began to
think about it and question it.

To Euripides the glory belongs of being the first to con-
demn it. "Slavery," he wrote:

> That thing of evil, by its nature evil,
> Forcing submission from a man to what
> No man should yield to.

He was, as usual, far in advance of his age. Even Plato, a
generation later, could not keep pace with him. He never
spoke against slavery; in his old age he actually advocated
it. Still, there are signs that he was troubled by it. He says,
"A slave is an embarrassing possession." He had reached a
point when he could not feel at ease with slaves, and he
does not admit them to his ideal Republic.

Except for this mild and indirect opposition and for
Euripides' open attack, we have no idea how or why the
opposition to slavery spread, but by Aristotle's time, a
generation after Plato, it had come out into the open.
Aristotle himself, for all his extraordinary powers of mind,
looked at the matter purely from the point of view of

common sense and social convenience. Slaves were necessary to carry on society as constituted, and he did not want any other kind of society. With no expressed or implied disapproval he defines a slave as "a machine which breathes, a piece of animated property," an instance of the cold, clear statement of fact which so often opens people's eyes and shocks them into opposition. Opponents to slavery increased. "There are people," Aristotle writes—he does not include himself—"who consider owning slaves as violating natural law because the distinction between a slave and a free person is wholly conventional and has no place in nature, so that it rests on mere force and is devoid of justice."

That is the point Greek thought had reached more than two thousand four hundred years ago. Less than a hundred years ago America had to fight a great war before slavery was abolished. The matter for wonder is not that Herodotus saw nothing odd in slaveowners being the champions of freedom, but that in Greece alone, through all ancient and almost all modern times, were there men great enough and courageous enough to see through the conventional coverings that disguised slavery, and to proclaim it for what it was. A few years after Aristotle the Stoics denounced it as the most intolerable of all the wrongs man ever committed against man.

Socrates, when the young Theætetus was introduced to him as a lad of brilliant promise, said to him that he felt sure he had thought a great deal. The boy answered, Oh, no—not that, but at least he had wondered a great deal. "Ah, that shows the lover of wisdom," Socrates said, "for wisdom begins in wonder."

There have been few men ever who wondered more than Herodotus did. The word is perpetually on his pen: "A wonder was told me"; "In that land there are ten thousand wonders"; "Wonderful deeds, those"; "It is a thing to be wondered at." In this disposition he was the true child of his age—the great age of Greece. During his life his countrymen were using their freedom, newly secured to them by the Persian defeat, to wonder in all directions. They were no longer obliged to spend their best powers on war. Fighting occurred, but only sporadically. The Athenians on the whole were peaceful and prosperous; they had leisure to sit at home and think about the universe and dispute with Socrates, or to travel abroad and explore the world. In any case, to be active. Leisure meant activity in those days. Nobody wanted anything else. Energy and high spirits and vitality marked the fifth century in Athens.

Herodotus, spiritually an Athenian although a native of Halicarnassus, summed up in himself the vigor of his times. He set out to travel over the earth as far as a man could go. What strength of will and also of body that called for under the travelling conditions of the day, it is impossible for us to realize. The first part of St. Paul's journey to Rome gives a picture of the hazards that had to be faced at sea four hundred years after Herodotus, and a companion picture for the land is Xenophon's description of the endless miles on foot or horseback through the burning wastes of Asia Minor to Babylon. It required a hungering and thirsting for knowledge and all the explorer's zest to send a man on the travels Herodotus undertook; undertook, too, with keen enjoyment. He was the first sight-seer in the world, and there has never been a happier one. If he could see something new, discomforts and difficulties and dangers were nothing to him. He seems never to have noticed them. He never wrote about them. He filled his book with the marvels to rejoice a man's heart—marvels of which the great earth was full. Oh, wonder that there were such goodly creatures in it!

Just how far he travelled is hard to say. What he heard he gives with as great interest as what he saw, and he is so objective, so absorbed in whatever he is describing, he generally leaves himself out. But he certainly went as far east as Persia and as far west as Italy. He knew the coast of the Black Sea and had been in Arabia. In Egypt he went up the Nile to Assouan. It seems probable that he went to Cyrene; his descriptions often read like those of an eye witness. That is less true of Libya and Sicily, but it is quite possible that he had been in both countries. In fact, his journeys practically reached to the boundaries of the

known world, and the information he gathered reached
far beyond. He knew a good deal about India. For instance, there were wild trees there that bore wool, superior
in whiteness and quality to sheep's wool. The Indians made
beautiful fine clothing from it. With India his information
about the East stopped. He had heard a report of great
deserts on the further side, but that was all. Of the West
he writes:

> I am unable to speak with certainty. I can learn nothing
> about the islands from which our tin comes, and though
> I have asked everywhere I have met no one who has seen
> a sea on the west side of Europe. The truth is no one has
> discovered if Europe is surrounded by water or not.

> I smile at those who with no sure knowledge to guide
> them describe the ocean flowing around a perfectly circular
> earth.

This is an example of the way the Greek mind worked.
The great river Ocean encircling the earth had been described by Homer, the revered, even sacred, authority, and
by Hesiod, second only to Homer, and yet Horodotus with
never a qualm at possible impiety permits himself a smile.
Quite as characteristic in his matter-of-fact statement that
the priestess at Delphi had been more than once bribed to
give an oracle favorable to one side in a dispute. This was
attacking the Greek holy of holies—like accusing the pope
of taking bribes. Herodotus had a great respect for the
Delphic oracle, but to his mind that was no reason to
suppress a charge which he had investigated and believed
to be true—and most assuredly no reason to abstain from
investigation. When an authority, no matter how tradition-
ally sacrosanct, came into conflict with a fact, the Greeks
preferred the fact. They had no inclination to protect
"sound doctrine taught of old." A new force had come
into the world with Greece, the idea of Truth to which
personal bias and prejudice must yield.

Herodotus is a shining instance of the strong Greek bent
to examine and prove or disprove. He had a passion for
finding out. The task he set himself was nothing less than

to find out all about everything in the world. He is always called the "father of history," but he was quite as much the father of geography, of archæology, of anthropology, of sociology, of whatever has to do with human beings and the places in which they live. He was as free from prejudice as it is possible to be. The Greek contempt for foreigners— in Greek, "barbarians"—never touched him. He was passionately on Athens' side in her struggle against Persia, yet he admired and praised the Persians. He found them brave and chivalrous and truthful. Much that he saw in Phœnicia and Egypt seemed admirable to him, and even in uncivilized Scythia and Libya he saw something to commend. He did not go abroad to find Greek superiority. An occasional inferiority quite pleased him. He quotes with amusement Cyrus' description of a Greek market as "a place set apart for people to go and cheat each other on oath."

"All men," he writes, "if asked to choose the best ways of ordering life would choose their own." Darius once asked some Greeks what would induce them to devour the dead bodies of their parents, and when they answered in horror that nothing could make them do an act so atrocious, he had some men from India brought in whose custom it was to do this very thing. He asked them how they could be persuaded to burn their dead instead of eating them. They cried out in abhorrence and begged him not to utter such abominable words. "As Pindar says," concludes Herodotus, "custom is king." The story is characteristic of his indulgent attitude toward all men's ways, however queer. He was that rare person, a lover of mankind. He liked people, all of them. But he liked them more than he admired them, and he never idealized them. Plutarch even accuses him, so markedly kind and fair-minded as he was, of actual malignity because heroes in his book are not consistently heroical. It is true that he lived in an age of heroism and never really believed in heroes. But his gentle scepticism worked both ways. He never judged or condemned. The weakness and fallibility of the human kind aroused only his sympathy. If his heroes are imperfectly great, his villains are never perfectly villainous. He looked at them all with dispassionate and equal interest.

Everything everywhere in the world of men was of interest to him. He tells us how the homely girls in Illyria get husbands, how the lake dwellers keep their children from falling into the water, what Egyptian mosquito nets are like, that the King of Persia when travelling drinks only boiled water, what the Adrymachidæ do to fleas, how the Arabians cut their hair, that the Danube islanders get drunk on smells, how the Scythians milk their mares, that in Libya the woman with the most lovers is honored, how the streets of Babylon are laid out, that physicians in Egypt specialize in diseases, and so on, and so on. Bits of information that have nothing to do with what he is writing about keep straying in; but he is so intensely interested in them himself, the reader's interest is caught too. Is not that really extraordinary? he says to us—or extremely diverting —or remarkably sensible? And we follow him; we are surprised and diverted and approving. Of course this is only to say that he has the *sine qua non* of a writer—he is never dull; but to avoid dulness in what is often a guidebook is an achievement. Some part of it is due to his perfect, his unsurpassed, ease in writing. He has no mannerisms, not a particle of self-consciousness; he is always simple, direct, and lucid, always easy to read. His countryman, Dionysius of Halicarnassus, said he was the first to give Greece the idea that an expression in prose could have the worth of a verse of poetry.

He is often accused of being credulous even to the point of silliness. It is said that he accepted with the naïve simplicity of a child everything he was told, no matter how preposterous. There is no truth whatsoever in the charge. Precisely the contrary is true: his turn of mind was sceptical; he was a born investigator. The word history, which was first used in our sense by him, means investigation in Greek. His book begins, "This is an account of the investigations [historia] made by Herodotus of Halicarnassus." He started on them prepared to scrutinize everything he heard. When different and equally probable accounts of an event were given him he wrote them all down and left the final judgment to his reader. "I cannot positively state whether this was done or that," he will say. "For myself," he remarks in a notable passage, "my duty is to report all that is said, but I am not obliged to believe it all—a remark which applies to my whole History."

Even these few quotations show the temper of his mind, his sense of responsibility as a reporter, and his care in weighing evidence. But of course in his day the unknown was so great, what was actually known was so limited, no borderline had yet been drawn between the credible and the incredible. It is often impossible to make out why Herodotus accepts one thing and rejects another purely on the ground of what can and cannot happen. Doves, he says firmly, do not ever speak even though the holy women at Dodona declare that they do, but he does not question the story that a mare gave birth to a rabbit. He is sure that no matter what the Egyptian priests assert, it is not true that the phœnix wraps up the dead body of his parent in a mass of myrrh and carries it from Arabia to the Temple of the Sun in Heliopolis where he buries it. On the other hand it seems to him quite reasonable that there are headless creatures in Libya with eyes in their breasts, and that cats in Egypt have the singular habit of jumping into the fire. He had a standard of what was possible and what was not, but it was so different from ours it escapes us. After all, wherever he went he saw so many strange things, it was easy to believe there were even stranger ones in the vast beyond.

But when he was on ground he knew he was a shrewd judge of the improbable. He writes:

> In the highest tower in Babylon, in the topmost chamber, there is a great couch on which the god himself is reported to sleep. So the priests told me, but I do not believe it.

> I cannot say with confidence how the man escaped, for the account given me made me wonder. They say he jumped into the sea and swam eighty stadia under water, never rising to the top. If I may give my own opinion, it is that he got off in a boat.

But he is always mildly tolerant of other people's explanations and never dogmatic about his own. Of the storm that wrecked Xerxes' fleet he writes:

> It lasted three days. At length the Magi charming the wind and sacrificing to the Nereids succeeded in laying the tempest—or perhaps it ceased of itself.

When he was sight-seeing in Thessaly he was told that a famous gorge he visited was caused by Neptune, and he remarks:

> It seemed plain to me that it was the result of an earthquake. Many people think earthquakes are the work of Neptune.

What he himself thought about the gods is not easy to make out. The heavenly powers play a leading part in his history, and omens, oracles, prayers, and prophets are very important to him. Yet it would be hard to find a more coldly rationalistic statement than the one he makes early in his book:

> Where the gods come from, whether they always existed, what they looked like, was, so to speak, unknown till yesterday. Homer and Hesiod lived not more than four hundred years ago and it was they who made the gods for the Greeks and gave them their names and shapes.

His book is really a bridge from one era to another. He was born in an age of deep religious feeling, just after the Persian Wars; he lived on into the scepticism of the age of Pericles; and by virtue of his kindly tolerance and keen intellectual interest he was equally at home in both.

Historians often forget that the proper study of history is men. Marshalled facts and reasoned analyses tend to cover up human nature. That was not Herodotus' way. People are always to the fore in his book. It is fortunate for us that he is the reporter of Marathon, Thermopylæ, Salamis, names which shine like stars through the endless, senseless wars that make up most of the world's history.

In his hands they are the scenes of a great drama written in plain human terms. The disposing causes are men's arrogance and greed for conquest and their power to defend what is dear to them against overwhelming odds.

Only the last part of the *History* has to do with the Persian Wars. Two thirds of the book are taken up with Herodotus' journeys and what he learned on them. These earlier chapters have the effect, more and more as one reads on, of a slowly unrolling stage setting. The whole of the known world is presented as the fitting background to the tremendous conflict that is to decide whether freedom or tyranny is the stronger, whether the West is to be enslaved by the East. Darius, the Great King, makes his appearance. He is ruler of most of the world. Myriads of men serve him; his wealth is limitless; his magnificence fabulous; his cruelty fantastic. He is the Orient in person, its barbaric pearl and gold, its helpless millions, its disregard for human life and suffering. Over against him stands Greece, "a rocky land and poor," a speaker in Herodotus tells Darius, where, as Pericles put it, the people "love beauty with economy"; economy, the very opposite to the lavishness and exaggeration of the grandiose East.

Herodotus describes the amused astonishment of the Persian Army at learning that the prize for an Olympic victory was a crown of wild olives. He tells about a pillar he saw, one of the many the Great King set up to mark his approbation when he passed a place that pleased him. It was inscribed: "These springs are the best and most beautiful of waters. They were visited by Darius, the best and most beautiful of men." By sheer force of contrast the words recall the epitaph on the dead at Thermopylæ: "Stranger, tell the Spartans that we lie here in obedience to their words."

The contrast is never stressed by Herodotus, but in one story after another it comes out so clearly that it needs no emphasis. "The immortals are near to men to watch over deeds of justice and kindliness," wrote Hesiod, and so all Greeks believed. Whatever the strange deities of the East required, it was not justice nor kindliness. "It is a Persian custom to bury people alive," says Herodotus.

"One of Darius' daughers-in-law had fourteen young children of the best Persian families buried alive." Imperial Rome, always inclined to Oriental ways, took over this custom of killing the young with the old. Little boys and girls were, if not buried alive, at any rate put to death with a guilty father. But Greece was different. When the young sons of a man who had betrayed his city to the Persians were brought to the general commanding the Spartan forces after Leonidas fell at Thermopylæ, he dismissed them. "They are boys," Herodotus reports him as saying. "What part could boys have in the guilt of siding with the Persians?"

What underlay the Spartan general's action was not only the belief that the innocent must not suffer with the guilty; even more basic was the conviction of the value of each individual, no matter how defenseless. This idea never touched even the surface of Oriental life. No law or custom there lent it support. In Greece it was based on something deeper than law or custom. Once, Herodotus says, ten of the ruling party in Corinth went to a house with the purpose of killing a little boy there who an oracle had declared would grow up to destroy the city.

> The mother, thinking it a friendly visit, brought her son when they asked to see him, and put him in the arms of one of them. Now they had agreed on the way there that whoever first received the child should dash it to the ground. But it happened that the baby smiled at the man who took it and so he was unable to kill it and handed it to another. Thus it passed through the hands of all the ten and no one of them would kill it. Then they gave it back to the mother and went away and began to blame each other, but especially him who had first held the child.

"A tyrant disturbs ancient laws," Herodotus writes, "violates women, kills men without trial. But a people ruling—first, the very name of it is so beautiful; and secondly, a people does none of these things." Only the tyrant was known throughout the East. When the Great King was on his march to Greece a very rich noble of Lydia entertained not only him and his courtiers, but his multitudinous host of soldiers as well. He set sumptuous feasts before all, Herodotus says, and in return begged humbly that one of his five sons, all in the army, might remain with him. "You make such a request?" said the king. "You who are my slave and bound to give me all that is yours, even to your wife?" He ordered the body of the eldest youth to be cut in two and placed on either side of the road where the army was to pass. The Persians were slaves, so called and so treated; the richest and most powerful claimed nothing as their right; they were completely at the disposal of the king. Herodotus tells another story. A noble, who had for years enjoyed the royal favor and then had lost it, was invited to dine with the king. After he had feasted on the meat placed before him, he was presented with a covered basket. Lifting the lid he saw the head and hands and feet of his only son. "Do you know now," the king asked pleasantly, "the kind of animal you have been eating?" The father had learned the lesson slaves must master, self-control. He answered with perfect composure, "I do know, indeed—and whatever the king is pleased to do pleases me." That was the spirit of the East from time immemorial, first clearly recorded for the world in Herodotus' book. Little, poor, barren Greece was free. "You know perfectly what it is to be a slave," Herodotus reports some Greeks as saying to a Persian official who was urging them to submit to Xerxes. "Freedom you have never tried, to know how sweet it is. If you had you would urge us to fight for it not with our spears only, but even with hatchets." As the war with the Persians draws nearer in Herodotus, it is seen more and more clearly as a contest not of flesh and blood only, but of spiritual forces which are incompatible.

A brief prologue introduces the action. A revolt broke out in the Greek cities on the coast of Asia Minor which were subject to Darius. Athens sent help. The Athenians marched to Sardis, the capital of Lydia, and they burned the splendid town. To Darius it was incredible that any people on earth should so defy him. "Who are the Athenians?" he demanded; and he ordered that every time he dined, an attendant should say to him three times: "Sire, remember the Athenians." There is no doubt that Herodotus understood dramatic requirements. The stage has been set for Marathon.

When the curtain rises for the drama proper the nephew of Darius, who has been entrusted with the charge of carrying out the vengeance of the king, is leading the Persian Army into Greece, vast forces by sea and by land. Before him heralds come demanding from the Greek cities "earth and water," the tokens of submission; and all as far south as Thebes give them. One, Eritræa, separated from Athens only by a narrow strait, refuses, but she is quickly captured and burned to the ground. Athens is next, seemingly a most trifling obstacle to that great host. She has no one in all Greece to help her except a little band of soldiers sent by Platæa, a town grateful for favors in the past. Away to the south the chief military power of Greece, Sparta, is no more ready to submit to Persia than Athens, and would be a strong ally. But, as democracies always do, Athens has waited too long to make her plans. The Persians are almost upon her when Pheidippides starts his race to enlist help for her. In Sparta the next day he urges: "Lacedæmonians, the Athenians entreat you. Do not suffer them to fall into bondage to barbarians." But there are some days yet to the full moon, and until the moon was full the Spartans would not march. "We will come as soon after that as we can," the herald is told. Events, however, do not wait on the moon. The Persian fleet is already at anchor in the curving bay of Marathon.

Herodotus was born about that time. The fight must often have been described to him by men who had taken part in it. He explains the strategy very clearly. The Athenian formation was the exact reverse of the enemy's who trusted to their centre, leaving their wings to inferior troops. Miltiades threw his chief strength into the wings. The centre was weak so that the Persians easily broke through it and rushed on in pursuit. Then the Athenian wings closed in behind, shutting the foe off from their ships and cutting them down. The defeat was complete. The fleet after sailing down the coast to within sight of Athens put out to sea. The Persians had gone. It was an incredible contest and an incredible victory. How could it happen like that—the little band of defenders victors over the mighty armament? We do not understand. But Herodotus understood, and so did all Greeks. A free democracy resisted a slave-supported tyranny. The Athenians at Marathon had advanced at a run; the enemy's officers drove them into battle by scourging them. Mere numbers were powerless against the spirit of free men fighting to defend their freedom. Liberty proved her power. A wave of exultant courage and faith swept through the city, and Athens started on her career.

Ten years passed before the curtain rose for the last act. Darius was kept fom the terrible vengeance he vowed he would take by a war which occupied him until he died. He had to leave it to his son to revenge the Persian defeat. He too was to remember the Athenians. Xerxes was not eager for the enterprise, but in actual fact he was helpless. It was written in the decrees of Fate that he should undertake it. The power of the Persians had grown too great, their self-confidence too assured. The gods who hated beyond all else the arrogance of power had passed judgment upon them. The time had come when the great empire should be broken and humbled. Insolent assurance will surely, soon or late, be brought low, Herodotus says, just as Æschylus wrote:

> All arrogance will reap a harvest rich in tears.
> God calls men to a heavy reckoning
> For overweening pride.

False dreams sent by heaven to Xerxes aroused his ambition and he determined to conquer Greece. Herodotus marshals with solemnity the preparations for the invasion: the slow assembling of the vast army; a canal dug across a great isthmus and the Hellespont bridged for an easy passage by sea and land; food commandeered and water supplies sought out; enormous stores of provisions amassed along the route. Then the pomp and splendor of the start which was signalled by the very heavens. As the army began its march "the sun quit his seat in the sky and disappeared. And yet there were no clouds and the air was serene." Science todays says that that eclipse happened two years later, but the ten-year-old Herodotus was then could not be expected to mark the date accurately, and a sense for dramatic appropriateness is so general, the older men he depended on for his facts would never have failed to bring together the darkening of the sun and the fall of the Persian power.

At the Hellespont a halt was made for the king to review his forces. On a lofty throne of white marble he watched the army filling shores and plain, and the ships crowding so close, they hid the water. Thus gazing he shed tears. "There came upon me," he told one standing by, "a sudden pity when I thought of the shortness of man's life and considered all this host, so numerous, fated so soon to die." "Nay, King," the other answered. "Weep rather for this, that brief as life is there never yet was or will be a man who does not wish more than once to die rather than to live."

The great army swept on to Greece, drinking the rivers dry as they advanced. Town after town at their approach sent the earth and water which showed that they were no longer free, but already under the Persian yoke. Athens did not send them. There was terror and despair there, too. The oracle at Delphi had spoken to Athenian envoys and had told them to fly to the ends of the earth and make their minds familiar with horrors. Still, the Athenians did not submit. Their cause seemed hopeless. Sparta was as determined as Athens to resist, but her policy was short-sighted. Her heart was in defending only the Peloponnesus; she refused at first to consider anything else. And still the Athenians stood firm. Xerxes' general sent an ambassador to Athens to offer most generous terms, everything good, in short—except freedom. "Tell the general," was the answer, "that the Athenians say, as long as the sun moves in his present course we will never come to terms with Xerxes." When that spirit takes possession of men miracles may be looked for.

Sparta was finally aroused. She sent a little band of soldiers north to defend Thermopylæ, the pass over which the Persians must advance. There was a long and heroic defense which in the end failed. Leonidas, the Spartan commander, sent away the other Greeks who had been fighting with him, "being anxious," Herodotus says, "that they should not perish, but he and the Spartans would not desert their post, for they held that to be dishonorable." As they waited for the attack which they knew would be the last, one of them said he had heard the Persians were so numerous that when they shot their arrows they hid the sky. "Good," said another. "Then we will fight in the shade." Men like that would make the enemy suffer before they fell. Herodotus describes them "advancing from the fortification which had hitherto protected them, as for certain death, while on the other side the Persian officers flogged their men forward. Thus they fought at Thermopylæ." And Xerxes, coming to the battlefield when all was over, looked at the many dead and sent for a Greek exile he had in his train. "In what way can we conquer these men?" he asked. "Come, tell me." But no one could tell him that.

Athens had been abandoned. The priestess at Delphi had spoken again. "Zeus gives a wooden wall to Pallas Athena," she said, "which shall preserve you and your children." When the messengers brought this answer back there was great dispute as to what it meant, but, Herodotus says, "a certain man lately risen to eminence whose name was Themistocles, prevailed." He said the wooden wall was the ships, and the entire populace left the city. The women and children were taken to places of safety; the fleet sailed to the island of Salamis, where the other Greeks assembled. Athens had the largest force and was entitled to the leadership, but she did not press her claim when she saw it would be bitterly contested. "She thought," Herodotus explains, "the great thing was that Greece should be saved," not that she should get the honor which was clearly her due. She withdrew and saw, without a protest, Sparta, always her rival, chosen in her stead. That was the greatest moment in her history. If she could have kept that vision of what was really important and what was not, there would have been no Peloponnesian War.

The victory, even so, belonged to the Athenian Themistocles. He made the plan which forced the Persians to fight
in the narrow waters around Salamis where their numbers
helped to defeat them. Xerxes watched the battle from
the shore.

> A king sat on the rocky brow
> That looks on sea-born Salamis,
> And ships by thousands lay below,
> And men by nations—all were his.
> He counted them at break of day,
> And when the sun set where were they?

The victorious Greeks distrusted the evidence of their
own eyes. They had gone into battle almost despairing.
"The night before," Herodotus says, "fear and dismay had
taken possession of them." Now they could not believe
the awful menace was ended. They held themselves ready
for another attack. But the Persian ships put out to sea;
they were gone never to return. Liberty had again proved
her power. Just before the attack the Greek leaders told
their men, "When we join battle with the Persians, before
all else remember freedom." Æschylus, who was there, says
they advanced upon the foe with a shout of:

> For freedom, sons of Greece,
> Freedom for country, children, wives,
> Freedom for worship, for our fathers' graves.

Awe fell upon the victors as they watched the mighty
armament depart. "It is not we who have done this,"
Themistocles said.

# Chapter IX

## THUCYDIDES

### THE THING THAT HATH BEEN IS THAT WHICH SHALL BE

### *The Spinning Ball*

THE greatest sea power in Europe and the greatest land power faced each other in war. The stake was the leadership of Europe. Each was fighting to strengthen her own position at the expense of the other: in the case of the sea power to hold her widely separated empire; in the case of the land power to challenge that empire and win one for herself. Both, as the war began, were uneasily conscious that an important and even decisive factor might be an Asiatic nation, enormous in extent of territory, which had a foothold in Europe and was believed by many to be interested in watching the two chief Western powers weaken and perhaps destroy each other until in the end she herself could easily dominate Europe.

The year was 431 B.C., when Athens was mistress of the sea, when Sparta had the best army in the world—and Persia saw a prospect of being rid of both at no more cost than encouraging first one and then the other.

Historians to-day generally reject the idea that history repeats itself and may therefore be studied as a warning and a guide. The modern scientific historian looks at his subject very much as the geologist does. History is a chronicle of fact considered for itself alone. There is no pattern in the web unrolled from the loom of time and no profit in studying it except to gain information. That was not the point of view of the Greek historian of the war between Athens and Sparta, whose book is still a masterpiece among histories. Thucydides would never have written his history if he had thought like that. Knowledge for the sake of knowledge had little attraction for the Athenians. They were realists. Knowledge was to be desired because it had value for living; it led men away from error to right action. Thucydides wrote his book because he believed that men would profit from a knowledge of what brought about that ruinous struggle precisely as they profit from a statement of what causes a deadly disease. He reasoned that since the nature of the human mind does not change any more than the nature of the human body, circumstances swayed by human nature are bound to repeat themselves, and in the same situation men are bound to act in the same way unless it is shown to them that such a course in other days ended disastrously. When the reason why a disaster came about is perceived people will be able to guard against that particular danger. "It will perhaps be found," he writes, "that the absence of story-telling in my work makes it less attractive to listen to, but I shall be satisfied if it is considered useful by all who wish to know the plain truth of the events which happened and will according to human nature happen again in the same way. It was written not for the moment, but for all time."

The man who looked thus at the historian's task was a contemporary of the events he related. Thucydides was one of the Athenian generals during the first years of the war. Then fate intervened and turned a soldier into an investigator, for he was exiled when the war was in its tenth year. He tells the reason:

> The general sent to the other commander of the district, Thucydides son of Olorus, the author of this history, who was about half a day's sail from Amphipolis, and urged him to come to their aid. He sailed in haste with seven ships which happened to be at hand, wishing above all to reach Amphipolis before it surrendered. But the citizens capitulated. On the evening of the same day Thucydides and his ships arrived.

He reached the town just too late. Athens punished unsuccessful officers, and from then on Thucydides occupied the post of an observer. "Because of my exile," he writes, "I was enabled to watch quietly the course of events."

Extraordinary as the statement is, it is proved true by the book he wrote. From being one of the men his country trusted most he had become a man without a country, a fate in those days little better than death, and, as far as we can judge, he had done nothing to deserve it. Yet he was able "to watch quietly the course of events," free from bitterness and bias, and to produce a history as coldly impartial as if it had dealt with a far-distant past. He looked at Athens exactly as he did at Sparta, with no concern to give a bit of praise here or blame there. What occupied his mind was something above and beyond the deadly and destructive contest he was recounting. He saw his subject in its eternal aspect—*sub specie æternitatis*. Underneath the shifting surface of the struggle between two little Greek states he had caught sight of a universal truth. Throughout his book, through the endless petty engagements on sea and land which he relates with such scrupulous care, he is pointing out what war is, why it comes to pass, what it does, and, unless men learn better ways, must continue to do. His *History of the Peloponnesian War* is really a treatise on war, its causes and its effects.

The war broke out in 431. A succession of petty quarrels had led up to it, insufficient, all put together, to give any adequate reason for a fight to the death between the two chief states of Greece. Aristophanes held them up to ridicule, declaring that the whole business started because some tipsy youngsters from Athens went off to a neighboring town and

> stole from Megara a hussy there.
> Then men of Megara came here and stole
> Two of Aspasia's minxes. And those three,
> No better than they should be, caused the war:
> For then in wrath Olympian Pericles
> Thundered and lightened and confounded Greece.

What Aristophanes parodied Thucydides dismissed. The real cause of the war was not this or that trivial disturbance, the revolt of a distant colony, the breaking of an unimportant treaty, or the like. It was something far beneath the surface, deep down in human nature, and the cause of all the wars ever fought. The motive power was greed, that strange passion for power and possession which no power and no posesssion satisfy. Power, Thucydides wrote, or its equivalent wealth, created the desire for more power, more wealth. The Athenians and the Spartans fought for one reason only—because they were powerful, and therefore were compelled (the words are Thucydides' own) to seek more power. They fought not because they were different—democratic Athens and oligarchical Sparta—but because they were alike. The war had nothing to do with differences in ideas or with considerations of right and wrong. Is democracy right and the rule of the few over the many wrong? To Thucydides the question would have seemed an evasion of the issue. There was no right power. Power, whoever wielded it, was evil, the corruptor of men.

A historian who lived some two hundred years later, Polybius, also a Greek, gives an admirably clear and condensed account of Thucydides' basic thesis. Human history, he says, is a cycle which excess of power keeps revolving. Primitive despots start the wheel rolling. The more power they get the more they want, and they go on abusing their authority until inevitably opposition is aroused and a few men, strong enough when they unite, seize the rule for themselves. These, too, can never be satisfied. They encroach upon the rights of others until they are opposed in their turn. The people are aroused against them, and democracy succeeds to oligarchy. But there again the evil in all power is no less operative. It brings corruption and contempt for law, until the state can no longer function and falls easily before a strong man who promises to restore order. The rule of the one, of the few, of the many, each is destroyed in turn because there is in them all an unvarying evil—the greed for power—and no moral quality is necessarily bound up with any of them.

The revolution of the cycle Thucydides watched brought results so terrible that he believed an account of them would be a warning which men could not disregard. The fact of first importance for them to realize, which the Peloponnesian War threw into clear relief, was that great power brought about its own destruction. Athens' triumphant career of empire building ended in ruin. Her immensely rich sea empire had seemed for a long time the exemplar of successful power politics. In reality she had grown too powerful. She acted in the invariable way with the invariable result; she abused her power and she was overwhelmingly defeated. So far Thucydides saw.

We can see farther. The cause of humanity was defeated. Greece's contribution to the world was checked and soon ceased. Hundreds of years had to pass before men reached again the point where Greek thought left off.

At the beginning of the sixth century, a hundred and fifty years before Thucydides' war, the Athens we know was born. She had been a little state ruled by a landed aristocracy that slowly as commerce increased turned into an aristocracy of wealth. Wars were infrequent. The main fighting up to the fifth century had been within the state itself, where the idea of the rights of man was gaining ground and the old order was weakening. Fortunately for the city, the early sixth century was marked by the coming forward of a great and good man, Solon, too great and too good to want power for himself. He saw as keenly as Thucydides that power worked out in evil and that greed was its source and its strength. "Men are driven on by greed to win wealth in unrighteous ways," he wrote, "and he who has most wealth always covets twice as much." Of power he said, "Powerful men pull the city down," than which there could be no greater condemnation from a Greek, utterly dependent as every man in those days was upon his city. Solon made over the government in accordance with the new spirit of the times. He gave the common people a share in it, and he laid the foundation for the first democracy in the world. It is true that an interlude followed after his retirement when a strong man profited by violent quarrels between the classes to take control himself, but on the whole he respected Solon's constitution. Democracy even under a tyranny continued to advance, and the city kept peace with her neighbors. The important island of Salamis, it is true, was taken away from Megara, a near neighbor, at the instigation of no less a person than Solon himself; but it was the only case of its kind.

That was well for Athens. A few years after the tyrant had been put down, in the great and memorable year 490 when the little city had to decide between fighting Persia or being enslaved, she did not have to guard also against enemies in Greece. There has never been a war fought for purer motives than the war against Persia. Marathon and Salamis are still words that "send a ringing challenge down through the generations." Their victories still seem a miracle as they seemed to the men who won them. The mighty were put down from their seats and those of low degree exalted, and for fifty years and more Persia could do nothing to Greece.

What followed was one of the most triumphant rebirths of the human spirit in all history, when the bitter differences that divide men were far in the background and freedom was in the air—freedom in the great sense, not only equality before the law, but freedom of thought and speech. Surely, we think, then, at any rate, in this sad and suffering world

> Joy was it at that season but to live.

There is no joy in the pages of Thucydides. A great change came over Athens in a brief space of time. Two quotations are enough to show it.

As the curtain rises in the *Suppliants* (held by many, and in my opinion with truth, to be one of Euripides' early plays) an expedition sent by Argos against Thebes has been defeated, and the Thebans have done what was utterly abhorrent to every Greek: they have refused to allow the enemy to bury their dead. Their leader comes to Athens for help "because," he tells Theseus, the Athenian king, "Athens of all cities is compassionate." As Theseus hesitates to take on the quarrel, however righteous, of another state his mother tells him it is his duty. The city's honor is at stake as well as his own.

> Look to the things of God,
> Know you are bound to help all who are wronged.

Bound to constrain all who destroy the law.
What else holds state to state save this alone,
That each one honors the great laws of right.

Theseus acknowledges that what she says is true. Athens is the defender of the defenseless, the enemy of the oppressor. Wherever she goes freedom follows.

Only a few years later, Thucydides has Pericles, his ideal statesman, give this warning to the Athenians:

Do not think you are fighting for the simple issue of letting this or that state become free or remain subject to you. You have an empire to lose. You must realize that Athens has a mighty name in the world because she has never yielded to misfortunes and has to-day the greatest power that exists. To be hated has always been the lot of those who had aspired to rule over others. In face of that hatred you cannot give up your power—even if some sluggards and cowards are all for being noble at this crisis. Your empire is a tyranny by now, perhaps, as many think, wrongfully acquired, but certainly dangerous to let go.

The difference between these two ideas of Athens is extraordinary. It cannot be explained by the difference between a poet and a historian. Euripides knew the world as well as Thucydides did. Few have ever known it better. It was Athens that was different. The two men were spokesmen each of his own time. In less than a generation the city that had been the champion of freedom had earned the name of the Tyrant City.

Back in 480, after the final defeat of the Persians, the Athenians had been chosen to lead the new confederacy of free Greek states. It was a lofty post and they were proud to hold it, but the role demanded a high degree of disinterestedness. Athens could be the leader of the free only if she considered the welfare of others on the same level with her own. During the war with Persia she had been able to do that. She had shown herself at a great crisis not meanly preoccupied with her own advantage, but honorable, generous, just as Euripides saw her. As head of the league, too, for a time she had not let her power corrupt her. But only for a short time. The temptation to acquire still more power proved as always irresistible. Very soon the free confederacy was being turned into the Athenian Empire. There are changes, even violent ones, in a state which do not affect the character of the people. But this change went deep down to the very roots of religion and morality.

To the men who fought against Persia, their astonishing victory was a proof of the belief that divine justice ruled the world. It worked, indeed, in a mysterious way; nevertheless, those who trampled on the rights of others would be punished no matter how strong they were, a nation as surely as an individual. The arrogance that springs from a consciousness of power was the sin Greeks had always hated most. In their earliest literature, throughout the stories of their mythology, it was sure to draw down the wrath of the gods upon the individual, and what it did to a nation they had seen for themselves when the proud power of Persia was crushed at Salamis. Their greatest leader Solon had declared that earthly justice mirrored the justice of heaven. Their greatest poet Æschylus wrote:

> Gold is never a bulwark,
> No defense to those who spurn
> God's great altar of justice.

But these convictions were swept away by the rising tide of money and power as Athens turned on her associates in the league and forced them to become her subjects. To the young men of the empire the old belief was proved false by the facts. Gold, as far as they could see, was actually an impregnable defense. Certainly they could see their city prospering by doing wrong to other cities. Where, then, was the divine power of justice? What was there to frighten a man if he injured those who could not injure him? Why should Thucydides and his contemporaries go on believing that the wicked would certainly be painfully punished and the good substantially rewarded? The younger generation of the Periclean age had only to use their eyes to be emancipated from the union between refraining from evil and being safe. A man who took every means to gain his own advantage at the expense of others most obviously did not have to live in terror of being struck dead by lightning. Suddenly, in imperial, invincible Athens the profit motive for doing right was taken away, along with the restraining fear of an odious penalty accurately meted out for each misdeed. The debit and credit system ceased to work, and the brilliant young men of the day, full of ambition and pride of possession, had nothing to take its place. To be sure, they continued to flock to the plays of Æschylus and Sophocles, but with all their intellect they did not understand them. They watched the *Oresteia* without a notion that the dramatist was showing them the supreme power of goodness, and they applauded the *Antigone,* never dreaming that they were looking at the lofty beauty of disinterested action.

This drastic change was understood by one person in that brilliant and corrupted city. Thucydides saw that the foundation stone of all morality, the regard for the rights of others, had crumbled and fallen away. It had been the acknowledged foundation when Euripides wrote the *Suppliants,* not only of dealings between man and man, but also between state and state. The state embodied the idea of honorable men. But when Thucydides wrote, Athens had won an empire by dismissing that idea. In the big business of power politics it was not only necessary, it was right, for the state to seize every opportunity for self-advantage. Thucydides was the first probably to see, certainly to put into words, this new doctrine which was to become the avowed doctrine of the world. He makes Pericles explicitly deny that fair dealing and compassion are proper to the state as they are to the individual. A country pursuing her own way with no thought of imposing that way on others might, he points out, keep to such ideas, but not one bent upon dominion. "A city that rules an empire," he writes, "holds nothing which is to its own interest as contrary to right and reason."

That was the spirit in Athens when the Peloponnesian War broke out. The growing power of the Athenian Empire aroused her most powerful competitor. Sparta took the field against her.

All readers approach Thucydides with a preconception in favor of Athens. The Spartans have left the world nothing in the way of art or literature or science. Nevertheless it must be said that the Spartan ideal has remained persistent from their day to our own, the manifestation of an instinct hardly weakened through the last two thousand years. It is not an adult point of view. Sparta looked at things the way schoolboys do, very much like Kipling's Stalky & Co. The ideal Spartan was plucky, indifferent to hardship and pain, a first-rate athlete. The less he talked or, for that matter, thought, the better. It was for him emphatically not to reason why, but always to do and die. He was a soldier and nothing else. The purpose of the Spartan state was war. The Athenians were realistic in their attitude toward war as toward everything else. They saw nothing attractive in dying on the battlefield. Pericles, in the oration Thucydides reports him as delivering over those who had fallen in battle, does not urge his hearers to go and do likewise, but bids them pray that if they fight it will be in less dangerous circumstances. War was a bad business in Athens. Nevertheless it was a necessity; the only way a state could take what belonged to others and, having taken, keep it. War could, of course, be very profitable.

The Spartans had the sentimental, not the business, view of war. It was by no means a necessary evil; it was the noblest form of human activity. They felt a great admiration for battlefields. Tyrtæus, the poet they adored, expressed to perfection their romantic emotions. In a poem which reaches a height of sentimentality rarely attained even by bards of martial lays, he says:

> The youth's fair form is fairest when he dies.
> Even in his death the boy is beautiful,
> The hero boy who dies in his life's bloom.
> He lives in men's regret and women's tears.
> More sacred than in life, more beautiful by far,
> Because he perished on the battlefield.

The idea that underlay the young Spartans' training was their obligation to maintain the power of the state and ignore everything that did not directly contribute to it. All the other possibilities of life—imagination, love of beauty, intellectual interests—were put aside. The goal of human aspiration and achievement was to uphold the fatherland. Only what helped the state was good; only what harmed it was bad. A Spartan was not an individual but a part of a well-functioning machine which assumed all responsibility for him, exacted absolute submission from him, molded his character and his mind, and imbued him with the deep conviction that the chief end of man was to kill and be killed. Plutarch writes:

> In Sparta, the citizens' way of life was fixed. In general, they had neither the will nor the ability to lead a private life. They were like a community of bees, clinging together around the leader and in an ecstasy of enthusiasm and selfless ambition belonging wholly to their country.

Athens was a democracy. The General Assembly to which every Athenian belonged was the final authority. The executive body was a Council of Five Hundred for which all citizens were eligible. Officials were chosen by lot or elected by the people.

The state did not take responsibility for the individual Athenian; the individual had to take responsibility for the state. The result was, of course, a totally different idea of what the state was from that in Sparta. In Athens there was never a notion that it was a kind of mystic entity, different from and superior to the people who made it up. Athenian realism blocked any idea like that. The idea of the Athenian state was a union of individuals free to develop their own powers and live in their own way, obedient only to the laws they passed themselves and could criticize and change at will. And yet underneath this apparently ephemeral view of law was the conviction peculiarly Athenian which dominated the thought and the art of the fifth century—that the unlimited, the unrestrained, the lawless, were barbarous, ugly, irrational. Freedom strictly limited by self-control—that was the idea of Athens at her greatest. Her artists embodied it; her democracy did not. Athenian art and Athenian thought survived the test of time. Athenian democracy became imperial and failed.

Imperial autocracy when it came to fighting proved the stronger. Year by year as the war went on the weakness of Athenian popular government became more and more evident in comparison with the stern discipline and undistracted policy of Sparta. Athens was moved this way or that as the man of the moment chose. One such person, the unprincipled but brilliant Alcibiades, from whom Socrates had expected great things, persuaded the people to send an expedition to conquer Sicily. He was a remarkable man, and in his hands the venture might have turned out well. Certainly the obvious reason why it failed is that it was carried out as badly as possible. Alcibiades was recalled almost as soon as the Athenian fleet reached Sicily. By that time popular feeling was hot against him because of a charge of sacrilege brought by his enemies. He had better sense than to face a populace seething with fervor to defend religion by making an example of the irreligious, and he transferred his allegiance to Sparta, where he proved very useful.

Sheer mismanagement wrecked the Sicilian expedition. The Athenian people were led by men too small for the part to which they aspired. They were misled. They underestimated the strength of the enemy until it was too late. They trusted implicitly to their sea power and it failed them. In the final sea fight around Syracuse the Athenians were outmaneuvered and the great fleet was defeated. The disaster was complete. The ships were abandoned and the army started to retreat by land with no food, no provisions of any sort. After days of marching, the desperate, starving men were divided; the van lost touch with the rear, and it was easy for the Syracusans to overwhelm first one and then the other. The last scene was on the bank of a river where the Athenians, mad with thirst, rushed down to the water not seeing or not caring that the enemy was upon them. The river was soon flowing red with blood, but they fought each other to get to it and they drank of it as they died.

All who were taken alive were made slaves. The greater

part of them were put in the stone quarries near Syracuse where nature did the torturing without need of human assistance. The frightful heat by day and the bitter cold by night insured the survival of very few. Thucydides writes their epitaph: "Having done what men could they suffered what men must."

There has never been, there could not be, a more complete defeat. To inflict on the enemy what the Athenians suffered in Sicily is still the brightest hope that can animate a nation going to war. But it was not the worst disaster the war brought Athens. The climax of Thucydides' history is his picture of what happened within the city to the individual Athenians during the years of fighting. It is a picture of the disintegration of a great people. He shows how swift the process was by two stories he tells, one early in the war, the other late. The first is about the revolt of an important island tributary. Athens sent a fleet to subdue her and then in furious anger voted to kill the men and enslave the women and children. In the debate before the vote was taken the popular leader of the moment warned the Athenians not to be misled by the three deadly foes of empire: pity, enjoyment of discussion, and the spirit of fair dealing. He carried the meeting, and a ship was dispatched with the fatal order. Then, still true to the spirit of Euripides' Athens, the Athenians came to themselves. A second ship was sent to overtake the first, or at any rate to get to the island in time to prevent the massacre. The eagerness was such that the rowers were fed at their oars, taking no rest until they landed in time.

The second story concerns another offending island, seven years later. This was little Melos, of no importance in herself, who wanted only to be neutral. But those seven years had left their mark on Athens. This time she did not have to be warned against pity and fair dealing. The conversation Thucydides gives between the envoys of the Athenians and the men of Melos shows what war did to the people who once had stood, as Herodotus said, in the perpetual choice between the lower and the higher, always for the higher.

To a plea from the Melians that they have done no

wrong and that to make war on them will be contrary to all justice, the envoys reply: "Justice is attained only when both sides are equal. The powerful exact what they can and the weak yield what they must."

"You ignore justice," the Melians answer, "and yet it is to your interest, too, to regard it, because if you ever are defeated you will not be able to appeal to it."

"You must allow us to take the risk of that," the Athenians say. "Our point is that we want to subjugate you without trouble to ourselves and that this will be better for you too."

"To become slaves?" ask the Melians.

"Well—it will save you from a worse fate."

"You will not consent to our remaining at peace, your friends, but not your allies?"

"No," the Athenians answer. "We do not want your friendship. It would appear a proof of our weakness whereas your hatred is a proof of our power. Please remember that with you the question is one of self-preservation. We are the stronger."

"Fortune does not always side with the strong," the Melians say. "There is hope that if we do our utmost we can stand erect."

"Beware of hope," the Athenians reply. "Do not be like the common crowd who when visible grounds for hope fail betake themselves to the invisible, religion and the like. We advise you to turn away from such folly. And may we remind you that in all this discussion you have not advanced one argument that practical men would use."

The Melians were unpractical and they fought. They were conquered with little trouble to Athens. She put the men to death and made slaves of the women and children. She had reached a point where she did not care to use fine words about ugly facts, and the reason was that they had ceased to look ugly to her. Vices by then, Thucydides says, were esteemed as virtues. The very meaning of words changed: deceit was praised as shrewdness, recklessness held to be courage, loyalty, moderation, generosity, scorned as proofs of weakness. "That good will which is the chief element in a noble nature was laughed out of court and vanished. Every man distrusted every other man." That was where the race for power brought the Athenians in the end.

Sparta was better off. Her ideal of the duty of death on a battlefield was guaranteed not to satisfy men for long, but it was better by far than the lack of any ideal shown in the Athenians' talk to the Melians. Athens was conquered in 404. Violent party strife divided the city, and the aristocratic coterie, always pro-Sparta, finally got the upper hand. There was another revolution of the power cycle.

The succeeding one came more quickly. Sparta could not rule other nations. Athens had taxed them heavily, but except for that she had not interfered with them. Sparta's methods are explained by the remark of an Athenian who admired her, to the effect that the will of any Spartan citizen was absolute law in the subject states. She was never able to understand any way but her own, and the other Greeks did not take kindly to that. They were not docile and they did not like obedience. She could not hold them long. The Spartan Empire lasted only a few years. Toward the end of the war she had made an alliance with her old arch-enemy, Persia, which helped her greatly in reducing Athens. But soon afterwards the two allies quarrelled. Sparta was defeated and Persia took away the sea empire she had taken away from Athens.

That was the result of twenty-seven years of war. It seems at first sight a triumph of futility, but it was worse than that. Very many Athenians were killed during those years. Fortunately for us, some who were of an age to fight—Socrates, Plato, Thucydides himself, and others equally familiar—did not die on battlefields; but it cannot be doubted that among all who did, there were those who would have led the world up to new heights. The flame that burned so brightly in fifth-century Athens would have given more and still more light to the world if these dead had not died, and died truly in vain.

The cause of all these evils was the desire for power which greed and ambition inspire.—*Thucydides* III, 83

# *Chapter* X

## XENOPHON

### THE ORDINARY ATHENIAN GENTLEMAN

To TURN from Thucydides to Xenophon is a pleasant, but surprising, experience. The lives of the two men overlapped, although Xenophon was much the younger. Both were Athenians and soldiers; both lived through the war and saw the defeat of Athens. Yet they inhabited different worlds; worlds so different, they seem to have no connection with each other. Thucydides' world was a place racked and ruined and disintegrated by war, where hope was gone and happiness was unimaginable. Xenophon's was a cheerful place with many nice people in it and many agreeable ways of passing the time. There was hunting, for instance. He writes a charming essay about it: of the delights of the early start, in winter over the snow, to track the hare with hounds as keen for the chase as their masters; in spring "when the fields are so full of wildflowers, the scent for the dogs is poor"; or a deer may be the quarry, first-rate sport; or a wild boar, dangerous, but delightfully exciting. Such rewards, too, as the hunter has: he keeps strong and young far longer than other men; he is braver, and even more trustworthy—although why that should be our author does not trouble to explain. A hunting man just is better than one who does not hunt and that is all there is to it. Ask any fox-hunting squire in English literature. Hunting is a good, healthy, honest pleasure, and a young man is lucky if he takes to it. It will save him from city vices and incline him to love virtue.

At what period in Thucydides' history were the Athenians going a hunting, one wonders. Did that man of tragic vision ever watch a hunt? Did he ever listen to stories about the size of the boar that had been killed? Was he ever at a dinner-party where any stories were told over the wine? The imagination fails before the attempt to put him there, even if Socrates had been a guest as he was at a dinner Xenophon went to and reported. It followed more closely, we must suppose, the fashion of the day for such parties than did Plato's famous supper at Agathon's house, where conversation was the only entertainment. Agathon's guests were the élite of Athens and wanted lofty discourse for their diversion. The guests at Xenophon's dinner, except for himself and Socrates, were ordinary people who would quickly have been bored by the speeches in the *Symposium*. But no one could possibly have been bored at the party Xenophon describes. It was from first to last a most enjoyable occasion. There was some good talk at the table, of course—Socrates would see to that; and now and then the discourse turned to matters sober enough to have engaged even Thucydides' attention. But for the most part, it was lighthearted as befitted a good dinner. There was a great deal of laughter when, for instance, Socrates defended his flat nose as being preferable to a straight one, and when a man newly married refused the onions. There was music, too, and Socrates obliged with a song, to the delighted amusement of the others. A pleasant interlude was afforded by a happy boy, and Xenophon's description reveals his power of keen observation and quick sympathy. The lad had been invited to come with his father, a great honor, but he had just won the chief contest for boys at the principal Athenian festival. He sat beside his father, regarded very kindly by the company. They tried to draw him out, but he was too shy to speak a word until someone asked him what he was most proud of, and someone else cried, "Oh, his victory, of course." At this he blushed and blurted out, "No—I'm not." All were delighted to have him finally say something and they encouraged him. "No? Of what are you proudest, then?" "Of my father," he said, and pressed closer to him. It is an attractive picture of Athenian boyhood in the brilliant, corrupt city where Thucydides could find nothing good.

As was usual, entertainment had been provided for the guests. A girl did some diverting and surprising feats. The best turn was when she danced and kept twelve hoops whirling in the air, catching and throwing them in perfect time with the music. Watching her with great attention Socrates declared that he was forced to conclude, "Not only from this girl, my friends, but from other things, too, that a woman's talent is not at all inferior to a man's." A pleasant thing to know, he added, if any of them wanted to teach something to his wife. A murmur passed around the table: "Xanthippe"; and one of the company ventured, "Why do not you, then, teach good temper to yours?" "Because," Socrates retorted, "my great aim in life is to get on well with people, and I chose Xanthippe because I knew if I could get on with her I could with anyone." The explanation was unanimously voted satisfactory.

A little desultory talk followed that finally turned upon exercise, and Socrates said, to the intense delight of all, that he danced every morning in order to reduce. "It's true," one of the others broke in. "I found him doing it and I thought he'd gone mad. But he talked to me and I tell you he convinced me. When I went home—will you believe it? I did not dance; I don't know how; but I waved my arms about." There was a general outcry, "Oh, Socrates, let us see you, too."

By this time the dancing girl was turning summersaults and leaping headfirst into a circle formed by swords. This displeased Socrates. "No doubt it is a wonderful performance," he conceded. "But pleasure? In watching a lovely young creature exposing herself to danger like that? I don't find it agreeable." The others agreed, and a pantomime between the girl and her partner, a graceful boy, was quickly substituted: "The Rescue of the Forsaken Ariadne by Bacchus." It was performed to admiration. Not a word was spoken by the two actors, but such was their skill that by gestures and dancing they expressed all the events and emotions of the story with perfect clarity to the spectators. "They seemed not actors who had learned their parts, but veritable lovers." With that the party broke up, Socrates walking home with the nice boy and his

father. Of himself Xenophon says nothing throughout the
essay except at the very beginning when he explains that
he was one of the guests and decided to give an account of
the dinner because he thought what honorable and virtuous
men did in their hours of amusement had its importance.
One can only regret that so few Greek writers agreed
with him.

Another pleasant picture he gives of domestic Athens
has an interest not only as a period piece but because it
shows a glimpse of that person so elusive in all periods,
the woman of ancient Greece. A man lately married talks
about his wife. She was not yet fifteen, he says, and had
been admirably brought up "to see as little, and hear as
little, and ask as few questions as possible." The young
husband had the delightful prospect of inscribing on this
blank page whatever he chose. There was no doubt in his
mind what he should start with. "Of course," Xenophon
reports him as saying, "I had to give her time to grow
used to me; but when we had reached a point where we
could talk easily together, I told her she had great responsibilities. I took up with her what I expected of her as a
housekeeper. She said wonderingly, 'But my mother told
me I was of no consequence, only you. All I had to do,
she said, was to be sensible and careful.' " Her husband
was quick to seize the cue. Kindly but weightily he explained to the young thing that her life henceforth was to
be a perpetual exercise in carefulness and good sense. She
would have to keep stock of everything brought into the
house; oversee all the work that went on; superintend
the spinning, the weaving, the making of clothes; train the
new servants and nurse the sick. At this point the girl's
spirits seem to have risen a little for she murmured that
she thought she would like to take care of sick people. But
her husband kept steadily on. Of course she would stay
indoors. He himself enjoyed starting the day with a long
ride into the country—very healthful as well as very
pleasant. But for a woman to be roaming abroad was most
discreditable. However, she could get plenty of exercise,
at the loom, or making beds, or supervising the maids.
Kneading bread was said to be as good exercise as one

could find. All that sort of thing would improve her health and help her complexion—very important in keeping herself attractive to her husband. Artificial substitutes were no good: husbands always knew when their wives painted, and they never like it; white and red stuff on the face was disgusting when a man was aware of it, as a husband must be. The essay ends happily with the declaration, "Ever since, my wife has done in all respects just as I taught her."

It is as hard to fit the dutiful young wife and the happily important husband and their immaculate household into Thucydides' Athens as it is to put Thucydides himself at the table beside Socrates watching the girl with the hoops. There is no use trying to make a composite picture out of Xenophon and Thucydides. The only result would be to lose the truth on each side. Thucydides' truth was immeasurably more profound. In life's uneasy panorama he could discover unchanging verities. He could probe to the depths the evils of his time and perceive them all grounded in the never varying evils of human nature. In Sparta's victory over Athens he saw what the decision of war was worth as a test of values, and that war would forever decide matters of highest importance to the world if men continued to be governed by greed and the passion for power. What he knew was truth indeed, with no shadow of turning and inexpressibly sad.

But Xenophon's truths were true, too. There were pleasant parties and well-ordered homes and nice lads and jolly hunters in war-wracked Greece. History never takes account of such pleasantries, but they have their importance. The Greek world would have gone insane if Thucydides' picture had been all-inclusive. Of course, Xenophon's mind was on an altogether lower level. Eternal truths were not in his line. The average man in Periclean Athens can be seen through Xenophon's eyes as he cannot be through Thucydides' or Plato's. In Xenophon there are no dark, greed-ridden schemers such as Thucydides saw in Athens; neither are there any Platonic idealists. The people in his books are ordinary, pleasant folk, not given to extremes in any direction and convincingly real, just as

Xenophon himself is. Here is a picture he draws of one
of them:

> He said that he had long realized that "unless we know
> what we ought to do and try our best to do it God has
> decided that we have no right to be prosperous. If we are
> wise and do take pains he makes some of us prosperous,
> although not all. So to start with, I reverence him and then
> do all I can to be worthy when I pray to be given health
> and strength of body and the respect of the Athenians and
> the affection of my friends and an increase of wealth—
> with honor, and safety in war—with honor."

These eminently sensible aspirations strike a true Greek
note. The man who uttered them and the man who recorded them were typical Athenian gentlemen. What
Xenophon was comes through clearly in his writings—a
man of good will and good sense, kindly, honest, pious;
intelligent, too, interested in ideas, not the purely speculative kind, rather those that could be made to work toward
some rational, practical good. His friends were like him;
they were representative Athenians of the better sort.

In another way, too, Xenophon represented his times.
His life shows the widely separated interests and varied
occupations which made the Periclean Athenians different
from other men. As a young man he came to Athens from
his father's estate in Attica, to be educated out of country
ways; he joined the circle around Socrates, where young
and old alike were, as Plato puts it, "possessed and mad-
dened with the passion for knowledge," or, as he himself
states, "wanting to become good and fine men and learn
their duty to their family, their servants, their friends and
their country." The Socrates he listened to did not, like
Plato's Socrates, discourse upon "the glorious sights of
justice and wisdom and truth the enraptured soul beholds,
shining in pure light," or anything like that. This Socrates
was a soberly thinking man, distinguished for common
sense, and in Xenophon's record of him, the *Memorabilia*,
what he chiefly does for his young friends is to give them
practical advice on how to manage their affairs. A budding
officer is told the way to make his men efficient soldiers;
a conscientious lad, burdened with many female relatives,

is shown how they can be taught to support themselves, and so on, while Xenophon listens entranced by such serviceable wisdom. How long Xenophon lived this delightful life of conversation is not known, but he was still young when he left it for the very opposite kind of life, that of a soldier. He was truly a man of his times, when poets and dramatists and historians were soldiers and generals and explorers.

In his campaigns he travelled far and saw the great world. He also got enough money to live on for the rest of his days by capturing and holding for ransom a rich Persian noble. Then he went back to Greece—but to Sparta, not Athens. Curiously, although he has left in his *Anabasis* an unsurpassed picture of what the democratic ideal can accomplish, he was himself no democrat. He came of a noble family and all his life kept the convictions of his class. He always loved Sparta and distrusted Athens. Even so, in the great crisis of his life, when he and his companions faced imminent destruction, he acted like a true Athenian, who knew what freedom was and what free men could achieve. When the Ten Thousand elected him general in order to get them out of their terrible predicament, he never tried out any Spartan ideas on them. He became as democratic a leader as there could possibly be of the freest democracy conceivable. The fact that the astonishing success which resulted had no permanent effect upon his point of view should not be surprising; a converted aristocrat is a rare figure in history. Xenophon never went back to Athens; indeed, a few years after his return to Greece he was fighting on the Spartan side against her and was declared an exile. The Spartans gave him an estate in the pleasant country near Olympia, where he lived for many years, riding and hunting and farming, a model country gentleman. Here he wrote a great many books on subjects as far apart as the dinner Socrates attended and the proper management of the Athenian revenues. With two or three exceptions the writings are quite pedestrian; sensible, straightforward, clearly written, but no more. There are a few sentences, however, scattered through them which show a surprising power of thought and far-reaching vision. Although, or perhaps because, he had fought much, he believed that peace should be the aim of all states. Diplomacy, he says, is the way to settle disputes, not war. He urges Athens to use her influence to maintain peace, and he suggests making Delphi a meeting place for the nations, where they can talk out their differences. "He who conquers by force," he says, "may fancy that he can continue to do so, but the only conquests that last are when men willingly submit to those who are better than themselves. The only way really to conquer a country is through generosity." The world has not yet caught up with Xenophon.

His best book, however, the book he really lives by, is on war. It is, of course, the *Anabasis,* the "Retreat of the Ten Thousand," a great story, and of great importance for our knowledge of the Greeks. No other piece of writing gives so clear a picture of Greek individualism, that instinct which was supremely characteristic of ancient Greece and decided the course of the Greek achievement. It was the cause, or the result, as one chooses to look at it, of the Greek love for freedom. A Greek had a passion for being left free to live his life in his own way. He wanted to act by himself and think for himself. It did not come natural to him to turn to others for direction; he depended upon his own sense of what was right and true. Indeed, there was no generally acknowledged source of direction anywhere in Greece except the oracles, difficult to reach and still more difficult to understand. Athens had no authoritarian church, or state either, to formulate what a man should believe and to regulate the details of how he should live. There was no agency or institution to oppose his thinking in any way he chose on anything whatsoever. As for the state, it never entered an Athenian's head that it could interfere with his private life: that it could see, for instance, that his children were taught to be patriotic, or limit the amount of liquor he could buy, or compel him to save for his old age. Everything like that a citizen of Athens had to decide himself and take full responsibility for.

The basis of the Athenian democracy was the conviction

of all democracies—that the average man can be depended upon to do his duty and to use good sense in doing it. *Trust the individual* was the avowed doctrine in Athens, and expressed or unexpressed it was common to Greece. Sparta we know as the exception, and there must have been other backwaters; nevertheless, the most reactionary Greek might at any time revert to type. It is on record that Spartan soldiers abroad shouted down an unpopular officer; threw stones at a general whose orders they did not approve; in an emergency, put down incompetent leaders and acted for themselves. Even the iron discipline of Sparta could not completely eradicate the primary Greek passion for independence. "A people ruling," says Herodotus, "—the very name of it is so beautiful." In Æschylus' play about the defeat of the Persians at Salamis, the Persian queen asks, "Who is set over the Greeks as despot?" and the proud answer is, "They are the slaves and vassals of no man." Therefore, all Greeks believed, they conquered the slave-subjects of the Persian tyrant. Free men, independent men, were always worth inexpressibly more than men submissive and controlled.

Military authorities have never advocated this point of view, but how applicable it is to soldiers, too, is shown for all time by the *Anabasis*. The Ten Thousand got back safely after one of the most perilous marches ever undertaken just because they were not a model, disciplined army but a band of enterprising individuals.

The epic of the Retreat begins in a camp beside a little town in Asia not far from Babylon. There, more than ten thousand Greeks were gathered. They had come from different places: one of the leaders was from Thessaly; another from Bœotia; the commander-in-chief was a Spartan; on his staff was a young civilian from Athens named Xenophon. They were soldiers of fortune, a typical army of mercenaries who had gone abroad because there was no hope of employment at home. Greece was not at war for the moment. A Spartan peace was over the land. It was the summer of 401, three years after the fall of Athens.

Persia, however, was a hotbed of plots and counterplots

that were bringing a revolution near. The late king's two sons were enemies, and the younger planned to take the throne from his brother. This young man was Cyrus, named for the great Cyrus, the conqueror of Babylon a hundred and fifty years earlier. His namesake is famous for one reason only: because when he marched into Persia Xenophon joined his army. If that had not happened he would be lost in the endless list of little Asiatic royalties forever fighting for no purpose of the slightest importance to the world. As it is, he lives in Xenophon's pages, gay and gallant and generous; careful for his soldiers' welfare; sharing their hardships; always first in the fighting; a great leader.

The Ten Thousand had enlisted under his banner with no clear idea of what they were to do beyond the matter of real importance, get regular pay and enough food. They earned their share of both in the next few months. They marched from the Mediterranean through sandy deserts far into Asia Minor living on the country, which generally meant a minimum of food and occasionally none at all. There was a large Asiatic contingent, a hundred thousand strong at the least, but they play very little part in the *Anabasis*. The Greeks are the real army Cyrus depends upon. As Xenophon tells the story they won the day for him when he met the king's forces. The battle of Cunaxa was a decisive victory for Cyrus. Only, he himself was dead, killed in the fighting as he struck at his brother and wounded him. With his death the reason for the expedition ceased to exist. The Asiatic forces melted away. The little Greek army was alone in the heart of Asia, in an unknown country swarming with hostile troops, with no food, no ammunition, and no notion how to get back. Soon there were no leaders either. The chief officers went to a conference with the Persians under a safe-conduct. Their return, eagerly awaited, was alarmingly delayed; and all eyes were watching for them when in the distance a man, one man all alone, was seen advancing very slowly, a Greek by his dress. They ran to meet him and caught him as he fell dying, terribly wounded. He could just gasp out that all the others were dead, assassinated by the Persians.

That was a terrible night. The Persian plan was clear.
In their experience leaderless men were helpless. Kill the
officers and the army would be a lot of sheep waiting to
be slaughtered. The only thing wrong with the idea was
that this was a Greek army.

Xenophon, all his friends dead, wandered away from
the horrified camp, found a quiet spot and fell asleep. He
dreamed a dream. He saw the thunderbolt of Zeus fall on
his home and a great light shine forth, and he awoke with
the absolute conviction that Zeus had chosen him to save
the army. On fire with enthusiasm, he called a council of
the under officers who had not gone to the conference.
There, young and a civilian, he stood up and addressed
them, hardened veterans all. He told them to throw off
despair and "show some superiority to misfortune." He
reminded them that they were Greeks, not to be cowed
by mere Asiatics. Something of his own fire was com-
municated to them. He even got them laughing. One man
who stubbornly objected to everything and would talk only
of their desperate case, Xenophon advised reducing to the
ranks and using to carry baggage; he would make an
excellent mule, he told his appreciative audience. They
elected him unanimously to lead the rear, and then had
the general assembly sounded so that he could address the
soldiers. He gave them a rousing talk. Things were black
and might seem hopeless to others, but they were Greeks,
free men, living in free states, born of free ancestors. The
enemy they had to face were slaves, ruled by despots,
ignorant of the very idea of freedom. "They think we are
defeated because our officers are dead and our good old
general Clearchus. But we will show them that they have
turned us all into generals. Instead of one Clearchus they
have ten thousand Clearchuses against them." He won
them over and that very morning the ten thousand generals
started the march back.

They had only enemies around them, not one man they
could trust as a guide, and there were no maps in those
days and no compasses. One thing only they were sure of:
they could not go back by the way they had come. Wherever they had passed the food was exhausted. They were

forced to turn northward and follow the course of the rivers up to the mountains where the Tigris and the Euphrates rise, through what is to-day the wilds of Kurdistan and the highlands of Georgia and Armenia, all inhabited by savage mountain tribes. These were their only source of provisions. If they could not conquer their strongholds and get at their stores they would starve. Mountain warfare of the most desperate character awaited them, waged by an enemy who knew every foot of the country, who watched for them on the heights above narrow valleys and rolled masses of rocks down on them, whose sharpshooters attacked them hidden in thickets on the opposite bank of some torrential icy river while the Greeks searched desperately for a ford. As they advanced ever higher into the hills, they found bitter cold and deep snow, and their equipment was designed for the Arabian desert.

Probably anyone to-day considering their plight would conclude that their only chance of safety would lie in maintaining strict discipline, abiding by their excellent military tradition, and obeying their leaders implicitly. The chief leaders, however, were dead; mountain fighting against savages was not a part of their military tradition; above all, being Greeks, they did not incline to blind obedience in desperate circumstances. In point of fact, the situation which confronted them could be met only by throwing away the rules and regulations that had been drilled into them. What they needed was to draw upon all the intelligence and power of initiative every man of them possessed.

They were merely a band of mercenaries, but they were Greek mercenaries and the average of intelligence was high. The question of discipline among ten thousand generals would otherwise certainly have been serious and might well have proved fatal, but, no less than our westward-faring pioneer ancestors who resembled them, they understood the necessity of acting together. Not a soldier but knew what it would mean to have disorder added to the perils they faced. Their discipline was a voluntary product, but it worked. When the covered wagons made their way across America any leader that arose did so by virtue of superior ability, which men in danger always follow willingly. The leaders of the Ten Thousand got their posts in the same way. The army was keen to perceive a man's quality and before long the young civilian Xenophon was practically in command.

Each man, however, had a share in the responsibility. Once when Xenophon sent out a reconnoitering force to find a pass through the mountains, he told them, "Every one of you is the leader." At any crisis an assembly was held, the situation explained and full discussion invited. "Whoever has a better plan, let him speak. Our aim is the safety of all and that is the concern of all." The case was argued back and forth, then put to the vote and the majority decided. Incompetent leaders were brought to trial. The whole army sat as judges and acquitted or punished. It reads like a caricature, but there has never been a better vindication of the average man when he is up against it. The ten thousand judges, which the ten thousand generals turned into on occasion, never, so far as Xenophon's record goes, passed an unjust sentence. On one occasion Xenophon was called to account for striking a soldier. " 'I own that I did so,' he said. 'I told him to carry to camp a wounded man, but I found him burying him still alive. I have struck others, too, half-frozen men who were sinking down in the snow to die, worn-out men lagging behind where the enemy might catch them. A blow would often make them get up and hasten. Those I have given offense to now accuse me. But those I have helped, in battle, on the march, in cold, in sickness, none of them speak up. They do not remember. And yet surely it is better—and happier, too—to remember a man's good deeds than his evil deeds.' Upon this," the narrative goes on, "the assembly, calling the past to mind, rose up and Xenophon was acquitted."

This completely disarming speech for the defense shows how well Xenophon knew the way to manage men. There is wounded feeling in his words, but no anger, no resentment, above all, no self-righteousness. Those listening were convinced by his frankness of his honesty; reminded, with-

out a suggestion of boasting, how great his services had
been; and given to understand that far from claiming to
be faultless, he appealed to them only to remember his
deserts as well as his mistakes. He understood his audience
and the qualities a leader must have, at least any leader
who would lead Greeks. In a book he wrote on the education of the great Cyrus he draws a picture of the ideal
general which, absurd as it is when applied to an Oriental
monarch, shows to perfection the Greek idea of the one
method that will make men who are worth anything independent, self-reliant men, willing to follow another man.
"The leader," he writes, "must himself believe that willing
obedience always beats forced obedience, and that he can
get this only by really knowing what should be done. Thus
he can secure obedience from his men because he can
convince them that he knows best, precisely as a good
doctor makes his patients obey him. Also he must be
ready to suffer more hardships than he asks of his soldiers,
more fatigue, greater extremes of heat and cold. 'No one,'
Cyrus always said, 'can be a good officer who does not
undergo more than those he commands.' " However that
may be, it is certain that the inexperienced civilian Xenophon was could have won over the Ten Thousand in no
other way. He was able to convince them that he knew
best and they gave up their own ideas and followed him
willingly.

He showed them too that even if they made him their
leader, it was share and share alike between him and the
army. On one occasion when he was riding up from his
post in the rear to consult with the van, and the snow was
deep and the marching hard, a soldier cried to him, "Oh,
it's easy enough for you on horseback." Xenophon leaped
from his horse, flung the man aside and marched in his
place.

Always, no matter how desperate things seemed, the
initiative which only free men can be counted on to
develop got them through. They abandoned their baggage
by common consent and threw away their loot. "We will
make the enemy carry our baggage for us," they said.
"When we have conquered them we can take what we

want." Early in the march they were terribly harassed by the Persian cavalry because they had none of their own. The men of Rhodes could throw with their slings twice as far as the Persians. They set them on baggage mules, directed them to aim at the riders, but spare their mounts and bring them back, and from that time on the Persians kept them in horses. If they needed ammunition they sent bowmen who could shoot farther than the foe to draw down showers of arrows that fell short and could be easily collected. One way or another they forced the Persians into service. When they got to the hills they discarded the tactics they had been trained in. They gave up the solid line, the only formation they knew, and the army advanced by columns, sometimes far apart. It was merely common sense in the rough broken country, but that virtue belongs peculiarly to men acting for themselves. The disciplined military mind has never been distinguished for it.

So, always cold and sometimes freezing, always hungry and sometimes starving, and always, always fighting, they held their own. No one by now had any clear idea where in the world they were. One day, Xenophon, riding in the rear, putting his horse up a steep hill, heard a great noise in front. A tumult was carried back to him by the wind, loud cries and shouting. An ambush, he thought, and calling to the others to follow at full speed, he drove his horse forward. No enemy was on the hilltop; only the Greeks. They were standing, all faced the same way, with tears running down their faces, their arms stretched out to what they saw before them. The shouting swelled into a great roar, "The sea! The sea!"

They were home at last. The sea was home to a Greek. It was the middle of January. They had left Cunaxa on the seventh of September. In four months they had marched well on to two thousand miles in circumstances never surpassed before or since for hardship and danger.

The *Anabasis* is the story of the Greeks in miniature. Ten thousand men, fiercely independent by nature, in a situation where they were a law unto themselves, showed that they were pre-eminently able to work together and proved what miracles of achievement willing co-operation can bring to pass. The Greek state, at any rate the Athenian state, which we know best, showed the same. What brought the Greeks safely back from Asia was precisely what made Athens great. The Athenian was a law unto himself, but his dominant instinct to stand alone was counterbalanced by his sense of overwhelming obligation to serve the state. This was his own spontaneous reaction to the facts of his life, nothing imposed upon him from outside. The city was his defense in a hostile world, his security, his pride, too, the guarantee to all of his worth as an Athenian.

Plato said that men could find their true moral development only in service to the city. The Athenian was saved from looking at his life as a private affair. Our word "idiot" comes from the Greek name for the man who took no share in public matters. Pericles in the funeral oration reported by Thucydides says:

> We are a free democracy, but we are obedient. We obey the laws, more especially those which protect the oppressed, and the unwritten laws whose transgression brings acknowledged shame. We do not allow absorption in our own affairs to interfere with participation in the city's. We differ from other states in regarding the man who holds aloof from public life as useless, yet we yield to none in independence of spirit and complete self-reliance.

This happy balance was maintained for a very brief period. No doubt at its best it was as imperfect as the working out of every lofty idea in human terms is bound to be. Even so, it was the foundation of the Greek achievement. The creed of democracy, spiritual and political liberty for all, and each man a willing servant of the state, was the conception which underlay the highest reach of Greek genius. It was fatally weakened by the race for money and power in the Periclean age; the Peloponnesian War destroyed it and Greece lost it forever. Nevertheless, the ideal of free individuals unified by a spontaneous service to the common life was left as a possession to the world, never to be forgotten.

# *Chapter* XI

## THE IDEA OF TRAGEDY

THE GREAT tragic artists of the world are four, and three
of them are Greek. It is in tragedy that the pre-eminence
of the Greeks can be seen most clearly. Except for Shakespeare, the great three, Æschylus, Sophocles, Euripides,
stand alone. Tragedy is an achievement peculiarly Greek.
They were the first to perceive it and they lifted it to
its supreme height. Nor is it a matter that directly touches
only the great artists who wrote tragedies; it concerns
the entire people as well, who felt the appeal of the tragic
to such a degree that they would gather thirty thousand
strong to see a performance. In tragedy the Greek genius
penetrated farthest and it is the revelation of what was
most profound in them.

The special characteristic of the Greeks was their
power to see the world clearly and at the same time as
beautiful. Because they were able to do this, they produced art distinguished from all other art by an absence
of struggle, marked by a calm and serenity which is
theirs alone. There is, it seems to assure us, a region where
beauty is truth, truth beauty. To it their artists would lead
us, illumining life's dark confusions by gleams fitful
indeed and wavering compared with the fixed light of
religious faith, but by some magic of their own, satisfying,
affording a vision of something inconclusive and yet of
incalculable significance. Of all the great poets this is
true, but truest of the tragic poets, for the reason that in
them the power of poetry confronts the inexplicable.

Tragedy was a Greek creation because in Greece
thought was free. Men were thinking more and more
deeply about human life, and beginning to perceive more

and more clearly that it was bound up with evil and that injustice was of the nature of things. And then, one day, this knowledge of something irremediably wrong in the world came to a poet with his poet's power to see beauty in the truth of human life, and the first tragedy was written. As the author of a most distinguished book on the subject says: "The spirit of inquiry meets the spirit of poetry and tragedy is born." Make it concrete: early Greece with her godlike heroes and hero-gods fighting far on the ringing plains of windy Troy; with her lyric world, where every common thing is touched with beauty —her twofold world of poetic creation. Then a new age dawns, not satisfied with beauty of song and story, an age that must try to know and to explain. And for the first time tragedy appears. A poet of surpassing magnitude, not content with the old sacred conventions, and of a soul great enough to bear new and intolerable truth—that is Æschylus, the first writer of tragedy.

Tragedy belongs to the poets. Only they have "trod the sunlit heights and from life's dissonance struck one clear chord." None but a poet can write a tragedy. For tragedy is nothing less than pain transmuted into exaltation by the alchemy of poetry, and if poetry is true knowledge and the great poets guides safe to follow, this transmutation has arresting implications.

Pain changed into, or, let us say, charged with, exaltation. It would seem that tragedy is a strange matter. There is indeed none stranger. A tragedy shows us pain and gives us pleasure thereby. The greater the suffering depicted, the more terrible the events, the more intense our pleasure. The most monstrous and appalling deeds life can show are those the tragedian chooses, and by the spectacle he thus offers us, we are moved to a very passion of enjoyment. There is food for wonder here, not to be passed over, as the superficial have done, but pointing out that the Romans made a holiday of a gladiator's slaughter, and that even to-day fierce instincts, savage survivals, stir in the most civilized. Grant all that, and we are not a step advanced on the way to explaining the mystery of tragic pleasure. It has no kinship with cruelty or the lust for blood.

On this point it is illuminating to consider our every-day use of the words tragedy and tragic. Pain, sorrow, disaster, are always spoken of as depressing, as dragging down—the dark abyss of pain, a crushing sorrow, an over-whelming disaster. But speak of tragedy and extraordinarily the metaphor changes. Lift us to tragic heights, we say, and never anything else. The depths of pathos but never of tragedy. Always the height of tragedy. A word is no light matter. Words have with truth been called fossil poetry, each, that is, a symbol of a creative thought. The whole philosophy of human nature is implicit in human speech. It is a matter to pause over, that the instinct of mankind has perceived a difference, not of degree but of kind, between tragic pain and all other pain. There is something in tragedy which marks it off from other disaster so sharply that in our common speech we bear witness to the difference.

All those whose attention has been caught by the strange contradiction of pleasure through pain agree with this instinctive witness, and some of the most brilliant minds the world has known have concerned themselves with it. Tragic pleasure, they tell us, is in a class by itself. "Pity and awe," Aristotle called it, "and a sense of emotion purged and purified thereby." "Reconciliation," said Hegel, which we may understand in the sense of life's temporary dissonance resolved into eternal harmony. "Acceptance," said Schopenhauer, the temper of mind that says, "Thy will be done." "The reaffirmation of the will to live in the face of death," said Nietzsche, "and the joy of its inexhaustibility when so reaffirmed."

Pity, awe, reconciliation, exaltation—these are the ele-ments that make up tragic pleasure. No play is a tragedy that does not call them forth. So the philosophers say, all in agreement with the common judgment of mankind, that tragedy is something above and beyond the dissonance of pain. But what it is that causes a play to call forth these feelings, what is the essential element in a tragedy, Hegel alone seeks to define. In a notable passage he says that the only tragic subject is a spiritual struggle in which each side has a claim upon our sympathy. But, as his critics have pointed out, he would thus exclude the tragedy of the suffering of the innocent, and a definition which does not include the death of Cordelia or of Deianira cannot be taken as final.

The suffering of the innocent, indeed, can itself be so differently treated as to necessitate completely different categories. In one of the greatest tragedies, the *Prometheus* of Æschylus, the main actor is an innocent sufferer, but, beyond this purely formal connection, that passionate rebel, defying God and all the powers of the universe, has no relationship whatever to the lovely, loving Cordelia. An inclusive definition of tragedy must cover cases as diverse in circumstance and in the character of the protagonist as the whole range of life and letters can afford it. It must include such opposites as Antigone, the high-souled maiden who goes with open eyes to her death rather than leave her brother's body unburied, and Macbeth, the ambition-mad, the murderer of his king and guest. These two plays, seemingly so totally unlike, call forth the same response. Tragic pleasure of the greatest intensity is caused by them both. They have something in common, but the philosophers do not tell us what it is. Their concern is with what a tragedy makes us feel, not with what makes a tragedy.

Only twice in literary history has there been a great period of tragedy, in the Athens of Pericles and in Elizabethan England. What these two periods had in common, two thousand years and more apart in time, that they expressed themselves in the same fashion, may give us some hint of the nature of tragedy, for far from being periods of darkness and defeat, each was a time when life was seen exalted, a time of thrilling and unfathomable possibilities. They held their heads high, those men who conquered at Marathon and Salamis, and those who fought Spain and saw the Great Armada sink. The world was a place of wonder; mankind was beauteous; life was lived on the crest of the wave. More than all, the poignant joy of heroism had stirred men's hearts. Not stuff for tragedy, would you say? But on the crest of the wave one must feel either tragically or joyously; one cannot feel tamely. The temper of mind that sees tragedy in life has not for its opposite the temper that sees joy. The opposite pole to the tragic view of life is the sordid view. When humanity is seen as devoid of dignity and significance, trivial, mean, and sunk in dreary hopelessness, then the spirit of tragedy departs. "Sometime let gorgeous tragedy in sceptred pall come sweeping by." At the opposite pole stands Gorki with *The Lower Depths.*

Other poets may, the tragedian must, seek for the significance of life. An error strangely common is that this significance for tragic purposes depends, in some sort, upon outward circumstance, on

> pomp and feast and revelry,
> With mask, and antique pageantry—

Nothing of all that touches tragedy. The surface of life is comedy's concern; tragedy is indifferent to it. We do not, to be sure, go to Main Street or to Zenith for tragedy, but the reason has nothing to do with their dull familiarity. There is no reason inherent in the house itself why Babbitt's home in Zenith should not be the scene of a tragedy quite as well as the Castle of Elsinore. The only reason it is not is Babbitt himself. "That singular swing toward elevation" which Schopenhauer discerned in tragedy, does not take any of its impetus from outside things.

The dignity and the significance of human life—of these, and of these alone, tragedy will never let go. Without them there is no tragedy. To answer the question, what makes a tragedy, is to answer the question wherein lies the essential significance of life, what the dignity of humanity depends upon in the last analysis. Here the tragedians speak to us with no uncertain voice. The great tragedies themselves offer the solution to the problem they propound. It is by our power to suffer, above all, that we are of more value than the sparrows. Endow them with a greater or as great a potentiality of pain and our foremost place in the world would no longer be undisputed. Deep down, when we search out the reason for our conviction of the transcendent worth of each human being, we know that it is because of the possibility that each can suffer so terribly. What do outside trappings matter, Zenith or Elsinore? Tragedy's preoccupation is with suffering.

But, it is to be well noted, not with all suffering. There are degrees in our high estate of pain. It is not given to all to suffer alike. We differ in nothing more than in our power to feel. There are souls of little and of great degree, and upon that degree the dignity and significance of each life depend. There is no dignity like the dignity of a soul in agony.

> Here I and sorrows sit;
> Here is my throne, bid kings come bow to it.

Tragedy is enthroned, and to her realm those alone are admitted who belong to the only true aristocracy, that of all passionate souls. Tragedy's one essential is a soul that can feel greatly. Given such a one and any catastrophe may be tragic. But the earth may be removed and the mountains be carried into the midst of the sea, and if only the small and shallow are confounded, tragedy is absent.

One dark page of Roman history tells of a little seven-year-old-girl, daughter of a man judged guilty of death and so herself condemned to die, and how she passed through the staring crowds sobbing and asking, "What had she done wrong? If they would tell her, she would never do it again"—and so on to the black prison and the executioner. That breaks the heart, but is not tragedy, it is pathos. No heights are there for the soul to mount to, but only the dark depths where there are tears for things. Undeserved suffering is not in itself tragic. Death is not tragic in itself, not the death of the beautiful and the young, the lovely and beloved. Death felt and suffered as Macbeth feels and suffers is tragic. Death felt as Lear feels Cordelia's death is tragic. Ophelia's death is not a tragedy. She being what she is, it could be so only if Hamlet's and Laertes' grief were tragic grief. The conflicting claims of the law of God and the law of man are not what make the tragedy of the *Antigone*. It is Antigone

herself, so great, so tortured. Hamlet's hesitation to kill his
uncle is not tragic. The tragedy is his power to feel. Change
all the circumstances of the drama and Hamlet in the
grip of any calamity would be tragic, just as Polonius
would never be, however awful the catastrophe. The suffering of a soul that can suffer greatly—that and only that,
is tragedy.

It follows, then, that tragedy has nothing to do with the
distinction between Realism and Romanticism. The contrary has always been maintained. The Greeks went to the
myths for their subjects, we are told, to insure remoteness
from real life which does not admit of high tragedy. "Realism is the ruin of tragedy," says the latest writer on the
subject. It is not true. If indeed Realism were conceived of
as dealing only with the usual, tragedy would be ruled out,
for the soul capable of a great passion is not unusual. But if
nothing human is alien to Realism, then tragedy is of her
domain, for the unusual is as real as the usual. When the
Moscow Art Players presented the *Brothers Karamazoff*
there was seen on the stage an absurd little man in dirty
clothes who waved his arms about and shuffled and sobbed,
the farthest possible remove from the traditional figures of
tragedy, and yet tragedy was there in his person, stripped
of her gorgeous pall, but sceptred truly, speaking the
authentic voice of human agony in a struggle past the
power of the human heart to bear. A drearier setting, a
more typically realistic setting, it would be hard to find,
but to see the play was to feel pity and awe before a man
dignified by one thing only, made great by what he could
suffer. Ibsen's plays are not tragedies. Whether Ibsen is a
realist or not—the Realism of one generation is apt to be
the Romanticism of the next—small souls are his dramatis
personæ and his plays are dramas with an unhappy ending.
The end of *Ghosts* leaves us with a sense of shuddering
horror and cold anger against a society where such things
can be, and these are not tragic feelings.

The greatest realistic works of fiction have been written
by the French and the Russians. To read one of the great
Frenchmen's books is to feel mingled despair and loathing
for mankind, so base, so trivial and so wretched. But to

read a great Russian novel is to have an altogether different experience. The baseness, the beast in us, the misery of life, are there as plain to see as in the French book, but what we are left with is not despair and not loathing, but a sense of pity and wonder before mankind that can so suffer. The Russian sees life in that way because the Russian genius is primarily poetical; the French genius is not. *Anna Karénina* is a tragedy; *Madame Bovary* is not. Realism and Romanticism, or comparative degrees of Realism, have nothing to do with the matter. It is a case of the small soul against the great soul and the power of a writer whose special endowment is *"voir clair dans ce qui est"* against the intuition of a poet.

If the Greeks had left no tragedies behind for us, the highest reach of their power would be unknown. The three poets who were able to sound the depths of human agony were able also to recognize and reveal it as tragedy. The mystery of evil, they said, curtains that of which "every man whose soul is not a clod hath visions." Pain could exalt and in tragedy for a moment men could have sight of a meaning beyond their grasp. "Yet had God not turned us in his hand and cast to earth our greatness," Euripides makes the old Trojan queen say in her extremity, "we would have passed away giving nothing to men. They would have found no theme for song in us nor made great poems from our sorrows."

Why is the death of the ordinary man a wretched, chilling thing which we turn from, while the death of the hero, always tragic, warms us with a sense of quickened life? Answer this question and the enigma of tragic pleasure is solved. "Never let me hear that brave blood has been shed in vain," said Sir Walter Scott; "it sends an imperious challenge down through all the generations." So the end of a tragedy challenges us. The great soul in pain and in death transforms pain and death. Through it we catch a glimpse of the Stoic Emperor's Dear City of God, of a deeper and more ultimate reality than that in which our lives are lived.

# Chapter XII

## ÆSCHYLUS

### THE FIRST DRAMATIST

WHEN Nietzsche made his famous defintion of tragic pleasure he fixed his eyes, like all the other philosophers in like case, not on the Muse herself but on a single tragedian. His "reaffirmation of the will to live in the face of death, and the joy of its inexhaustibility when so reaffirmed" is not the tragedy of Sophocles nor the tragedy of Euripides, but it is the very essence of the tragedy of Æschylus. The strange power tragedy has to present suffering and death in such a way as to exalt and not depress is to be felt in Æschylus' play as in those of no other tragic poet. He was the first tragedian; tragedy was his creation, and he set upon it the stamp of his own spirit.

It was a soldier-spirit. Æschylus was a Marathon-warrior, the title given to each of the little band who had beaten back the earlier tremendous Persian onslaught. As such, his epitaph would seem to show, he merited honor so lofty, no mention of his poetry could find place beside it.

Æschylus, the Athenian, Euphorion's son, is dead. This tomb in Gela's cornlands covers him. His glorious courage the hallowed field of Marathon could tell, and the long-haired Mede had knowledge of it.

Did he fight elsewhere too? There is no answer to this or to any other question about him except in so far as it can be found in what he wrote. The epitaph, a statement that he was descended from an aristocratic family,

and a few dates—of the production of this or that play,
and of his death—make up all the facts that have come
down. There was no Plato to draw his portrait with sure,
intimate touches and make him a living human being
forever. As with Shakespeare, we know him only as he
permits us through his plays, a doubtful matter in the
case of the greatest poets whose province is the whole of
life and who can identify themselves with everything there
is, delight in conceiving an Iago equally with an Imogen,
as Keats once said. Even so, Æschylus' work, what we
have of it, that is—seven plays only left from ninety—
shows the main lines of his character and the temper of his
mind as Shakespeare's, with its boundless range, does not.
A conclusion, however, to be checked by the consideration
that if we had all those ninety plays, and of Shakespeare's
only seven tragedies, the exact reverse might appear to be
the truth. And yet such is the overpowering impression
each of Æschylus' plays makes of his grandeur of mind
and spirit, of the heroic mold he was cast in, it is not
possible to conceive of his writing anything that would
not have been so stamped.

So much we can conclude about the man himself, but
of his actual life there are almost no indications. He was
used to the ways of a great house, we gather, and despised
the *nouveau riche*—he takes him off in the Zeus of the
*Prometheus*, "the upstart god" who "shows forth his power
for his brief day, his little moment of lording it." If one is
a slave, Clytemnestra tells the captive Trojan princess,

> It is very well to serve in an old family,
> Long used to riches. For indeed the man
> Who reaps a sudden harvest beyond hope,
> Is savage to his slaves above the rule.

In this matter of his soldiering, too, there are passages
that would appear to strike unmistakably the note of
personal experience: "Our beds were close to the enemy's
walls; our clothes were rotting with the wet; our hair full
of vermin." That is not war as the novice sees it. Even
more pointed are the words in Clytemnestra's announce-

ment that Troy has fallen, when she pauses in the full
flight of her tale of triumph to give a strange little realistic
picture of a newly captured town:

> The women have flung themselves on lifeless bodies,
> husbands, brothers—little children are clinging to the old
> dead that gave them life, sobbing from throats no longer
> free, above their dearest. And the victors—a night of
> roaming after battle has set them down hungry to break-
> fast on what the town affords, not billeted in order, but as
> chance directs.

That speech sounds oddly on a great queen's lips. It
seems an old soldier's reminiscence, each clear detail part
of a picture often seen. But these few passages are all
there are that throw any light upon his way of life.

We are, the greatest of us, the product of our times.
Æschylus lived in one of those brief periods of hope and
endeavor which now and again light up the dark pages
of history, when mankind makes a visible advance along
its destined path without fear or faltering. A mere handful
of men had driven back the hosts of the ruling world-
power, so defeated that Persia was never again to repeat
an invasion that had brought only disaster. The success of
that great venture went thrillingly through the land. Life
was lived at an intenser level. Peril, terror, and anguish
had sharpened men's spirits and deepened their insight.
A victory achieved past all hope at the very moment when
utter defeat and the loss of all things seemed certain had
lifted them to an exultant courage. Men knew that they
could do heroic deeds, for they had seen heroic deeds
done by men. This was the moment for the birth of
tragedy, that mysterious combination of pain and exaltation, which discloses an invincible spirit precisely when
disaster is irreparable. Up to that time the poets of Greece
had looked with a direct and un-self-conscious gaze upon
the world and found it good. The glory of brave deeds and
the loveliness of natural things had contented them.
Æschylus was the poet of a new era. He bridged the
tremendous gulf between the poetry of the beauty of the

outside world and the poetry of the beauty of the pain of
the world.

He was the first poet to grasp the bewildering strangeness of life, "the antagonism at the heart of the world."
He knew life as only the greatest poets can know it; he
perceived the mystery of suffering. Mankind he saw fast
bound to calamity by the working of unknown powers,
committed to a strange venture, companioned by disaster.
But to the heroic, desperate odds fling a challenge. The
high spirit of his time was strong in Æschylus. He was,
first and last, the born fighter, to whom the consciousness
of being matched against a great adversary suffices and
who can dispense with success. Life for him was an adventure, perilous indeed, but men are not made for safe
havens. The fullness of life is in the hazards of life. And,
at the worst, there is that in us which can turn defeat into
victory.

In a man of this heroic temper, a piercing insight into
the awful truth of human anguish met supreme poetic
power, and tragedy was brought into being. And if
tragedy's peculiar province is to show man's misery at its
blackest and man's grandeur at its greatest, Æschylus is
not only the creator of tragedy, he is the most truly tragic
of all the tragedians. No one else has struck such ringing
music from life's dissonance. In his plays there is nothing
of resignation or passive acceptance. Great spirits meet
calamity greatly. The maidens who form the chorus of the
*Prometheus* demand full knowledge of all the evil before
them: "For when one lies sick, to face with clear eyes all
the pain to come is sweet." Antigone, about to do what
means certain death to her, cries, "Courage! The power
will be mine and the means to act." When Clytemnestra
has struck her blow and her husband has fallen dead, she
opens the palace doors and proclaims what she has done:

Here I stand where I struck. So did I. Nothing do I
deny. Twice did I strike him and twice he cried out, and
his limbs failed and he fell. The third stroke I gave him,
an offering to the god of Hell who holds fast the dead. And
there he lay gasping and his blood spouted and splashed

me with black spray, a dew of death, sweet to me as
heaven's sweet raindrops when the cornland buds.

Prometheus, helpless and faced by irresistible force,
is unconquered. There is no yielding in him, even to pronounce the one word of submission which will set him free;
no repentance in dust and ashes before almighty power.
To the herald of the gods who bids him yield to Zeus'
commands, he answers:

> There is no torture and no cunning trick,
> There is no force, which can compel my speech,
> Until Zeus wills to loose these deadly bonds.
> So let him hurl his blazing thunderbolt,
> And with the white wings of the snow,
> With lightning and with earthquake,
> Confound the reeling world.
> None of all this will bend my will.

HERALD
Submit, you fool. Submit. In agony learn wisdom.

PROMETHEUS
Seek to persuade the sea wave not to break.
You will persuade me no more easily.

With his last words as the universe crashes upon him,
he asserts the justice of his cause: "Behold me, I am
wronged"—greater than the universe which crushes him,
said Pascal. In this way Æschylus sees mankind, meeting
disaster grandly, forever undefeated. "Take heart. Suffering, when it climbs highest, lasts but a little time"—that
line from a lost play gives in brief his spirit as it gives the
spirit of his time.

He was a pioneer who hews his way through by the
magnificence of sheer strength and does not stay to level
and finish. There is no smooth perfection of form in him
such as ever gives a hint that the summit has been reached
and just beyond lies decadence. He could have heaved
the mighty stones of the Mycenæan gate; he could not
have polished the lovely beauty of the Praxiteles Hermes.
Aristophanes, keenest of critics and true lover of Æschylus

even when caricaturing him, describes his adjectives, those touchstones of a poet, as "new, torrent-swept timbers, blown loose by a giant at war," and the words recall that storm of "high-engendered battles," of "sulphurous and thought-executing fires, vaunt-couriers of oak-cleaving thunderbolts" that beat upon Lear's head. A kind of splendid carelessness goes with surpassing power. The labor of the file was not for Æschylus as it was not for Shakespeare. These are not to be pictured pacing the floor through nights of anguish, searching for *le mot unique.*

There is a kinship between the two. Shakespeare also had seen men achieve and suffer on a plane above the level of mere human life and had been moved by the high hope of courage of an age when heroes like those of Marathon and Salamis walked the earth. The sense of the wonder of human life, its beauty and terror and pain, and the power in men to do and to bear, is in Æschylus and in Shakespeare as in no other writer.

> Thy friends are exultations, agonies,
> And love and man's unconquerable mind.

These words from a nineteenth-century poet are as characteristic of both Shakespeare and Æschylus as anything either of them ever wrote.

One of Shakespeare's plays, indeed, *Macbeth,* is completely like Æschylus in conception, more so by far than any of Sophocles' or Euripides' plays. The atmosphere of Macbeth's castle and Agamemnon's palace is the same. It is always night there; a heavy murk is in the air; death drifts through the doorways. It is not a mere case of dark deeds done in both. Œdipus' palace is as deeply stained with blood; horror is there, and the slow footsteps of fate, clearly heard, ever inexorably drawing nearer to the doom that must be. But in the *Oresteia* and *Macbeth* the horror consists of the fact that those footsteps are not clearly heard; they are muffled; the ear listens and is not sure; what moves on is shrouded in blackness; the unknown is there and the mystery of evil.

It is impossible to show by quotations the similarity in

the general impression the two tragedies make, but the way each is continually pointing to an undefined terror to come can be illustrated by many passages. Again and again in both plays the note of foreboding is struck. Some dreadful deed is impending—what, none may say, but any moment we may be face to face with it.

MACBETH
*Act I, sc. 3*

MACBETH: Why do I yield to that suggestion
Whose horrid image doth unfix my hair,
And make my seated heart knock at my ribs,
Against the use of nature? Present fears
Are less than horrible imaginings.

*Act I, sc. 4*

MACBETH: Stars, hide your fires!
Let not light see my black and deep desires;
The eye wink at the hand; yet let that be
Which the eye fears, when it is done, to see.

LADY MACBETH: Come, thick night,
And pall thee in the dunnest smoke of hell,
That my keen knife sees not the wound it makes,
Nor heaven peep through the blanket of the dark,
To cry: "Hold, hold!"—

*Act III, sc. 4*

MACBETH: Avaunt! and quit my sight! Let the earth hide
thee!
Thy bones are marrowless, thy blood is cold!
Thou hast no speculation in those eyes
Which thou dost glare with . . . Hence, hor-
rible shadow!
Unreal mockery, hence!

AGAMEMNON
CHORUS: But dark fear now
Shows me dim
Dreadful forms
Hid in night.
Men who shed the blood of men,
Their ways are not unseen of God.
Black the spirits that avenge . . .

Why for me so steadfastly
Hovers still this terror dark
At the portals of my heart prophetic . . .
Spirit of vengeance, your music is sung to no
   lyre.
> Heart that throbs,
> Breast that swells,
> Tides of pain that shake the spirit,
> Are you but fools?
Nay, you presage what shall be . . .

CASSANDRA: Where have you brought me—and to what a
house!

CHORUS: The house of Atreus' sons—

CASSANDRA: No—but a house God hates.
Murders and strangling deaths—
Kin . . . striking down kin. Oh, they kill men
here.
House that knows evil and evil!—the floor
drips red.
O God, O God. What would they bring to
pass?
Is there a woe that this house knows not?
Oh, dark deed, beyond cure, beyond hope.
—And help stands far away.

CASSANDRA: See them—those yonder by the wall—there,
there!
So young—like forms that hover in a dream.
Children they seem, murdered by those they
loved.
And in their hands is flesh—It is their own!
And inward parts—O load most horrible!
I see them . . .
Vengeance, I swear, from these is shaping still.

The similarity in the effect produced by these quotations
is unmistakable, and it could be illustrated at far greater
length. It is not a chance resemblance that through one
drama come and go the weird sisters and through the other
three avenging furies of crime. Neither band could have
found a place in Œdipus' palace.

Another notable resemblance: both poets can laugh.

That can be said of no other tragedian. The poets, indeed, of whatsoever description, are not given to laughter; they are a serious company. Æschylus and Shakespeare alone stand for the soundness of Socrates' opinion, that it is within the province of the same writer to compose both tragedy and comedy. Lesser men would feel the intrusion of the comic into the tragic a fault against good taste, as witness all the critics who have suffered over the porter in *Macbeth*. But the great two, one surmises, were not concerned with good taste. They did what they pleased. A moment of tragic suspense, hardly to be equalled, is when the doors of Agamemnon's palace close upon the son who has come to kill his mother and has gained admission to her by pretending to be the bearer of the news of his own death. As he passes into the palace and the mind is full of the awful deed to be done, an old woman enters whom the chorus addresses as Orestes' nurse. She is crying:

> Oh, I'm a wretched woman. I've known troubles enough but never any like this. Oh, Orestes, my darling! Oh, dear, he was the trouble of my life. His mother gave him to me to nurse, and the shrill screams at night that routed me out of bed, and all the useless bother of him. I had to put up with it. A child hasn't any sense, any more than a dumb beast. You've got to follow its whims. A baby can't tell you when it's hungry or thirsty or going to wet its clothes. And a child's stomach can do it all alone—and sometimes I knew what was coming, but often I didn't, and then all the clothes had to be washed. I wasn't only nurse, I was washerwoman too—

And so exits the forerunner of Juliet's nurse and the play moves on to the murder of the mother by her son.

Shakespeare, it may be said, was above all a man of the theatre as Æschylus, it is the current opinion, was not. He is generally held to be a philosophic poet who strayed by some mischance upon the stage. So far is this from being true that he was first and foremost the born dramatist, a man who saw life so dramatically that to express himself he had to invent the drama. For that is what he did. Until he came there was only a chorus with a leader. He added a second actor, thus contriving the action of character upon character which is the essence of the drama. He was at least as much a man of the theatre as Shakespeare, not only the founder of it, but an actor and a practical producer as well. He designed the dress all Greek actors wore; he developed stage scenery and stage machinery; he laid down the lines for the Attic theatre.

Small wonder that with all this on his shoulders his technique was often faulty. No doubt he could write bad lines and bad scenes; he was a careless workman, negligent of detail. Sometimes he ignored legitimate minor interests; sometimes he dragged them out to a wearisome length, as in the *Libation-Bearers,* where Orestes' recognition by Electra is given briefly and tamely, while the discovery of the lock of hair on the tomb holds the stage for a hundred and fifty long lines. But he always realized the essential drama of the story he was dramatizing, and he always went straight to it. There he was not careless. The great central theme of each play he presented with consummate theatrical skill as well as dramatic power. The plays of his two great successors are often better theatre than his. They were more skillful craftsmen and had a far more developed technique, but there are scenes in his plays of a dramatic intensity which is beyond anything in Sophocles or Eurpidies. He not only invented the drama, he raised it to a height which has only once been equalled, and in the glory of that twofold achievement he stands alone.

One quotation to support the point must suffice, for the reason that only a fairly long passage can show this special power of dramatic effect. In the *Libation-Bearers* Clytemnestra learns that Orestes is alive and has killed her lover. She knows then what is to come. She bids a slave:

> Swift! Bring me an axe that can slay. I will know now
> if I am to win or lose. I stand here on the height of misery.
> ORESTES *enters with* PYLADES.
> ORESTES: It is you I seek. The other has had his fill. You
> love him—you shall lie in the same grave.
> CLYTEMNESTRA: Stop—oh, my son. Look—my breast.
> Your heavy head dropped on it and you slept, oh, many a

time, and your baby mouth where never a tooth was, sucked the milk, and so you grew—

ORESTES: Oh, Pylades, what shall I do? My mother—Awe holds me. May I spare?

PYLADES: Where then Apollo's words and the dread compact? Make all men enemies but not the gods.

ORESTES: Good counsel. I obey. You—follow me. I lead you where he lies to kill you there.

CLYTEMNESTRA: It seems, my son, that you will kill your mother.

ORESTES: Not I. You kill yourself.

CLYTEMNESTRA: I am alive—I stand beside my grave. I hear the song of death. [*They go out and the* CHORUS *sing that her fate is just.*]

Lift up your head, oh, house. The light! I see the light.

[*The palace doors roll back.* ORESTES *stands over two dead bodies.*]

ORESTES: I am blameless of the one. He died the death adulterers must die. But she who planned this thing of horror against her husband by whom she had borne beneath her girdle the burden of children—what think you of her? Snake or viper was she? Her very touch would rot a man.

CHORUS: Woe—woe—Oh, fearful deeds!

ORESTES: Did she do it or did she not? The proofs you know—the deed and the death. I am victor but vile, polluted.

CHORUS: One trouble is here—another comes.

ORESTES: Hear me and learn, for I know not how it will end. I am borne along by a runaway horse. My thoughts are out of bounds. Fear at my heart is leaping up. Before my reason goes—oh, you my friends, I say I killed my mother—yet not without reason—she was vile and she killed my father and God hated her—Look—Look—Women—there—there—Black—all black, and long hair twisting like snakes. Oh, let me go.

CHORUS: What fancies trouble you, O son, faithful to your father? Do not fear.

ORESTES: No fancies. My mother has sent them. They throng upon me and from their eyes blood drips, blood of hate. You see them not? I—I see them. They drive me. I cannot stay.

[*He rushes out.*]

CHORUS: Oh, where will this frenzy of evil end?

And on this note the play closes. There is not in all literature any scene more dramatic.

This inventor of a new form of art was by temperament an innovator who saw the old go down and joyfully helped make the new. He was the leader of thought for Greece at that moment when ideas the world had never known before were stirring, but he soon left his followers far out of sight. That piercing intellect of his saw through false and foolish notions which were to hold the world enslaved for many a century to come. He was the fore-runner of Euripides, the arch-rationalist. Long before Euripides had brought his terrible indictment against war in the *Trojan Women*, Æschylus, Marathon-warrior though he was, had stripped away its glory. He had fought in the ranks and he knew what war was like as only the man can who has seen it at close quarters. It is curious that he perceived how money and war are bound up together:

> For all who sped
>   forth from Greece,
>     joining company,
> such grief as passes power to bear
>   in each man's home,
>     plain to see.
> Many things
>   there to pierce a heart through.
> Women know whom they sent forth,
>   but instead of the living,
>   back there comes to every house
>   armor and dust from the burning.
> And war who trades
>   men for gold,
>   living for dead,
>   and holds his scales
> where the spear-points meet and clash,
>   to their beloved,
>   back from Troy
>   he sends them dust
>   from the flame,
>   heavy dust,
>   dust wet with tears,
>   filling urns in seemly wise,
>   freight well-stowed, the dust of men.

There are many passages like that in the *Agamemnon*.

In one brief sentence he dismisses a central—perhaps the central—dogma of the Greeks, that great prosperity is viewed jealously by heaven and ends in misery: "I hold my own mind and think apart from other men. Not prosperity but sin brings misery."

It is usually held that the radical and the religious temperaments are antagonistic, but in point of fact the greatest religious leaders have been radicals. Æschylus was profoundly religious and a radical, and so he pushed aside the outside trappings of religion to search into the thing itself. The gods come and go bewilderingly in his plays for the reason that they are only shadows to him, whose inconsistencies and incongruities do not interest him. He is looking past them, beyond the many to the one, "the Father, Ancient of Days, who fashioned us with his own hand." In Him, in God, he holds, rests the final and reconciling truth of this mystery that is human life, which is above all the mystery of undeserved suffering. The innocent suffer—how can that be and God be just? That is not only the central problem of tragedy. It is the great problem everywhere when men begin to think, and everywhere at the same stage of thought they devise the same explanation, the curse, which, caused by sin in the first instance, works on of itself through the generations—and lifts from God the awful burden of injustice. The haunted house, the accursed race, literature is full of them. "The sins of the fathers shall be visited upon the children." Œdipus and Agamemnon must pay for their forefathers' crimes. The stolen gold dooms the Volsungs. It is a kind of half-way house of explanation which satisfies for a time men's awakening moral sense. It did not satisfy Æschylus.

He was a lonely thinker when he began to think "those thoughts that wander through eternity." The Hebrew Ezekiel at about the same time perceived the injustice of this way of maintaining God's justice and protested against the intolerable wrong of children's suffering for their father's sins, but his way out was to deny that they did. As ever, the Jew was content

with a "Thus saith the Lord," an attitude that leaves
no place for tragedy in the world. He could accept the
irrational and rest in it serenely; the actual fact before
him did not confront him inescapably as it did the
Greek.

Æschylus was conscious of his own isolation when
he went beneath the accepted explanation. "I alone do
not believe thus," he wrote. He took the problem at
its worst, a wife driven to murder her husband, a son
driven to kill his mother, and back of them an inheritance of black deed upon black deed. No easy way out
that would "heal the hurt" of the world "slightly" would
do for him. He saw the inexorable working out of the
curse; he knew that the sins of the fathers are visited upon
the children; he believed in the justice of God. The truth
to reconcile these truths he found in the experience of
men, which the men of his generation must have realized
far beyond others, that pain and error have their purpose
and their use: they are steps of the ladder of knowledge:

> God, whose law it is that he who learns must suffer. And
> even in our sleep pain that cannot forget, falls drop by
> drop upon the heart, and in our own despite, against our
> will, comes wisdom to us by the awful grace of God.

A great and lonely thinker. Only here and there in the
very greatest have the depth and penetration of his thought
been equalled, and his insight into the riddle of the world
has not yet been superseded.

# *Chapter* XIII

## SOPHOCLES

### QUINTESSENCE OF THE GREEK

TRAGIC pleasure, Schopenhauer said, is in the last analysis a matter of acceptance. The great philosopher of gloom was defining all tragedy in terms of one tragedian. His definition applies to Sophocles alone, but it compresses into a single word the spirit of the Sophoclean drama. Acceptance is not acquiescence or resignation. To endure because there is no other way out is an attitude that has no commerce with tragedy. Acceptance is the temper of mind that says, "Thy will be done" in the sense of "Lo, I come to do thy will." It is active, not passive. Yet it is distinct from the spirit of the fighter, with which, indeed, it has nothing in common. It accepts life, seeing clearly that thus it must be and not otherwise. "We must endure our going hence even as our coming hither." To strive to understand the irresistible movement of events is illusory; still more so to set ourselves against what we can affect as little as the planets in their orbits. Even so, we are not mere spectators. There is nobility in the world, goodness, gentleness. Men are helpless so far as their fate is concerned, but they can ally themselves with the good, and in suffering and dying, die and suffer nobly. "Ripeness is all."

This is the spirit of Sophocles, as unlike that of Æschylus as the spirit of a man on a foundering vessel who stands aside to let the women and children fill the life-boats and accepts death calmly as his portion, is unlike that of the Elizabethan gentleman who sailed the little *Revenge* against the Spanish Armada in that most glorious fight of history. There were scarcely two decades between the two tragedians, but the tremendous stream of the life of Athens flowed so swiftly that by the time Sophocles had reached manhood the outlook on life which had made Marathon, Thermopylæ, Salamis, possible had passed away. Their very names have power to-day to move us to great memories. "Gods then were men and walked upon the earth." Even to-day we can catch a glimpse of what it must have meant to watch the decline of that heroic endeavor and the failure of those high hopes. Athens had brought to birth freedom for the world, and then straightway turned to compass the destruction of her own glorious offspring. She grew powerful, imperial, tyrannical. She was for bringing all Greece beneath her yoke so that the rest of Greece turned upon her, and before Sophocles died, Sparta was at her gates and her sun was setting. As a very old man, when death the deliverer was close at hand, he wrote the well-known lines:

> The long days store up many things nearer to grief than
>    joy.
> . . . Death at the last, the deliverer.
> Not to be born is past all prizing best.
> Next best by far when one has seen the light
> Is to go thither swiftly whence he came.
> When youth and its light carelessness are past,
> What woes are not without, what griefs within,
> Envy and faction, strife and sudden death.
> And last of all, old age, despised,
> Infirm, unfriended.

These words are not his creed. They were written when he was as full of grief as age, wretched in both. They are a record of his life: his youth in the bright day of Athens' hope; his manhood when war and party strife were assailing the city; and his old age when the enemy of beauty and tolerance and fair living, of all that Athens had stood for, was conqueror. An old man summing up his life after all the taste for life and all the reason for it, too, were gone, not the great poet's final judgment passed upon it. He gave that judgment in no uncertain words. Such times as those he lived in test the temper of men. To the weaker spirits they bring the despair of all things. The starry heavens are darkened and truth and justice are no more. But to men like Sophocles outside change does not bring the loss of inner steadfastness. The strong can keep the transient and the eternal separate. Sophocles despaired for the city he loved; to him himself evil had come and not good; but, as he saw life, outside circumstance was in the ultimate sense powerless; within himself, he held, no man is helpless. There is an inner citadel where we may rule our own spirits; live as free men; die without dishonoring humanity. A man can always live nobly or die nobly, Ajax says. Antigone goes to her death not uncomforted: death was her choice, and she dies, the chorus tell her, "mistress of her own fate." Sophocles saw life hard but he could bear it hard. When Deianira is being told of her husband's infidelity and her unwilling informant falters in his tale, she bids him, "Do not cheat me of the truth. Not to know the truth—that indeed would be my hurt." The last words of the second *Œdipus* strike the dominant note of all his plays: "Cease lamentation, for verily these things stand fast." He offers no refuge from things as they are except the refuge of suffering and death accepted in calm of mind, with strength unshaken.

For the rest, in the outside world nothing is sure and most things are sad. Sophocles is melancholy, not with a black or bitter melancholy; Milton's "pensive nun." "Friendship is often false"; "Faith does not abide"; "Human life is a shadow"—such sayings are on every page:

> For never all days free from pain
> are given mortals by the son of Kronos.
> But joy and grief
> the wheels of time
> roll round to all,
> even as the circling pathways of the stars.
> Nothing abides for men, not bright-bespangled night,
> not doom, not death.

Wealth comes and goes,
and grief and gladness.

The danger of this kind of moralizing is that it is easy and separated by a hair's-breadth only from the commonplace. Sophocles often grows sententious: "For all men it is appointed to die"; "Before he sees it no man can read the future or his fate"; "The honor of life lies not in words but in deeds." Not even the sweep of his mighty wing can lift this sort of thing into the realm of poetry, but here as in all else he is a Greek of the Greeks, lovers ever of antithesis and of a pithy saying. The wonder is not that Sophocles must draw the moral but that Æschylus signally does not. The point is only one of many that mark the fundamental difference between the two.

Sophocles was conservative, the upholder of an established order. In theology the conservative temper tends to formalism. Sophocles puts on the same level "to walk with no regard for justice" and to have "no reverence for images of gods." He took contentedly the orthodox view of the hierarchy of Olympus, but a mind and a spirit such as his could not rest there. His beatific vision has nothing to do with the fancies and fables of a childish mythology. The word forever on his lips is law and when he searches the heavens seeking to understand, what he found was, "Law of purity and reverence which no forgetfulness shall ever put to sleep, and God through them is great and grows not old." He has substituted law for that proud word freedom which Æschylus so loved. Athens is to him the city which has "the perfect fear of Heaven in righteous laws." He loves "order" and "fair harmony" and "sobriety." Freedom, one suspects, looked to him a noisy, disorderly, intemperate business, not to be contained within decent limits. "And ever shall this law hold good," sing the chorus in the *Antigone*, "nothing that is vast enters into the life of mortals without a curse." That is the Greek speaking. All Greek words that mean literally *boundless, indefinite, unlimited*, have a bad connotation. The Greek liked what he could see clearly. The infinite was unpleasant to him.

In every way Sophocles is the embodiment of what we know as Greek, so much so that all definitions of the Greek spirit and Greek art are first of all definitions of his spirit and his art. He has imposed himself upon the world as the quintessential Greek, and the qualities pre-eminently his are ascribed to all the rest. He is direct, lucid, simple, reasonable. Excess—the word is not to be mentioned in his presence. Restraint is his as no other writer's. Beauty to him does not inhere in color, or light and shade, or any method of adornment, but in structure, in line and proportion, or, from another point of view, it has its roots not in mystery but in clear truthfulness. This is the classic spirit as we have conceived it, and contrasted with Sophocles, Æschylus is a romanticist. How sober is Sophocles' utterance even in despair. His most desperate sayings have an air of reasonableness:

> Only the base will long for length of life
> that never turns another way from evil.
> What joy is there in day that follows day,
> now swift, now slow, and death the only goal.
> I count as nothing him who feels within
> the glow of empty hopes.

And how romantic is Æschylus' despair:

> Black smoke I would be,
> nearing the clouds of God.
> All unseen, soaring aloft,
> as dust without wings I would perish.
> Oh, for a seat high in air,
> where the dripping clouds turn snow,
> a sheer, bare cliff, outranging sight,
> brooding alone, aloft.
> Down I would hurl myself, deep down,
> and only the eagles would see.

The last words spoken by the two Antigones bring into clear relief the difference between the two men's temperaments. Sophocles' Antigone mourns:

> Unwept, unfriended, without marriage song,
> I pass on my last journey to my grave.
> Behold me, what I suffer and from whom,
> because I have upheld that which is high.

Not so Æschylus' heroine:

> No one shall ever thus decree for me.
> I am a woman and yet will I make
> a grave, a burying for him . . . With my own hands!
> Courage! For I will find the power to act.
> Speak not to stay me.

Aristophanes in the *Frogs* gives a sketch of Sophocles which is in singular contrast to the mocking portraits of everybody else. The rest brawl like fishwives and fight like bad little boys, Æschylus and Euripides foremost. Sophocles stands aloof, gentle and courteous and ready to give place to others, "blameless in life and blameless, too, in death." Not even Aristophanes could then jeer at Sophocles to an Athenian audience.* There is no other proof so convincing of the general level of intelligence and cultivated understanding in Athens as the fact that Sophocles was the popular playwright. But however great and sad the difference between the taste of the theatre public then and now, in one respect they are the same: general popularity always means warmth of human sympathy. In Sophocles' plays one may catch a glimpse here and there of that tender and gentle spirit which so endeared him to the Athenians, and which is moving as only the tenderness and the gentleness of the very strong can be. The blinded Œdipus begging for his children:

> Let me touch them—Oh, could I but touch them with my hands, I would think that they were with me as when once I could behold them. Do I hear weeping? My beloved near me? Come to me, my children. Come here to my hands.

---

*There is, of course, the comparison with Simonides in the *Peace*, but that was many years earlier.

That is a new note. There is nothing like it in Æschylus.

Warmth of nature does not argue a passionate soul. Sophocles is warm, but underneath all he is passionless. A great tragedian and a supremely great poet, and yet a detached observer of life. Of another such it was said, "Thy soul was like a star and dwelt apart," and those who love Milton will always understand Sophocles best. The periods the two men lived in were as alike as the periods of Æschylus and Shakespeare were alike. Milton, too, passed through a time of exultant hope, when Cromwell put England on the map of Europe, and he, too, had to watch the failure of all he cared for and die at last, a very old man, seeing his country, to use his own words, "shamed and defiled." He, too, learned to accept life and view it as a thing apart from himself "in calm of mind, all passion spent." His world of lofty and solemn poetry is the world of the *Antigone* and the *Œdipus at Colonus*.

The supreme excellence of both men is the same. Alas for us, that it is one which for Sophocles was lost in its complete perfection when classic Greek ceased to be a spoken language. A great thought can live forever, passed on from tongue to tongue, but a great style lives only in one language. Of all English poets Milton is least read by non-English-speaking people. Shakespeare may almost be called German as well as English, but Milton is English alone. Sophocles and Milton are the two incomparable stylists. They are always artists of the great style. They maintain a continuous level of loveliness of word, of phrase, of musical sweep and pause. Compared to them Æschylus and Shakespeare are faulty workmen, capable of supreme felicity of expression side by side with grotesque distortion. Milton's poetry is typically English in its genius; it is poetry of magnificent opulence, of weighted phrase and gorgeous adjective, but there are times when he becomes so limpid, simple, clear, direct, that he is classic, and for one who cannot read Greek easily the surest way to catch a glimpse of that flawless perfection of utterance which is Sophocles, is to read Milton:

Sabrina fair,
Listen where thou art sitting

Under the glassy, cool, translucent wave . . .
While the still morn went out with sandals gray . . .

That is the way Sophocles can write.
And completely Sophoclean in substance and in style is:

Come, come; no time for lamentations now,
Nor much more cause. Samson hath quit himself
Like Samson and heroicly hath finished
A life heroic. . . .
Nothing is here for tears, nothing to wail
Or knock the breast, no weakness, no contempt,
Dispraise or blame; nothing but well and fair,
And what may calm us in a death so noble.

It is hard to believe that Sophocles did not write that.

Milton was no dramatist. Thought was his great interest, not action. Sophocles turned naturally to the
drama. He was a man of Periclean Athens where pre-
eminently the play was the thing, but it is open to question
whether his own bent would have led him that way. It is
certain that he is a greater poet than dramatist. In dramatic power he stands below Æschylus. On the other
hand, in good theatre, as distinguished from sheer drama,
he is his superior, but that is only to say that he possessed
in the highest degree the Athenian technical gift: in whatever direction he turned he was a consummate workman.
If he wrote a play it would be done as well as it could be
done from every point of view of theatrical craftsmanship.
One imagines the young man watching a performance of
Æschylus' *Libation-Bearers* and noting every crude detail
and the passing over of many a chance for a tense moment:
that lock of Orestes' hair they will never have done talking
about; the patent silliness of Electra's divining that her
brother has arrived because the footprints she has found
are like her own; the scene where she recognizes him, so
quickly passed over when it held most admirable dramatic
possibilities. And off he goes to do a really well-made play.
Such is the *Electra*. So brief, but not a word wasted;
Electra's character given in a moment by the sharp contrast to her sister; the intense, compressed dialogue, where

every word means something different to the speakers and
the spectators, and the effect is electric; that lock of hair
relegated far to the background; the recognition scene
worked to the full of all its possibilities; and in the end a
thrilling moment. The son has come to avenge his father's
death at the hands of his wife and her lover by murdering
the two murderers. He has killed his mother, having gained
admission to her by declaring that he is bringing her news
of his own death. His sister waits at the palace door. To
her comes their mother's lover, rejoicing that the one man
they feared is dead:

ÆGISTHUS: Where are the strangers who have brought
us news of Orestes slain?
ELECTRA: Within. They have found a way to the heart
of their hostess.
ÆGISTHUS: Can I look upon the corpse with my own
eyes?
ELECTRA: You can indeed.
[*The palace doors open. The shrouded corpse of*
CLYTEMNESTRA *lies just within.* ORESTES *stands over it.*]
ÆGISTHUS: Uncover the face that I, who was his kins-
man, may pay my due tribute of mourning.
ORESTES: Do you yourself lift the veil.
ÆGISTHUS: So be it—but you, Electra, call me Clytem-
nestra if she is near.
ORESTES: She is. Look no farther for her.
[ÆGISTHUS *lifts the face cloth.*]
ÆGISTHUS: What do I see—
ORESTES: Why so terrified? Is the face strange to you?

The lifting of that cloth is a supreme theatrical touch.
It is the great moment in the play. But the story Sophocles
was dramatizing centered around a situation which could
not be surpassed for dramatic opportunity, the murder of
a mother by her son. No attention is focused on this fact
in the play. When the son comes out after killing his
mother, he and his sister agree briefly that it is well done,
and turn instantly to the real climax, the killing of
Ægisthus. Sophocles deliberately avoided the horror of that
first murder. He substituted for it the righteous punishment of a murderer, a death that could move no one to

pity and awe. "Thoughts too great for man," he ever held, are not for man to utter. He had the sure instinct of the consummate artist: what was too tremendous ever to be done in finished perfection he would not attempt. The high passion that is needed for the very highest drama was not in him. He had a supreme gift of poetic expression, a great intellect, and an unsurpassed sureness of beautiful workmanship, but he did not rise to the heights where Æschylus and Shakespeare alone have walked.

# *Chapter* XIV

## EURIPIDES

### THE MODERN MIND

EURIPIDES "with all his faults the most tragic of the poets," said Aristotle, supreme among critics, whose claim to pronounce ever the final verdict has only of late been called into question. His judgment here points the latter-day attitude toward him: the great critic was wrong; he confused sadness and tragedy. Euripides is the saddest of the poets and for that very reason not the most tragic. A very great tragedian, beyond all question, one of the world's four greatest, to all of whom belongs that strangest power, so to present the spectacle of pain that we are lifted to what we truly call the height of tragedy.

Euripides can indeed walk "those heights exalted" but the dark depths of pain are what he knows best. He is "the poet of the world's grief." He feels, as no other writer has felt, the pitifulness of human life, as of children suffering helplessly what they do not know and can never understand. No poet's ear has ever been so sensitively attuned as his to the still, sad music of humanity, a strain little heeded by that world of long ago. And together with that, something then even more unheeded, the sense of the value of each individual human being. He alone of all the classic world so felt. It is an amazing phenomenon. Out of the pages written more than twenty-three hundred years ago sound the two notes which we feel are the dominants in our world to-day, sympathy with suffering and the conviction of the worth of everyone alive. A poet of the antique world speaks to us and we hear what seems peculiarly our own.

There is an order of mind which is perpetually modern. All those possessed of it are akin, no matter how great the lapse of time that separates them. When Professor Murray's translations made Euripides popular in the early years of this century, what impressed people first of all was his astonishing modernity: he seemed to be speaking the very accent of 1900. To-day another generation who have little care for the brightest stars of those years, George Meredith, Henry James, any or all of the great later Victorians, read Euripides as belonging to them. So the younger generation in 400 B.C. felt, and so will they feel in many a century to come. Always those in the vanguard of their time find in Euripides an expression of their own spirit. He is the great exponent of the forever recurring modern mind.

This spirit, always in the world and always the same, is primarily a destructive spirit, critical not creative. "The life without criticism," Plato says, "is not worthy to be lived." The modern minds in each generation are the critics who preserve us from a petrifying world, who will not leave us to walk undisturbed in the ways of our fathers. The established order is always wrong to them. But there is criticism and criticism. Cynical criticism is totally opposed to the temper of the modern mind. The wise king who looked upon all the works that his hands had wrought and on all the labor that he had labored to do, and beheld that all was vanity and vexation of spirit, was not a modern mind. To read Ecclesiastes is to feel, "This is what men have always thought at times and will always think"; it never carries the conviction, "This, just this is modern. It is the new note of to-day." The same is true of Voltaire, that other wisest man and greatest critic, whose mighty pen shook the old unhappy things of his day until their foundations gave way. He is not a modern mind. His attitude, given in brief by his *"Je ne sais pas ce que c'est que la vie éternelle, mais celle-ci est une mauvaise plaisanterie"* is of another order. His is the critical intellect, directed upon human affairs but quite separated from "the human heart all ages live by," and that is a separation the modern-minded know nothing of.

Above all, they care for human life and human things and can never stand aloof from them. They suffer for mankind, and what preoccupies them is the problem of pain. They are peculiarly sensitized to "the giant agony of the world." What they see as needless misery around them and what they envisage as needless misery to come is intolerable to them. The world to them is made up of individuals, each with a terrible power to suffer, and the poignant pity of their own hearts precludes them from any philosophy in the face of this awful sum of pain and any capacity to detach themselves from it. They behold, first and foremost, that most sorrowful thing on earth, injustice, and they are driven by it to a passion of revolt. Convention, so often a mask for injustice, they will have none of; in their pursuit of justice at any cost they tear away veils that hide hateful things; they call into question all pleasant and comfortable things. They are not of those who take "all life as their province"; what is good in the age they live in they do not regard; their eyes are fixed upon what is wrong. And yet they never despair. They are rebels, fighters. They will never accept defeat. It is this fact that gives them their profound influence, the fact that they who see so deep into wrong and misery and feel them so intolerable, never conclude the defeat of the mind of man.

Such a spirit, critical, subversive, destructive, is very rarely embodied in a poet. On the great secular scale of literature the modern minds for the most part are negligible. It is in the nature of things that it should be so. Genius moves to creation, not to destruction. Only a very few have combined both. Three hundred years before Euripides there was such a one, completely a modern mind, who felt, as no one has ever felt more, the pitifulness of human life and the intolerable wrong of human injustice, and whose eyes were keen to pierce beneath fair surfaces—the greatest prophet of Israel, Isaiah. A burning coal was placed upon his lips and he uttered the most magnificent indictment ever delivered against those who work evil, and, in words as beautifully tender as any ever spoken, the pity for those who suffer.

Isaiah stands with Euripides as the great example of
the modern mind in literature. On every page he speaks
his protest against the wrongdoing of men: "We look for
judgment, but there is none; for salvation, but it is far off
from us . . . and justice standeth afar off: for truth is
fallen in the street, and equity cannot enter. Yea, truth
faileth. . . . Everyone followeth after rewards; they judge
not for the fatherless, neither doth the cause of the widow
come into them, which justify the wicked for reward and
grind the faces of the poor, . . . which call evil good and
good evil. . . . If one look to the land, behold the light is
darkened in the heavens, behold trouble and darkness and
dimness of anguish."

Side by side with the burning of his anger appears the
depth of his pity: "He hath sent me to bind up the broken-
hearted. . . . As one whom his mother comforteth, so will
I comfort you. . . . Can a woman forget her sucking child,
that she should not have compassion on the son of her
womb? Yea, they may forget, yet will I not forget thee. . . .
I, even I, am he that comforteth thee, to open the blind
eyes, to bring out the prisoners from the prison, and them
that sit in darkness out of the prison house. . . . Oh, thou
afflicted, tossed with tempest . . . in a little wrath I hid
my face from thee but with everlasting kindness will I
have mercy upon thee."

Parallel passages in Euripides must not be sought for,
or even passages strictly comparable; the method of writing
is too unlike. Euripides' indictment of evil is to be found
not in this or that statement but in the entire body of his
plays. The years of his manhood were the years of the
great war between Athens and Sparta. His own country's
victories at first, her immensely spreading power, never
dazzled his eyes. He looked at war and he saw through all
the sham glory to the awful evil beneath and he wrote
the *Trojan Women*—war as it appears to a handful of
captive women waiting for the victors to carry them away
to all that slavery means for women. The fall of Troy,
the theme of the most glorious martial poetry ever written,
ends in his play with one old broken-hearted woman,
sitting on the ground, holding a dead child in her arms.

So too it is impossible to show adequately by quotation his spirit of tender compassion for all the unfortunate and his sense of the worth of human life. He sets a poor ignorant peasant beside a royal princess and shows him at least her equal in nobility. Not Plato, the idealist, would have done that. Slaves, who, in the antique scale of human values were not persons any more but only goods and chattels, stand forth in his pages justified, men among men. Euripides has another standard to measure by: "A man without fear cannot be a slave." Old people, old women even and old slaves, completely negligible to the age he lived in, he touches with the deep pity of his perfect understanding. Hecuba remains with Lear the tenderest study in literature of desolate old age.

That spirit of compassionate love made him see deep into the human heart, deeper far than either of his two great predecessors. Not Æschylus, not Sophocles, nobody indeed but he himself, could have drawn the picture of utter pain so utterly human that closes the *Trojan Women*. The herald of the victorious Greeks comes to tell Andromache that her son is to be thrown from the wall of Troy. She speaks to the child:

Go, die, my best-beloved, my cherished one,
In fierce men's hands, leaving me here alone.
                    . . . Weepest thou?
Nay, why, my little one? Thou canst not know.
And Father will not come; he will not come;
Not once, the great spear flashing, and the tomb
Riven to set thee free!
How shall it be? One horrible spring . . . deep, deep
Down. And thy neck. . . . Ah God, so cometh sleep? . . .
And none to pity thee! Thou little thing
That curlest in my arms, what sweet scents cling
All round thy neck! Belovèd; can it be
All nothing, that this bosom cradled thee
And fostered; all the weary nights, wherethrough
I watched upon thy sickness, till I grew
Wasted with watching? Kiss me. This one time;
Not ever again. Put up thine arms and climb
About my neck: now, kiss me, lips to lips. . . .
Quick! take him: drag him: cast him from the wall,

If cast ye will! Tear him, ye beasts, be swift!
God hath undone me, and I cannot lift
One hand, one hand, to save my child from death.

When the little boy has been killed, his mother is gone, on her way to Greece in a Greek ship, and the dead body is brought to the grandmother, who holds it in her arms and speaks to it:

Ah, what a death hath found thee, little one.
                    . . . Poor little child!
Was it our ancient wall so savagely hath rent
Thy curls . . . here, where the bone-edge frayed
Grins white . . . Ah, God, I will not see!
Ye tender arms . . . how from the shoulder loose
Ye drop. And dear proud lips, so full of hope
And closed forever! What false words ye said
At daybreak, when he crept into my bed,
Called me kind names, and promised: "Grandmother,
When thou art dead I will cut close my hair,
And lead out all the captains to ride by
Thy tomb." . . . 'Tis I—old, homeless, childless,
That for thee, must shed cold tears.

These are no austere figures, awfully remote, lifted to heights of tragedy inaccessible. The human heart was what Euripides cared about, and the mythical princess and queen of far-fabled Troy have become suffering women, who feel what women everywhere have felt, their only throne that which sorrows build. A supreme master in human nature added those slight touches that bring them close to us: the sweet smell of the baby's neck as the mother buried her face there for the last time; the old woman remembering the small boy climbing on to her bed of a morning to tell her how he would lead his captains out gloriously for her when she was dead. No tragic exaltation is here but the most poignant pain perhaps ever painted. Few passages in all the literature of pain can be set beside it.

The speculative side of the modern mind, the spirit that is forever examining and calling into question, is less easy to do justice to by quotation. In Isaiah it underlies all the denunciations, and the most cursory reading discovers it. Here and there, too, it finds expression in some isolated piece of acute critical judgment. His keen, questioning mind saw evils which even yet, after twenty-six hundred years, are not clearly seen as such: "Woe unto them that join field to field that they may be placed alone in the earth"—the evil of great landed estates given in brief, England's land question to-day. Euripides' well-known words about women in the *Medea*, familiar quotation to woman-suffragists so short a time ago, are a perfect parallel of far-sighted criticism:

> But we, they say, live a safe life at home,
> While they, the men, go forth in arms to war.
> Fools! Three times would I rather take my stand
> With sword and shield than bring to birth one child.

But in truth the critical spirit is stamped upon Euripides as upon no other poet. He lived in a day when criticism was dominating more and more the thought in Athens. Life went at a rapid pace in that brilliant city, and the bare half century that separated Euripides from Æschylus saw astonishing changes. Signs of them are not to be sought for in Sophocles. Even though his long life did not end until a year or two after Euripides' death, he belonged to an earlier day. Or rather is it true that Sophocles was aloof from the spirit of his age and would always have been so no matter what the age. He was first and last the artist, who looked at human beings apart from himself as subjects for his art and who took life as he found it. Passionate protest in face of the facts of life would have seemed to him the action of a child. "Such was the pleasure of the gods, angry, haply, at my race of old," is the final comment of the innocent but blinded, blackened, ruined Œdipus. Questions where none could answer, Sophocles would not ask.

Over against him stand the other two, greatly different but akin. The spirit of inquiry dawning in Æschylus' day had moved him, too, to wonder and surmise. He was never one to acquiesce in what he found because it

was there. He, too, saw war with clear eyes, and Sophocles'
tranquil acceptance of "all Olympus' faded hierarchy"
was never possible to him. Completely a modern mind
he was not. He would never, under no circumstances,
in no age, have seen mankind as chiefly pitiable. Indeed
pity was not a major emotion with him. He had the soldier's temper which faces what is next to come with
never a look back to mourn what is past. But even more
than this, stamped upon his whole work is the conviction that human beings are capable of grandeur, and that
calamity met greatly is justified. Passionate protest against
the facts of life is no more to be found in him than in
Sophocles, but for a totally different reason: a hero's death
awakens neither pity nor indignation.

Completely unlike him in this point, Euripides is
nevertheless his spiritual son; he inherits directly from
him, passing over Sophocles as though he had never been.
Æschylus disregarded the current religion; Euripides directly attacked it. Again and again he shows up the gods
in accordance with the popular conception of them, as
lustful, jealous, moved by meanest motives, utterly inferior to the human beings they bring disaster upon, and
he will have none of them:

> Say not there are adulterers in Heaven,
> Long since my heart has known it false.
> God if he be God lacks in nothing.
> All these are dead unhappy tales.

His final rejection, "If gods do evil then they are
not gods," is essentially a rejection of man's creating
God in his own image, a practice that was to hold the
world completely for centuries after him and is to-day
more common than not. So can a master mind outstrip
the ages. Of certainties he had few:

> For who knows if the thing that we call death
> Is life, and our life dying—who can know?
> Save only that all we beneath the sun
> Are sick and suffering, and those gone before
> Not sick, not touched with evil.

Aristophanes' indictment of him in the *Frogs* is summed up in the charge that he taught the Athenians "to think, see, understand, suspect, question, everything."

He was, the stories that have come down about him say, an unhappy man. He withdrew from the world and lived the life of a recluse in his library; "gloomy, unsmiling, averse to society," duns an ancient description of him. A misanthrope, they said, who preferred books to men. Never was a judgment less true. He fled from the world of men because he cared for men too much. He could not bear the poignant pity of his own heart. His life had fallen on unhappy times. As final defeat drew ever nearer, Athens grew terrified, fierce, cruel. And Euripides had a double burden to carry, the sensitiveness of a great poet and the aching pity of a modern mind. How could such a one endure to come into contact with what his city had learned to tolerate and to commend? One thing alone to help her he had been fitted to do: he could so write as to show the hideousness of cruelty and men's fierce passions, and the piteousness of suffering, weak, and wicked human beings, and move men thereby to the compassion which they were learning to forget.

On these two scores it is easy to explain what at first sight seems puzzling, his great unpopularity in his lifetime and his unexampled popularity shortly after his death. Only five of his plays were awarded a first prize, whereas Sophocles gained over twenty. Aristophanes has good words for Æschylus and higher praise for Sophocles but nothing is too bad for him to say about Euripides. The modern mind is never popular in its own day. People hate being made to think, above all upon fundamental problems. Sophocles touched with the radiant glory of sublime poetry the figures of the ancient gods, and the Athenians went home from his plays with the pleasing conviction that old things were right. But Euripides was the archheretic, miserably disturbing, never willing to leave a man comfortably ensconced in his favorite convictions and prejudices. Prizes were not for such as he. And yet, very soon after his death, the verdict swung far to the other side and extraordinary tales of the way he was loved by all manner of men have come down to us.

The dogmatisms of each age wear out. Statesments of absolute truth grow thin, show gaps, are discarded. The heterodoxy of one generation is the orthodoxy of the next. The ultimate critique of pure reason is that its results do not endure. Euripides' assaults upon the super-structure of religion were forgotten; what men remem-bered and came to him for was the pitying understanding of their own suffering selves in a strange world of pain, and the courage to tear down old wrongs and never give up seeking for new things that should be good. And gen-eration after generation since have placed him securely with those very few great artists

> Who feel the giant agony of the world,
> And more, like slaves to poor humanity,
> Labor for mortal good . . .

# Chapter XV

## THE RELIGION OF THE GREEKS

WHAT the Greeks did for religion is in general not highly esteemed. Their achievement in that field is usually described as unimportant, without any real significance. It has even been called paltry and trivial. The reason people think of it in this way is that Greek religion has got confused with Greek mythology. The Greek gods are certainly Homer's Olympians, and the jovial company of the *Iliad* who sit at the banqueting board in Olympus making heaven shake with their shouts of inextinguishable laughter are not a religious gathering. Their morality, even, is more than questionable and also their dignity. They deceive each other; they are shifty and tricky in their dealings with mortals; they act sometimes like rebellious subjects and sometimes like naughty children and are kept in order only by Father Zeus' threats. In Homer's pages they are delightful reading, but not in the very least edifying.

If Homer is really the Greek Bible and these stories of his are accepted as the Greek idea of spiritual truth, the only possible conclusion is that in the enormously important sphere of religion the Greeks were naïve, not to say childish, and quite indifferent to ethical conduct. Because Homer is far and away the best known of the Greeks, this really is the prevailing idea, absurd as it must appear in face of the Greek achievement. There is no truth whatever in it. Religion in Greece shows one of the greatest of what Schopenhauer calls the "singular swing to elevation" in the history of the human spirit. It marks a great stage on the long road that leads up from savagery, from senseless and horrible rites, toward a world still so very dim and far away that its outline can hardly be seen; a world in which no individual shall be sacrificed for an end, but in which each will be willing to sacrifice himself for the end of working for the good of others in the spirit of love with the God who is love.

It would be impossible to compress Greek religion into the compass of a single chapter, but it is perhaps possible to give an idea of the special Greek stamp which marked it out from the others. Greek religion was developed not by priests nor by prophets nor by saints nor by any set of men who were held to be removed from the ordinary run of life because of a superior degree of holiness; it was developed by poets and artists and philosophers, all of them people who instinctively leave thought and imagination free, and all of them, in Greece, men of practical affairs. The Greeks had no authoritative Sacred Book, no creed, no ten commandments, no dogmas. The very idea of orthodoxy was unknown to them. They had no theologians to draw up sacrosanct definitions of the eternal and infinite. They never tried to define it; only to express or suggest it. St. Paul was speaking as a Greek when he said the invisible must be understood by the visible. That is the basis of all great art, and in Greece great artists strove to make the visible express the invisible. They, not theologians, defined it for the Greeks. Phidias' statue of Zeus at Olympia was his definition of Zeus, the greatest ever achieved in terms of beauty. Phidias said, so Dion Chrysostom reports, that pure thought and spirit cannot be portrayed, but the artist has in the human body a true vessel of thought and spirit. So he made his statue of God, the sight of which drew the beholder away from himself to the contemplation of the divine. "I think," Dion Chrysostom writes, "that if a man heavy of heart, who had drunk often of the cup of adversity and sorrow should stand before it, he would remember no longer the bitter hardships of his life. Your work, O Phidias, is

Grief's cure,
Bringing forgetfulness of every care."

"The Zeus of Phidias," said the Roman Quintilian, "has added to our conception of religion."

That was one way the Greeks worked out their theology. Another way was the poet's, as when Æschylus used his power to suggest what is beyond categorical statement:

> God—the pathways of his purpose
> Are hard to find.
> And yet it shines out through the gloom,
> In the dark chance of human life.
> Effortless and calm
> He works his perfect will.

Words that define God clamp down walls before the mind, but words like these open out vistas. The door swings wide for a moment.

Socrates' way was the same. Nothing to him was important except finding the truth, the reality in all that is, which in another aspect is God. He spent his life in the search for it, but he never tried to put what he had seen into hard and fast statements. "To find the Father and Maker of all is hard," he said, "and having found him it is impossible to utter him."

The way of Greek religion could not but be different from the ways of religions dependent not upon each man's seeking the truth for himself, as an artist or a poet must seek it, but upon an absolute authority to which each man must submit himself. In Greece there was no dominating church or creed, but there was a dominating ideal which everyone would want to pursue if he caught sight of it. Different men saw it differently. It was one thing to the artist, another to the warrior. "Excellence" is the nearest equivalent we have to the word they commonly used for it, but it meant more than that. It was the utmost perfection possible, the very best and highest a man could attain to, which when perceived always has a compelling authority. A man must strive to attain it. We needs must love the highest when we see it. "No one," Socrates said, "is willingly deprived of the good." To win it required all that a man could give. Simonides wrote:

> Not seen in visible presence by the eyes of men
> Is Excellence, save his from whom in utmost toil
> Heart-racking sweat comes, at his manhood's height.

Hesiod had already said the same:

> Before the gates of Excellence the high gods have placed
>      sweat.
> Long is the road thereto and steep and rough at the first.
> But when the height is won, then is there ease,
> Though grievously hard in the winning.

Aristotle summed up the search and struggle: "Excellence much labored for by the race of men." The long and steep and rough road to it was the road Greek religion took.

In the very earliest Greek records we have, a high stage has been reached. All things Greek begin for us with Homer, and in the *Iliad* and the *Odyssey* the Greeks have left far behind not only the bestialities of primitive worship, but the terrible and degrading rites the terror-stricken world around them was practicing. In Homer, magic has been abolished. It is practically nonexistent in the *Iliad* and the *Odyssey*. The enormous spiritual advance this shows—and intellectual, no less—is hard for us to realize. Before Greece all religion was magical. Magic was of supreme importance. It was mankind's sole defense against fearful powers leagued against mankind. Myriads of malignant spirits were bent on bringing every kind of evil to it. They were omnipresent. A Chaldean inscription runs:

> They lie in wait. They twine around the rafters. They take their way from house to house and the door cannot stop them. They separate the bride from the embraces of the bridegroom; they snatch the child from between his father's knees.

Life was possible only because, fearful as they were, they could be appeased or weakened by magical means. These were often terrible as well as senseless. The human mind played no part at all in the whole business. It was enslaved by terror. A magical universe was so terrifying because it was so irrational, and therefore completely incalculable. There was no dependable relation anywhere between cause and effect. It will readily be seen what it did to the human intellect to live in such an atmosphere, and what it did to the human character, too. Fear is of all the emotions the most brutalizing.

In this terror-haunted world a strange thing came to pass. In one little country the terror was banished. For untold ages it had dominated mankind and stunted its growth. The Greeks dismissed it. They changed a world that was full of fear into a world full of beauty. We have not the least idea when or how this extraordinary change came about. We know only that in Homer men are free and fearless. There are no fearful powers to be propitiated in fearful ways. Very humanlike gods inhabit a very delightful heaven. Strange and terrifying unrealities—shapes made up of bird and beast and human joined together by artists who thought only the unhuman could be divine—have no place in Greece. The universe has become rational. An early Greek philosopher wrote: "All things were in confusion until Mind came and set them in order." That mind was Greek, and the first exponent of it we know about was Homer. In the *Iliad* and the *Odyssey* mankind has been delivered from the terror of the unhuman supreme over the human.

Homer's universe is quite rational and well ordered and very well lit. When night comes on, the gods go to sleep. There are no mysterious doings that must shun the eye of day either in heaven or on the earth. If the worship of the powers of darkness still went on—and there are allusions to practices that point to it—at least literature takes no notice of it. Homer would have none of it, and no writer after him ever brought it back. Stories like that of the sacrifice of Iphigenia, which clearly point back to brutal rites, always represent what was done as evil.

An ancient writer says of Homer that he touched

nothing without somehow honoring and glorifying it. He was not the Greek Bible; he was the representative and spokesman of the Greeks. He was quintessentially Greek. The stamp of the Greek genius is everywhere on his two epics, in the banishment of the ugly and the frightful and the senseless; in the conviction that gods were like men and men able to be godlike; in the courage and undaunted spirit with which the heroes faced any opponent, human or divine, even Fate herself; in the prevailing atmosphere of reason and good sense. The very essence of Greek rationality is in the passage in which Hector is advised to consult the flight of birds as an omen before going into battle and cries: "Obedience to long-winged birds, whether they fare to the right or to the left—nay; one omen is best, to fight for our country." Homer was the great molding force of Greece because he was so Greek himself. Plato says: "I have always from my earliest years had an awe of Homer and a love for him which even now [when he is about to criticize him] make the words falter on my lips. He is the great leader and teacher."

The Greeks never fell back from the height they had reached with him. They went further on, but not in the directions he had banned, away from reason to magic, and away from freedom to creeds and priests. His gods, however, could not continue long to be adequate to men fired by the desire for the best. They were unable to satisfy people who were thinking soberly of right and wrong, who were using their critical powers to speculate about the universe, who, above all, were trying to find religion, not the doubtful divinities of Olympus, but a solution of life's mystery and a conviction of its purpose and its end. Men began to ask for a loftier Zeus, and one who cared for all, not only, as in the *Iliad*, for the great and powerful. So in a passage in the *Odyssey* he has become the protector of the poor and helpless; and soon after, the peasant poet Hesiod, who knew by experience what it was to be weak and have no defense against the strong, placed justice in Olympus as Zeus' companion: "Fishes and beasts and fowls of the air devour one another. But to men Zeus has given justice. Beside Zeus on his throne Justice has her seat."

Delphi, the oracle of oracles, took up this implied criticism of Homer and put it into plain words. Moral standards were applied to what went on in Homer's heaven. Pindar, Delphi's greatest spokesman, denounced Homer as speaking falsehoods about the gods. It was wicked and contrary to reason, he protested, to tell unedifying tales about divinities: "Hateful is the poet's lore that utters slander against the gods." Criticism of this kind came from all sides. The rationalizing spirit, which was Homer's own, turned against him. The idea of the truth had dawned, to which personal preferences had to give way; and in the sixth century one of the leaders in what was the beginning of scientific thinking, wrote:

> One God there is, greatest of gods and mortals,
> Not like to men in body or in mind.
> All of him sees and hears and thinks.
> We men have made our gods in our own image.
> I think that horses, lions, oxen too,
> Had they but hands would make their gods like them,
> Horse-gods for horses, oxen-gods for oxen.

Homer's Olympians were being attacked by the same love for the rational which had brought them to birth in a mad and magical world. Not only new ideas but new needs were awakening. Greece needs a religion for the heart, as Homer's signally was not, which could satisfy the hunger in men's souls, as the cool morality of Delphi could not.

Such a need is always met sooner or later. A new god came to Greece who for a time did very strange things to the Greek spirit. He was Dionysus, the god of wine, the latest comer among the gods. Homer never admit him to Olympus. He was alien to the bright company there, a god of earth not heaven. The power wine has to uplift a man, to give him an exultant sense of mastery, to carry him out of himself, was finally transformed into the idea of the god of wine freeing men from themselves and revealing to them that they too could become divine, an idea really implicit in Homer's picture of human gods and godlike men, but never developed until Dionysus came.

His worship must have begun in a great religious revival, a revolt very probably against the powerful centre of worship Delphi had become. At any rate, it was the very antipodes to Delphi, the shrine of Apollo the most Greek of all the gods, the artist-god, the poet and musician, who ever brought fair order and harmony out of confusion, who stood for moderation and sobriety, upon whose temple was graven the great Delphic saying, "Nothing in excess." The new religion was marked by everything in excess—drunkenness, bloody feasts, people acting like mad creatures, shrieking and shouting and dancing wildly, rushing over the land in fierce ecstasy. Elsewhere, when the desire to find liberation has arisen, it has very often led men to asceticism and its excesses, to exaggerated cults bent on punishing the body for corrupting the soul. This did not happen in Greece. It could not happen to a people who knew better than any other that liberty depends on self-restraint, who knew that freedom is freedom only when controlled and limited. The Greeks could never wander very far from the spirit of Apollo. In the end, we do not know when or how, the worship of Apollo and the worship of Dionysus came together. All we are told of this momentous meeting is that Orpheus, the master musician, Apollo's pupil, reformed the violent Bacchic rites and brought them into order.

It must have been after this transformation that Dionysus was admitted to the Eleusinian mysteries, the great solemnity of Greece, and took his place beside Demeter in whose honor they had been founded. It was natural to associate the two—the goddess of the corn and the god of the vine, both deities of earth, the benefactors of mankind from whom came the bread and the wine that sustain life. Their mysteries, the Eleusinian, always chiefly Demeter's, and the Orphic, centering in

Dionysus, were an enormously important force for religion throughout the Greek and Roman world. Cicero, clearly an initiate, says: "Nothing is higher than these mysteries. . . . They have not only shown us how to live joyfully, but they have taught us how to die with a better hope." In view of their great importance, it is extraordinary that we know almost nothing about them. Everyone initiated had to take an oath not to reveal them, and their influence was so strong that apparently no one ever did. All we are sure of is that they awakened a deep sense of reverence and awe, that they offered purification from sin, and that they promised immorality. Plutarch, in a letter to his wife about the death of a little daughter during his absence from home, writes her that he knows she gives no credence to assertions that the soul once departed from the body vanishes and feels nothing, "because of those sacred and faithful promises given in the mysteries of Bacchus. . . . We hold it firmly for an undoubted truth that our soul is incorruptible and immortal. . . . Let us behave ourselves accordingly, outwardly ordering our lives, while within all should be purer, wiser, incorruptible."

A fragment of Plutarch's apparently describes the initiation ceremonies. "When a man dies he is like those who are initiated into the mysteries. Our whole life is a journey by tortuous ways without outlet. At the moment of quitting it come terrors, shuddering fear, amazement. Then a light that moves to meet you, pure meadows that receive you, songs and dances and holy apparitions." Plutarch lived in the last half of the first century A.D. There is no possible way of telling how much of all that carefully arranged appeal to the emotions belonged to the mysteries of the Periclean age, but some great appeal there was, as Aristophanes shows beyond question in the *Frogs:*

HERACLES
Then you will find a breath about your ears
Of music, and a light about your eyes
Most beautiful—like this—and myrtle groves,
And joyous throngs of women and of men—
The Initiated.

At first sight, this whole matter of an ecstatic religion of salvation, wrapped in mystery and highly emotional, is foreign to our idea of the Greek. Delphi and Pindar, teaching practical morality and forever emphasizing moderation, seem the true representatives of Greece. But they would never by themselves have reached the loftiest and the deepest expression of the Greek spirit. Noble self-restraint must have something to restrain. Apollo needed Dionysus, as Greeks could be trusted to perceive. "He who not being inspired," Plato says, "and having no touch of madness in his soul, comes to the door and thinks he will get into the temple by the help of art—he, I say, and his poetry are not admitted."

The Delphic way and the way of Dionysus reached their perfect union in the fifth-century theatre. There the great mystery, human life, was presented through the power of great art. Poet and actors and audience were conscious of a higher presence. They were gathered there in an act of worship, all sharing in the same experience. The poet and the actors did not speak to the audience; they spoke for them. Their tasks and their power was to interpret and express the great communal emotion. That is what Aristole meant when he said tragedy purified through pity and awe. Men were set free from themselves when they all realized together the universal suffering of life. For a moment they were lifted above their own griefs and cares. They ceased to be shut-in, lonely individuals as they were swept away in a great onrush of emotion which extraordinarily united instead of isolating. Plato said the perfect state was one of which the citizens wept and rejoiced over the same things. That deep community of feeling came to pass in the theatre of Dionysus. Men lost their sense of isolation.

The religion of the mysteries was individual, the search for personal purity and salvation. It pointed men toward union with God. The religion of the drama brought men into union with one another. Personal preoccupations fell away before the soul-shaking spectacle of pain presented on the stage, and the dammed-up flood within was released as the audience wept their hearts out over Œdipus and Hecuba.

But in the long and terrible struggle of the Peloponnesian War, ideals grew dim. Safety, not salvation, was in men's thoughts, the spirit of getting what one could while one could in a world where nothing seemed certain; nothing indeed, for the gods and the old morality were failing. Euripides had succeeded to Æschylus, and a new criticism of all things was in the air. In Pericles' Athens a noted teacher was declaring that "whether there are gods or not we cannot say, and life is too short to find out." The state took alarm and there was a persecution, so slight in comparison with mediæval and later times that it would not deserve notice if it were not for the last victim of it who was Socrates.

One form of religion perpetually gives way to another; if religion did not change it would be dead. In the long history of man's search for God and a basis for right living, the changes almost always come as something better. Each time the new ideas appear they are seen at first as a deadly foe threatening to make religion perish from the earth; but in the end there is a deeper insight and a better life with ancient follies and prejudices gone. Then other follies and prejudices come in, and the whole process has to be gone over again. So it was at this time in Greece, when the supports of all belief seemed to be giving way. Socrates taught and died because of his teaching. In the bitter disillusion caused by the long-drawn-out suffering of the endless war, and even more by the defeat of the Athenian spirit before the hard, narrow, intolerant Spartan spirit, Athens needed above all to be brought back to a fresh realization of the old ideal which her three tragedians had presented so magnificently. She needed a restatement of excellence, and that is what Socrates did for her and all the world to come.

He can never be separated from Plato. Almost all Plato wrote professes to be a report of what Socrates said, a faithful pupil's record of his master's words; and it is impossible to decide just what part belongs to each.

Together they shaped the idea of the excellent which the classical world lived by for hundreds of years and which the modern world has never forgotten.

Socrates believed that goodness and truth were the fundamental realities, and that they were attainable. Every man would strive to attain them if he could be shown them. No one would pursue evil except through ignorance. Once let him see what evil was and he would fly from it. His own mission, Socrates believed, was to open men's eyes to their ignorance and to lead them on to where they could catch a glimpse of the eternal truth and goodness beneath life's confusions and futilities, when they would inevitably, irresistibly, seek for a fuller and fuller vision of it. He had no dogma, no set of beliefs to implant in men's minds. He wanted to awaken in them the realization that they did not know what was good, and to arouse in them the longing to discover it. Each one, he was sure, must seek and find it for himself. He never set himself up as a guide. "Although my mind is far from wise," he said, "some of those who come to me make astonishing progress. They discover for themselves, not from me—and yet I am an instrument in the hands of God."

He was always the seeker, asking, not teaching; but his questions upset men's confidence in themselves and in all the comfortable conventions they lived by. The result at first was only perplexity, and sometimes extreme distress. Alcibiades told the company at Agathon's dinner table:

> I have heard Pericles and other great orators, but they never stirred my soul or made me angry at living in a way that was no better than a slave. But this man has often brought me to such a pass that I felt I could hardly endure the life I was leading, neglecting the needs of my soul. I have sometimes wished that he was dead!

Aristotle says happiness is activity of soul. That defines precisely Socrates' way of making men happy. He believed that the unexamined life, the life of those who knew nothing of themselves or their real needs and desires, was not worthy to be lived by a human being. So he would sting into activity the souls of men to test their lives, confident that when they found them utterly unsatisfying they would be driven to seek what would satisfy.

His own life did as much to arouse the divine discontent as his words did. He was aware of a counsellor within him which guided him in all his dealings and enabled him to maintain a perfect serenity of spirit always. When he was taken to court on a life-and-death charge of corrupting young men—and no pupil of Socrates could take seriously Homer's gods, still the state religion—he jested with his accusers in a spirit of perfect good will, refused with complete courtesy to save his life by a promise to give up teaching—and ended by comforting his judges for condemning him to death! "Be of good cheer," he told them, "and know of a certainty that no evil can happen to a good man either in life or after death. I see clearly that the time has come when it is better for me to die and my accusers have done me no harm. Still, they did not mean to do me good—and for this I may gently blame them. And now we go our ways, you to live and I to die. Which is better God only knows."

In the prison cell when the time had come to drink the hemlock, he had a kind word for the jailor who brought him the cup, and he broke off his discourse with his friends when he was telling them that nothing was surer than that beauty and goodness have a most real and actual existence, by exclaiming: "But I really had better go bathe so that the women may not have the trouble of washing my body when I am dead." One of those present, suddenly recalled from the charm of his talk to the stark facts, cried: "How shall we bury you?" "Anyway you like," was the amused answer. "Only be sure you get hold of me and see that I do not run away." And turning to the rest of the company: "I cannot make this fellow believe that the dead body will not be me. Don't let him talk about burying Socrates, for false words infect the soul. Dear Crito, say only that you are burying my body."

No one who knew of Socrates could fail to believe

that "goodness has a most real and actual existence." He exemplified in himself that excellence of which Greece from the beginning had had a vision. Four hundred years before Christ the world took courage from him and from the conviction which underlay all he said and did, that in the confusion and darkness and seeming futility of life there is a purpose which is good and that men can find it and help work it out. Aristotle, through Plato a pupil of Socrates, wrote some fifty years after Socrates died:

> There is a life which is higher than the measure of humanity: men will live it not by virtue of their humanity, but by virtue of something in them that is divine. We ought not to listen to those who exhort a man to keep to man's thoughts, but to live according to the highest thing that is in him, for small though it be, in power and worth it is far above the rest.

# Chapter XVI

## THE WAY OF THE GREEKS

CHARACTER is a Greek word, but it did not mean to the Greeks what it means to us. To them it stood first for the mark stamped upon the coin, and then for the impress of this or that quality upon a man, as Euripides speaks of the stamp—character—of valor upon Hercules, man the coin, valor the mark imprinted on him. To us a man's character is that which is peculiarly his own; it distinguishes each one from the rest. To the Greeks it was a man's share in qualities all men partake of; it united each one to the rest. We are interested in people's special characteristics, the things in this or that person which are different from the general. The Greeks, on the contrary, thought what was important in a man were precisely the qualities he shared with all mankind.

The distinction is a vital one. Our way is to consider each separate thing alone by itself; the Greeks always saw things as parts of a whole, and this habit of mind is stamped upon everything they did. It is the underlying cause of the difference between their art and ours. Architecture, perhaps, is the clearest illustration. The greatest buildings since Greek days, the cathedrals of the Middle Ages, were built, it would seem, without any regard to their situation, placed haphazard, wherever it was convenient. Almost invariably a cathedral stands low down in the midst of a huddle of little houses, often as old or older, where it is marked by its incongruity with the surroundings. The situation of the building did not enter into the architects' plans. They were concerned only with the cathedral itself. The idea never occurred to them to think of it in relation to what was around it. It was not part of a whole to them; it was the whole. But to the Greek architect the setting of his temple was all-important. He planned it, seeing it in clear outline against sea or sky, determining its size by its situation on plain hilltop or the wide plateau of an acropolis. It dominated the scene, indeed; it became through his genius the most important feature in it, but it was always a part of it. He did not think of it in and for itself, as just the building he was making; he conceived of it in relation to the hills and the seas and the arch of the sky.

To see anything in relation to other things is to see it simplified. A house is a very complicated matter considered by itself: plan, decoration, furnishings; each room, indeed, made up of many things; but, if it is considered as part of a block or part of a city, the details sink out of sight. Just as a city in itself is a mass of complexity but is reduced to a few essentials when it is thought of as belonging to a country. The earth shows an infinite diversity, but in relation to the universe it is a sphere swinging in space, nothing more.

So the Greek temple, conceived of as a part of its setting, was simplified, the simplest of all the great buildings of the world, and the Gothic cathedral, seen as a complete whole in itself, unrelated to anything beyond itself, was of all buildings the most elaborated in detail.

This necessity of the Greek mind to see everything in relation to a whole made the Greek drama what it is just as it made the Greek temple. The characters in a Greek play are not like the characters in any other drama. The Greek tragedians' way of drawing a human being belongs to them alone of all playwrights. They saw people simplified, because, just as in the case of their temples, they saw them as part of a whole. As they looked at human life, the protagonist was not human; the chief role was played by that which underlies the riddle of the world, that Necessity which brings us here and takes us hence, which gives good to one and evil to another, which visits the sins of the fathers upon the children and sweeps away innocent and guilty in fire and pestilence and earthquake shock. "Shall the thing formed say to him that formed it, Why hast thou made me thus? Hath not the potter power over the clay to make one vessel unto honor and another unto dishonor?" To St. Paul the puzzle was easy to solve. To the Greek tragedians it was the enigma never to be answered and they thought of human beings first and foremost in relation to that mystery. So placed against "the background of infinity," part of an immeasurable whole, human complexities are simplified. The accidental and the trivial, from the point of view of the whole, drop out of sight, as in a wide landscape figures can be seen only in outline, or as the innumerable lines on one of Rembrandt's old women's faces would disappear if she were placed in a spacious setting.

For us it is the other way about. Each human being fills an entire canvas. We have dismissed from our scheme of things fate that spins the thread and cuts it. Human nature is the great enigma to us; the mystery of life is the mystery of a man's own self and the conflict we care about goes on within. A man's life is seen not as what is done to him but as what he does to himself, the fault not in our stars but in ourselves, and there is a stage where each one of us is the only actor. We differ from the Greeks in nothing so much as in the way we look at the individual, isolated, in and for himself. Our drama, all our art, is the very reverse of simplified. It is a work of most subtle individualization.

But to the Greek, human beings were not chiefly different but chiefly alike. The Greek dramatists, placing their characters on the tremendous stage whose drama is the conflict between man and the power that shapes him, man "created sick, commanded to the whole," saw as important in them only the dominant traits, the great emotions, the terrors and desires and sorrows and hatreds, that belong to all mankind and to all generations and make the unchanging pattern of human life. Put any character from a Greek tragedy beside one of Shakespeare's and the difference that results from the different points of view is clearly to be seen. One is simple and uncomplicated; the other complex and contradictory too.

An obvious comparison is that between the Clytemnestra of Æschylus and Lady Macbeth, the two outstanding examples of splendid evil embodied in a woman. The greatest poet of classic times drew the one; the greatest poet of modern times the other; the two characters point the way their creators looked at the world of men.

Clytemnestra in the Greek play is magnificent from beginning to end. When she enters, we have been prepared for her hatred of her husband and her determination to kill him as soon as he comes back from Troy; we have heard most pitifully told the tale of how, ten years before, her young daughter was killed by her own father when the gods demanded a human life to speed the ships to Troy. There is one sentence in her first speech which hints at what she has felt:

Even though the victors wend their way securely home,
what those dead suffered yet may work them ill—
that pain which never sleeps.

It has never slept for her throughout the years—that pain which one dead girl suffered. So much to win our sympathy the poet allows himself, but in all that follows he draws boldly in clear, firm outline the picture of a strong woman without a single weakness; calm and proud and sure of herself; scornful of opposition; never doubting that what she determines she can carry through alone, with help from no one. So does she do; she murders her husband and coming out through the palace doors, she proclaims her deed:

Lies, endless lies I spoke to serve my purpose.
Now I gainsay them all and feel no shame.
Long years ago I planned. Now it is done.
Old hatred ended. It was slow in coming,
but it came—
I stand here where I struck. So did I.
Nothing do I deny. I flung around him
a cloak, full folds, deadly folds. I caught him,

fish in a net. No way to fly or fight.
Twice did I strike him and he cried out twice
and his limbs failed him and he fell. Then—then
I gave him the third stroke—
So there he lay and as he gasped, his blood
spouted and splashed me with black spray—a dew
of death, sweet to me as heaven's sweet raindrops
When the cornland buds. . . . Oh, if such a thing might be
over the dead to pour thank-offerings,
over this dead it would be meet and more,
who caring not, as if a beast should die
when flocks are plenty in the fleecy folds,
slew his own daughter—dearest anguish borne
by me in travail—slew her for a charm
against the Thracian winds.

#### CHORUS
Loud words of boasting—and the man your husband.

#### CLYTEMNESTRA
Call me to trial, like any silly woman?
Curse me or bless—all one to me.
Look: this is Agamemnon,
my husband, dead, struck down by my right hand,
a righteous workman. So the matter stands.
Here lies the man who scorned me, me, his wife,
the fool and tool of every shameless woman
beneath Troy's walls.

Her last words, addressed to her lover angered at the people's outcry, and the last words of the play,* are:

> Dogs will bark. Who cares to listen? What avails this empty talk?
> You and I are lords here. We two now will order all things well.

Lady Macbeth is a second Clytemnestra through the earlier acts, as sure of her purpose, as resolute, as untroubled by a doubt. When Macbeth wavers she has strength enough to make him strong. Would he, she

---

*i.e. of the *Agamemnon*, which is the first of the trilogy dealing with all that happened after Agamemnon's return, to Orestes' final acquittal for his mother's death.

asks him, by failing to carry through his determination, live a coward in his own esteem? The words have the very ring of Clytemnestra's. So too in her great speech she is one with the Grecian queen exulting in the strains upon her from her husband's blood:

> I have given suck, and know
> How tender 'tis to love the babe that milks me:
> I would, while it was smiling in my face,
> Have plucked my nipple from his boneless gums,
> And dash'd the brains out, had I so sworn as you
> Have done to this.

When Duncan is dead and Macbeth comes to her with the daggers that should have been left by the attendants as proof they were guilty, she bids him carry them back and smear the men with blood, and to his horrified refusal:

> I am afraid to think what I have done;
> Look on't again I dare not.

she answers scornfully,

> Infirm of purpose!
> Give me the daggers. The sleeping and the dead
> Are but as pictures . . .

Even so would Clytemnestra have spoken and have done. The portrait of Lady Macbeth is drawn up to her last appearance as simply, in as clear outline, as Æschylus could have done it, with only one slight and yet significant exception. While she is waiting for Macbeth to kill the king, and fearing that his purpose will not hold, she speaks to herself:

> Had he [i.e. the king] not resembled
> My father as he slept, I had done't.

That sentence blurs the clear outline. Did Clytemnestra have a moment of anguish, a sharp memory to stab her, when her husband rose from the bath for her to throw the cloak around him? Be sure if she had, Æschylus would never have put it in his picture. Clytemnestra's inmost personal life was not his concern. To him her significance, her importance, lay in what was clear for all to see, outstanding, uncomplicated, a great and powerful nature brought to ruin by a hatred within her she could not resist because it was the instrument of fate. When death at her own son's hand came upon her she met it as unflinchingly as she had dealt it. Lady Macbeth at the end, broken, pitiful, forever washing the hands which all the perfumes of Araby will never sweeten, shows a contradiction completely foreign to the Greek stage. She is the victim of her own most individual reaction to the murder she had planned and desired above all things. Her tragedy is within. Shakespeare was looking at what was deepest and what was loneliest in her.

Clytemnestra's tragedy was without; her adversary was fate. Æschylus, like the Greek architect building his temple, was not looking at her alone; he did not see her isolated with her fate in her own hands, or rather, within her own self, as Shakespeare saw Lady Macbeth. He had in view much else besides; he saw her against the background of the past, terrible deeds of old that must work out in evil for her and hers; the thread of her web of life spun far back in dim years of old; she herself, for all her great spirit, doomed before ever she began. Crime upon crime through the generations behind her; the Trojan War brought about by her sister; because of it her daughter made to die, and she, killing her husband, killed in turn by her son. That is life, said the Greek tragedian, human beings each weaving a bit of the web of sorrow and sin and suffering, and the pattern made by a power before which the heart stands still. Against that background an individual vagary or inconsistency does not stand out. Only a clear outline can be discerned, simplified down to the dominating, the essential, that which past all question stamps a man for what he is.

Hecuba in Euripides' *Trojan Women* is in all outside circumstances comparable to Lear. She too is old and royal and most miserable. She was queen of Troy; now Troy has fallen, husband, sons, are dead; she and her daughters wait beside the ruined walls while the Greek princes draw lots for them. Hecuba's opening speech shows her complete. All the rest of the drama only confirms that first impression of a woman able to suffer to the uttermost, in misery and helpless old age, unbroken. When the play begins she wakes from her bed on the ground and speaks:

> Up from the earth, O weary head!
> This is not Troy, about, above—
> Not Troy, nor we the lords thereof.
> Thou breaking neck, be strengthened!
> Endure and chafe not . . .
> Who am I that I sit
> Here at a Greek king's door,
> Yea, in the dust of it . . .
> A woman that hath no home.
> Weeping alone for her dead—
> > All kings we were,
> And I must wed a king. And sons I brought
> My lord King, many sons . . . all, all are gone.
> And no hope left that I shall look upon
> Their faces any more, nor they on mine.
> And now my feet tread on the utmost line:
> An old, slave woman . . .

The Greek herald tells her one of her daughters has been sacrificed on Achilles' Tomb; the Greek soldiers carry her other daughters one by one; they cry to her,

> Mother, see'st then what things are here?

She answers:

> I see God's hand that buildeth a great crown
> For littleness and hath cast the mighty down.

The last to go, Andromache, her son Hector's wife, she counsels:

Lo, yonder ships: I ne'er set foot on one,
But tales and pictures tell when over them
Too strong breaks the o'erwhelming sea: lo, then
All cease and yield them up as broken men
To fate and the wild waters. Even so
I in my many sorrows bear me low,
Nor curse, nor strive that other things may be.
The great wave rolled from God hath conquered me.
Thou—thou—let Hector and the fate that fell
On Hector, sleep. Weep for him ne'er so well,
Thy weeping shall not wake him. Honor thou
The master that is set above thee now,
And make of thine own gentle piety
A prize to lure his heart.

Such is Hecuba from first to last, placed by the mysterious workings of fate, through no fault of her own, upon the height of misery, and able to remain there; outside, a pitiful old woman, but within, no variableness nor shadow of turning; raised above human weakness even though completely human in her power to suffer.

The contrast Lear shows is obvious the moment one thinks of him, his passionate temper, his unreasoning folly, that brought him to such a pass; the Trojan War and all that followed it, could do no worse to Hecuba. As Goneril and Regan carelessly comment to each other:

'Tis the infirmity of his age; yet he hath ever but slenderly known himself.
The best and soundest of his time hath been but rash.

Yet so lovable, a high and careless spirit, slow to mark a slight:

### KNIGHT
—to my judgment, your highness is not entertained with that ceremonious affection as you were wont . . . for my duty cannot be silent when I think your highness wronged.

### LEAR
I have perceived a most faint neglect of late; which I have rather blamed as mine own jealous curiosity than as

a very pretense and purpose of unkindness. I will look further into 't—But where's my fool?

All the little touches that bring him near us. His struggle to control his rage when terror is at his heart:

### LEAR
Deny to speak with me? They are sick? They are weary? . . .
Fetch me a better answer.

### GLOUCESTER
                My dear lord,
You know the fiery quality of the duke . . .

### LEAR
The king would speak with Cornwall; the dear father
Would with his daughter speak, commands her service;
Are they informed of this? My breath and blood!—
Fiery? The fiery duke?—Tell the hot duke, that—
No, but not yet—may be he is not well—

And most endearing, most moving of all, his weakness:

                No, you unnatural hags,
I will have such revenges on you both
That all the world shall—I will do such things—
What they are, yet I know not; but they shall be
The terrors of the earth. You think I'll weep;
No, I'll not weep—
I have full cause of weeping—

Toward the end those most piteous words that strip him bare:

I am a very foolish fond old man,
Four score and upward, not an hour more nor less;
And, to deal plainly,
I fear I am not in my perfect mind.

So, just as Clytemmnestra and Lady Macbeth, the old queen and the old king stand over against each other, she the victim of fate, he of his own self; her character given broadly without detail, simplified down to the dominant; his individual composition, like no one's else, given to us unanalyzed. Lear has the whole stage to himself; Hecuba only a part. We have no need to question what she stands for; we look past her; her pain and her ruin point us to that which no one ever shall understand, what Ajax saw when he was driven innocent to death:

> All strangest things the multitudinous years
> bring forth and shadow from us all we know.
> Falter alike great oath and steeled resolve,
> and none shall say of aught, This cannot be.

A Greek temple makes the spectator aware of the wideness and the wonder of sea and sky and mountain range as he could not be if that shining marvel of white stone were not there in sharp relief against them, and, in the same way, a Greek tragedy brings before us the strangeness that surrounds us, the dark unknown our life is bounded by, through the suffering of a great soul given to us so simply and so powerfully, we know in it all human anguish and the mystery of pain.

But simplicity of characterization is not the same thing as lack of characterization. It is true in fact that characters simply drawn are almost never distinctly individualized, but Greek tragedy is the great example of how it can be done. The personages of a Greek play are clearly characterized. Hecuba is not in any respect one with Clytemnestra; each of them has her own way of meeting the determined things of destiny. Shift about the scene for them and Hecuba would never have avenged her daughter's death upon her husband; with Clytemnestra in Hecuba's place the Greek soldiers would have found their task less easy. Their portraits have been simplified; much is omitted from them, but all is there that is necessary to make each live, her own self and no one's copy. An artist can make an outline of a face which shows the individual as unmistakably as a minutely detailed portrait could, and in the same way the Greek tragedian while simplifying could individualize.

The point is one that must be stressed because it is

generally held that the personages of the Greek drama
were not people at all but only types, abstractions of humanity. This is not true in fact and it could not be true in
theory. As regards the fact, an example of individualization more easily perceived than either Hecuba or Clytemnestra, is Electra as each of the three tragedians saw
her. They all left dramas in which she is a chief figure,
and they all conceived her in a completely different way.
She is Clytemnestra's daughter who has continued to live
on in the palace after her father's death, with one hope
only, that her brother Orestes will come back from exile
and avenge the murder. All three plays open when Orestes
returns to find her living in utter wretchedness, refusing to
make terms with her father's murderers and insulted and
ill-treated by them.

   In Æschylus' play when she enters, she is carrying offerings to her father's grave, sent by her mother, who is
terrified because of a dream. Her first words, addressed
to the chorus, slave-women of the household and devoted
to her, show her troubled and uncertain:

> Women, who order well all in our house,
> be my advisers,
> These offerings of sorrow—while I pour them
> upon the grave, tell me the words to say.
> What can I speak of good? How voice my prayer?
> Say that I bring this from a loving wife
> to a loved husband—sent by my own mother?
> Not that—I have not courage. What then? Speak.
> Shall I in shame and silence, as he died,
> pour out the offering for the earth to drink?

The chorus bid her pray for "one to come who shall take
life for life," but she shrinks back:

> Can it be righteous for me to make prayer
> to God for such a gift?

Assured by them it is her very duty, she prays, but in
veiled words. She cannot ask for her brother to come
and take vengeance upon her mother:

> My father, pity me, and dear Orestes.
> I pray, may he come home with happy fortune.
> And I—O grant that I may be more pure
> of heart, more innocent of hand, than she,
> my mother. For your enemies, my father,
> may retribution come, the slayers slain.

That is the utmost she can say. No passionate reproaches against her mother, no crying out for revenge. She is not passionate but very quiet, self-contained in all her sorrow, and yet when Orestes appears and she knows him, she is eagerly, warmly loving. She calls him:

> My joy, my four loves, father, mother, sister,
> so pitilessly killed—my brother, trusted, reverenced,
> you are them all to me.

And in the dialogue that follows while the chorus cry exultantly that they will shout in triumph when the murderers are killed, and Orestes says:

> Let me but take her life, then let me die.

she wishes only that her father's murderers had been slain in some far-off land. Her final prayer is that no mortal hand but Zeus himself would bring down justice on the murderers. So she passes from the scene. From first to last she never speaks of her brother's killing her mother, and she has no share in the deed. As Æschylus has drawn her, she could not have.

Completely different is Sophocles' Electra. She is burning with resentment for every wrong that she has ever suffered. She tells the chorus that she lives like a servant in her father's halls:

> Clad in mean clothing, eating a slave's food,

taunted and insulted by "that woman," her mother, and "that abject dastard," Ægisthus, her mother's lover. When her sister tells her they have decided to imprison her in a dungeon as soon as he returns from his journey, she cries:

> If that be all, then may he come with speed
> that I may be removed far from you, every one.

To her mother who reproaches her for perpetually insulting her and thinking only of her father, never of her sister whom her father killed, she retorts:

> Call me disloyal, insolent, outrageous.
> If I am so accomplished, then be sure
> I am your very child.

But now and again there is something pitiful in her. At the beginning of the play she prays:

> Send me my brother, for I have no more
> The strength to bear alone my load of grief—

To the chorus who reproach her gently for her "sullen soul" that must "forever be breeding conflicts," she answers:

> I know my passion—it escapes me not—
> I am ashamed before your chiding.

And when Orestes arriving speaks kindly to her before they recognize each other, she says:

> Know this, you are the first to pity me.

But when he goes within to kill their mother and a shriek is heard:

> Oh, I am struck down—smitten.

she cries to him:

> Smite if you can once more!

As he comes out from the murder she greets him exultantly:

> The guilty now is dead—is dead . . .

THE WAY OF THE GREEKS

At the end when her mother's lover pleads for his life, she bids her brother:

> No—slay him and forthwith, and cast him dead
> Far from our sight, to dogs—to birds of prey.

They are her last words.

Euripides' Electra is unlike both of the others. In his play she has been married to a peasant so that her children might never have power to work harm to Clytemnestra and Ægisthus. Her first words are addressed to him as she comes out from their hut. Tenderness and gratitude are in them:

> O friend, my friend, as God might be my friend,
> Thou only hast not trampled on my tears.
> Life scarce can be so hard, 'mid many fears
> And many shames, when mortal heart can find
> Somewhere one healing touch, as my sick mind
> Finds thee.

He bids her gently not to work so hard for him:

> So soft thy nurture was—

but she answers as a generous nature would:

> Not pour
> My strength out in thy toiling fellowship?
> Thou hast enough with fields and kine to keep.
> 'Tis mine to make all bright within the door.

But when he departs she speaks to herself what she really feels:

> Onward, O laboring tread,
>    As on move the years;
> Onward amid thy tears,
>    O happier dead!
> Let me remember: I am she,
> Agamemnon's child, and the mother of me
> Clytemnestra, the evil queen . . . My name

Electra . . . God protect my shame.
Oh, toil, toil is a weary thing,
And life is heavy.

She cannot endure the peasant's life of squalor and unending work, she who was once a princess. When Orestes comes and tells her at first that her brother has sent him to find out how matters are, she speaks with fierce passion. If he will but come back she will stand with him and kill her mother:

Yea—with the selfsame axe that slew my father.
Let me shed my mother's blood and I die happy—

And then she pours out all her misery and her humiliation and her hatred:

Tell him this grime and reek of toil that choke
My breathing; this low roof that bows my head
After a king's. This raiment—thread by thread
'Tis I must weave it or go bare . . .
                              And she—she! The spoils
Of Troy gleam round her throne, and by each hand
Queens of the East, my father's prisoners, stand,
A cloud of Orient webs and tangling gold.
And there upon the floor, the blood, the old
Black blood, yet crawls and cankers, like a rot
In the stone.

When Orestes has revealed himself to her, she is passionate with him to kill their mother and never spare. He sees Clytemnestra coming from afar and memory stirs in him:

My mother comes, my mother, my own
That bare me.

But she is exultant:

Straight into the snare!
Aye, there she comes—

And then that ever-present wrong of her rough clothing that she loathes, and her mother's soft Eastern gold-embroidered stuffs, stings her again. She says:

> All in her brave array—

Orestes is thinking only of one thing:

> What would we with our mother? Didst thou say
> Kill her?

> ELECTRA
> What? Pity? Is it pity?

> ORESTES
>                                       She gave me suck.
> How can I strike her?

> ELECTRA
>                                   Strike her as she struck
> Our father!

When her mother arrives she goes with her into the house so that she can help in the murder, with never a hesitation, never a thought to hold her back. But after it is done and brother and sister re-enter, all her passion has gone. She is horror-struck, but her thought is for Orestes, not herself. She wants to take all the guilt and spare him, warm and generous as in the first scene with the peasant:

> Brother, mine is the blame—
> And I was the child at her knee—
> "Mother," I named her name.
>                     What clime shall hold
> My evil or roof it above?
> I cried in my heart for love—
> What love shall kiss my brow
> Nor blench at the brand stamped there?

Orestes cries that the deed was his:

> I lifted over mine eyes
> My mantle: blinded I smote

As one smiteth a sacrifice,
And the sword found her throat.

But she will have it the guilt is hers who planned and urged him on:

I gave thee the sign and the word.
I touched with mine hand the sword—

Then she kneels to cover the body:

Her that I loved of yore,
Her that I hated sore—

her last words, except at the end to bid her brother farewell.

The three women have nothing in common but their situation. Æschylus' Electra is gentle and loving and dutiful, driven on against her own nature by the duty so all-important in antiquity, to exact vengeance for a father's death; but not only completely incapable herself of carrying it out, not even equal to facing her brother's doing so.

To Sophocles she is an embittered, stern, strong woman, who lives for one thing only, vengeance. Completely brave, never stooping to submit to those who have absolute power over her; resolved if Orestes does not return, to try to kill her father's murderers herself or die; knowing no least hesitation before killing her mother or shadow of regret when she is dead; and yet touched here and there with something of pathos.

Euripides' picture is by far the most carefully studied. He too draws an embittered woman, but one in whom the lesser insults rankle as much as the great wrongs done her. She hates her poverty and her grimy hut and her poor clothes, along with her father's murderers. She is as determined as Sophocles' heroine that her mother shall be killed, indeed she helps in the murder, as Sophocles does not have her do, but the moment the deed is done she turns upon herself with a passion of loathing and remorse, and at the end, covering her mother's body, she remembers that she loved her.

Each of the three is an individual woman different from the other two but all are drawn with complete clarity. There is nothing complicated in them, nothing to be doubtfully analyzed. There they stand, unmistakeably outlined, each herself, a person, greatly suffering and able to exalt us by the passion of her pain, but simple, direct, easy to understand, an example of "the plain reporting of the significant." Our attention is to be directed elsewhere, to matters of a wider scope than the inner conflicts of a complex nature.

If types were what the Greek drama had centered in, bloodless representatives of humanity, and all three Electras were essentially the same—a woman, any woman, possessed by the spirit of vengeance—the plays so written would not have been tragedies. The idea of the type is as indefensible theoretically as it is false actually. A tragedy cannot take place around a type. There is no such thing as typical suffering except in the mind, a pallid image of the philosopher's making, not the artist's. Pain is the most individualizing thing on earth. It is true that it is the great common bond as well but that realization comes only when it is over. To suffer is to be alone; to watch another suffer is to know the barrier that shuts each of us away by himself. Only individuals can suffer and only individuals have a place in tragedy. The personages of the Greek drama show first and foremost what suffering is in a great soul, and therefore they move us to pity and awe. Emotions are not aroused by an abstraction of the mind, but Hecuba is forever something to us to stir the feelings and quicken the spirit. Tragedy belongs to the domain of poetry which has nothing to do with the type.

The type belongs to comedy, intellectual comedy, the comedy of wit and satire. According as an art is strongly intellectual or not, the balance is tipped toward the type or toward the individual. In modern days the art which is inclined toward the typical, which is centered in what the mind and the eye perceive, is best exemplified by the French. The individualizing tendency, the preoccupation with the deep and lonely life of each human being, marks the English. The French are interested in what things are;

the English in what things mean. They are the great poets of the modern world as the French are the great intellectualists.

In a Molière comedy the central character is a type, only slightly individualized. Tartuffe is not a hypocrite, he is the hypocrite. His creator has not only depicted his hypocrisy with such complete fidelity that the vice is stamped clearly forevermore, but he has at the same time so heightened it—*l'exagération juste* is the French phrase—that hypocrisy is embodied in Tartuffe. He is a great artistic creation; he is not a living human being. Like all Molière's characters he moves on the stage, not in real life. Molière is called by common consent a great comic poet but he has nothing of the poet in him unless the word is used to cover all creative genius. His comedy of wit, irony, and satire is the creation of the crystal-clear intellect, the farthest remove from that which allies the lunatic, the lover, and the poet. But to Shakespeare, the poet, types meant nothing at all. His characters are people in real life, never thought of as personages of the stage. Falstaff sits at his ease in his inn; he walks the London streets; always he moves against the background of life; it is inconceivable that he should be placed forever on the theatre boards. Is it a stage wood and moonlight of the electric arc that come to mind with Bottom and his crew? The green plot is their stage, the hawthorn brake their tiring house, the chaste beams of the wat'ry moon their light. To think of Beatrice and Benedict is to be transported to an orchard as inevitably as to think of Alceste and Célimène is to be in fancy seated before the footlights.

Life is what the spirit is concerned with, the individual. Abstractions from life are what the mind is concerned with, the classified, the type. The Greeks were concerned with both. They wanted to know what things are and what things mean. They did not lose the individual in the type nor the type in the individual, Tartuffe's universal truth or Falstaff's living reality. The most familiar of all the sayings that has come down to us from classic times was spoken indeed by a Roman but it is a purely Greek conception, the basic idea of one of the greatest of Greek philosophies,

"I am a man and nothing in mankind do I hold alien to me."

In Greek tragedy the figures are seen very simply from afar, parts of a whole that has no beginning and no end, and yet in some strange fashion their remoteness does not diminish their profoundly tragic and individual appeal. They suffer greatly and passionately and therefore they are greatly, passionately alive.

There is only one other masterpiece that can help us to an understanding of this method, the life of Christ. It is the supreme tragedy but it is tragedy after the Greek model. The figure of Christ is outlined with complete simplicity, and yet by no possibility could He be thought of as a type. In a Shakespeare tragedy the moving power is that the characters are so shown to us, we can look deep into the mystery of the human soul, as we cannot even with our nearest and our dearest. And the result is that we identify ourselves with them; we ourselves become in our degree Hamlet or Lear. That is not the moving power of a Greek drama nor has it anything to do with what moves us in the Gospels. The Evangelists never let us know what went on within when the words they record were spoken and the deeds they tell of done. "And Peter said, Man, I know not what thou sayest. And immediately while he yet spake, the cock crew. And the Lord turned and looked upon Peter."

Our sense of the tragedy of the Gospels does not come from our identifying ourselves with Christ nor from any sense of deep personal knowledge. He is given to us more simply drawn than any other character anywhere, and more unmistakable in His individuality than any other. He stands upon the tremendous stage of the conflict of good and evil for mankind, and we are far removed; we can only watch. That agony is of another sort from ours. Yet never, by no other spectacle, has the human heart been so moved to pity and to awe. And after some such fashion the Greek dramatists worked.

It is an achievement possible only when mind and spirit are balanced. The mind simplifies, for it sees everything related, everything part of a whole, as Christ in the Gospel story is the mediator between God and man. The spirit individualizes. The figure of the Son of Man, so depicted that throughout the centuries a great multitude which no man could number, of all nations and kindreds and peoples and tongues, have suffered with Him and understood through Him, is the creation of the spirit.

So too the characters in Greek drama were the result of the Greek balance, individuals that showed a truth for all humanity in every human being, mankind in a man. The Greek mind that must see a thing never in and for itself but always connected with what was greater, and the Greek spirit that saw beauty and meaning in each separate thing, made Greek tragedy as they made Greek sculpture and Greek architecture, each an example of something completely individual at once simplified and given its significance by being always seen as connected with something universal, an expression of the Greek ideal, "beauty, absolute, simple, and everlasting . . . the irradiation of the particular by the general."

# *Chapter* XVII

## THE WAY OF THE MODERN WORLD

IN ITS ultimate analysis the balance between the particular and the general is that between the spirit and the mind. All that the Greeks achieved was stamped by that balance. In a sense, it was the cause of all they did. The flowering of genius in Greece was due to the immense impetus given when clarity and power of thought was added to great spiritual force. That union made the Greek temples, statues, writings, all the plain expression of the significant; the temple in its simplicity; the statue in its combination of reality and ideality; the poetry in its dependence upon ideas; the tragedy in its union of the spirit of inquiry with the spirit of poetry. It made the Athenians lovers of fact and of beauty; it enabled them to hold fast both to the things that are seen and to the things that are not seen in all they have left behind for us, science, philosophy, religion, art.

But since the days of Greece that balanced view has been the rarest of achievements. The Western world has not taken outright the way of the spirit, nor the way of the mind, but wavered between the two, giving adherence now to one, now to the other, never able finally to discard either yet powerless to reconcile their claims.

When the Greek city-state came to an end, in the bewilderment and insecurity that followed, men turned away from the visible world of the mind to the Stoics and the unshakable security of their kingdom of the spirit. In like manner, during the first centuries after Christ the trend of the Church, poor and weak and persecuted, was strongly away from the visible. Those were the years that saw the anchorites of the desert; the saint who lived upon a pillar; they saw self-torture and self-mutilation exalted. The things that are seen began to be viewed not only as negligible but as evil, drawing men away from the pure contemplation of the invisible. With the coming of the great monastic orders, that extreme tendency was checked; learning and art had a place and austerities were moderated, but the misery that underlay the lovely superstructure of the Middle Ages worked as misery has always done, turning men against the bitter reality of life, and freedom of thought was as unknown as if Greece had never lived. With the Renaissance and the rediscovery of Greece the pendulum swung far over to the other side. Grim wretchedness had ceased to be a matter of course in the Italian cities. People had begun to enjoy themselves and they were using their minds. They demanded liberty to think and to love life and the beauty of earth, but in their turn they ended by regarding as negligible the things that are not seen and they made their gain finally at the cost of morality and ethics. The Reformation asserted both morality and man's right to think for himself, but denied beauty and the right of enjoyment. The last great swing of the pendulum was in the late nineteenth century when the battle was fought for scientific truth, and in the victory religion and art and the claims of the spirit were all slighted or discarded.

Never since Greek days has the balance been maintained throughout; only very seldom has it been achieved even in a single field. Here and there through the ages, however, it has come to pass in this matter or in that, and always, even when so circumscribed, it has accomplished something great and of lasting good. When the wisest of Roman lawgivers said that the enforcement of an absolutely just law without any exceptions, irrespective of particular differences, worked absolute injustice, he was declaring in effect that Rome had been able in this one matter to perceive the balance between the individual and the general, between the claims of the single man and the majority, between men's sympathy and their reason. In this one field Rome reached the balance Greece reached in every field she entered, and Rome has been the lawmaker for the world.

The only balance we can see with any degree of clearness that we are struggling toward to-day is in some sort like that achieved by Rome. The opposition between the spirit and the mind which we are chiefly conscious of is that between the individual and the community. Our great achievement that which our age will stand for above all, is Science, but modern science, unlike that of Greece, has kept to the mind alone, and the balance there between the law and the exception, the particular and the general, is only intellectual; the spiritual does not enter in. As regards our art and our literature nothing certain can be perceived. The trend toward the individual reached its height in Shakespeare and the Renaissance painters; nothing since has approached in greatness what was then done, but the individual has continued to be the focus of all our art.

At the moment, there seems to be discernible a turning away from this extreme individualization, but the movement is too new for us to know whether it has any real importance or promise for the future. The balance we are seeing more and more distinctly before us will be, if ever it is achieved, a new one, because we are directing our chief energies toward new fields of social and economic forces, and, most of all, because we have a knowledge and a point of view about the individual which have never been in the world before.

For nineteen hundred years the West has been undergoing a process of education in the particular versus the general. We have been in school to the foremost individualist of all time who declared that the very hairs of each man's head were numbered. That intense individualization has molded our spirit, and it has brought to us problems new in the history of mankind, together with trouble of mind and bitter disagreement where once there was ease and unanimity. It is not men's greed, nor their ambition, nor yet their machines, it is not even the removal of their ancient landmarks, that is filling our present world with turmoil and dissension, but our new vision of the individual's claim against the majority's claim.

Things were simple in days of old when the single man had no right at all if a common good conflicted, his life taken for any purpose that served the public welfare, his blood sprinkled over the fields to make the harvest plentiful. Then a new idea, the most disturbing ever conceived, dawned, that every human being had rights. Men began to question what had been unquestioned since the world began: a father's authority, a king's, a slaveholder's. Perplexity and division came where all had been plain and simple. The individual had made his appearance and nothing was to be plain and simple again; no clear distinction could be drawn any more between what was just and unjust. To-day we see, fitfully and dimly, but more constantly and clearly, the individual sacrificed to the greatest good of the greatest number—the coal miner, the criminal in the death-house. Everywhere we are distracted by the claim of the single man against the common welfare.

Along with this realization of each unit in the mass has come an over-realization of ourselves. We are burdened with over-realization. Not that we can perceive too clearly the rights and wrongs of every human being but that we feel too deeply our own, to find in the end that what has meaning only for each one alone has no real meaning at all.

Greek scientists in their century or two of life remade the universe. They leaped to the truth by an intuition, they saw a whole made up of related parts, and with the sweep of their vision the old world of hodge-podge and magic fell away and a world of order took its place. They could only begin the detailed investigation of the parts, but, ever since, Science has by an infinite labor confirmed their intuition of the whole. Greek artists found a disorganized world of human beings, a complex mass made up of units unrelated and disordered, and they too had an intuition of parts all belonging to a whole. They saw what is permanently important in a man and unites him to the rest.

We cannot recapture the Greek point of view; the simplicity and directness of their vision are not for us. The wheels of time never turn backward, and fortunately so. The deep integration of the idea of the individual

gained through the centuries since Greece can never be
lost. But modern science has made generalizations of
greater truth than the Greeks could reach through a greater
knowledge of individual facts. If we can follow that method and through our own intense realization of ourselves
reach a unity with all men, seeing as deeply as the great
tragic poets of old saw, that what is of any importance
in us is what we share with all, then there will be a new
distribution in the scales and the balance held so evenly
in those great days of Greece may be ours as well. The
goal which we see ourselves committed to struggle toward
without method or any clear hope, can be attained in no
other way: a world where no one shall be sacrificed against
his will, where general expediency which is the mind of
mankind, and the feeling for each human being which is
the spirit and the heart of mankind, shall be reconciled.

"For we war not against flesh and blood," wrote St.
Paul, "but against principalities and powers. . . ." The
bitterest conflicts that have divided the minds of men and
set family against family, and brother against brother,
have not been waged for emperor or king, but for one
side of the truth to the suppression of the other side. And
yet, as our struggle to-day is again proving, there is something within us that will not let us rest in the divided truth.
Even though the way of the West since Greece has been
always to set mind against spirit, never to grasp the twofold aspect of all human things, yet we are not able to give
ourselves wholly up to one and let the other drop from
our consciousness. Each generation in turn is constrained
to try to reconcile the truth the spirit knows with the truth
the mind knows, to make the inner world fit into the ever-
changing frame of the outer world. To each in turn it appears impossible; either the picture or the frame must go,
but the struggle toward adjustment never ends, for the
necessity to achieve it is in our nature.

The East can let the frame go and give up the struggle. We of the West, slaves to the reason, cannot. For
brief periods we have thought that we could let the picture
go, but that negation of the things each man knows most
surely for himself is always partial and of short duration.

In our present effort after adjustment which not only seems to us, but is, more difficult than any before because we are aware of so much more, it is worth our while to consider the adjustments achieved in the past. Of them all, the Greek was the most complete. The Greeks did not abstract away the outside world to prefer the claims of the world within; neither did they deny the spirit in favor of its incarnation. To them the frame and the picture fitted; the things that are seen and the things that are not seen harmonized.

For a hundred years Athens was a city where the great spiritual forces that war in men's minds flowed along together in peace; law and freedom, truth and religion, beauty and goodness, the objective and the subjective—there was a truce to their eternal warfare, and the result was the balance and clarity, the harmony and completeness, the word Greek has come to stand for. They saw both sides of the paradox of truth, giving predominance to neither, and in all Greek art there is an absence of struggle, a reconciling power, something of calm and serenity, the world has yet to see again.

# REFERENCES

PAGE LINE

20  25   A summary of Plato's comparison in *Laws,* VII, 819: All freemen should learn as much of these branches of knowledge (i.e. the Mathematical) as every child in Egypt is taught when he learns the alphabet. Arithmetical games have been invented for the children, which they learn as a pleasure.

23  2   Pindar, N., VII, 6.

23  8   e.g., Thuc., I, 126.

23  21   Plato, *Tim.,* 22 C.

23  28   The Roman games played an important part in the life of the Romans, but, as has often been remarked, the Greeks played; the Romans watched others play. Pliny asks how any man of sense can enjoy seeing the dreary round of fights. As a result—or as a cause—the contests were brutal. At the games for Anchises in the *Æneid,* the challenger flings into the ring his cæstus, stiff with lead and iron and spattered with blood and brains. Many a Latin epigram bears witness to the brutal doings. One on a victor in Nero's reign runs:

      This victor, glorious in his olive wreath,
      Had once eyes, eyebrows, nose, and ears,
        and teeth.
      [*Anth. Pal.,* XI, 75, tr. Gilbert West. Quoted
         by Gardner, *The Greek Games.*]

24  15   Pindar, *Pyth.,* VIII, 135.

24  28   Sophocles, *Antig.,* 1142. (Whenever the name of the translator is not given, the author is responsible for the translation.)

24  30   Idem, *Ajax,* 692.

PAGE LINE

24  34  Idem, *Œd. Col.*, 670.

25  7  These words are put into the mouth of a Phæacian (*Odys.*, VIII, 245), but it would be splitting hairs to argue that therefore they do not express a Greek feeling. The Phæacians are not represented as Sybarites but as good athletes and master-seamen.

25  12  Xenophanes, *ap. Athen.*, 54.

25  17  Aristophanes, *Clouds*, 1007.

26  2  Pindar, *Pyth.*, IV, 524. R. W. Livingstone, tr.

26  16  Æschylus, *Persians*, 241. Hdt., VII, 104.

27  16  Æschylus, *Agam.*, 1132. (The author has reproduced here the metre of the original, as in all the quotations from the choruses of the *Agamemnon.*)

28  21  Plato, *Laws*, X, 908.

28  37  Idem, X, 909.
There is a long passage in the *Prometheus*, which has to do with divination, "the dark and riddling art" (*Prom.*, 497), with omens from the flight of birds, from the inward parts of the sacrifice, etc. But as early as Homer the characteristic Greek attitude is expressed in Hector's words: "The one best omen is to fight for our country." (*Iliad*, XII, 243.)

29  17  Hdt., I, 53.

29  22  Plato, *Charm.*, 164 D.

31  14  This comparison is adapted from that given by R. W. Livingstone in *The Greek Genius and Its Meaning to Us*.

31  34  Socrates was executed; Anaxagoras banished; Protagoras and Diagoras of Melos obliged to flee.

32  14  Plato, *Meno.*, 99–100.

33  2  Idem, *Protag.*, 310*ff.* (abridged).

33  20  Idem, *Rep.*, IV, 435 E.

34  11  Aristotle, *Eth.*, 1177 b. 27.

35  18  Quoted by D'A. W. Thompson in *The Legacy of Greece*.

36  14  Æschylus, *Supp.*, 592.

36  30  Idem, 93.

37  1  Plato, *Apol.*, 41 C.

37  14  Idem, *Phædo*, 91*ff.*

PAGE LINE
59  24  Idem, 396.
59  28  Plato, *Phæd.*, 234–5.
        In this, as in all quotations from Plato, Jowett's translation has been used. In practically every case the passage quoted has been abbreviated.
60   1  Thuc., II, 40.
60  26  Pindar, *Pyth.*, IX, 66.
62   8  Horace, *Carm.*, IV, 2.
69  27  O. II, W. III.
69  33  O. IX.
69  35  P. VI.
70   6  W. III.
70  26  O. I.
70  29  W. VII.
70  37  P. I.
71   3  W. V.
71   6  O. IX.
71   9  O. I.
71  16  O. II.
73   3  O. V.
73   6  P. XI.
73  30  P. VIII.
75  25  The tale is told by a literary gossip, Aulus Gellius, who lived in the late second century, A.D.
76  32  Thuc., II, 40.
78  19  Idem, II, 35*ff.* (abbreviated).
79  12  Sophócles, *Œd. Tyr.*, 338.
79  28  Pindar, *Pyth.*, XI, 75, Professor Paul Shorey tr.
81   4  Plato, *Protag.*, 314 E.*ff.*
81  26  Plato, *Theætetus*, 173 D.
82   9  Idem, *Phæd.*, 227, 228, 230 C.
83  10  Idem, *Symposium*, 175 B.*ff.*
85   4  Thuc., II, 41.
85  16  Plato, *Theæt.*, 175 D. E.
85  23  Plato, *Menexenus*, 235 E.*ff.*
86  16  Idem, *Symp.*, 194 D.
86  23  Idem, 214 A., 219 E.*ff.*
87   7  Idem, 223 C.
87  19  Idem, *Lysis*, 207 C. 223.
87  40  Idem, *Cratylus*, 384 B. 440 C.
88  28  Idem, *Symp.*, 173 C.
88  31  Idem, *Phæd.*, 229 B.
        In all of the quotations from Aristophanes that

follow, the passages have been abridged.

In reproducing the original metres I have not attempted any accurate, syllabic correspondence, as I have done in the translations from the choral parts of the *Agamemnon*, but only a reproduction of the general effect of the verse. I have not hesitated to make Aristophanes' favorite seven-foot line end on an accent, as is practically essential in a rhymed version. And I have never reproduced the trimetre. To my mind the true English version of the Greek six-foot line is the five-foot line. English trimetre is not swift and light, but slow and weighted:

> A shielded scutcheon blushed with
>      blood of queens and kings.

The effect of the Greek is essentially the same as that of:

> St. Agnes' Eve—Ah, bitter chill it was.

E. H.

| | | |
|---|---|---|
| 92 | 9 | *Acharn.*, 515*ff.* |
| 92 | 27 | *Wasps*, 71*ff.* |
| 93 | 24 | *Thesmoph.*, 29*ff.* One of the very rare examples of the use of rhyme in Greek is found in lines 54–7. |
| 95 | 12 | *Clouds*, 218*ff.* |
| 96 | 21 | *Clouds*, 1355*ff.* |
| 97 | 14 | *Plutus*, 26*ff.* |
| 101 | 33 | *Clouds*, 961*ff.* |
| 102 | 31 | *Acharn.*, 309*ff.* |
| 103 | 31 | Lawrence Housman **tr.** |
| 104 | 21 | *Thesmoph.*, 3*ff.* |
| 106 | 6 | *Birds*, 904*ff.* (except first four lines, not in the original metre). |
| 107 | 32 | *Knights*, 3*ff.* |
| 109 | 31 | *Plutus*, 901*ff.* |
| 111 | 7 | *Knights*, 149*ff.* |
| 112 | 34 | *Thesmoph.*, 785*ff.* |
| 118 | 3 | Æschylus, *Agam.*, 1042. |
| 118 | 22 | Euripides, *Hecuba*, 330. |
| 118 | 29 | Plato, *Rep.*, 563 B. |
| 119 | 4 | Aristotle, *Pol.*, I, 4, 13. |
| 119 | 25 | Plato, *Theæt.*, 155 D. |
| 121 | 3 | *History*, III, 106. |

PAGE LINE

121  14  Idem, IV, 36.
122  15  Idem, I, 182.
122  17  Idem, III, 38.
124   3  Idem, VII, 152.
124  17  Idem, II, 73.
125   4  Idem, VII, 191.
125  19  Idem, II, 53.
126  28  Idem, IV, 9.
127  10  Idem, IX, 88.
127  20  Idem, V, 92.
128  32  Book VI gives the account of Marathon.
130  12  Book VII tells of Xerxes' advance.
130  26  Æschylus, *Pers.*, 820.
131  23  Book VII tells of his defeat and flight.
133  21  Æschylus, *Pers.*, 402.
135  31  *Hist.*, IV, 104, 1.
136  31  Aristoph., *Acharn.*, 515*ff*.
137  18  Polybius, *Hist.*, VI.
137  40  *Hist.*, I, 74.
138  23  Solon, frg. 3.
139  37  Euripides, *Supp.*, 310*ff*.
140   9  *Hist.*, II, 65.
141  22  Æschylus, *Agam.*, 378.
142  30  *Hist.*, II, 66.
144  12  Plutarch, *Lycurgus*, 24.
145  11  Book VII gives the Sicilian Expedition.
146  15  *Hist.*, III, 36, 1*ff*.
146  30  Idem, V, 84*ff*.
147  35  Idem, III, 82, 3.
148  16  Xenophon, *Œcon.*, II.
149  12  *Cyneget.*, V*ff*.
150   6  *Symp.*
152   8  *Occonom.*, VII*ff*.
154  31  *Memorabilia.*
162   6  *Cyropædia.*
164  18  *Thuc.*, II, 37, 2.
166   7  W. Macneile Dixon, *Tragedy*, page 51.
174  29  Æschylus, *Agam.*, 1042.
175   4  Idem, 326*ff*.
176  35  Idem, 1379*ff*. (with omissions).
177   9  Idem, *Prom.*, 989 (with omissions).
178   5  *Frogs*, Professor Gilbert Murray tr.

PAGE LINE

179  7  Æschylus, *Agam.*, 459. (In the metre of the original.)

179  12  Idem, *Agam.*, 976 . . . 90. (In the metre of the original.)

179  17  Idem, 1087 . . . 1101. (In the metre of the original.)

180  25  Idem, 1217.

181  18  Idem, *Choeph.*, 743*ff.*

182  34  Idem, 889 (with omissions).

184  18  Idem, *Agam.*, 429*ff.* (In the metre of the original.)

185  4  Idem, 757*ff.*

188  20  Sophocles, *Œd. Tyr.*, 1215*ff.* (with omissions).

189  17  Idem, *Antig.*, 821.

189  20  Idem, *Trach.*, 458.

189  32  Idem, 128*ff.*

190  19  Idem, *Œd. Tyr.*, 883*ff.*

190  26  Idem, 864*ff.* (with omissions).

191  18  Idem, *Ajax*, 472*ff.*

191  25  Æschylus, *Supp.*, 779*ff.* (with omissions).

192  1  Sophocles, *Antig.*, 878*ff.*

192  6  Æschylus, *Septem.*, 1042.

192  16  The comparison with Simonides in the *Peace* was sixteen years earlier, a long time in the swift life of Athens.

192  30  Sophocles, *Œd. Tyr.*, 1471*ff.* (with omissions).

195  12  Idem, *Electra*, 1448*ff.* (with omissions).

201  23  All the passages quoted from Euripides are taken from Professor Gilbert Murray's translations.

209  7  Æschylus, *Supp.*, 95.

209  20  Plato, *Tim.*, IX.

210  5  Hesiod, Op. 289.

211  22  Anaxagoras.

212  40  Hesiod, Op. 276.

213  9  Pindar, O. IX, 28.

213  18  Xenophanes of Colophon.

215  3  *De Legib.*, II, 4, 36.

215  12  Plutarch, *Consol.*

215  24  Idem, frg. *de Anima.*

215  35  *Frogs*, 153*ff.*

217  10  Protagoras.

218  35  Aristotle, *Eth.*, I, 13, 6.

219  14  *Apol.*, 41 D.

PAGE LINE

219  27  *Phæd.*, 115 A.

220  11  *Eth.*, X, 7, 7.

224  18  Æschylus, *Agam.*, 346.

224  31  Idem, 1372*ff.* (with omissions).

242   7  Sophocles, *Ajax,* 644*ff.* Calverley tr.

242  18  Plotinus.

248  11  For this idea compare Professor Gilbert Murray, *Euripides* preface, XXIII.

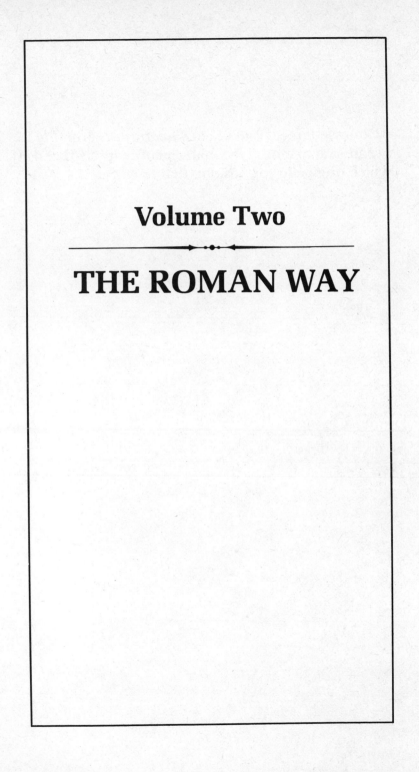

Volume Two

# THE ROMAN WAY

Acknowledgment is made to *Theatre Arts Monthly* for permission to reprint the material in chapters II and III which originally appeared in that magazine.

To
D·F·R·

*—nostrorum sermonum*
*candide iudex*

# CONTENTS

# PREFACE

IF *a personal confession may be allowed, although I have read Latin ever since my father, who knew nothing about methods for softening the rigors of study, started me at the age of seven on* Six Weeks' Preparation for Caesar, *I have read it, except during the brief intermission of college, for my own pleasure merely, exactly as I would read French or German. I open a volume of Cicero or Horace or Virgil purely for the enjoyment of what they write, not in the slightest degree because they write in Latin or because they are essential to a knowledge of Roman history. What the Romans did has always interested me much less than what they were, and what the historians have said they were is beyond all comparison less interesting to me than what they themselves said.*

*It was inevitable, therefore, that when I came to think about the outline of* The Roman Way, *I should see it entirely as it was marked out by the Roman writers. I have considered them alone in writing this book. It is in no sense a history of Rome, but an attempt to show what the Romans were as they appear in their great authors, to set forth the combination of qualities they themselves prove are peculiarly Roman, distinguishing them from the rest of antiquity. A people's literature is the great text-book for real knowledge of them. The writings of the day show the quality of the people as no historical reconstruction can. When we*

263

read Anthony Trollope or W. S. Gilbert we get an incomparably better view of what mid-Victorian England was like than any given by the historians. They will always be our best text-books for an understanding of the force back of those years of unparalleled prosperity for the favored few—the character and the outlook of the upper-class Englishman.

That is the kind of text-book I have depended upon exclusively. For each period I have taken only the accounts given by contemporary writers. The contents of the book are the result of a selection based not upon personal preferences but upon how much a writer shows of the life and character of the men of his own times. Plautus and Terence from this point of view are of the greatest importance, as they not only paint the very first picture we have of Rome, but do so in great detail. The century in between Terence and Cicero is, of course, passed over, since none of the writings have survived. Cicero's Rome is taken up at greater length than any other period because his letters are the best source of information we possess for any age, not of Rome only, but of all antiquity.

The force Rome had to mould her people is evident on every page of her literature. All her men of letters were Romans first, individual artists only second. Different, of course, from each other, as Cicero, for instance, is different from Tacitus, or Horace from Juvenal, their differences are yet superficial compared to their fundamental resemblances. During the four centuries which saw the beginning and end of Latin Literature as it has come down to us, every writer shows the main outlines of the Roman way.

# CHAPTER I

## COMEDY'S MIRROR

WHEN the curtain rings up for the stupendous drama which we know as Ancient Rome, it is raised surprisingly on two comic writers. They are the first to make their appearance on that mighty stage. The oldest piece of Roman literature we have is a collection of comedies. Only two earlier writers are known to us and of their work a few lines is all that is left. Not only Latin literature, but our own direct knowledge of Rome, have their source in comedy, and that not of a rude, popular sort, but sophisticated, a true comedy of manners. The fact, seldom meditated upon, is a little disturbing. We all have our idea of the Romans, implanted by education, by many books: an indomitable people, stern and steadfast and serious beyond all others. It is disconcerting that the fountainhead of our knowledge should be the very reverse of all this. Our notion of the proper beginning for the literature of the mistess of the world would be something martial and stirring, old ballads of valiant men and warlike deeds with spirited bards to sing them, culminating in a great epic, a Latin *Iliad*. But it actually begins as far away from that as the wide realm of letters allows, in a series of comedies which are avowedly founded upon the popular Greek comedy of the day.

265

No other great national literature goes back to an origin borrowed in all respects. In Greece the development was the natural one, from songs and stories handed down by word of mouth and added to through unknown ages. There was a spontaneous desire in the people—the farmers, shepherds, fighting men—for imaginative expression, which ultimately took literary shape and was preserved. With the Romans it was just the other way about. The literary shape came first, across the sea, from Greece. The desire for expression was secondary, following upon the discovery of an appropriate form ready-made to hand. The fact is full of significance for the Roman mentality.

Rome literature appears suddenly, during the third century B.C., in the generation after the First Punic War, and not only comedy, but everything else as well is modelled upon the Greek. There is hardly even a suggestion anywhere of a native product supplanted by the imported. We find, indeed, a metre never met with elsewhere which the first translator from the Greek used, and a few references in later writers to old ballads heard in boyhood, but that is all. Whether the truth is that the Roman shepherds and farmers, with the strong practical bent that later marked them, had little inclination to spend valuable time in singing songs and making up stories, or whether the literary men, when they finally appeared, despised the popular productions as beneath the notice of writers who were out to bring culture to Rome and bring it quick, the fact is equally illuminating. A sense for poetry was not strong in the Roman people. Their natural genius did not urge them on to artistic expression. Rome was said to have been founded in the year 753 B.C., and the earliest piece of literature we know about is a translation of the *Odyssey* made at the end of the First Punic War, some five hundred years later. For all these centuries it would seem that the Romans felt little impulsion to express in any form what the world was showing them and life bringing them. Later Roman critics speak of a native comedy, dramatic improvisations at festivals, but there is no warrant for supposing that it was ever written down and it is certain that it had no direct literary descendants.

For us, Roman literature begins with Plautus, writer of comedies after the Greek fashion, and what he shows us of Roman life is the first glimpse we have of Rome. It is a brief glimpse. The curtain raised for him and his successor, Terence, is quickly lowered. When it is raised again we are looking at the age of Cicero. With the exception of a treatise on agriculture, curiously the one surviving work of the indomitable old censor of morals, Cato, we have only fragmentary bits of the literature in between, no secure basis upon which to reconstruct the city that was already the dominating power in the world. It is true that while Terence, the younger of the two comedians, was producing his plays the Greek Polybius was writing a great history on the rise and growth of the Roman power, of which a considerable part remains, but his concern is with Rome's wars and with the Romans as men of war. The only contemporary information given us about the rest of Roman life up to the first century B.C. comes from the work of the two playwrights.

We may perhaps account ourselves fortunate that comedy was the survivor. There is no better indication of what the people of any period are like than the plays they go to see. Popular drama shows the public quality as nothing else can. But comedy does more. It must present the audience, as tragedy need not, with a picture of life lived as they know it. The comedy of each age holds up a mirror to the people of that age, a mirror that is unique. Ancient comedy, made up for us of four playwrights whose work alone has survived, the Greek Aristophanes and Menander, and the Roman Plautus and Terence, is a mirror where may be seen vividly reflected the Greek and Roman people in periods of notable significance to us: the great day of Greece, an influence still felt in all our thought

and our art, together with the age directly succeeding
it; the Rome of a hundred years later, when Carthage
had been twice defeated and the foundations were
solidly laid of the Roman civilization to which our own
goes directly back. What we want most of all to know
about these two greatest nations of antiquity, is the
kind of people that made them up, the every-day men
and women, and this history in its concern for wars
and laws does not give us. They were the theatre crowd,
above all, the comic theatre. It is there we can find
them. Popular comedy reflects the average person.

If the Greek tragedians had been lost and we had
only Aristophanes left, we should have a very fair idea
of the private citizen in Periclean Athens. How little
resemblance he had to the theatre-going man elsewhere,
what a completely different sort of amusement he
wanted, may be seen in every one of Aristophanes'
plays. Aristophanes has his own receipt for comedy,
unlike, so he himself tells us, all that went before him
and certainly never followed by any dramatist since. In
choruses of the *Wasps* and the *Peace,* the methods are
described which were used by the most popular playwright in Athens to draw his public:

> Your poet in all of his plays has scorned to show you
>     upon the stage
> A few paltry men and their mean little ways. A great
>     theme he gave you—the age.
> He has stripped bare the monster with eyes flaming red,
>     foul vice with his vile perjured band.
> He has battled with spectral shapes, the pains and
>     pangs that are racking our land.[1]
> It was he that indignantly swept from the stage the
>     rabble that cluttered its boards,
> Greedy gods, vagabonds, swindling scamps, whining
>     slaves, sturdy beggars, despicable hordes.
> Such vulgar, contemptible lumber at once he bade from
>     the theatre depart,

[1] *Wasps,* v. 1027.

And then like an edifice stately and grand he raised
and ennobled the art.
High thoughts and high language he brought to the
stage, a humor exalted and rare,
Nor stooped with a scurrilous jest to assail some small-
man-and-woman affair.[a]

Here is clearly written what Aristophanes and his
audience wanted from the Comic Muse. In their eyes
she was great Comedy, fit to stand beside Tragedy, of
equal dignity and with essentially the same deep seriousness. The Old Comedy of Athens stands alone. It is as
unlike the comedy of all other countries and periods as
the age of Pericles is unlike all others. No small-man-
and-woman affair for Aristophanes. Great themes, a
grandiose conception of the world, belonged to Comedy,
as he saw her, just as much as they did to Tragedy, as
Æschylus saw her. That rabble he swept from the
stage, those stock characters, each with his fixed form
of antics, his thread-bare joke—"a few paltry men and
their mean little ways"—gave place to marvelous
figures: birds building a city in the sky that put all
earthly cities to shame; a band of tight-waisted buzzing
wasps to show up the law-courts; radiant Peace in all
her beauty; the inexorable world of the dead where art
receives its final award. This was Aristophanes' idea of
Comedy's province. It died with him and was never
found again within the theatre.

The old kind of fun-making came to the fore when
he and his audience were gone. That edict of banishment he had proclaimed in great Comedy's name did
not hold beyond his lifetime. Back came the exiles,
the tricky servant, the braggart, the quack, the drunk-
ard, the cunning thief, familiar stock characters, so his
words tell us, four hundred years and more before
Christ. The depth of our ignorance about the past is not
often so vividly brought to mind. None of that crowded,
busy theatre is known to us, nothing of what must often

*Peace*, v. 739.

have been brilliant entertainment made by brilliant minds. A marvelous sense for the absurd and a very genius for observing and characterizing human nature put first upon the stage the personages which have held their place there ever since, with the brief exception of Aristophanes' lifetime. Latin comedy and through it all modern comedy have drawn upon the figures of fun unknown Greek playwrights made in the dim past. The small-man-and-woman affair, too, disdained by the great Athenian and his age, took lasting possession not only of the stage, but of literature as well. Aristophanes stands alone indeed. The men who fought at Salamis and planned the Acropolis and carved the Parthenon sculptures gave the laws to the Athenian drama, and when they died there was no audience any more for great Tragedy and great Comedy.

Athens, we are always told, was a democracy, based, of course, upon slavery because that was the prerequisite to civilized life in the ancient world; but except for that, a place where all men were free and politcally equal. But there are democracies and democracies. The Periclean pattern was not like that which succeeded it. There is a marked difference between a young and a full-grown democracy. In the first, aristocracy still lingers. Aristocratic standards are abroad. The democracy of Washington at Mt. Vernon wears another look from that of Mr. Coolidge in Vermont. Pericles was an aristocratic democrat and there is an extremely qualified democracy in Plato's young men. The theatre audiences of that day were people of highly cultivated tastes who could not be amused with the commonplace. But fourth century Athens was another matter. The aristocrats were gone and democracy was in secure possession. There was no need of fighting and suffering in its behalf. Athens was comfortable and undistinguished; life was lived on an easy middle-class level. The New Comedy, one ancient writer after another assures us, reflected the age, in especial the chief ornament and exponent of the innovation, Menander. An enthusiastic Alexandrian exclaims: "O Life, O Menander, which of you two was the plagiarist?"

Of all his fellow artists he alone has survived, but only in small part. No complete play has come down to us. Indeed, up to a few years ago he was directly known through short extracts merely, lines cited to illustrate some point, and the like. Indirectly, however, much was deduced from the unqualified praise and devoted imitation of him by ancient critics and writers. But the discovery of nearly the whole of one play and considerable portions of several others has made it dubious how far that great reputation was deserved. They are pleasantly written, these plays, the characters not infrequently drawn with skilful and delicate touches, the dialogue occasionally entertaining, the plot contrived with some ingenuity; but more than that cannot be said of them at their best and at their worst they are very dull indeed. They are not funny. They are little dramas of little folk; a miniature art done in very quiet tones; subdued pictures of a well-to-do, completely commonplace society, showing the bad punished and the good rewarded, but moderately as the vices and virtues are moderate, and always a happy marriage to bring down the curtain. What would Aristophanes have made of them, one wonders. There is not the faintest reminiscence of his soaring imagination, not the most distant echo of his roaring laughter. The difference between the two playwrights illumines as nothing could better the change that had come over the Athenians in the space of hardly fifty years.

That brief flowering of genius, the golden age not of Greece alone but of all our western world, had been brought about by a lofty and exultant spirit, conscious of heroic deeds done and full of joyous courage for great enterprises to come. It had lived in the audiences who shouted at Aristophanes' riotous nonsense, who delighted in every brilliant bit of his satire, appreciated each delicate parody, with minds keen to follow his master mind. But the flame, so intense, so white-hot, quickly sank, leaving behind only a comfortable fireside warmth. Menander's audiences wanted nothing in the very least Aristophanic. They were out for pleasant, unexciting entertainment, reassuringly like their every-day life, and, above all, guaranteed to make no demands upon the intelligence. Comfort, prosperity, safety, was the order of the new day that produced the New Comedy. Under their soothing influence the Athenians changed so swiftly they were themselves surprised, and seeking for a cause laid it to Sparta's account. The world ever since has echoed them, but to read Menander is to understand perfectly how inevitable was the passing of the Periclean age, to perceive other far more potent causes than the victory of Sparta in the Peloponnesian War.

In Rome, comedy has an even greater significance for us. The two Roman comedians are immensely important, beyond the Greek even from one point of view, in that they made the actual models upon which European comedy formed itself. With them we enter the great sphere of Latin influence, mighty in moulding our civilization, direct and all-penetrating as never was that of Greece. Aristophanes founded no school. He had no followers, ancient or modern. Menander has lived only as a shadow in Roman plays. Plautus and Terence were the founders of the drama as we know it today.

But how far they hold up comedy's mirror to the life of their own times is a matter not easily determined. As has been said, they are all the literature of that period which we possess. There is not one contemporary record by which their credibility can be tested as a source of information about Rome. The question how closely they imitated the Greek New Comedy, to what degree they translated or followed their own genius, is one to delight the scholarly mind because it never can be settled by scholarly standards. The battle of the learned can be waged forever. Too little is left of Menander's work for even the most erudite to give the victory on that score to either side, and of his fellow-comedians nothing is left at all. However, the absence of clear-cut facts, with which alone the scholars are really concerned, is not fatal to the argument. In deciding the matter there are certain general aspects of the question which cannot be passed over and they tell conclusively for the originality of the two Romans.

Their own evidence in all they say about their work is strongly in favor of Menander. Their prologues give the names of the Greek plays, Menander's or one of his school, upon which they declare their own are modelled. Neither man ever lays claim to originality beyond the trifling degree involved in making occasionally one play out of two. In one of Terence's prologues he quite plumes himself on having translated a certain incident word for word. But on this point it must be remembered that in antiquity a copyist, far from being thought less of, was highly esteemed if he copied what was known to be good. Plautus and Terence would have every motive to emphasize their connection with the admired Menander. And against this evidence there is a consideration so weighty, it turns the scale decisively in favor of the plays being a veritable Roman product: the essential quality of a comic play.

Those who argue that they gave their audiences not Rome but Greece, foreign folk whose ways were strange to Romans, do not take into account the nature of comedy. It must present the familiar. An easy understanding of what is going on is essential. Let puzzlement or what follows inevitably in its train, disapproval, come in and comedy is at an end. The audience are not there to have their minds enlarged geographically or ethnologically. They want to see people they know about and life lived in the way they live it. A stray foreigner acting according to his own foolish foreign notions is a capital figure of fun, but a stage peopled with such would not be funny at all. In one of Plautus' plays a slave is rewarded for good service by being given a cask of wine and permission to entertain his friends. The feast that follows was essential to the plot of the Greek original so that Plautus could not leave it out, but he knew that it would seem strange to his hearers, indeed quite shocking to their ideas of how slaves should be treated, and he makes the slave turn to the audience and say: "Don't you be surprised that slaves drink, court, give invitations to dinner. That is allowed us at Athens." Plautus' instinct as a comedian was sure. He would not have his actors out of touch with his public. But this is the only occasion when he feels an explanation necessary.

The people who laughed at these plays were on terms of friendly intimacy with their characters and found nothing "foreign" in their ways. Those who hold to the contrary might as well argue that Antipholus and Dromio, whose originals are in a play by Plautus, are Romans—or Greeks—and not Elizabethans. Shakespeare would never have attempted to people his plays with Romans. *The Comedy of Errors* has no more to do with Rome—or with Ephesus—than *A Midsummer-Night's Dream* has to do with Athens. The English stamp is upon the two Dromios just as clearly as upon Bottom and his crew. *Les Fourberies de Scapin* follows Terence's *Phormio* so closely in many scenes that occasionally the dialogue is a direct translation, but Molière would never have fallen into the fatal mistake of making his personages anything but French. As Molière well knew, comedy's range does not reach beyond the national frontier—not even in our own age of Internationalism. Every continental comedy transported to us today must suffer a change on the way to make it acceptable to Americans.

It is true that both the Romans always state that the scene of their comedies is a Greek city, just as the names of the characters are Greek, but the fact has really no bearing at all upon the argument. There was an excellent reason for that convention which had nothing to do with the nationality of the people of the plays. It was of great practical importance for a Roman comedian to choose a far country for his fun. The

stage has always been a most attractive field for
legislators, and the Romans, who had a very passion for
passing laws about everything in the world, revelled in
the censorship. A law of the Twelve Tables condemned
people to be whipped who wrote anything defamatory,
and one of Plautus' contemporaries had been imprisoned
and then exiled—a punishment only less terrible than
death in those days—for writing a play in which there
was a single disrespectful allusion to dignitaries. Back
of this procedure was a fixed idea about what a Roman
citizen must be. A kind of divinity hedged him in and
no scurrilous playwright was to make him ridiculous.
Faced with this dilemma, comedy a matter of fun but
no fun to be made of Romans, the comedians sensibly
turned to foreign parts for their scenery. Further than
that they did not trouble themselves. These people with
Greek names walk in the forum, go to the capitol,
worship the Roman household gods, allude con-
temptuously to "those Greeks," and so on. To be consistent was not important, but to escape the censor was.

Political allusions, too, would have been equally
dangerous. Nothing really is more inconceivable than
Aristophanes at Rome. The Roman formula of condemnation when a man had done ill by the state, was:
*For diminishing the Majesty of the Republic.* The fate
of that arch-diminisher of majesties would have been so
swift in Rome, he would never have written a second
comedy. The thought has significance for Plautus at
least. Something in his rollicking, jovial spirit, his
exuberant vitality, recalls though ever so faintly the Old
Comedy. It is not hard to imagine his turning those
shrewd, twinkling eyes of his upon public as well as
private follies and giving us a picture of the Rome of
statesmen and politicians and great affairs, which would
make it live in some sort as Athens lives in Aristophanes.
But the Roman way was far from the Greek way. A
free stage or anything else free was not for Romans.
Order, well enforced by magistrates, was the Roman
idea.

Theories that go counter to the facts of human nature are foredoomed. Comedy in Rome to be comedy had of necessity to be Roman and no argument, linguistical, historical, archæological, can have any counterbalancing weight against this fundamental truth. The mirror of Plautus and Terence reflects not a strange, shadowy Greece, but their own day and their own city, the veritable Rome of the Republic.

# *CHAPTER II*

## ANCIENT ROME REFLECTED IN
## PLAUTUS AND TERENCE

ROMAN comedy plays the same rôle that all comedy everywhere plays. It takes us behind the scenes of history's stately drama. In Plautus' mirror the curious may see how that austere figure fixed in our minds from early schoolroom days, the Ancient Roman, appeared to view when he was out to be amused.

What do the words Republican Rome call to mind? Discipline, first and foremost, then frugality, hardihood; white-toga-ed figures of an incomparable dignity; ranks of fighting men drilled to the last degree of military precision; an aura of the simple life lived, not quite on heroic heights, but at any rate on perpetual battlefields; Cincinnatus at the plough; the death of a son decreed by a father for disobedience of orders even though a victory resulted. That is the sort of thing we think of as early Rome. This edifying picture is considerably enlarged and diversified by Roman comedy. In Plautus we get the reverse of the shield, the senator not in his toga but in the Roman equivalent of dressing-gown and slippers; the soldier dispensing alike with armour and discipline; dignity, iron resolution, the stern compulsion of duty, the entire arsenal of the antique Roman virtues, completely in the discard.

In the *Merchant,* one of Plautus' most entertaining

277

plays, a young fellow, sent on a business trip by his father, bought a lovely lady while away and has just landed bringing her back with him. As he comes on the stage his slave enters running, breathless, able only to gasp out: "Terrible—dreadful—awful—awful news— Oh, it's bad, bad."

MASTER
(*after repeated petition for something clear*)

*Speak it out. What *is* the matter? Don't dare say bad news again.

SLAVE

Oh, don't ask me. It's too awful.

MASTER

By the Lord, you'll be so thrashed—

SLAVE

If I must, I must. Your father—

MASTER
(*terrified*)
Father! What?

SLAVE

He saw the girl.

MASTER

Hell! How could he?

SLAVE
With his eyes.

*In the following translation, as in all others, the text has been condensed. Very few plays lend themselves to quotation. The actors are essential, and rightly so, to any real appreciation of them. But even more than most, Roman comedy would be wronged by a word for word rendering. These plays afford excellent scope for an actor, but they move slowly for a reader. To give the passages as they stand would mean to lose the point completely in any citation brief enough to be included here. In each case the metre of the original has been reproduced.

MASTER
But how, you fool?

SLAVE
By opening 'em.

MASTER
Damn you. Quibbling when my life's at stake.

SLAVE
Oh, cheer up. Worse to come.
Soon's he saw her the old blackguard started petting.

MASTER
Heavens! Her?

SLAVE
(*snorting*)
Strange it wasn't me—
(*The two young men go off to try to get the girl
safely away, and the father enters with a friend of his
own age, his next door neighbor.*)

FATHER
(*very sprightly*)
Come, how old d'you think I look?

FRIEND
(*dispassionately, looking him over*)
Decrepit. One foot in the grave.

FATHER
(*dashed for a moment, then recovering*)
Oh, your eyesight's failing. I'm a boy, old friend—not
eight years old.

FRIEND
Are you daft? Oh—second childhood. Yes, I quite agree.

FATHER
No, no.
(*archly*) I've begun to go to school, old man—four letters
learned today.

FRIEND

Eh? Four letters?

FATHER
LOVE

FRIEND
(*surveying him unsympathetically*)
              You in love with that gray head?
(*turning to audience*) If you ever saw a portrait of a
lover there he is.
The old dotard—feeble, tottering. A nice picture you'll
agree.
(*Appealed to for old acquaintance' sake, however, he
agrees to go to the ship and buy the girl for his friend,
and offers until the other can find a place for her, to take
her to his own house, as his wife is away. In the next
act he enters with the girl, who seems much agitated.*)

FRIEND
Come along, my girl. Don't cry. Don't spoil those pretty
eyes of yours.

GIRL
(*sobbing*)
Do be nice to me and tell me—

FRIEND
              There, there. Just be a good girl
And you'll see a good time's coming.

GIRL
Oh, dear, dear. Poor little me.

FRIEND
How's that?

GIRL
Where I come from it's the naughty girls
that have the fun.

FRIEND
That's to say there are no good ones?

GIRL
                                No, indeed. I never say
Things that everybody knows.


FRIEND
(*beginning to think she is far too nice for the old fool
next door*)
                By Jove, the girl's a perfect pearl.
Worth more than she cost to hear her talk. Well, come
my beauty, now.
Into the house with you quickly.


GIRL
                So I will, you dear old thing.


The selection could be duplicated over and over again.
Plautus loves the senator in his lighter moments. An
equal favorite is the soldier. In the first scene of his
*Braggart Captain* the captain enters with an attendant,
Artotrogus, and several orderlies carrying an enormous
shield.


CAPTAIN
(*strutting back and forth, Artotrogus at his heels,
mimicking him*)
Make ye my buckler's sheen outshine the radiant sun
To dazzle in the fray the myriad hosts that seek me.
Now do I pity this poor blade (*drawing his sword*) that
idle hangs
When so it longs to slash to bloody shreds my foes.
Artotrogus!


ARTOTROGUS
(*popping out with a wink at the orderlies*)
                Here, sir, beside our warrior bold.
Oh what a hero!


CAPTAIN
(*wrapped in great memories*)
                Who was he—that man I saved—


ARTOTROGUS
The time you puffed the foe away as with a breath?

CAPTAIN

A trifle really—a mere nothing, that, to me.


ARTOTROGUS

Indeed, sir, yes, compared with other feats I know
(*Aside*) You never did. (*Aloud*) In India that elephant—
My word, sir, how you smashed his foreleg into pulp
Just with your fist.


CAPTAIN
Oh, that? A careless tap, no more


ARTOTROGUS

Oh, sir, that other day too when you nearly killed
Five hundred at one stroke.


CAPTAIN
Ah, yes, mere infantry.
Poor beggars—so I let them live.


ARTOTROGUS
Oh, unsurpassed!
And all the women mad about you, simply mad.
Those two girls yesterday—


CAPTAIN
(*very careless*)
What did they talk about?


ARTOTROGUS

About you, sir, of course. Says one, Is he Achilles?
Says I, His brother. Oh, the other says, That's why
He looks so noble. And then didn't both of them
Beg me to lead you past their house like a parade,
To feast their eyes on.


CAPTAIN
(*yawning*)
It's a real affliction to me
To be so handsome.


Such is the appearance of the Father of the State, in
history's sober pages the pillar of the Republic's Majesty,

and of the martial ancestor of Caesar's legions, when they are presented in their lighter aspects, from what might be called the point of view of the home. The domestic drama, which is essentially the drama as we know it today, has its direct origin in these Latin plays. The intimate domesticity of family life in one of its most impressive manifestations, the Roman family, is the pivot they all turn on, and character after character is shown which the theatre has never let go of since. Here is the very first appearance upon the world's stage of the figure so dear to audiences everywhere, the Mother, essentially what she is to be through all the centuries down to our own with the white carnation and Mother's Day. Greece never knew her. The Mother, capitalized, was foreign to Greek ideas. But the Romans in such matters were just like overselves and often more so. One of Terence's good young men, finding on his return from a journey that his newly married wife has gone back to her father's house presumably because of a quarrel with her mother-in-law, is instantly aware of what he should do:

> Since she thinks it's not for her to give in to my
>     mother's ways,
> Says her self-respect won't let her, it seems clear I've
>     got to choose,
> Either leave my wife, or mother. A son's duty must
>     come first.

FATHER

Right, my boy. Your mother first. There's nothing you should put ahead.

The father has a place even more prominent. What they called in Rome the *Patria Potestas*, the Father's Authority, was clearly an awful matter. There was no rebelling against it. In Plautus' *Comedy of Asses* a father, much taken with a girl his son is in love with, is sitting at table beside her, very jovial. The son, very mournful, sits opposite:

FATHER

Come, my boy, you don't mind, do you, if she sits 'longside
o' me?

SON
(*dolefully*)

I'm your son. I know my duty, father. I'll not say a word.

FATHER

Young men must be modest, son.

SON

Oh, yes, I know. Do what you want.

FATHER
(*briskly*)

Well, fill up—good wine, good talk. No filial awe, my
boy, for me.
It's your love I want.

SON
(*more doleful*)

Of course, I give you both as a son should.

FATHER

I'll believe it when you take that look off.

SON

Father, I *am sad*.

It isn't that I don't wish everything you wish. You know
I do.
But I really love her. Any other girl I wouldn't mind.

FATHER

But it happens I want this one. Come, tomorrow she'll be
yours.
That's not much for me to ask.

SON
(*wretchedness complete*)

You know I want to please you first.

But the authority of the master of the house had its
limits. Plautus' Rome was the Rome of the Mother of

the Gracchi and it is not difficult to understand that the Roman *Pater Familias*, weightily endowed though he was by law and edict and tradition, might meet his match in the determined virtues of the Roman matron. Indeed that resolute lady seems to be responsible for the creation of one of the most popular characters in literature, the hen-pecked husband. He makes his very first bow upon the stage in these plays.

His sufferings give Plautus great delight. In the *Merchant*, a wife returning unexpectedly from a visit in the country finds a very questionable young person very much at home in her house. She runs out proclaiming her wrongs.

WIFE

Oh, never was a woman so abused as I,
Or never will be. Married to a man like that—
And I who brought him two good thousand pounds in gold.
(*Husbands enters. Stops and eyes her in great alarm*)

WIFE

Such insults. Bring that creature to my house—

HUSBAND

Ye Gods!

I'm in for it. She's seen her.

WIFE

Heaven help me now!

HUSBAND
(*feelingly*)
Oh, no. Me, me. I'd better speak to her—My dear,
You're back? So soon? Well, this *is* pleasant.

WIFE

Who's the girl?

HUSBAND
(*tentatively*)
You saw her?

WIFE

Yes, I did.


HUSBAND

Well, she's—oh, she's—oh, damn.


WIFE

You're stuck.


HUSBAND
(*sulkily*)
The way you keep at me.


WIFE

Of course, it's I.
No fault of yours. (*with change of voice*) I've caught you
in the act. That girl—
Say who she is.


HUSBAND
(*aside*)
Oh, this is all too much for me.


In such scenes, of course, the end is always that he is
reduced to the state of a helpless victim while she
triumphs. "Mayn't I even have my dinner first?" one
of them pleads when his wife appears to drag him home
from the party. "I'll see you get the dinner you deserve,"
is her answer, and he follows her unprotestingly. "I kept
telling you, father, you'd better not try any tricks on
mother," the son says smugly as the slaves bring in the
food. And with the contrast between the gay dinner
table and the dark door-way through which "mother"
relentlessly drives "father" the play ends. Perhaps the
most familiar passage in Virgil is the one in which he
bids the men of Rome remember that to them belongs
the rule of the earth. They are to "spare the submissive
and war down the proud." It would seem that this high
charge was subject to modifications within the home.

The plays leave no possibility of doubt that although
public life was denied the Roman woman, she could

find a very fair outlet for her energy in the domestic circle. In Plautus' *Casina*, a representative of the character Plautus is perhaps fondest of, the true ancestor of Pantaloon, is in love with his wife's protégée and plans to have his bailiff marry her and then give her over to him. The wife counterplans with her maid to dress up the footman as the bride and take a spectacular vengeance. The maid opens the scene. She comes out from the house in high glee.

### MAID

No games, I don't care where, not even the Olympic,
Are half the sport the joke we're playing our old man.
He's bustling in and out in such a mighty hurry.
And there's the bailiff all rigged up, so spick and span,
And mistress in her room is dressing up—the footman!
And oh, the lovely way she does pretend—They're here!
(*Enter old man. He speaks through door to his wife*)

### OLD MAN

I'll take the bride and groom out to the farm. It's safest.
Enjoy yourself here. I'll dine there. But hurry, please,
And send them out. Until tomorrow then, my dear.
(*Enter footman dressed and veiled as bride, wife and
maid escorting him*)

### MAID

Now, do be gentle with this innocent young girl.

### BAILIFF

Indeed I will.

### OLD MAN

Go in. (*nervously as the door shuts*) My wife—is she still there?

### BAILIFF

She's gone.

### OLD MAN
(*dancing excitedly around bride*)
Hurrah! Oh, sweetheart, honey, flower of spring—

*(They go off, and some time is supposed to have passed before the next scene, which discovers wife and maid waiting for the result of the instructions given the footman.)*

### MAID
*(tittering)*
I'd like to see that bride and bridegroom now, I would.

### WIFE
I'd like to see the old scamp's face well battered in.
*(They draw back as the old man enters, much dishevelled, tunic torn, all the signs of rough handling.)*

### OLD MAN
I don't know how I'll ever face my wife again.
But there—In I must go and pay her damages.
*(to audience)* Would one of you here like to substitute
for me?
*(Pauses a moment, then shakes his head)*
I just can't stick it.
*(Makes as if to run when enter footman)*

### FOOTMAN
           Stop right where you are, old man.
*(coyly)* Now if you want to fondle me, sir, here's your
chance.

### WIFE
*(stepping out, followed by maid)*
Good day to you, young lover.

### MAID
*(joining in)*
           How did your courting go?

### FOOTMAN
*(sobbing)*
He doesn't love me any more.

### OLD MAN
           Wish I was dead—

The entire scene could have been played just as it stands by any *commedia dell' arte* troupe. Not a character there that would not have been perfectly familiar to actors and spectators.

But there is one notable difference between what an audience would accept from women in Plautus' day and in later times. The deceived husband, so familiar for so many centuries to the European stage, never appears in Roman comedy. There is no indication of any other bar to the activity of the Roman wife, but she could not put horns upon her husband's head. No Puritan morality could be more unyielding on this point. The fact is thrown into high relief by the complete absence of any sex-morality in other directions. The courtesans are important characters in nearly every play and Terence's most estimable youths have affairs with them which their mothers on occasion hotly defend. One of his irreproachable young men, passionately in love with such a lady, agrees to share the possession of her with a blustering bully in order that his own purse may be spared. Familiar characters, too, are the panderer or his female equivalent. In Plautus' *Comedy of Asses* a lover is raging up and down before a house where doors and windows are all conspicuously closed:

LOVER
Thrown out of doors! That's the reward I get
For all I've spent upon them. You'll be sorry.
I'm off to the police—leave your names with 'em.
I'll humble you, your girl too—
(*Enter Madam from house, very calm and pleasant*)

MADAM
Go right on threatening. Such a state of mind
Means money down. Get off. Away with you.
The more you try, the quicker you'll come back.

LOVER
And all I've given you! If I could have her
Just for myself now, why you'd owe me sums.

MADAM
(*cheerfully*)

Oh, you can always have her—on condition
You give what's asked—and more than other men.

LOVER

Be just a little kind. I'll last you longer.

MADAM
(*coolly*)

You miss the point. A lover's like a fish
Where we're concerned—no good unless he's fresh.
Your sweet, fresh, juicy ones—ah, they're the men.
They don't care what it costs. They *want* to give.
To please their girl they'll give to me, the servants.
Make up even to my little dog. Now come—(*reasonably*)
A woman's got to look out for herself.

Such passages, side by side with the idea steadily
presented throughout the plays of a sacrosanct family
life, throw a flood of light on the kind and the degree of
morality abroad in the Republic. The Romans were
franker than our grandfathers were, but their basic notions of what could and could not be done were the
same. Strict virtue within the house for everyone. Outside, all the pleasant vices for the men. A hard and fast
division of ethics into male and female received its final
consummation in Rome. The double standard which
has been the world's standard for all these centuries
since, is formulated, complete to the last detail, in
Roman comedy. In this respect the men of Greece were
dull of wit compared with the men of Rome. Their
astuteness did not rise beyond the four walls of the
house for their women folk, with occasional assistance
from bolts and bars, most futile of defenses, as story-
tellers the world over have shown. Aristophanes has
many a joke about the way Athenian women eluded
them and the husbands they deceived. Nothing of the
kind passed with a Roman audience of the Republic.
The men saw to it that they were not deceived, and the
way they did it was a triumph of Roman intelligence as
well as of Roman determination. One of Rome's great-

est achievements, which has passed almost unnoticed, was the successful education of their women in the idea that their supreme duty was to be chaste. The popular story of Lucretia who killed herself when she was violated by force, completely innocent though she was in reality, and the story, even more popular, of the father acclaimed a hero because he killed his daughter with his own hand rather than have her live as the tyrant's mistress, testify eloquently to the thoroughness of the women's training. Thus disciplined they were safe to go abroad and enjoyed a degree of freedom civilized women had never known before. But the lesson was taught so cleverly, the idea that men's pleasures, too, should be curtailed never entered the women's minds. Their conviction of the all-importance of chastity, side by side with the conviction that it had nothing to do with men, is a proof of what the Roman mentality could accomplish when faced with a practical problem.

The whole matter bears directly upon the Roman character of the plays. Plautus' women, who have so influenced the women of all later drama, were never drawn from Greek originals. In the *Amphitryon*, Alcumena is the model Roman matron complete, and the line of her descendants upon the stage is too long to be reckoned. On her—supposed—husband's departure for the war she soliloquizes in words which recall all the soliloquies spoken by noble women the world over when the necessities of the drama require them to be abandoned by their lawful protectors:

> Absent from me
>   So let him be,
> If fame and glory come
> With him triumphant home.
> Bear and forbear,
> Make my heart strong,
> Through bitter care,
> Days sad and long,
> All this I can endure, all and yet more,
> If I may hear him hailed at last victor in war.

That prize enough for me.
His valor's prize shall be
Mine. What is all the rest?
Valor is best.

(*As she concludes, Amphitryon, her real husband, enters.
The circumstances are complicated: Jupiter has been assum-
ing Amphitryon's form while the latter is away fighting, and
has thus gained access to Alcumena with whom he is in love.
It is he Alcumena has just taken leave of. Upon Amphitryon's unexpected return, Jupiter has decamped, telling her
he is due at headquarters. When Amphitryon enters she, of
course, thinks they parted only a few moments ago. In this
delicate situation she is the perfect Roman lady, indeed,
the perfect lady of every age and clime.*)

AMPHITRYON
(*entering eagerly, followed by his slave*)
Joyfully I greet my wife, my own, my hope, the very
best,
So her husband thinks, of all the ladies that the city
holds.
You are well? Glad I am come?

ALCUMENA
Oh dear. Please don't. I hate such jokes.
Why pretend we haven't met before?

AMPHITRYON
We haven't!

ALCUMENA
(*not condescending to notice this*)
Back so soon?
Weather? Bad news? Or what's the cause? You told me
you were due in camp.

AMPHITRYON
Told you? When?

ALCUMENA
Why keep on teasing? When? Some time
ago—just now.

AMPHITRYON
(*to slave*)

Why, she's raving.

SLAVE

She's asleep.

ALCUMENA

I? What's this nonsense?

AMPHITRYON

Greet me, dear.

ALCUMENA

Yesterday I greeted you.

AMPHITRYON

When we made harbor just last night!

ALCUMENA

Nonsense. You were here last night and told me all about
the war.
Here we dined and slept together.

AMPHITRYON

O my God!

ALCUMENA

What *do* you mean?

AMPHITRYON

She has had her lover here. She's lost—seduced—my wife
no more.

ALCUMENA

Sir, you neither know me nor my family. Take care.
You will find
We are not that sort of people.

AMPHITRYON

You are bold.

ALCUMENA

No, innocent.
The real dowry that I brought you was not gold but
   purity,
Honor, self-control and reverence for the gods, my parents
   too,
Love to all my kin, obedience to my husband, serving
   him
In true faithfulness.


AMPHITRYON

My word, I'm so dazed I don't know myself.
Madam, I'll investigate the matter.


ALCUMENA

Dear me. Do, I beg.


Talk like this is so familiar to us, it is difficult for
us to realize how new it was in the second century
before Christ. It bears the true Roman stamp. There
is nothing like it in Greek literature. Conscious virtue,
noble declamation, a fine gesture—none of that is Greek.
Where the Romans were all for exalted sentiments, the
Greeks were singularly matter-of-fact, and this difference is an important reason, perhaps the chief reason,
why we feel instinctively at home in the Roman way
and strangers to the Greek. A certain amount of
heroics is necessary for us.

Another point in this passage which is new to the
student of Greek literature is the exaltation of woman
and her purity. That, too, began in Rome. Greek
tragedy, indeed, shows women of a greatness unsurpassed anywhere. The greatest figures are women, but
the fact that it is so is never directly brought to mind.
We are never made to feel, how wonderful that a woman
should be like that, any more than, how wonderful
that a man should be. Antigone and Iphigenia are as
they are, just as Œdipus and Orestes are as they are.
The sex is as little to the fore in the one case as in
the other. But in Roman literature, as in our own, a

woman is always a woman. Her sex is never in the background of the picture.

The idea, too, which our literature for hundreds of years has made familiar to us, that she is on a higher plane than any man has reason to be, goes back to Rome. It resulted, of course, from the insistence that chastity was strictly for women only.

Roman sentimentality, also, appeals to us, just as the lack of it in Greek literature repels us. Along with the comedy there is invariably in Terence and often in Plautus a love interest, a pair of unhappy lovers, whose troubles find a perfect solution as the curtain falls. The girl is always a model of beauty and virtue, the young man madly in love with her. They are never touched by any of the indecencies the other characters may indulge in; they are never humorous. The Roman audience wanted both sides: greedy courtesans and easily-tricked panderers and senile dotards to laugh at; good, sweet young people to sympathize with.

But the character that stands out first of all, far beyond even the dominating figures of the father and the expensive lady, is the slave. He is the ancestor of all the devoted and agile servitors, models of fidelity and never fazed by any of their masters' difficulties, whom literature everywhere has made so familiar, but in Rome the rôle he played was more important than any given him since. The portrait of the Roman family would lack its chief feature without the slave and no Roman comedy could be written without him. In every play he is the chief personage, the only one with brains, who succeeds in fooling all of the people all of the time. But in spite of his gay assurance and his triumphant success, his terrible lot in Rome is continually suggested. One of Terence's characters, represented as loveliest and kindest of ladies, offers her maid-servants for examination by torture to prove her innocence. The punishments the slaves are perpetually threatened with might well have given points to the inquisitors, and, obviously, the reason for the detailed descriptions is that they were delightfully humorous to the audience. The cross—the slave's penalty, they called it in Rome— is often on the master's lips. Sometimes, but only once or twice, there is a hint as to the slave's side. In Plautus' *Braggart Captain* a master is denouncing his slave, who in this case is innocent. As the list of tortures in wait for him is unrolled he turns on the speaker:

> Don't go on threatening. Well I know the cross will be my end,
> My place of burial. There is where my ancestors all rest,
> My father, my grandfather, and my great-grandfather, too.
> My great-great grandfather. D'you think just words mean much to us?

It is difficult to understand how the hearers could have laughed at this and yet we must suppose they did. No doubt at all, the tide of human kindness, never high anywhere in the ancient world, ebbed perceptibly when Rome came to the fore, but on the other hand the actual suffering of the slave is very seldom shown upon the stage and the end is always that he is forgiven and rewarded. The enjoyment from the spectacle of actual danger to life and limb the Romans of the day reserved for the circus shows. They did not care for it in the theatre.

On the whole, the general impression the plays leave is that they were written for fairly decent, sober-living folk, completely moral within their homes and even outside wanting nothing decadent. The obscenity is moderate judged by Aristophanic standards. There is a genuine feeling, too, for justice and fair play, and vice and virtue must always have their deserts. Once only Plautus fails to live up to this ideal and at the end of a play shows two bad old men enjoying themselves with two girls who had begun by making fun of their white hairs. The curtain falls on their triumph, but Plautus knew his public and was ready with an

antidote. There is an epilogue holding up to reproba-
tion all the elderly who act like that. Terence never
had to apologize for his endings. He assigns rewards and
punishments with impeccable correctness.

It is a world far removed from Elia's "land of
Cuckoldry, the Utopia of gallantry, where pleasure is
duty and manners perfect freedom." No fancy roams
in it, whether to Utopia or anywhere else; gallantry is
undreamed of; freedom is equally remote; pleasure, of
the physical variety alone. It is a sordid place, inhabited
by people whose standards are at best those of a dull
respectability, whose ideas are completely ordinary, not
to say stodgy. There is no suggestion of distinction or
charm anywhere. Terence, to be sure, shows now and
again a flash of insight, as in his famous "I am a man
and nothing in mankind do I hold alien to me." The
younger comedian was intellectually superior to the
elder, but even so the flashes are few. Terence's world,
too, lies on the dead level of the commonplace.

Fragments of Menander have come down to us
which show that neither he nor his audience had quite
forgotten the great Greek tradition:

> I hold him happiest
> Who before going quickly whence he came,
> Hath looked ungrieving on these majesties,
> The world-wide sun, the stars, water and clouds
> And fire. Hast thou a hundred years to live or but
> The briefest space, these thou canst always see.
> Thou wilt not ever see a greater thing.

There is not a passage in Plautus or Terence that recalls
ever so faintly anything like this, not one that points
to something poetical in their model, however dimly
apprehended. A single sentence of Plautus', perhaps,
should be excepted; at any rate it gives one pause, it is
so strangely unlike the self he shows elsewhere:

> The poet seeks what is nowhere in all the world,
> And yet—somewhere—he finds it.

Did he himself occasionally wander away from this actual, solid world, one wonders, and was it his audience that held his plays so fast down to it?

A good-humored crowd, those people who filled the Roman theatre in its first days of popularity, easily appealed to by any sentimental interest, eager to have the wicked punished—but not too severely—and the good live happily ever after. No occasions wanted for intellectual exertion, no wit or deft malice; fun such as could be passively enjoyed, broad with a flavor of obscenity. Most marked characteristic of all, a love of mediocrity, a complete satisfaction with the average. The people who applauded these plays wanted nothing bigger than their own small selves. They were democratic.

That audience of two thousand one hundred years ago looks oddly familiar. The reflection shown in the mirror of Plautus and Terence has "nothing alien" to us as we watch it. The close family life and the masterful lady of the house and the elderly-man-in-search-of-a-mistress and the nice young lovers—we know them all only too well and we cannot feel ourselves strangers to the theatre-crowd that flocked to see them in Rome of the Republic.

A Roman comedy 200 B.C., a Broadway musical comedy, 1932 A.D.—the gulf between can be passed without exertion. Save in respect of time only, it is neither wide nor deep. This swiftly changing world we must all run so hard to keep up with suddenly looks strangely static.

# CHAPTER III

## THE COMIC SPIRIT IN PLAUTUS
## AND TERENCE

PLAUTUS and Terence, as has been pointed out, are the founders of our theatre. Their influence has been incalculable. The two main divisions of comedy under which all comic plays except Aristophanes' can be grouped, go back to the two Roman playwrights. Plautus is the source for one, Terence for the other. The fact is another and a vivid illustration of how little the material of literature matters, and how much the way the material is treated. Both dramatists deal with exactly the same sort of life and exactly the same sort of people. The characters in the plays of the one are duplicated in the plays of the other, and in both the background is the family life of the day, and yet Plautus' world of comedy is another place from Terence's world. The two men were completely unlike, so much so that it is difficult to conceive of either viewing a play of the other with any complacency. Plautus would have been bored by Terence, Terence offended by Plautus. Precisely the same material, but a totally different point of view, and the result, two distinct types of comedy.

Plautus was the older by a generation. His life fell during a restless period when Rome was fighting even more than usual. He could have taken part in the

Second Punic War and the wars in the east which followed it, but whether he did or not is pure conjecture. All that is actually known about him is that he was the son of a poor Umbrian farmer, that he worked once in a mill and wrote three of his plays there, and that he was an old man when he died in 184 B.C. But it is impossible to read him without getting a vivid impression of the man himself. A picture emerges, done in bold strokes and unshaded colors, of a jovial, devil-may-care vagabond, a Latin Villon; a soldier of fortune who had roamed the world hobnobbing with all manner of men, and had no illusions about any of them; a man of careless good humor, keen to see and delighting to laugh at follies, but with a large and indulgent tolerance for every kind of fool.

Terence was a man of quite another order. He was born a slave in one of Rome's African colonies and brought up in a great Roman house where they recognized his talents, educated and freed him. These talents, too, found him a place in a little circle of young men who were the intelligentsia and the gilded youth of Rome combined. The leader was the young Scipio, but the elegant Laelius, no mean poet, and the brilliant Lucilius, the inventor of satire, were close seconds, and it was an astonishing triumph that the former slave, once admitted, proved inferior to none of them. It requires no imagination to realize his pride and happiness at being made one of their number. When envious people declared that his grand friends wrote his plays for him, he answered proudly that he boasted of their help.

It was a very youthful company. Terence is said to have died before he was twenty-six and they were all much of an age. The plays show nothing more clearly than that the audience they were primarily written for was this little band of close friends and not the vulgar crowd. Every one is laid in the Utopia of a young man about town in Republican Rome. Undoubtedly the members of the group in their bringing up had had a great deal required of them in the way of the antique Roman virtues. The father and mother of the day, as Plautus shows them, were not given to overindulgence, and Scipio Africanus Maior, the young Scipio's grandfather by adoption, must have been a man very much to be reckoned with in the family circle, while the ladies of the Scipio household were notable for their practice of the domestic virtues. The redoubtable Cornelia herself was his aunt and her jewels were his cousins. No doubt at all he and his friends had had to walk a narrow path with watchful guardians on either side.

But under Terence's guidance, art, the liberator, set them free. He took them away to an enchanted world where fathers were what they ought to be and young men had their proper position in the world. Plautus' fathers were hard on their sons and—more intolerable still—the young fellows were held up to ridicule. Terence altered all this delightfully. For the most part his fathers are of an amiability not to be surpassed. "Does my darling son want that pretty flute girl? The dear boy—I'll buy her for him at once." "Extravagant do you call him? Well, all young men are like that. I was myself. I'll gladly pay his debts." There is never any joking at that sort of thing. Such sentiments are the part of a right-minded man. Indeed, there are no jokes at all where the young men are concerned. They are all wonderfully serious and completely noble and accorded the deepest respect. Plautus' young lover on his knees before the door that shuts in his lady-love, undoubtedly moved the audience to laughter when he declaimed:

Hear me, ye bolts, ye bolts. Gladly I greet you, I love you.
Humbly I pray you, beseech you, kneel here before you to beg you,
Grant to a lover his longing, sweetest bolts, fairest and kindest.
Spring now like ballet-girls dancing, lift yourselves up from the door-post.

Open, oh open and send her, send her to me ere my life
    blood
Drains from me wasting and waiting.

But who would laugh at Terence's estimable young man,
so admirably concerned for his love:

I treat her so? And she through me be wronged, made
    wretched,
She who has trusted love and life, her all, to me?
So will I never do.

They are all like that. Whatever the audience thought
of them, they were certainly not amused. But whereas
Plautus was out to get a laugh by any and every means
possible, Terence had an entirely different object in
view. Plautus talked directly to the spectators when
the action failed to get a response, calling out to the
man in the back row not to be so slow to see a joke,
or to the women in front to stop chattering and let
their husbands listen, or making an actor warn another,

Softly now, speak softly.
Don't disturb the pleasant slumbers of the audience
                                           I beg.

His object was to amuse. But Terence's mind was bent
upon the approval of what he thought the most fastidious, polished people that ever there had been, and he
worshipped where they did, at the shrine ever dearest
to youth, good taste, as laid down by the canons of
each youthful circle, "the thing," which is and isn't
"done." Plautus makes fun of everyone, gods included.
Terence has few comic characters, and they are in
general confined to the lower classes. One catches a
glimpse of an English public-school feeling for good
form in that little circle of serious young men of which
he was so proud a member. Making gentlemen ridiculous was simply not "done." Fortunately, in the
circumstances, Terence's sense of humor was such that

it could be perfectly controlled. No doubt to him Plautus was a terrible bounder—Plautus, the comedian pure and simple, who when he is not funny, is nothing at all. Terence is a serious dramatist, able to write an amusing scene; but seldom choosing to do so. His interest is in his nice people, above all his nice young men, and in their very well-bred-man-of-the-world doings. It is not to be presumed that Plautus knew anything about well-bred men, and no one ever had less concern for good taste. His quality is Rabelaisian—diluted—and certainly he would have been as much disconcerted by Terence's fine friends as they would have been uncomfortable with him.

With dissimilarities so marked it is not surprising that they disagreed about the whole business of drama-making. The fundamental question of how to secure dramatic interest each solved in his own way, completely unlike the other's. They constructed their plays differently and two forms of comedy, widely divergent from each other, were the result.

There are only two main sources for dramatic interest in a comedy. The first is the method of suspense and surprise, depending upon plot or upon the reaction of character to character, or to situation. But the second method is precisely the reverse: it acts by eliminating suspense and making surprise impossible. The dramatic interest depends upon the spectators knowing everything beforehand. They know what the actor does not. It is a method found in both tragedy and comedy; it is common ground to the sublime and the ridiculous. The Greeks who made great use of it, called it irony. Nothing in tragedy is more tragic. Œdipus invokes an awful curse upon the murderer of his wife's first husband:

> I charge you all: Let no one of this land
> Give shelter to him. Bar him from your homes,
> A thing defiled, companioned by pollution.
> And solemnly I pray, may he who killed,
> Wear out his life in evil, being evil.

And we know it is he himself he is cursing, he is the murderer; he killed his father, he married his mother. This is tragic irony. It lies at the very foundation of Greek tragedy. The audience knew beforehand what the action of each play would be. They sat as beings from another world, foreseeing all the dire results of every deed as it took place, but perceiving also that thus it must be and not otherwise. The feeling of the inevitability of what is being done and suffered upon the stage, of men's helplessness to avert their destiny, which is the peculiar power of Greek tragedy, depends in the last analysis upon irony, upon the spectators' awareness and the actors' unconsciousness of what is really happening. The darkness that envelops mortal life, our utter ignorance of what confronts us and our blinded eyes that cannot see the ruin we are bringing down upon ourselves, is driven home so dramatically and with such intensity as is possible to no other method.

The use of it may be as comic as it is tragic. We, the audience, are in the secret that there are two men who look exactly alike. The poor, stupid actors do not dream that it is so. How absurdly unable they are to escape their ridiculous mishaps, and what a delightfully superior position our omniscience assures to us.

We cannot trace back the use of the suspense method. Plot is as old as the very first story-teller and the interest of what the effect will be of a situation or of one character upon another is at least as old as Homer and the Bible. But irony begins with Greek tragedy, and, as far as our evidence goes, comic irony begins with Roman comedy. Among the fragments we have of Menander there are two in which irony is evident, but in neither passage is it used humorously. It is found so used for the first time in Plautus. If he was indeed the originator of it, if it was he who perceived to what comic uses tragic irony could be turned, he deserves a place in literature far higher than that now given him. Irony is his chief source of dramatic interest and he is a master of it. It follows, of course, that he offers nothing notable in plots. Suspense is automatically shut out when irony is used. Plautus' plots, when he has one, are extremely poor, and there is a distressing similarity between them. But no one ever put irony to better comic use. His usual way is to explain the action of the piece in a very long and exceedingly tiresome prologue, but the result of the detailed explanation is that the spectators are free to give their entire attention to the absurdities they are now in a position to see through.

In the *Amphitryon*, it will be remembered, Jupiter is in love with Amphitryon's wife, Alcumena. When Amphitryon is away at war Jupiter assumes his form to gain access to Alcumena. Mercury, who guards the house whenever Jupiter is in it, under the form of Amphitryon's slave, Sosia, absent with his master, speaks the prologue, and explains in minutest detail all that is going to take place throughout the play. Jupiter and Amphitryon will look exactly alike, he warns the audience, and so will he and Sosia, but in order that they may have no bother as to which is which, Jupiter will have a bright gold tassel hanging from his hat and

> I shall wear this little plume on mine,
> Note well: the other two are unadorned.

With this the play begins. The scene is a street at night before Amphitryon's house where Mercury stands on guard. To him enters his duplicate, Sosia, sent ahead by Amphitryon to prepare his wife for his unexpected return. It is too dark for Sosia to see how Mercury looks. As he goes up to the door the latter stops him.

#### MERCURY
May I know where you come from, who you are, and why you're here? Just you tell me.

#### SOSIA
Well, I'm going in there. I'm the master's slave. Do you know it all now? Just you tell me.

MERCURY

Is that your house?

SOSIA

Haven't I said so?

MERCURY

Then who is the man that owns you?

SOSIA

Amphitryon. General commanding the troops. He's got a wife—name Alcumena.

MERCURY

What stuff are you giving me? What's your name?

SOSIA

It's Sosia. My father was Davus.

MERCURY

Well, you've got your cheek. You're Sosia? You? What's your game? Didn't know I was he? Eh? (*Strikes him.*)

SOSIA

Oh, you'll kill me!

MERCURY

You'll find if you keep this up there are
                things a whole lot worse than dying.
Now, say who you are.

SOSIA

I'm Sosia, please—

MERCURY

He's mad.

SOSIA

                I'm not. Why, you rascal.
Didn't a ship bring me in from the battlefield this very night? Didn't my master

Send me here to our house? And you say I'm not—
Well, I'll go straight in to my mistress.

### MERCURY

Every word a lie—I'm Amphitryon's slave. We stormed the
    enemy's city,
Killed the king—cut his head off, Amphitryon did.

### SOSIA
(*awestruck*)
He knows it all.
(*pause, then recovering*)
Just you tell me
If you are me, when the fight was on, where were you?
What were you doing?

### MERCURY

A cask full of wine in the tent and my own pocket flask.
What d'you think I'd be doing?

### SOSIA
(*overwhelmed*)
It's the truth. Wretched man that I am.
(*shakes head, then suddenly holds lantern up so that the
    light falls on Mercury*)
Well, well. He's as like me as I myself was.
Oh, immortal gods! When was I changed? Did I die?
Have I lost my memory?
Did they leave me behind in foreign parts? I'm going
    straight back to my master.
(*Runs off, and re-enters following Amphitryon who is
    completely nonplussed at the report of what has
    happened.*)

### AMPHITRYON
(*angrily*)
The boy's drunk. You, speak up. Tell the truth, where
    you got the stuff.

### SOSIA
But I didn't.

AMPHITRYON
(*uneasiness getting the better of his anger*)
Who's that man you saw?

SOSIA
I've told you ten times. I'm there at the
house and I'm here, too.
That's the straight truth.

AMPHITRYON
(*trying to persuade himself it's all nonsense, but uncomfortable*)
Get out. Take yourself off. You're sick.

SOSIA
I'm just as well as you are.

AMPHITRYON
Ah, I'll see that you aren't. If you're not mad, you're
bad.

SOSIA
(*tearfully*)
I tell the truth. You won't hear me.
I was standing there in front of the house before I got
there.

AMPHITRYON
You're dreaming.
That's the cause of this nonsense. Wake up.

SOSIA
No, no. I don't sleep when you give me an order.
I was wide awake then—I'm wide awake now. I was
wide awake when he beat me.
He was wide awake too. I'll tell you that.

AMPHITRYON
(*gruffly*)
It'll bear looking into. Come on then.

This is the way Plautus handles comic irony. Molière
follows him closely. In his *Amphitryon* the dialogue

between Mercure and Sosie is essentially a reproduction of the Latin and no one can say that the great master of comedy used the device at any point more skillfully than the Latin poet.

Playwright after playwright took it over from him. Shakespeare's ironical play, *The Comedy of Errors,* is not as close a parallel to Plautus' *Menaechmi* as Molière's is to the *Amphitryon,* but the entire play is only a variation on Plautus' theme. Scenes in Shakespeare and Molière where the comedy depends upon irony are so many, to run through them would mean making a résumé of a large part of their comedies. The basis of the fun in *Much Ado About Nothing* is the spectators' knowledge of the plot against Beatrice and Benedict. The great scene in *L'Avare* is funny because we know the miser is talking about his money box and the young man about his lady-love, while each supposes the other has the same object in mind. Here, too, Molière drew directly from Plautus. Whether the latter first employed the method or whether he got it from the Greek New Comedy, it is certain that its use upon our own stage goes directly back to him.

Terence never used it. It seems strange at first sight that he did not, but upon consideration reasons appear. A plot intricate enough to supply a full measure of suspense and surprise can be enjoyed only by an intelligent and attentive audience, especially when programmes, outlines, synopses of scenes, all the sources of printed information, have to be dispensed with. Plautus' audience was not up to that level; Terence's was—the real audience he wrote for, his little circle of superior people. Plautus had to hold the attention of a holiday crowd, and hold it too, as he says in many a prologue, against such competitors as chattering women and crying babies. No method of playwriting requires so little effort on the part of the spectator as comic irony. Comedies based upon it are merely a succession of funny scenes strung on the thread of a familiar story. There was sound sense in Plautus' preference for it, and equally good reason for Terence's rejection. His audience enjoyed using their minds on an ingenious plot. He could dispense with the obviously comic and follow his own strong bent toward character and situation. The germ of the novel lies within his plays. His plots are never poor. Perhaps the best of them is that of the *Mother-in-Law*, where the suspense is excellently sustained to the very end. Indeed, as the curtain falls the two chief characters pledge each other to keep the solution of the mystery to their own selves. "Don't let's have it like the comedies where everyone knows everything," one of them says.

It is a good story throughout and the characters are well drawn. Nevertheless when the play was presented to the public it failed. The prologue, spoken at a second presentation, declares the reason was that

A rope-dancer had caught the gaping people's mind.

Yet another prologue—for still another presentation, presumably—says that the theatre was thrown into an uproar by the announcement of a gladiatorial show, and the play could not proceed. Clearly the road of the early dramatist in Rome was not an easy one, but there is never a hint that Plautus found it hard. Perhaps he had the happy faculty of not taking himself too seriously, and merely went along with the crowd when such occasions worked havoc with his play. One feels sure that even so he would have enjoyed the rope-dancer. But the young playwright, hardly more than a boy, felt poignantly the hurt to his feelings and the wrong to his genius. Every one of his prologues contains an attack upon his critics or his public. They are fearfully serious productions, warranted to make any audience restless and any other show irresistibly attractive, but to his own inner circle, those very sober and cultured young men, no doubt they appeared admirably distinguished from the well-worn, old-fashioned method of appeal to the vulgar.

The marked difference between the two writers is another proof of the Roman character of Roman comedy. Plautus and Terence owed something, no doubt, much perhaps, to their Greek originals, but much more to their own selves. They were Roman writers, not Greek copyists, and the drama they bequeathed to the world which still holds the stage today, is a witness to the extent of our legacy from Rome.

# *CHAPTER IV*

## CICERO'S ROME: THE REPUBLIC

WHILE Terence was writing his plays a very remarkable man came to Rome. He did not come voluntarily; he was brought there as a hostage and there he had to stay for seventeen years. In all that length of time the city grew to be a home to him instead of a prison, and after he was released he came back again for another long stay. He was Polybius, the Greek historian, and except for Plautus and Terence, what he has to say about Rome is the only contemporary record before Cicero which has come down to us. He was a man of great ability, a true scientist in his love of truth, a keen observer of human affairs, qualified as few could be more to weigh the good and the bad in the great city which even then he saw as the coming mistress of the world. His testimony is overwhelmingly in her favor. He has a profound admiration for the Republic and for the Roman character. To be sure, his keen eyes saw signs of moral weakening after Carthage was conquered; even so, his history is a great testimonial to the city he knew through and through, to Roman uprightness and patriotism, and to the Roman mastery of the art of ruling men.

He was not a flatterer, trying to win for himself the favor of a powerful nation. When he wrote he was an old man, living far from Rome in his early Greek home. He dared to praise Hannibal, to blame Rome sharply for more than one breach of faith. If the government had been corrupt, he would certainly have known it and certainly recorded it. He never so much as hints at such a condition. His Romans are simple and hardy in ways of life, upright, steadfast, devotedly and disinterestedly patriotic.

But an enormous change has taken place when next we have a contemporary's account of the city; the government is corrupt through and through and the people completely indifferent. Only a hundred years— less than that—changed Polybius' great Republic into one of which we have as black a picture as could well be painted. Indeed, to the historian Sallust, a man with something of Polybius' passion for accuracy, the change was fully consummated a generation earlier. A foreign prince, so he tells the story, came to Rome at the beginning of the first century to engineer a deal. He was rich and he succeeded, and as he left the town he said, "City in which everything is for sale."

That is the city shown in the next authentic record of Rome. It is a remarkable record. During the strange and exciting days when the great Republic was coming to an end and the Empire was looming just ahead, there lived the most distinguished letter-writer the world has ever known, one of Rome's very great men, Cicero the orator.

Hundreds of his letters have been preserved, along with many letters from his friends. They are of all sorts: letters of condolence, letters of affection, letters of apology, literary criticism, philosophical discussion, town gossip, business letters, and outnumbering all the rest a hundred to one, political letters. Such a ratio would be a matter of course to a Roman. The thing of paramount importance, away beyond everything else, was politics. Throughout the great days of the Republic it had been the field both of duty and honor. A good man, a great man—both terms were synonymous with a patriotic man. Goodness apart from patriotism did not exist to the Roman. All the men who counted, whether by birth or property, had been brought up in the tradition that they were bound to be politicians first; whatever else they might take up must be treated as of secondary importance. Our letter-writer in any other age would have had no leanings toward politics. He belonged by nature to the men of thought, not of action. He was a student, a lover of books, a critic and a man of artistic tastes, too, the very last sort of person in our eyes to enter public life. Rome made him into a politician, so devoted to his calling that when events removed him from it he was inconsolable. What of comfort could philosophy, literature, art, give to a Roman forced to lead a private life? Cicero was disgraced and contemptible in his own eyes.

That was the conception which had enabled the Republic to endure for hundreds of years perpetually encompassed by unnumbered perils. The best brains, the strongest characters, had always been at the absolute disposal of the state. Her service had been at once their chief obligation and their greatest joy.

A wonderful help in ensuring brave men and men capable of self-sacrifice to manage state affairs was the fact that politics and war were inextricably connected. Any day a successful politician might find himself compelled to desert his constituency, don his armor, and march against a foe whose forces outnumbered his own. The practice of politics in Republican Rome had never been for those in search of an easy berth. It was ever a dangerous pursuit. The odds were that favors voted by the people would have to be paid for on the battlefield.

It would have been unthinkable to a Roman that high personal courage was not an essential part of the equipment of a politician. Officials, party chiefs, "bosses" big and little, must face an ever present possibility of having to die for their country. Ex-officials were allowed no more comfortable prospects. Consulars, as they called

them, men who had been consuls—Rome's ex-presidents
—became oftenest commanders in the wars Rome was
always waging in one or another part of the world.
Cicero, pre-eminently a man of peace, sensitive in the
extreme and timid, a lover of ease and luxury, in his
fastitdious culture a typical man of letters, must yet put
himself at the head of an army and live for months at
a time as a fighting general. It was the price he paid for
once having been placed at the head of the state. In
none of the many letters he wrote from the seat of war
is there a word of complaint against the fate that carried
him away from his beloved city and his books and the
comforts of his country houses and his pleasant ways of
life, to far distant Cilicia and the hardships of a guerilla
war. He was merely doing what he had expected when
he came forward as candidate for the consulship.

The high distinction which always attends the fighting
forces of a nation at war marked out the Roman politician as well, the distinction which only conspicuous
danger and death can give.

And yet when Cicero was carrying on his Cilician
campaign in strict accordance with Rome's great tradition, the Republic was dying and all but dead. That was
in 51 B.C. Nine years before, three powerful party
leaders had come together; they agreed to pool their
resources and take the government into their own hands.
But it was all completely unofficial and no one need
take cognizance of it if he chose not. The senate met;
the consuls presided; the old respected political forms
were strictly adhered to. The fact that Caesar, Pompey,
and Crassus held the reins did not seem to matter much,
if they kept, as they did, in the background. People got
used to the idea of them and when four years later
their powerful organization was completed and they
began to act openly, honored and honorable patriots
could find excellent reasons for acquiescing in their
running the city. Indeed, it seemed exceedingly probable
that if they did not do so there would be nobody to
run it. As regards the senate, once and through so many

centuries Rome's great guide, the only question that could be raised was whether it was more incompetent than it was corrupt or the other way about. Something had happened to Roman morale. The people were safe and at ease. Rome's enemies were outside Italy now, far away, shut off by mountains or sea, and although civilian commanders were the rule, fighting in other respects had become a matter for professionals. Wealth was pouring into the city from conquered countries; easy money had become possible for a great many and the ideal for most. To have three able men take the responsibility of looking after Rome's wide interests, saved a vast deal of trouble for others. The old Republic had exacted a great deal from her citizens and left them poor. Now people wanted politics at a profit; they were out for a share in the riches they saw around them.

Politics have seldom offered a better field for that purpose than they did then. Rome had in very truth become the city where everything was for sale. Cicero's letters make it possible to see the inwardness of the political situation clearly as in hardly any other period of history. Bribery here, there and everywhere, he writes over and over again, not an official exempt, not even the highest. Politics have become a money-making business; votes are bought and sold, so are judges. Everyone knows that there is one sure way to being elected or being acquitted, and nobody cares. One day, Cicero writes, there was read out in the senate an agreement a candidate for the consulship had made with the two consuls to pay each of them a large sum of money in case he was elected, but failed to get for them the offices they wanted when their term was over. The compact called for false oaths not only from the principals but from two ex-consuls as well. "It was regularly drawn up," Cicero continues, "with the sums promised, and drafts on the bank added, and so on. It does throw a lurid light on the consuls, but it was all the same to Appius Claudius [one of them]—he had nothing to lose by it."

The reason for that remark was that in the eyes of all Rome no Claudius had anything left to keep or lose in the way of reputation. Once the Claudii had been citizens Rome was proud of. The Appian Way was the achievement of an ancestor; so was the first water system, and the splendid aqueduct. They had been great people and no house was more aristocratic. The present representatives, however, were not of the antique stamp. Appius, his brother Publius, and their three sisters, all noted for brilliancy and personal beauty, were talked of throughout the city for their reckless ways, their extravagance, dissipation, and worse. There was nothing so bad that Rome was not ready to whisper about them and believe. The *cause célèbre* of that day and many a day to come centered in Publius, and Caesar's young wife, Pompeia, was co-respondent.

As Cicero tells the story it is a cynical drama of corrupt politics. It began at the festival of the Good Goddess, a highly important ceremony in which women alone took part. During the celebration no male could enter the house where it was held. The master must find other lodgings; even pictures and statues of men were banished. Juvenal says no male mouse dared to stay. Caesar was pontifex maximus at the time and his house was chosen for the sacred rite. This suited Clodius, as Cicero always writes the name, exceedingly well. His affair with Pompeia was not coming off, Plutarch thinks because of the strict chaperonage of her mother-in-law, "a very discreet woman," and here was an occasion when the most vigilant duenna might relax. His smooth boyish beauty fitted well a woman's dress and he arranged with Pompeia to go to the house disguised as a singing girl and be met at the door by her own maid. No doubt the dare-devil adventure urged him on quite as much as his passion. The maid was on hand as he entered and bidding him wait slipped away to find her mistress. But she was long in coming back and Clodius, who, to be sure, was never one to wait patiently for anything, started to find his lady for himself. But something had gone wrong. Perhaps Pompeia's courage failed; more probably the very discreet woman had had her suspicions aroused, for as he went through the house her maid ran up to him and called out gaily that he must come and play with her, a custom, Plutarch says, at the festival—it would be pleasant to know what they played at—and upon his drawing back, asked him what was wrong. Clodius had the folly, inconceivable on the part of anyone except his arrogant, reckless self, to speak to her in answer and his voice betrayed him. She shrieked, "A man—a man!" and the fat was in the fire. Great was the to-do. The "sacred things" were covered; the holy rites pronounced null and void; the house ransacked. To no purpose, however; Clodius had been smuggled out by Pompeia's maid. All the same, he had been recognized and of course next morning the town buzzed with the delightfully horrific scandal.

The women made the most of it. A tribune was found to impeach the offender for profaning sacred ordinances, and a number of husbands were persuaded to bring forward in addition to this clearly substantiated charge, another which every Roman lady had shuddered at and passed on to her friends, but which obviously could not be clearly substantiated, that he had committed incest with one of his sisters, or indeed, with all three. Clodius contented himself with declaring that he was out of town at the time of the festival and had witnesses to prove it. Caesar put the best face he could on the matter: swore he did not believe a word of it; Clodius had never been in the house; a lot of women's talk. It was true he divorced Pompeia, but then he was ready with a reason which commended itself to every masculine heart, voiced in the famous saying about Caesar's wife.

Clodius, we may well believe, enjoyed himself. A trial for sacrilege was certain, but he knew the way out from that. Cicero was drawn into the affair. He was in a position to testify that Clodius had been in town, for he had called to see him the very evening of the festival. Rumor had it that he was extremely reluctant to move in the matter and that the reason was the lovely Clodia, the most beautiful and notorious of the three sisters. It is certain that he oftens speaks of her in his letters, and his nickname for her, "our ox-eyed goddess"—elsewhere he mentions her great flashing eyes—would point to some intimacy. At all events, Cicero's wife, a lady built on the lines of Plautus' Roman matrons, laid down an ultimatum and Cicero came forward as the chief witness for the prosecution. The enmity he aroused thereby followed him implacably through his life and even after. It was the part of a wise man to avoid giving offense to people like the Claudii, and the supple politician that lived in Cicero along with several widely divergent characters, was perfectly aware of the fact—but then there was Terentia, a violent lady, says Plutarch.

One of Cicero's letters gives a full account of the proceedings: "If you want to know about the trial, the result of it was incredible. The challenging of the jury took place amidst an uproar, since the prosecutor, like a good censor, rejected the knaves, and the defendant, like a kind-hearted trainer of gladiators, set aside all the respectable people. When the jury finally took their seats, a more disreputable lot never got together even in a gambling hell. All the same, these noble talesmen declared that they would not come to court without a guard [in a previous letter Cicero says that Clodius has several gangs of ruffians at his command]. No one thought Clodius would even defend his case.

" 'Tell me now, ye Muses, how first the fire fell.' Well, Baldpate [Cicero's name for Crassus, the richest man in Rome] managed the whole job in a couple of days with the help of just one slave. He sent for everybody, made promises, gave security, paid money down. Some of the jury were even presented with the time—at night—of certain ladies, and some with introductions to young men of good family. Even so, five and twenty of them were brave enough to prefer to risk their lives, but thirty-one were more influenced by famine than fame. Catulus meeting one of them later remarked, 'Why did you ask for a guard? For fear of having your pocket picked?' There you have the trial in brief and the reason for the acquittal. But I was the man who revived the fainting courage of patriots. I was speaking before the Senate soon after and by a happy inspiration I introduced into my speech this passage: You are mistaken, Clodius. The jury saved you for the gallows, not for public life. Keep up your heart, senators. We have merely discovered an evil that existed unnoticed. The trial of one villain has revealed many as guilty as himself. But there, I've nearly copied the whole speech for you. Up gets the pretty boy and reproaches me with spending my time at Baiae [as we should say at night clubs or at Monte Carlo]. It was a lie and anyhow what did it matter? 'You've bought a house,' he says. 'You seem to think it's the same as buying a jury,' I answer. 'They did not credit you on your oath,' he retorts. To which I answer, 'Twenty-five credited me. The other thirty-one gave you no credit but took care to get their money first.' Loud applause and he collapsed."

Yes, but nothing happened. Well-meaning citizens would applaud, but when it came to doing anything that meant personal effort, not to say inconvenience and even possible danger, that was another matter. Not long after this impressive demonstration of patriotic feeling, Clodius was elected to high office.

To the modern reader of the record it seems incredible that anyone, let alone those shrewd, competent Romans, should have believed that such a state of things could go on and on and a republic in which no one trusted either the electorate or the courts could in the nature of things endure. But so it was. Not even Cicero, superman that he was, read the handwriting on the wall. To be sure, he is perpetually saying that this or that piece of perfidy has dealt a death-wound to the state, but he never for a moment believes it. The laws are disregarded; the courts are despised; armed gangs face each other in the forum; the elections are a farce; the man with the largest purse always gets in, and nobody cares. Why should they? Life goes on most comfortably and agreeably in the great city, more so by far than ever in the world before. A violent change in government or in anything else is inconceivable. Business is good; great fortunes are made quickly in the provinces; at home it is not hard to keep the rank and file contented. Citizens of a republic where every man has a vote have easy ways open to them for getting money, and even wide-spread unemployment, when it occurs, no longer threatens danger. The people are kept contented not only by cheap food but also by the Roman equivalent of free tickets to the theatres and the major league games. Let the courts and the Big Three carry on as they like; nothing is really important but a pleasant, easy life which sensible people can have if they choose. Cicero, during a temporary lapse of his ruling passion, writes his brother: "Anything more corrupt than the men and times of today cannot be conceived. And so since no pleasure can be got of politics, I don't see why I should fret myself. I find my pleasures in literature and my favorite pursuits and the leisure of my country houses and, most of all, in our boys."

Ten years after that letter was written the Republic was ended; Antony and Augustus were dividing between them the Roman world; Cicero's headless body was lying on the seashore. In one of his letters he says that it is easy to know how to pull the ropes in a bad cause, but hard in a good cause, and "it is a difficult art to rule a republic."

# CHAPTER V

## CICERO HIMSELF

OF most famous people we know only the imposing façade. We have no key to open the door and let us enter. Cicero belongs to the very few who have left the key behind.

The general outline of what he did is familiar to us all: he was one of the two greatest orators of antiquity and everything else about him is in comparison negligible. This is the traditional idea of him, and from one point of view it is quite true. Today, after two thousand years, there are speeches of his which still live; the roll of their grand periods can still stir an emotion, and nothing else that he wrote has this power of independent life. His treatises, his politics, philosophy, rhetoric, have gone the way of all the books that decorate the library and are never read. And yet, even so, they have a claim upon the world's respect and admiration: few writings have had as many and as devoted readers. To run through the most famous of them now, the essay on Old Age, on Friendship, is to feel the impatience a perpetual mental "Of course" always awakens, but once these truisms were strangely new and it was Cicero who made them common. For centuries he was the main channel by which Greek standards reached mankind. He had the power so to write them down that people

322

everywhere read and believed them. He harnessed Greek thought to his heavy Roman car and the huge shapeless mass of men Rome was to form to civilized ways, caught a glimpse of what would else have soared far above them.

This achievement hardly needs illustration; it is acknowledged. Also, quotations of truisms are less enlightening than boring. Yet a few may perhaps be permitted. Some remembrance is due to the standards Cicero set, the effect he had upon this stubborn world. The gentleman, the English gentleman, who has meant much to many generations, may well have had his beginning in, certainly he was fostered by, the English schoolboys' strenuous drilling in Cicero. Our orator knew a great deal about the matter—which is not to say that he always lived up to his knowledge. His orations are not specimens of gentlemanly restraint, but there he followed, as he was bound to do, the customs of the courts. In his letters, where he is really himself, he always shows a perfect good breeding.

The fundamental precept of the gentleman, that if in a bargain one of the parties is to come out worsted, he must be the one, is laid down uncompromisingly in one of his essays. Liberality in spending, too, he knew was part of the code; he is firm against economy that might be a cover for meanness. In political matters if gentlemen take different sides, there can be no heat of controversy between them, however burning the question; they are well-bred men first and always, politicians and opponents second. And never, under any provocation, must a gentleman (N.B., *not* a lawyer) allow himself to refer to his antagonist's private life. Such points of conduct rank with the most important in his eyes. Among the terrible charges he brings against Mark Antony in the Second Philippic is the one of violating the gentleman's code: "He has quoted openly a letter he said I once wrote him! What man knowing even a little the ways of honorable men, ever because of some later offence, quoted a letter written by one who was at that time a friend?" Words like these were seeds in fruitful soil when they became part of the Englishman's education.

To teach mankind so effectively that the teacher ceases to be needed because the lessons have permanently affected men's fundamental convictions is a very great achievement. Nevertheless, it is a second-rate achievement. The greatest writers do not enter into the general consciousness and then cease to be. We cannot drain them dry and pass on, revived but never called back to find refreshment there. They belong in the city which was built

> to music, therefore never built at all,
> and therefore built forever.

Plato does not merely fill a shelf in our libraries. But Cicero is the man in Plato's parable of the poet who cannot be admitted to the temple, "being uninspired and having no touch of madness in his soul." In his greatest orations, there is fire. When he pleaded for unfortunate men or the unfortunate Republic—to him the most precious thing on earth, he writes a friend—he had passion and the power to put it into great words. But in the austere regions of the impersonal it failed and died.

He was not a typical Roman, but he had the training given all Romans by the most practical and efficient city the world had ever seen or was to see for two thousand years, and the undivided mind which thought demands was not only never his, he did not want it. He wanted to be doing something and if in a crowd, so much the better. Alone, unoccupied, he was bored. "I am so driven from pillar to post I can hardly find time for these few lines and even that I must snatch from important matters." The surface complaint does not conceal the deep satisfaction. In all the letters from Rome this tired-business-man attitude is to the fore, and in the country, in one of his delightful villas, the case is hardly better: "Writing is impossible. My house is a public hall, it is so crowded with the village people. Of course, the small fry don't bother me after ten o'clock, but Arrius lives next door, or, more truly, with me. On the other side is Sebosus!" In the next letter: "Just as I was writing these words in comes Sebosus and I had hardly time to sigh when there was Arrius saying good morning. This is going out of town!" All the same, when the bores spare him and leisure enfolds him, the result is not happier and certainly the letters are duller. "Nothing could be pleasanter than this solitude. All is more charming than you can imagine, the shore, the sea view, the hillocks, and everything. But they don't deserve a longer letter—and I have nothing else to say—and I am very sleepy—." Something more exciting than nature and meditation was necessary to keep Cicero awake. He wanted the movement of the great world; he wanted political life and a foremost part in it.

He achieved his ambition: he was the most important man in Rome when he put down Catiline's conspiracy, and for nearly twenty years he fought in the vanguard of all the political fighting, a great figure, thundering denunciations in the forum, pleading with passion against injustice, firing a feeble senate to stand by the state, a devoted republican, a patriot of the antique Roman stamp.

That is the façade, stately, imposing: and if it were not for his letters that is all we should see, as it is all we see of the heroes of history everywhere. But of these many letters, which number over eight hundred, more than half are written to a man with whom he was on terms of closest intimacy. He had nothing to hide from Atticus; with him he put up no pretense; he was content to appear just what he was. In his letters to other friends he remembered and would have them remember that he was one of Rome's leading men, moved, as Rome's leaders had ever been, by loftiest motives. To them he is sure that "only the honorable is the truly profitable," that "true worth is always victorious," that "nothing is expedient but what is right," but he never writes in this strain to Atticus. With him he is completely at ease. He can talk as he wants about everything and make jokes of matters he would feel bound in writing anyone else to take with decorous solemnity.

Of the letters Atticus wrote Cicero not a single one has been preserved and the so-called life of Atticus which has come down is hardly more than a long-drawn encomium. It is known, however, that he kept his large property intact through all the political convulsions of the times, and that he lived to be an old man, in those days quite as signal a triumph of worldly wisdom, and with the added light thrown by Cicero's correspondence he stands out clearly, a cool-headed man of business, whose standards were the expedient and the profitable and who made it comfortable for people to dispense with all pretensions to any other standards in his company. "There is no one, not even myself, with whom I talk as freely as with you," Cicero writes him. With this key Cicero unlocked his heart and the contents lie open for inspection.

He tells him that his son-in-law has been left property by a lady; he is to share with two others a third of her estate, but upon condition that he change his name. "It's a nice point," is Cicero's cheerful comment, "if it's the right thing for a noble to change his name under a woman's will—but we can decide that more scientifically when we know how much a third of a third amounts to."

He sets down with complete candor what many have felt and few been willing to say: "When I write you praising any of your friends I do wish you would let them know. I mentioned lately in a letter Varro's kindness to me and you answered you were glad to hear it. But I had much rather you had written him that he was doing all I wished—not that he was, but to make him do it."

His oratorical effects—"the mature outcome of my

talent, the finished product of my industry," when he speaks of them to others—to Atticus become delightfully something to poke fun at: "All that purple patch I so often use to decorate my speeches—the passage about fire and sword. You know the paints I have on my pallet. Ye Gods, how I showed off! You know how I can thunder. This time it was so loud I expect you heard it right over there."

When he must come to terms with Caesar whom he hated and had denounced over and over again as the destroyer of everything good in the state, he can find very fine words to dress up his motives for other friends: "To speak of him who has all the power in his hands—just as I used to think it was my duty to speak freely, since through me freedom still lived, now that it is lost I do not think I have any right to say a word against his wishes. In the opinion of those philosophers who alone grasp the true meaning of Virtue, the wise man will prefer nothing to the avoidance of wrong doing." But to Atticus he puts it differently: "As to the letter to Caesar, what view ought I to have taken except what I thought he wanted? What other purpose had my letter save to kow-tow to him? Do you suppose I should have been at a loss for words if I had wanted to tell him what I really thought? But what will the conservatives say? [This in another letter.] That I have been bribed to change my opinions? And what will history be saying of me six hundred years hence? That is a thing I fear much more than the petty gossip of today. Perhaps you will say. 'Hang dignity. It's prehistoric. Look after your own safety.' Oh, why aren't you here! Perhaps I *am* blinded by my passion for high ideals."

When his actions invade the realm of the Moral Duties, on which he wrote a famous treatise, he has the comfortable assurance that Atticus knows the ways of a politician in handling constituents must be judged by some other standard and he never has to bother how to cloak them nicely. His son-in-law, Dolabella, has become politically important, and Cicero writes him a long letter of glowing commendation: "Though I take the greatest pleasure in the glory you have won, I confess the crown of my joy is that in the popular opinion my name is associated with yours. Lucius Caesar said to me, 'My dear Cicero, I congratulate you on the influence you have with Dolabella. He is the first consul since yourself who can really be called a consul.' Why then exhort you and set distinguished examples before you? There is none more distinguished than your own." Cicero sends Atticus a copy of this letter and comments: "What a shameless fellow Dolabella is. He has lost your good graces for the same reason that he has made a bitter enemy of me."

Mark Antony writes to ask a favor and Cicero sends a charming answer: "Your friendly letter makes me feel that I am receiving a favor, not giving one. Of course I grant your request, my dear Antony. I wish you had made it in person. Then you could have seen the affection I have for you." Atticus gets a copy of both letters with the remark: "Antony's request is so unprincipled, so disgraceful and so mischievous, that one almost wishes for Caesar back again."

Occasionally, but very rarely, he mixes his Atticus style with his style of grandeur: "Two of my shops have fallen down. People call it a calamity, but I am not even annoyed. O Socrates, I can never thank you enough. Ye Gods, how insignificant all such things are to me. However, I have got a plan of rebuilding which will make my loss a profit." One can see Atticus first dismayed at the news, next a bit irritated by Socrates, and finally relieved by the profitable plan. Cicero had a way of drawing upon Atticus' resources as if they were his own.

But on the whole one closes the volumes with a sense of disappointment. These intimate letters, written at one of the most interesting moments of history about one of the two nations most interesting to us in all antiquity, are nearly always very dull. They are not history, they are daily life, nonconsecutive, full of trivialities, repetitions. Often they are hardly to be called letters; memoranda, rather, hastily jotted down, the day-book of a busy man. Personal concerns fill them. The great city into which everything in the world, civilized and barbarian, was pouring, becomes Cicero's own little stage monopolized by his own drama. He is too hard-pressed for anything else. Here is a political matter which must be decided at once, or a matter of buying a house, or of choosing a husband for Tullia, or of getting some money for Terentia. Will Atticus write back instantly what he advises? That is the way nine-tenths of the letters are written and it is the reason why he who was not commonplace hardly ever wrote a letter that was anything else. Elevation, power, distinction, were saved up for the orations. He may be writing from Athens (he had lodgings on the Acropolis!), or from Delos, "the marvelous isle," or from strange cities and lonely mountain camps in the unknown east: as far as the letters are concerned he might as well be in his house on the Palatine. There is never the least sign of interest in his surroundings. He is in a hurry. The messenger must be despatched and let him get on to the next piece of work. He is a man of big business.

But through all this mass of unassorted detail a singularly convincing picture emerges of the writer, and in the midst of the tiresome trivialities comes every now and then a comment, a story, a description, which suddenly stirs to life that faraway dead city.

If only Cicero had not been such a keen politician! The political life over-shadows the social to such a degree that while there are dozens of letters discussing in deadly detail the chances for election of this or that long, long ago forgotten candidate, or the effects of some, ages since, dead and buried measure, only a sentence here and there, at the best a few stray passages, throw a little light on the way of the world as the smart society of Ciceronian Rome pursued it.

Luxury is plain to see. Cicero pays nine hundred

dollars for some statues "of Megaric marble," on Atticus'
advice, and bids him also "send the figures of Hermes
in Pentelic marble with bronze heads, which you wrote
about, for the gymnasium and colonnade. I have fallen
in love with them. Don't hesitate. My purse is long
enough." What the house with gymnasium and colonnade must have been like, can be seen in a letter about
his brother's house: "All's right on your estate—nothing
left to do but the baths and a promenade and the
aviary. The paved colonnade gives dignity. The columns
have been polished and the handsome curve of the ceil-
ing will make it an excellent summer room. I will see
to the stuccoing. In the bathroom I moved the stove
to the corner of a dressing room because it was so
placed that the steam pipe was directly under the bed-
rooms. Your landscape gardener has won my praise;
he has enveloped everything in ivy—even the Greek
statues seem advertising it. It's the coolest, greenest
retreat. Statues, wrestling ground, fish pond, water system—all are fine. Really, an edifice worthy of Caesar—
and there is no more fastidious connoisseur." His brother
was in Gaul with Caesar, and it may be assumed Cicero
knew he could be depended upon "when I write praising
any of my friends, to let them know." The letter ends
with one of those touches of nature: "I love your boy,
but I am allowing him to leave me, because when he
is away from his mother the amount he eats appalls me."

Sometimes we get a glimpse of the vast slave world
which did all the work and provided all the amusements. "Do send me two of your library slaves," Cicero
writes Atticus, "to help glue pages, and tell them to
brings bits of parchment for title-pieces. I say, you *have*
bought a fine troupe of gladiators. I hear they fight
splendidly. If you had cared to hire them out you
would have cleared expenses on those two shows.
Enough of that—but, as you love me, remember the
library slaves."

Of the shows themselves, the most conspicuous feature of the life as we see it, Cicero speaks only once in

detail, an often quoted passage: "The games were of course most magnificent, but they would not have been to your taste. I infer that from my own feelings. Why, they were not as attractive even as games on a moderate scale often are. For what pleasure can there be in the sight of six hundred mules in the *Clytemnestra* or of three thousand bowls in the *Trojan Horse?* Two wild-beast hunts a day for five days—magnificent, of course. But what possible pleasure can it be to a man of culture when a puny human being is mangled by a tremendously powerful beast, or a splendid beast transfixed by a spear? And even if it is a spectacle, you've seen it all often, and there was nothing new that I saw. The last day came the elephants—very impressive, but the crowd took no pleasure in them. Indeed, there was a kind of compassion—a feeling that the huge creatures have some sort of fellowship with humans." Gladiatorial contests Cicero rather inclined to—from moral considerations. People call them cruel, he says, and perhaps they are, as conducted today. But certainly the spectators receive an incomparable training in despising suffering and death.

All through the letters there are allusions to the love the great, luxurious, corrupt and vice-ridden city had for passing prohibtions against luxury, corruption and vice. There is an amusing passage in a letter from a young scoffer Cicero was very fond of, Caelius Rufus, where Cicero is urged to come home to divert himself with the censor's activities: "He's performing prodigies in the matter of pictures and statues. Seems to feel his censorship is to be a kind of soap. Hurry home and join the laugh. Appius busy with pictures and statues!" It was of course delightful. Appius was Clodia's brother and the man who had bribed the consuls.

Only a very mild and limited edition of the *chronique scandaleuse* of the day is to be found. The decorum of the letters is amazing in that day and in that city. There is hardly a suggestion of impropriety even. A sample of his scandal-mongering—there are not above half a dozen in all—is a story he tells Atticus about an unfortunate gentleman who had his baggage searched and among his goods "were found five diminutive busts of Roman ladies—married, all of them! One was Brutus' sister, another, Lepidus' wife. *He* won't fret." This is as far Cicero will go in the way of an off-color story, and yet he wrote at a time when Rome was full of the vilest vice and the foulest talk. In an age notable for indecency, when Cicero was at his ease and writing just as he felt, he was invariably decent-minded. The scandalous tales passed him by all unheeded. In that respect his letters might have been written by Gladstone to John Bright. "I like modesty in speech," he once wrote. "The Stoics say that nothing is shameful or obscene in the saying of it. Wise men will call a spade a spade. Well, I shall keep as I always have, to Plato's reserves." He goes back to the Greek for his example; all the same, one catches a glimpse of a grave, disciplined restraint which through the centuries had ordered Roman life.

Dinner parties figure largely in the letters. On one occasion Cicero finds himself in very questionable company, "where next me reclined Cytheris [respectable women sat at table]. At such a dinner, say you, was Cicero! Upon my oath, I never dreamed she would be there. However, even when I was young I was never tempted by anything of that sort, much less now that I am old. But I do dearly love a dinner party where I may talk on anything and everything." What he has to eat there is of much less importance; still he never professes to be indifferent to that, either. "I do like high-class food and of a delicate quality," he writes, "but even if you persist in putting me off with the kind of dinner your good mother gives, I won't refuse." The standards of what one ought to have at a party are truly exalted: "Behold my audacity," he tells the same friend. "I have given a dinner to Hirtius without a peacock!"

His own private life figures very little. He divorced his wife when he was sixty and their daughter was old enough to have been married three times, but he never alludes to the divorce or to anything that led up to it. There are many letters to Terentia which are full of affection. "To think that you of all people, noble, faithful, upright, generous, as you are, should have fallen into misery because of me. Nothing is or ever has been dearer to me than you are," he writes her during his exile. "Tullius sends his best love to his wife Terentia and to his sweetest daughter Tullia, the two darlings of his heart." Such a beginning is quite usual in his letters, but gradually the tone grows cool and the last of all is rather a written order than a letter: "I think I shall arrive at my Tusculan villa on the 7th. See that everything is ready. I may have several others with me. If there is no basin for the bath, provide one and all else necessary. Goodbye." Terentia was not a submissive lady, and the divorce followed soon after. A few months later he had married a rich young ward of his and in as many weeks was bitterly regretting his rashness. He tells Atticus: "Publilia writes that her mother is coming to see me and that she will, too, if I will let her. She begs me urgently and humbly to do so and to answer her. You see what a nuisance it is. I answered that I was even worse than when I told her I wanted to be alone and she must not think of coming. I thought if I did not answer she would come; now I don't think she will. But I want you to find out how long I can stay here without being caught." Of course in Rome of easy divorces the marriage was soon ended.

Cicero's reason for wanting to be let alone was that that sweetest daughter of his had just died. He had only two children and his son was never very satisfactory. But Tullia was all that he could desire and he gave her his most devoted love. When she died, about two years before he did, he was utterly desolate. "While she lived," he wrote a friend, "I always had a sanctuary to flee to, a haven of rest. I had one whose sweet converse could help me to drop all the burden of my anxieties and sorrows." For months after, his letters to Atticus show a broken-hearted man. "I don't speak to a soul. In the morning I hide myself in the wood where it is wild and thick and I don't come out till evening. After you I have not a better friend than solitude. I fight against tears as much as I can, but as yet I am not equal to the struggle." It was the deepest personal sorrow of his life.

Through the letters great figures pass perpetually, great still to us today. Mark Antony, "a wretched, insignificant subordinate of Caesar's," Pompey from his height of aloof superiority calls him; "the toy captain," Cicero dubs him jeeringly to Atticus, "who carries round with him that actress Cytheris [the lady of the dinner party?] and in an open litter too. Indeed, they say he had seven litters with him full of his vile creatures, men and women both." Pompey appears often, contradicting on one page what was said on the page before, now the great statesman and superlatively great general who had been the leading man in Rome for years, and then at the crisis of his life when he faced Caesar to see which would rule the world, suddenly showing himself neither a statesman nor a general, as devoid of resolution as of common sense. "His way is to want one thing and say another," that engaging young scamp, Caelius Rufus, writes Cicero, "and yet he's not clever enough to hide what he wants. But," he adds gaily, "he's undergoing a reducing treatment at Bauli and is so extremely hungry, even I am sorry for him."

It will be seen that the letters puncture balloons; magnificence has a way of collapsing. The noblest Roman of them all bears no resemblance whatever to the personage we have watched so often on the stage. Cicero hears that Brutus is to marry Portia, and a good thing, too—the only way to stop the gossip. He goes to Greece and finds that Brutus is insisting that the people of Salamis shall pay him forty-eight percent on the money he has loaned them. "I can't go back on my own edict fixing twelve percent as the rate, even for Brutus," he writes Atticus. "A letter from Brutus"—

this shortly after Caesar's assassination. "I enclose a copy. One must confess it's of rather a dubious description—still he does show some sparks of manly courage."

Brutus' mother at any rate was not deficient in that respect. One day in his country house, shortly after Caesar's death, Cicero is present at a meeting of three great ladies, Servilia, Tertulla and Portia, Brutus' mother, sister and wife. They talk over the situation: both Brutus and Cassius have been insulted by receiving from the senate appointments to insignificant offices, Cassius' being merely to buy corn in Sicily. As they deliberate, "in came Cassius with flashing eyes and declared he would not go to Sicily." Whereupon Servilia promised she would take the matter in hand herself: "Servilia says she will cut the corn supply business out of the senatorial decree." It is a curious little picture of those elusive persons, the Roman women. Obviously, Servilia knew that she had the senate in her pocket.

The great Augustus, first Emperor of Rome, the autocrat whose word was final throughout the civilized world, appears a very human young man before the splendid trappings of royalty covered him up. Cicero shakes his head over him many a time. "It's a grave question how far one can trust one of his age and bringing up," he writes a few months after Caesar's death. "His father-in-law whom I saw at Astura thinks he is not to be trusted at all." "He's such a boy," this in a letter dated a year before Augustus handed Cicero over to Antony to be murdered. "He thinks he can call the Senate right away. Who will come? Yet the country towns are enthusiastic about the lad. Crowds to meet him and cheer him. Would you ever have believed it?" "A praiseworthy youth who had better be rewarded—and removed," is his final pronouncement. That remark was repeated to Augustus; three months later he agreed to Cicero's assassination.

Cleopatra, unfortunately, enters rarely and only once at any length. To Cicero she was not precisely the queen

Whom everything becomes, to chide, to laugh,
To weep—

"Cleopatra. How I detest the woman. You know she lived just across the river from me for several months. Anything more insolent—." Clearly a royal snub had been administered. Something on Cicero's part royalty had deemed presumptuous. It is a pity the interview has been lost. Cicero was not the man to submit in silence. A consular of Rome and a petty barbarian potentate would have been his evaluation of the opposing forces.

So at the touch of the letters, magnificence even in the most magnificent vanishes. The stately personages great tragedy has made live for us upon exalted heights, through these day-by-day records come down to the same levels where we live ourselves. Yet it is true that every one of them, Pompey, the solemnly inefficient, Brutus, the usurer, Portia, the indiscreet, Antony, the waster, even the insolent queen, were able to rise to greatness on occasion. If they could not maintain it during their lives they could reach it in the way they died, perhaps a matter of hardly less importance.

# CHAPTER VI

## CAESAR AND CICERO

CAESAR, the greatest man Rome produced, as we all believe with perhaps no very definite notion why, is seen less distinctly than any of the other notable personages Cicero discusses with his friends. That is our great loss, for Caesar was not given to explaining himself. A book, no matter on what subject, could hardly be less personal than his *Gallic War*. It is the one example in literature of an impersonal autobiography. Caesar figures on nearly every page, but in exactly the same way as all the other characters do. In a narrative which shows him overcoming incredible obstacles, facing almost insuperable odds, carrying overwhelming responsibilities, in perpetual danger of defeat and death— through all the account of what must have filled him with joy and grief and despair and triumph, there are only two exceptions to the perfect detachment of the record, only two passages, both very brief, in which there is a trace of personal feeling.

The first is merely a sentence, at the end of the account of his first campaign: "The Senate, informed of these successes by Caesar's letters, decreed a thanksgiving of fifteen days, a number never allowed to any general before." The statement is almost naïve enough to be Cicero's. A little ray of light shoots from it into that

inscrutable thing, Caesar's heart. He was proud of that
thanksgiving; he loved being more honored than any
man before. With the words he comes down for a moment from the unhuman heights on which he sets himself.

In the second passage, which belongs to the narrative
of the war, the emotion is unmistakable. Once a man
he loved was sent by him into what proved to be the
extremest peril, and Caesar suffered so much, the story
bears the impress. "A young man," he describes him, "of
great merit and politeness and of a singular integrity,"
was despatched as envoy to the German camp, where
he was seized and held. For all Caesar knew, they
killed him. He attacked and routed them, and then "the
young man, bound with a triple chain, dragged along
by his keepers in their flight, fell in with Caesar himself
as he pursued the Germans. Nor was the victory itself
more grateful to the general than his good fortune in
rescuing his intimate and familiar friend and to have
the success of the day no way diminished by the loss
of one he esteemed so highly."

With the words, the polite and meritorious young
man vanishes from history, and in all the rest of Caesar's
writings, the seven books of the *Gallic War* and the
three of the *Civil War* (often judged not his) there is
nothing comparable to his story. Even the annihilation
of a legion and the rescue of another just on the point
of annihilation are recounted with no more feeling than
if the narrator were a historian of deeds done centuries
before him.

It is not to be supposed that he followed a deliberate
plan to leave himself out. He had one thing alone in
his mind, his campaigns, and he thought of himself only
as he was concerned in them. Certainly he wrote without an idea that he would ever have a reader who would
think of anything else. He was always a man of few
words; about himself he did not talk at all. A result of
this reticence was that legend became extremely busy
with him; indeed, it took possession of him not long

after his death when his first biographer gratified a curious world. For years he was the most talked-of man in Rome and the stories, of course, grew always bigger and usually blacker. It is the greater pity that Cicero, who knew him from boyhood and was the one man among his contemporaries with ability enough to understand him, should mention him only briefly and rarely. No clear picture of him can be drawn from the letters. The truth is that Cicero did not try to see him clearly and was always shifting his point of view. But not his feelings; they remained the same: he never liked him. That is as plain to see as is Caesar's liking for him. Up to the crossing of the Rubicon the letters mention Caesar's name oftenest because of some service he has done or wishes to do Cicero. Caesar wanted his friendship and Cicero never gave it to him.

And yet Cicero was a good friend. Perhaps more than any other quality, the letters show his warmth of heart and the many people he was able to spend it upon. Expressions of devoted affection are common. He writes a man for whom he had got a post abroad: " 'How hard to please are those who love'—at first I was annoyed that you did not like being where you are; and now it gives me a pang of pain when you write that you do. I am distressed that you can find pleasure without me!" He is laughing at himself, but even so the words ring true and others like them are found again and again. "All men believe," he wrote elsewhere, "that life without friendship is no life at all."

No doubt these friends were often among the powerful; nevertheless some of the very warmest and sweetest of the letters are written to the slave who was his secretary. He was not strong, and Cicero showed a constant and tender anxiety for him: "Let your health be your only care; leave everything else to my care. Manifest as much regard for yourself as you do for me. Add this to the numberless services you have done and I shall value it more than them all. Take care, take care of yourself, Tiro mine." There are many such little notes to this beloved servant.

But what was given to a slave in full measure Caesar never won for himself, although year after year he tried. To be sure, away back in 63 (B.C., N.B.) he had voted against putting Catiline's fellow-conspirators to death, than which he could have done nothing worse in Cicero's eyes. All the same, when three years later he formed the coalition with Pompey and Crassus he invited Cicero to join, as great a proof of his esteem as he could have given. Cicero refused, why, can only be conjectured; the letters do not mention the offer nor indeed the coalition, except for a single reference to "three unbridled men." He refused, too, Caesar's next friendly move made soon after, when he had been given an office as notable in its results as any that has ever been given, the governorship of "Cisalpine Gaul and the Provinces beyond the Alps." He asked Cicero to go with him. Atticus is told, "Caesar most liberally invites me to take a place on his personal staff."

Back of that offer was the hero of the Good Goddess festival, young Clodius, although no one would have been more surprised than he to know it. He was easily the most popular man in Rome at the moment and as dangerous an enemy as one could have. It might be supposed that he was Caesar's enemy, too, but not at all. The scandal and the divorce and Pompeia's disgrace had somehow all been wiped off the slate, to Caesar's lasting shame, Plutarch says, but political expediency is always abominable in Plutarch's eyes. Clodius was to defend Caesar's interests during his absence. Caesar knew he was planning a spectacular vengeance on Cicero, and the invitation was given to get him away where he would be safe, and also, perhaps, where he would be harmless. After he refused to join the coalition, Caesar's idea of him was always that as a politician he was a liability. But life outside Rome was desolation to him and Caesar's company certainly nothing by way of compensation. He would not go, and soon after,

Clodius triumphantly passed the law which cut him completely off from his beloved city and sent him into exile, the most forlorn, homesick wanderer that ever there was.

Pompey, who, Cicero writes Atticus, "swears he will not see me injured [by Clodius] if it costs him his life," acted as was his way at a crisis, held grandly aloof and would take no part at all. When Cicero went to beseech his help and even flung himself at his feet, he answered coldly that he could not interfere, and he did not so much as stretch out his hand to raise the stricken man. Unforgivable, one would suppose, from a friend, and Pompey was an old friend; and yet when after more than a year of misery in foreign parts Cicero was recalled with Pompey's approval, he not only forgave him, he felt himself ever after deep in his debt. Inexplicably—nothing in the record gives any reason why—the plaster god which Pompey throughout the letters appears to be, all gilding outside and inside all hollow, had Cicero's unspeakable devotion. Years later when the war had begun for the leadership of the Roman world and Pompey fled before Caesar, abandoning Italy to him, Cicero could write: "The one thing that tortures me is that I did not follow Pompey when he was rushing to ruin. Since then I never have approved his course and he has never ceased to commit one blunder after another. And never a letter to me. But yet, now my old love breaks forth; now I miss him intolerably. Day and night I gaze at the sea and long to take flight to him."

With Caesar it was just the other way about. Cicero would not like him, no matter what he did. Caesar sent him many letters during the years he was in Gaul; he succeeded at least in convincing him that he could count upon him. All of the letters have been lost, but one of them Cicero quotes from in his answer: "A letter has just come from you saying, 'As to the man you have recommended to me, I will e'en make him king of Gaul. Send me somebody else to give a post to!'" It is delightfully said. The words, so few, are like a tiny snapshot—no pose; for the moment the great general has gone: a laughing face looks out and there is something warm beneath the gaiety. He wrote Cicero, so the latter tells his brother, "a most beautiful letter," when his dearly loved daughter died, the young Julia, Pompey's wife, who as long as she lived kept peace between the two men who both adored her.

Even on his arduous campaigns he took the trouble to write often. "A most cordial letter from Caesar," Cicero writes Atticus. "The result of the war in Britain is looked forward to with anxiety. There is not a scrap of silver on the island, no booty either except slaves— and I don't fancy there will be any with literary or musical talent among *them*." And again, some three weeks later: "On October 24th I had a letter from Caesar in Britain, dated September 25th. Britain is settled, hostages taken. No booty, but a tribute imposed, [it was never paid], and they are bringing back the army."

That was in the year 54. Then for several years Caesar drops out of the letters except now and then in those Caelius Rufus writes Cicero in Cilicia: "Lots of talk about Caesar—not so very nice. One fellow says he's lost his cavalry, which I don't doubt; another that he's hemmed in among the Bellovaci, cut off from the rest of the army. All secrets these. Domitius puts his finger to his lips before he even begins to speak."    )

The date of that letter is 50, the year when, frightened by Caesar's triumphs in the west and his increasing popularity in Rome, the senate and Pompey lightly determined to put him down. Caelius writes: "Pompey is resolved not to allow Caesar to be consul unless he hands over his army; Caesar is convinced there is no safety for him without the army; he wants to compromise—have both give up their armies." This fair proposal was rejected. Rome had no idea yet what Caesar was like. "When Pompey was asked," Caelius continues, " 'What if Caesar is minded to be consul and keep his army too?' he replied with the utmost suavity, 'What if my son is minded to lay his stick across my shoulders?' "

"Pompey has a perfect contempt for Caesar," Cicero writes Atticus. The result of this attitude was that Caesar crossed the Rubicon early in the next year and the fight was on, to end eighteen months later in Pompey's defeat and death.

Almost at once Caelius Rufus, the gay adventurer, and Atticus, the far-seeing and prudent, go over to Caesar, significant straws, both of them. Caelius flings himself into the cause with enthusiasm. "Did you ever see a sillier fellow that your Pompey," he writes Cicero from Caesar's quarters in northern Italy, "stirring up all this mud with his feeble inefficiency? And did you ever read or hear of anyone keener in action than our Caesar or more moderate in victory?" Of Atticus' right-about-face we know only from a letter Cicero writes him: "When men like you and Peducaeus are going to meet him [Caesar] at the fifth milestone, surely his belief that he is right will be strengthened. 'What harm in that?' you ask. None—but yet the outward signs of the distinction between true feelings and pretense are all upset." Poor Cicero. Atticus is merely acting according to the principles of expediency that he and Cicero had always acknowledged to each other they followed, but when it comes to the point of deserting Pompey and the senate just because they are not succeeding, Cicero cannot do it and it is bitter to him that Atticus can. And yet a few months earlier he had written him: "What am I to do? I know if it comes to fighting it would be better to be beaten with Pompey than conquer with Caesar. But consider by what trick I can keep Caesar's good will."

From then on until Pompey's defeat there is nothing in the letters Cicero himself writes that helps to explain Caesar. He is only denunciatory. Caesar is "that viper we have cherished in our bosom"; "the prince of scoundrels"; a "wretched madman" who has "never seen the shadow of honor and right." But there are two letters of Caesar's included in the correspondence which are remarkable documents. During Cicero's long and agonizing struggle to follow what he felt was the path of honor and take his stand with Pompey and the losing cause, Caesar never ceased begging him—not to join him, that, it is clear, he instantly saw Cicero would not do—but not to join Pompey either. He writes him— the letter is inscribed *On the march* and the year is 49—"You will have done a serious injury to our friendship and consulted your own interest very little if you show that you have condemned anything that I have done, the greatest harm you could do me. By the right of our friendship, I beg you, do not take such a step. What better befits a good and peaceful man and a good citizen than to keep out of civil dissension? There are some who approved such a course and were unable to follow it because of danger." He means himself and the words, so carefully impersonal, are yet one of the few personal expressions of his feelings on record. "But for you," the letter continues, "the evidence of my life, your conviction of my affection, must show you there is no safer or more honorable course than to keep clear of the struggle."

Urgent words, written with strong feeling. It is not to be supposed that politically Cicero was important to Caesar. He had always been a weak and wavering politician. What must have dictated that letter was Caesar's genuine friendship, and also, perhaps no less, his hatred of civil war. He wanted to enlist in the cause of peace the eloquent tongue he had himself often been moved by.

When his letters failed he arranged for a meeting, and Cicero's account of it to Atticus shows how little those two able men who had known him all his life, understood him. "We were mistaken," so the letter runs, "in thinking he would be easy to manage. I have never seen anyone less easy. After much talk he said, 'Well, come and work for peace.' 'On my own terms?' I asked. 'Am I to dictate to you?' he said. 'Well,' I said, 'I shall oppose your invasion of Spain and I shall mourn for Pompey.' He replied, 'That is not what I want.' 'So I

fancied,' said I. 'But that is what I must say if I go to
Rome.' So we parted. I am sure he has no liking for
me, but I like myself as I have not for a great while. He
is very wide-awake and bold—"

Most significant of all is another letter which one of
Caesar's officers sent Cicero in an effort to show him
Caesar's real aims and so win him over. It is unique in
military correspondence. Caesar had written his subordinate: "I made up my mind to act with the greatest
moderation and do my best to bring about a reconciliation with Pompey. Let us see if in this way we can win
all hearts and secure a lasting victory. It is a new way
of conquering, to use compassion and generosity as our
defenses. I captured one of Pompey's officers. Of course
I acted according to this plan of mine and set him free
at once."

There was nothing weak and wavering in Caesar. He
kept to his plan; he followed this new way of conquering. When Pompey was defeated, one after another of
the men who had supported him were given a free
pardon. There has never been a victor more merciful.
In that pitiless ancient world he stands alone. Cicero,
eagerly forgiven and welcomed back to Italy, was won
to an apparent admiration. He writes one and another
of his friends, "We find him daily more yielding and
conciliatory"; "He has a mild and merciful nature"; "I
continue to enjoy his extreme kindness to me." And on
one occasion when Caesar pardons a man who had
not only opposed him but deeply insulted him, Cicero
even has a moment of enthusiasm. "It seemed to me
so glorious a day that I imagined I saw before me some
fair vision of the Republic rising from the dead."

Such expressions, however, are all in letters to other
people, never to Atticus. The only praise he ever gave
Caesar in the letters where he spoke the truth was praise
of his writing: "I forgot to enclose a copy of my letter
to Caesar—not, as you suspect, because I was ashamed
of seeming a flatterer. I have a high opinion of those
books of his, so that I wrote without flattery, and yet

I think he will read it with pleasure." For the rest, the allusions are brief and cautious: "I give you a free hand. Only take care that nothing is done to offend the great man." Atticus would not have welcomed just then any denunciations of the great man, nor would Cicero have dreamed of writing them. He was doing everything in his power to stand well with Caesar, and postal messengers did not always carry mail to the right person.

The last glimpse of Caesar is in a letter dated about six months later and less than three months before the Ides of March. Cicero gives him a dinner party, a very splendid affair. "It passed off perfectly delightfully," he tells Atticus. "A formidable guest, but he left no regret behind. Until one o'clock he admitted no one: at his accounts, I believe. Then he took a walk, and after two, his bath, and then, when he had been anointed sat down to dinner. He was undergoing a course of emetics so he ate and drank as he pleased—a lordly dinner and well served,

> Well cooked, well seasoned and the truth to tell,
> With pleasant discourse all went very well.

We were all friends together. Still he isn't the sort of guest to whom one would say, 'be sure to look me up on your way back. Once is enough. There was no serious talk but plenty of literary—" a sentence typically Roman in its evaluation of what was really worth men's sober attention.

In Cicero's next letter Caesar is dead. The conspirators did not ask Cicero to join them, to his never-ending regret, he protests in several letters. There were no bounds to his enthusiasm at first: "Though all the world conspire against us, the Ides of March console me. Our heroes accomplished most gloriously and magnificently all they could." So for the next two months. Then there is a change. He begins to distrust Brutus and Cassius as leaders. They will not take any decisive steps. They keep away from Rome and do nothing. "The deed was done with the courage of men, but with the blind policy of a child," he writes Atticus in May. And when he goes to see them a month later he finds "a ship breaking up or rather in wreckage. No plan, no reason, no system." Then for a moment he remembers the friend who had stood by him through just such a shipwreck: "For Caesar, somehow, was most patient with me." But that touch of regret and wonder stands quite alone. His final words are as sweeping a condemnation as has ever been spoken of one man by another. In the treatise on moral duties, written in the year of Caesar's death and the year before his own, he says: "So great was his passion for wrongdoing that the very doing of wrong was a joy to him for its own sake." This is Cicero's obituary over Caesar.

It is not possible to explain his feeling as due merely or mainly to his devotion to the Republic and consequent hatred of the man who took the supreme power himself. To the end of his life he loved and praised and mourned Pompey, but long before he joined his camp in Greece he had seen clearly that he was fighting for one thing only, his own domination. "Absolute power is what Pompey and Caesar both have sought," he wrote Atticus. "Both want to be kings." "Pompey's idea from the first has been to bring savage tribes to ravage Italy." Nevertheless, his affection for him never failed. Something else was responsible for his steady dislike of Caesar. Alone among his contemporaries he was qualified to understand him, and no doubt Caesar felt this. His powerful and brilliant mind could find a companionship in Cicero no one else could give him. Except for him he was surrounded by petty minds, mean and limited spirits. But Cicero would have none of him, and so far as is known, except for Mark Antony, Caesar never had a close and steadfast friend. The two officers he most trusted turned against him; Brutus whom he loved killed him, and no other men are mentioned as being on terms of intimacy with him.

The devotion of his soldiers to him, affirmed in many

stories, must be a fact. He could not have done what he did without it. The speech in which it is always said he quelled a mutiny with a single word, calling his men not fellow-soldiers as was his custom, but citizens, civilians, shows a great deal more about his methods than the mere clever use of a term.

It was a most critical moment for him. He was in Rome after Pompey's defeat, on the point of sailing for Africa, to put down the powerful senatorial army there. In the city he was surrounded by bitter enemies. His whole dependence was his army, and the best and most trusted legion in it mutinied. They nearly killed their officer; they marched to Rome and claimed their discharge; they would serve Caesar no longer. He sent for them, telling them to bring their swords with them, a direction perfectly characteristic of him. Everything told of him shows his unconcern about danger to himself. Face to face with them, he asked them to state their case and listened while they told him all they had done and suffered and been poorly rewarded for, and demanded to be discharged. His speech in answer was also characteristic, very gentle, very brief, exactly to the point:

"You say well, citizens. You have worked hard—you have suffered much. You desire your discharge. You have it. I discharge you all. You shall have your recompense. It shall never be said of me that I made use of you when I was in danger, and was ungrateful to you when danger was past."

That was all, yet the legionaries listening were completely broken to his will. They cried out that they would never leave him; they implored him to forgive them, to receive them again as his soldiers. Back of the words was his personality, and although that can never be recaptured, something of it yet comes through the brief, bald sentences: the strength that faced tranquilly desertion at a moment of great need; the pride that would not utter a word of appeal or reproach; the mild tolerance of one who knew men and counted upon nothing from them.

One more speech famous in antiquity is reported which shows the same characteristics. It was made to his officers during the war in Africa. The senatorial forces there had formed an alliance with a barbarian king of whom frightful stories were told. Caesar heard that his centurions were nervous at the report of the king's approach with an overwhelming army, and he called them together. "You are to understand," he said, "that within a day King Juba will be here. He has ten legions" (their own force was very inferior), "thirty thousand horse, one hundred thousand skirmishers, three hundred elephants. Your part is neither to think about the situation nor to ask questions. I tell you the truth and you must prepare for it. If any of you are frightened I will provide you with means for going home."

"I am told," Cicero said to him in a speech made in the senate a few weeks before his assassination, "that you often say you do not wish for longer life. I have myself with sorrow heard you say that you have lived long enough." The night before the Ides of March, a chronicler relates, he was at supper with a number of others when the talk turned on what was the best kind of death. Caesar, who was signing papers while the rest argued, looked up and said: "A sudden one." The story, of course, is too apposite, but the man who first told it understood character. It is just what Caesar would have said.

Two other accounts of him by contemporaries have come down. Sallust, who wrote a history of Catiline's conspiracy, describes Caesar at some length, but dwells only upon his kindness and leniency. He was always "giving, relieving, pardoning, a refuge for the unfortunate"; "He was marked out by his humanity and benevolence"; "He cared for his friends' interests and neglected his own." It is undoubtedly the report of a partisan; Sallust was an officer of Caesar's and Caesar thought highly of him, but it agrees in general with

Cicero's account—who was no partisan. The speech
Caesar made against putting the conspirators to death,
Sallust gives in full, and all the probabilities are that it
is essentially accurate. Certainly Sallust was not present
when it was spoken, but there were short-hand writers
in Rome, and the occasion was a great and notable one.
Furthermore, those who had heard the speech would
be Sallust's readers and the very ones whose approval
would mean most. It is not credible that he wrote what
the senate would know was false. The speech is brief
and calm, a closely reasoned, unemotional appeal to
abide by the law. Laws are made to be men's defenses
not only against others but against their own selves.
They are man's safeguards against man's passions. The
proposal before the house is to put citizens to death. It
is illegal. Whenever in the past the great bulwark of
the law has been weakened, the consequences have
invariably been calamitous. If by any act now it should
be seriously impaired, the danger is that it may be
ultimately completely overthrown, to the disaster of all
within the state.

But what could this impersonal rationality mean to
furious, frightened men whose ears still rang with
Cicero's impassioned appeals to everything mortal and
immortal except the rational? Cicero is an authority for
Caesar's brilliant promise at the bar when in his youth
he began a career as a lawyer. None of his speeches
there have survived and all that can be said is that he
must then have changed his style completely in his
later years. Cicero was the model for the Roman bar;
his powers of terrific invective, of playing upon people's
emotions, of firing them to anger or melting them to
tears, of making the eagle scream—the bronze Roman
eagle—with appeals to republican glory and ancestral
purity of hearth and home—this overpowering onrush of
eloquent language would surely never have found a
rival in the direct, terse, simple words which are all
that Caesar has left behind him.

There is still another portrait of Caesar drawn by

a contemporary. In those last years of the Republic a fierce young poet was walking the streets of Rome and noting with passionate scorn in bitter, jeering verses the corruption he met with there. It would be hard to find in all the range of literature anything more different from Cicero's letters than Catullus' poems. To pass from one to the other is rather like passing from Archdeacon Grantley and the pleasant people of Barset to Swift at his most violent. Cicero by birth and by nature is the decent, comfortable bourgeois always; Catullus, the aristocrat by temperament turned rebel against the world and everything decent and comfortable in it.

The first of the two poems in which he expresses his opinion of Caesar turns on one Mamurra, of whom Cicero wrote to Atticus: "Do I approve of Caesar's military power being extended? If I did I would approve of the throwing away of the Campanian lands, of my own banishment, of the wealth of Mamurra—" Catullus thought the same about that wealth: "Who can witness, who endure, this thing? Only he who is himself without shame, greedy, a swindling gamester. Mamurra have the wealth of Gaul beyond the Alps and farthest Britain? O Rome, decadent in your debauchery, will you witness these things and endure? Now, arrogant, money rolling off him, he goes to every bed of all alike. Was it for this, O general, great as never another, that you went to the farthest island of the west? You foster this thing of evil? Is it for this, O Caesar, Pompey, that you have brought ruin upon all."

The second poem leaves nothing further to be said in the way of personal malediction: "How prettily they agree, Mamurra, Caesar, each as vile as the other with the vice of decadents. No wonder either. The dirt that fouls both has sunk deep in, nor will be washed away. Sick alike, in the same bed, sweet twins, elegantly learned in adultery, both, and one as greedy for it as the other— how prettily they agree."

Did that loud furious voice, shouting out filth of vilest abuse, not reach Cicero's ears when Caesar seemed to him, too, all that was most hateful? He never mentions Catullus; he never hints at any sort of vice in Caesar. With all their decent propriety, the letters give a clear enough picture of Mark Antony's habits. It would seem natural to find in them some allusion of the kind to Caesar's if they had been as Catullus made out. But Cicero is completely silent. Once in a speech he remarked that there was no young man in Rome with any attraction against whom such things had not been said.

The century after Caesar's death heard other tales about him that bore out Catullus' accusation, as well as endless stories of ladies who loved him, but they are not for the chronicler to pass on. There is no contemporary evidence in the case except Catullus, and a complete absence of the judicial quality seems to have distinguished that passionate young man beyond all else. It will be with Caesar as with other men accused of infamies which cannot be proved or disproved, people will believe or not according to their own temperament.

As his contemporaries saw him he was a contradiction, and so he remains. Plutarch quotes a description of him from Cicero which makes credible the many accounts that he was excessively dandified, always an elegant. "When I see his hair so carefully arranged and observe him adjusting it with one finger, I cannot imagine it should enter such a man's thoughts to subvert the Roman State." Yet all reports agree that he could fight—and swim—with the best of his soldiers, and that he not only endured exceptional hardships easily, but practiced always a notable temperance in food and drink. If he was really sick with the diseases of the sewer his vigor was truly astounding. He was—probably—nearing fifty-eight when he died. During the three years preceding he had carried on successful wars in Greece, Egypt, Asia Minor, Africa, Spain, in the accounts of which occur constant references to his outstanding characteristic, swiftness—of mind, in anticipating the enemy's next move, of body, in always arriving long before it seemed possible.

He was reported as fearfully cruel in Gaul and notably merciful in Italy. As regards the first, he is the chief witness against himself. Four times he tells of terrible severity, of whole tribes of Gauls or Germans wiped out or sold into slavery. Each time the people in question had broken an agreement—or Caesar thought so—and he was fighting in a hostile country with no possibility of help from anywhere. In all other cases he makes himself out a lenient conquerer, and the fact that during the long struggle with the Pompeians there was no rising in Gaul against his rule speaks for his wisdom in exercising it.

Before he left Rome for the west the splendor of the gladiatorial games he held had outdone all others and were always spoken of as a cause of his popularity with the lower classes, and yet a curious little story of him has come down in a life of Augustus: "As often as Augustus attended the gladiatorial games, he would take special pains to appear absorbed by the spectacle, because he wished to avoid the odium incurred by his relative (Caesar) who had been used, when present on such occasions, to turn away and occupy himself with reading or writing."

In the end he remains an enigma except in a single respect, his generalship. Quite possibly that is the way he himself would have had it. At any rate, he cared to put himself before the world only as a soldier. He was too great to be easily pigeonholed. He must be given a place among the men of thought; he was preeminent as a statesman and he wrote a book which has held its own for two thousand years. Nevertheless, it is the book of a man interested only in what is outside, in things, which to him included most men and all soldiers. His real place is, of course, with the great captains of the world, who whether they rule over war or industry, act and do not explain.

At the opposite pole stands Cicero. He can be understood through and through. All the hidden things within the heart, the meannesses and weaknesses we least wish seen in ourselves, in his case lie open, completely exposed to strange, critical eyes. His vanity, his hypocrisy, his falsehoods, his cowardice, his dependence upon praise, his love of ease, his terrible difficulty in making up his mind, all these and more he wrote down for the friend he knew would never hold a single one against him, and so he preserved them plain to see forever. It was a hard fate for a man to bring down upon himself who wanted most of all to stand a glorious figure in the halls of history.

"He was without magnificence of mind," Plutarch says in his grave summary of his character. The words are arresting; they bring vividly before us the difference between our scale of values and the Greek and Roman. Magnificence of mind is not among our best-prized virtues today. Caesar had it. When his most trusted officer deserted to the enemy in a time of crisis he sent after him all the possessions he had left behind, horses, slaves, baggage, without a word. After Pompey's defeat they brought him a great mass of correspondence found in Pompey's tent, for him to read and find out who were his enemies in Rome. He burned the whole unread. Behind the action lay fearlessness and self-confidence, both of the essence of magnificence. Cicero had neither. He let Catiline go when he had him under his hand. He denounced him sitting before him in the senate-house; he showed him up to the whole senate as a convicted traitor; he thundered and lightened against him—and allowed him to walk out undisturbed, free to leave the city and put himself at the head of a hostile army. He was consul; a word from him and Catiline would have been in prison, but he was not sure that people were with him, and without that surety he never could act. He had no surety within himself.

Magnificence in a man means one who will live on his own terms, not on those imposed by others. A story which illustrates the point is told by Plutarch. When

Caesar was very young, Sulla, the all-powerful, bade him as he had already bidden the obedient Pompey, to divorce his wife and take another of Sulla's choosing. Caesar refused; his property was confiscated; he still refused; a price was put upon his head; he fled and still refused. In the end it was Sulla, the terrible autocrat, who gave in to a boy not yet out of his teens. Cicero lived all his life on terms imposed by others. The matter of chief importance to him was to have approval. To the day of his death this was a source of terrible trouble to him. It made him jealous of everyone else who was approved. Even of Pompey he could write: "The thought that his services to the country might in the dim future be reckoned higher than mine used to prick me to the heart." It was the reason he was forever explaining himself, excusing himself. He could not get on without support, or even without praise.

Plutarch was right, he was never magnificent. But all the same he had virtues to command respect. The negative one of complete personal integrity which Pompey shared with him, and Caesar probably too, is by no means to be lightly regarded. In a city where everything was for sale, to be the exception was admirable. But far beyond that is the fact that whenever it came to a definite choice between what he thought was right and what he knew was safe, he chose the former, at a cost of suffering such as only a man timid and sensitive as he was could feel—such suffering as a man like Caesar never felt. But in spite of the agony it cost him, he held fast to duty when he saw it. "One may do some time-serving," he once wrote, "but when one's hour has come one must not miss it." Nor did he. He joined Pompey when he believed his cause was hopeless and that he was bidding farewell to all that made life worth living. He was a tired old man, too. He wrote Atticus at the time: "And to speak truth, my life's evening, following peacefully after my long labors, has made me lazy with the thought of home pleasures." All the same he found his way to Pompey's camp across the sea.

Lucan's famous line about another faithful adherent of the Republic applies as truly to Cicero in that moment:

Conquering causes are dear to the gods, the conquered to Cato.

Once more, when Caesar was dead and there seemed to him a possibility of restoring the Republic, he gave up going to Greece where safety lay, to come back to Rome and fight against the man of the hour, Mark Antony, the greatest power then in Italy, whom he saw as an imminent danger to the state. He died in consequence. He was forced to leave Rome; he went first to one country house, then another. At last he decided to take ship and sail somewhere—anywhere. He was all alone. Not one of the many friends of the letters came forward to stand by him. (The record does not say where Atticus was, but we may feel sure the situation was advantageous.) He embarked, and then—no reason is given—left the boat and returned to the house and lay down upon his bed. He had come to the end of his desire for life. But his servants got him up and into a litter and were hurrying him back to the seashore when Antony's men caught up with them. He told them to set the litter down, and, Plutarch says, continuing to stroke his chin as he was wont to do, he looked steadfastly upon his murderers. Only one man dared strike him; the others stood by, covering their faces. "There is nothing," he once wrote to his son-in-law, "absolutely nothing fairer, more beautiful, more to be loved, than high courage." He had not always been able to show it in his life. In his death he was more fortunate.

# CHAPTER VII

## CATULLUS

ONE holiday morning in the year 57 B.C., the year after Cicero returned from exile, the Roman forum was filled with a gathering unusual to the place. In spite of the festival just beginning, a trial was to be held, and not only the size of the crowd but the fact that many notables were to be seen who would normally never think of coming to court, showed that it was judged an occasion quite out of the ordinary. Ladies of fashion were conspicuous; of all the wits of the town every one had his place there; and not a single young man with any pretensions either to wit or fashion but was well to the fore. There was reason enough for their presence. One of Rome's very great ladies had brought a charge of murder and attempt to poison against one of the most brilliant young elegants in the city. Even more alluring than that, the two had been lately, very lately, closely associated, their names linked together in everyone's mouth. It had really been an acknowledged fact; he had even lived for a time in her house, neither of them being people who would dream of giving up anything they wanted because of what might be said. And now they sat facing each other, accuser and defendant on a capital charge, Clodia, once Cicero's friend, the sister of the hero of the Good Goddess festival and herself

357

the heroine of a thousand scandals, and Cicero's gay
and cynical and delightful young correspondent, Caelius
Rufus.

Clodia had taken her seat in the front row beside the
men who had preferred the accusation for her, not one
of them important enough to draw even a passing glance
away from her. At this time she had not a shred of
reputation left; her name was a byword; yet she sat
there as disdainfully superior to the staring, covertly
sneering crowd as if she had never strayed an inch
from the traditions of the great aristocratic house which
had fathered her. Of so much the reader of the record
may be sure. The Claudii all had magnificence of a sort:
they lived their lives on their own terms and what
people thought of them mattered not in the very least.
In the crowded forum Clodia saw two persons only,
the man who had yielded to her for a brief space, lived
in her house, taken her money, and then all in a moment
scornfully shaken himself free of her, and the man who
was to defend him, the bitter enemy of her and hers,
home in triumph from the exile her brother had brought
down upon him. No one in Rome but knew Cicero's
tongue. Another woman would have stayed safe at
home. Clodia took a front seat and faced her foe with
eyes that never wavered and a faint smile upon her lips.

One may conjecture that the defendant was less at
ease. He was at least ten years younger than the lady
and twenty years less experienced. Furthermore, if the
verdict went against him, he was ruined, and a life of
fairest promise had stretched before him when this terrible accusation loomed up in his path. He might well
be thinking that he had acted with reckless folly when
he had wearied of an older woman's passion and on
the instant flung himself away from her. Care was
necessary in dealing with the Claudii. He had not
troubled to take any. He had laughed at her advances
and gone from her to make the city laugh too. *Quadran-
taria* he called her, the lady whose price is a penny, and
the taunt went through the town. Whenever Clodia ap-

peared someone would whisper it and everyone catch it up and pass it on. He had scorned her openly, and she had been used only to scorn others herself, to throw carelessly away man after man when they had served her turn. Caelius had been a fool and his only hope to escape paying a terrible price for his folly lay in his advocate.

To Cicero the case was heaven-sent. He had come back to Rome to find that Clodius had had his beloved house razed to the ground and a temple erected on the site. It was the insult added to injury which seemed hardest of the two to bear. And now was his enemy delievered into his hands. Plutarch says of him that before he started on a speech he was always cold with fright and even when launched into the full current of it could hardly leave off shaking and trembling. It is a credible account. Such high tension and quivering sensitiveness are very often the companions of genius. But, it may well be believed, upon this occasion there was not a trace of either. Cicero was at ease and happy; he was perfectly aware of what he could do.

The case for the prosecution was at an end: Caelius had hired men to assassinate the envoy of the King of Egypt with money Clodia had given him; with this same money also he had bribed slaves to administer poison to her. Witnesses were present to swear to both charges. Cicero rose to answer. He knew the Roman crowd as a master musician his instrument; he could play upon them as skillfully and as surely.

"The whole case, gentlemen of the jury, rests upon Clodia, a woman known not only by her noble birth but by the crowd's complete familiarity with her [laughter]. I wish I need not name her, the more that there has been enmity between me and her husband—I mean, her brother. I am always making that mistake—[a wave of delighted amusement passes over the audience, well aware of the scandal of Clodia's relations with her brother]. And indeed, I never thought to take upon me a quarrel with a woman, especially with one who far

from being considered any man's adversary is universally held to be the intimate of all [laughter]. I would not
offend her. Let me ask her how she would prefer me
to address her—in the grave, old-fashioned style or in
the lighter manner of today? If the first, I must summon
one to rise from the dead, that grand old blind man, of
all her family the most renowned, not sorry today that
he cannot see who sits before him. He shall stand here
and speak in my stead: Clodia, what have you to do
with Caelius? How is it that you were either so intimate
with him as to give him money, or so hostile to him as
to fear to be poisoned by him? You, your father's
daughter, the descendant of generations of men who
were Rome's consuls, the wife of a man Rome delighted
to honor—why did you seek this intimacy? Was he your
husband's friend—was he related to you by blood or by
marriage? None of these, O daughter of a house where
the women have ever equalled the men in glorious
renown. Did I break off a base peace with Rome's
bitter foe that you might enter into the alliance of a
shameful love? Did I bring water to the city for you
to wash away your filthiness? Did I build the great high-
way that you might take your pleasure on it with
strange men?

"But perhaps, Clodia, you prefer me to speak to you
as a man of the world? Let me dismiss that stern, rugged
figure and choose as my spokesman, most appropriately,
that perfect man of the world, your youngest brother,
who loves you very much. He asks you what all this to-
do is about. Are you out of your head, sister, making
such a molehill into a mountain? You took a fancy to
the young man next door—to his handsome face and
figure. His father gave him little money; you tried to
bind him to you with some of yours. But he found
he must pay too high for your gifts and he has done
with you. What of it? Are there no others? Those
gardens of yours by the Tiber which you have fitted up
so that all the young men want to take their swim
there—what is the use of them if you cannot pick

and choose as you want? Why make yourself a nuisance to someone who does not want you?"

The delight of the audience may be imagined, but Cicero has not yet done with Clodia. Caelius he treats indulgently, with a touch of humorous despair over youth's careless pursuit of pleasure. Very sad, no doubt. His client cannot be defended on that score; he did what he ought not. "And yet, gentlemen of the jury, we ourselves can remember the hot youth of some among us today. Understand me, gentlemen, I have no intention of naming anyone, but if I had, you will bear me out, I should have no trouble. To speak plain truth, if any woman throws her house open to whosoever desires, if without disguise she leads a courtesan's life, if she so acts here in the city, in her gardens, at Baiae, that what she is is apparent not only by her gait, her dress, her burning eyes, her freedom of speech, but by such entertainments as only women of that kind offer, would you judge a young man who approached her guilty of wrong or merely bent on a moment's pleasure? Tell me, Clodia, would a man who had intercourse with that sort of woman—completely unlike yourself, of course—[laughter] be disgraced and degraded in your eyes? If you are not such a one, as I grant you, how could Caelius act with you as he is said to have done? If you are, your life makes null and void any testimony from you."

Then he passes on to the charge of poison and his mocking voice takes on the deep sonorous accents of the righteously indignant: "Gentlemen, I saw—I myself saw and with as bitter pain as ever I felt in my life, the excellent Metellus, this lady's husband, dying, him whom the day before I had met in the senate house, enjoying the full strength of his vigorous prime. I saw him struggling to speak, his voice choked with agony, striking the wall in his paroxysms. From that house Clodia comes and dares to speak of the effect of swift poison?" Cicero knew his case was won. No one in the audience but was glad to believe the worst of the woman whose beauty and wealth and arrogance had made bitterly envious enemies for her everywhere. The shrewd lawyer brought his speech to a swift close. It ends with the statement astonishing to the modern reader, that the charge rested on nothing substantial, no logical argument, no conclusion necessitated by the premises, but only on the word of witnesses (everyone there knew they were to be hired for any statement desired, on every street corner) and with a pathetic picture of the poor, wronged, innocent young Caelius and the misery of his noble old father, all due to the vilest of women. The verdict was not so much a vindication of Caelius as an overwhelming condemnation of Clodia. Such was the woman whom life's irony made the heroine of one of the world's great love stories.

It is in the highest degree improbable that Clodia ever realized that she had achieved immortality or that if she had she would have cared. The present was her concern, not the future, to extract from each moment the utmost possible of exciting pleasure. The empty immortality of a name would have meant nothing to her at all. Nevertheless it is hers, not because of her charms or her sins or even her great prosecutor, but only because once she loved for a moment a man who had the power, as few before him or since, to put love's passion into poetry.

This was the young Catullus, the fiery poet who blackened Caesar's name. He came to Rome from Verona, sent by a careful father to be cultivated and polished out of small town ways. He was perhaps twenty or so when he was introduced to the grand house on the Palatine where its brilliant mistress held a salon for all the great world. We must conceive him on his first entrance a very shy young provincial, hesitating on the edge of the gay company. But there is much in his verse to prove that he was extraordinarily attractive and it is impossible not to believe him beautiful, too, with the beauty so strangely given to poets in all ages everywhere. At all events, he drew to himself the attention of

the lady of the house and by swift degrees he became
her close companion. Clodia was a woman of mind and
taste, able to see a distinguished talent. She liked to
play the critic and the connoisseur with the gifted young
Veronese and they had delightful times tearing bad
writers to pieces: "My lady has sworn that if I will
make no more bitter, biting verses she will choose out
the very worst of all poets and offer up his effusions in
a fiery sacrifice. Here they are, the poems of Volusius,
so superlatively bad, the gods will have a merry laugh
when they see the sacrifice offered them."

This was strong wine for a young head, a country
boy preferred to all the elegant worldlings by a most
beautiful great lady, full ten years his senior. Of course
he fell madly in love and for a time he moved her to
love him, perhaps surprised at herself that a youthful
rustic could make her feel so much. The story is plain
to read in the poems. They have come down to us helter-
skelter, in no chronological order; poems that belong
to the end of his life are among the first in the collection;
but about the order of the love poems there can be no
doubt. They speak for themselves.

They are a unique chapter in the literature of love,
these "Poems to Lesbia"—it was the fashion for a young
man to write to his mistress under an assumed name.
Their like cannot be found in all the range of English
literature. Only a few poems scattered through the centuries approach them in passion and poignancy. Poets of
love there have been many in England, but poets of
passion almost none. The truth is that it is nature, not
a mistress, who really holds the hearts of English poets,
and the lady in the case is apt to be lost sight of amid
trees and clouds and birds and, above all, the flowers
that grow in English gardens:

Say Rose, say Daffodil, and Violet blue, with Primrose
fair,
Since ye have see my nymph's sweet dainty face and
gesture rare,

Did not (bright Cowslip, blooming Pink) her view (White
lily) shine
(Ah, Gillyflower, ah, Daisy!) with a grace like stars
divine

The only poems really comparable to those of Catullus
are Shakespeare's sonnets and in respect of passion
alone. In every other way the two poets are a world
apart: Shakespeare torturing language to express not
only passion, but the entire universe of man's heart,
with death and time and eternity and life's tragedy of
joy never fulfilled; and Catullus seeing nothing in the
universe but Lesbia and able to speak with perfect
simplicity because he felt nothing that was not simple.
Never did there hover in his restless thoughts what his
pen could not write down. He was Lesbia's most uncomplicated lover whose place was this earth, whose
precinct was strictly confined to his own loves and
hates. In every way he was limited except one only,
intensity. He was a great poet, but he was a Roman,
and Romans, however poetically inclined, were not given
to thoughts that wander through eternity. There is only
one exception in all of Latin literature, Catullus' great
contemporary Lucretius, the poet of Greek philosophy.

Catullus could write on other themes, too. He could
turn out a charming bit of verse on whatever he pleased,
his sailing boat, his little "almost island" home where
the lake water laughed in the wind, a dinner party, a
friend's grief, or what not. He could honor a marriage
with a lovely song and divert himself by telling fairy
stories. And he could write any number of diatribes like
the one on Caesar and Mamurra, as violent and as
coarse as anything found in literature, if indeed they
belong to that realm. But a poet is judged by his best;
his bad makes no difference whatever in the final esti-
mation of him. Catullus was Clodia's lover-poet and his
fame is secure.

His distinguishing characteristic, beyond that of all
other poets, is to put love's rapture and agony into

words so direct, they seem to leave no veil between the reader and the poet's heart. He pours out what he feels with a burning passion that will have nothing but the plainest expression. Figures of speech, embroidery of lovely phrase and delicate fancy, all the decorations of poetry, are swept aside. When he chose he could use them excellently well. The few long poems he wrote on impersonal subjects he ornamented, often very delightfully, in poetry's usual way, but they are negligible beside the love poems. Only rarely, when an unhappy love is his theme or when, in the midst of most unlikely mythological figures, Lesbia suddenly enters—Catullus cannot keep her out—then the voice is once more his own passionate, ecstatic, anguished voice, speaking in words so fused by his fire, we seem to dispense with them and see only the flame.

The love-story he tells is the concentrated story of all loves. He traverses the whole gamut of lovers' feelings everywhere. But this is not to say that he is the typical lover; such fervor of feeling can never be typical; rather he is the quintessential lover. Into a few brief poems he puts the essence of the passion of love.

The story begins very delicately and exquisitely as young love is wont to begin. Clodia—Lesbia—had a pet bird and the youthful stranger watched her adoringly as she played with it, and one night when he went home he wrote her a poem. No doubt he hesitated long before sending it to her:

*Sparrow, dearest delight of my sweet lady,
whom she plays with, who nestle in her bosom,
Swooping down on her, small, sharp beak all ready,
when she teases and holds out a swift finger,

*It is not necessary to say that such poems are untranslatable. All poems are. Still, the burning fusion of feeling and expression certainly has its own peculiar difficulties for the translator, and the following translations are offered in the hope of giving the reader an idea not so much of what Catullus' poetry is like, but only of what he himself was like. In each case the original metre of the poem has been reproduced accurately enough to give the reader the feeling of the rhythm.

and my radiant lady, my desire,
answers back with I know not what sweet nonsense,
solace finds for a moment from her heartache,
as one sick with a fever feels a respite.
Would I too could so play with you, sweet sparrow,
I would lift from my spirit its dark trouble.

Lesbia was pleased with the poem and began to distinguish its author with her notice more and more, and he sent her a second, written in the same strain. But now that dark trouble has been lifted, Catullus is happy; he can make tender fun of his wonderful lady:

Gods and goddesses all, of love and beauty,
you too, all who are men of finer feeling,
mourn. A sparrow is dead, my lady's sparrow,
my own lady's delight, her sweetest plaything,
dear to her as her eyes—and dearer even.
Little honey bird, knowing its sweet mistress
Well as ever a girl her own dear mother,
Close to her she would hold him, sweetly nestled.
Where she went he went after, here now, there now,
piping only to her his little bird-note.
Who now goes down the sombre road of shadows,
down where never a one comes back, they tell us.
Ill attend you, O evil gods of darkness.
All things beautiful end in you forever.
You have taken away my pretty sparrow,
Shame upon you. And, pitiful poor sparrow,
it is you that have set my lady weeping,
Dear eyes, heavy with tears and red with sorrow.

When a rival of Lesbia's was praised her poet was quick to attack and defend, and Lesbia laughed delightedly at the verses and, one may be sure, passed them on to others:

Quintia, so says the crowd, is beautiful. I grant her fairness.
Tall she is, too, and erect. So much I give her—no more.

Beautiful? Utterly not. What, beauty where charm is
all wanting?
Never a spice of salt seasons that heavy flesh.
Lesbia—ah, there is beauty. From top to toe she is
lovely.
Venus has lost her grace. Lesbia stole it away.

All of a sudden, it would seem, Lesbia was won. She
was a connoisseur of lovers and a poet-lover had not
come her way before; she found the combination attractive. Catullus was in heaven:

Live, my Lesbia, love. I live—I love you.
Not a fig will we care what grim old men say.
Setting sun will come back again tomorrow.
We, when once our brief daylight has faded,
needs must sleep an unending night forever.
Give me a thousand kisses—then a hundred.
Now a thousand again—and now a hundred.
Still a hundred—and in one breath a thousand.
And when a thousand thousand we have added,
stop the count and throw them all together.
So no envious eye bring evil on us,
spying out all the number of our kisses.

But the situation was difficult—how to meet, how
to avoid the good Metellus' suspicions—all the troubles
that have beset true lovers everywhere. Lesbia of course
was experienced in handling a husband under such
circumstances:

Lesbia, if her husband is near, speaks ill of me always,
greatest delight thereby giving the blind old fool.
Idiot, not to see she remembers me when she upbraids
me.
Silence would prove her heart-whole. Now all her jeers
and her taunts
show she never forgets. Oh, more than that. Through
her anger
I see a heart a-flame—she is on fire for me.

But the first trembling, incredible rapture had gone.
Catullus was on tenterhooks all the time. Would she

come—would she not? When—where—how? He grew
irritable from misery:

> Lesbia laughs me to scorn all day and never is silent.
> But, may I die else, I swear, Lesbia loves me alone.
> How can I know? I am like her. I laugh her to scorn
>    all the day through.
> But, may I die else, I swear, Lesbia only I love.

Ecstatic hours came still, but through them, far underneath, there was a fear.

> Dearest, my life, my own, you say our love is forever,
> What is between us shall be joy of love without end.
> Gods almighty, give her the power to promise truly,
> speak to me only truth, speak to me from her heart.
> So through all our years we shall keep faith, each to
>    the other,
> bound by a holy bond, lovers eternally.

This poem stands for the culmination of Catullus'
love and so of his life that was bound up with his love,
and yet already he was learning the agony of doubt. He
longed to believe; he could not quite. Into his lines he
put the true lover's invariable feeling of the holy purity
of a great love, no matter what—a husband in the
background or anything else. A passion conceived of
as eternally faithful has always been felt to be its own
justification and through his life Catullus loved Lesbia
only.

But his descent from that high point of—almost—
believing that the same holy bond bound her was swift.
No doubt the mature woman of the world soon found
it trying to be a poet's ideal and something less than
passion's lofty heights more agreeable for every day in
the year. She wearied of perpetual ecstasies. His agony
when he first realized that she was unfaithful to him
must be imagined. If he made a poem of it, it has not
come down to us. Perhaps it was too terrible for even
a poet to be able to write it out. But he was very young

and very eager for happiness, and humble, too, with the
humility of true love. She was so great, so wonderful—
how could he hope she would be his alone? Should he
not be content that she, the marvelous lady, loved him
best? And he wrote:

> So my light, my love, came to me in my arms,
> came with Cupid dancing, joyously circling around her,
> radiant, shining boy, wrapped in a saffron cloak.
> Past are those days. No more can Catullus alone now
>     content her.
> She goes to others now—only a few—I forgive—
> I am no fool like the rest to plague her with jealous
>     complainings.
> For she came not to me by right from the hand of a
>     father,
> here to my house—these rooms, sweet with Assyrian
>     scents,
> but through the secret night to give me love's wonder-
>     ful bounty,
> gifts that she stole away, robbed from a husband's heart.
> Therefore this is enough, if only when I—I—am with
>     her,
> that day a white stone marks, shining bright in her
>     heart.

Lesbia, however, was used to varied entertainment.
She never had an idea of confining herself to "only a
few," and Catullus' forgiveness mattered less and less
to her. From then on he was living in the specially fiery
hell reserved for great ·passions wronged. In his first
agony he wrote two lines which express within their
brief compass what that experience is like:

> I hate and I love. Why—how—can it be, perhaps
>     you will ask me.
> That I know not. What I feel, that I do know. I am
>     tortured.

He knew her now, and her sweet words meant nothing
any more:

Ah, what a woman says in the arms of a lover who
  wants her,
Write on the wings of the wind, give to the rushing
  stream.

He knew everything, but he could not free himself:

Lesbia, once you would say none knew you, only
  Catullus,
nor would you choose in my stead even a god—Jove
  himself.
Then I loved you not as the common herd loves a
  mistress,
but as a father his son—so you were dear to me.
Now I know you indeed. The flame that is in me burns
  fiercer,
yet I see you clear, small and shallow and cheap.
What? You cannot understand? The wrongs you do to
  your lover
force him to love you more, but, ah my dear, prize you
  less.

He had come far from that young fresh world of
enchantment where he watched the sparrow play. He
was only in his early twenties, but he would never enter
it again:

Yours is the guilt, my Lesbia, to this pass you have
  brought me,
  where love's duty works ruin to love itself.
So that I have no power to wish you were best among
  women,
Yet no power to cease loving you through all you do.

She had certainly been trying to hold him in spite of
all this anguish of bitterness, but a day came when she
did not try any more. She had done with him and in
his passion-torn, despairing young heart he found courage to face the truth:

Poor wretch Catullus, end this frantic folly now,
and what you see is dead give up for lost, poor fool.

A time was once when golden suns shone bright for
   you,
when you went only where a girl was pleased to go,
a girl more loved than any will be loved again.
Then there was merry sport for two, unstinted joys,
what you would have and what your lady, too, liked
   well.
Then golden suns in very truth shone bright for you.
She wants no more. Then do not you, infirm of will.
When she would flee, will you run after—live a wretch?
Now force your heart—now steel your stubborn will—
   be hard.
Goodbye, my girl, Catullus has made hard his heart.
No more pursuit—to cold reluctance no more prayers.
It is you will suffer pain when no one prays to you.
Oh, you are evil. Yet what life awaits you now—
Who now will go to you? To whom will you seem
   fair?
Whom will you love now—swear that you are his
   alone?
Whom kiss and kissing keenly, hotly, bite his lips?
But you, Catullus, come, an end. Make hard your
   heart.

His dearly loved brother had lately died in the distant
east; his grief for him, his old father who needed him,
his sick longing for change, called him home from the
city of his suffering and he went back to Verona. There
he found money troubles, and as the quickest way to
be free of them, he got a post with a new governor on
the point of leaving for his province, and he went to
the east in his train. He made no money, the province
having been already drained dry by Roman fortune
hunters, but one great wish he did fulfill, he went to
his brother's grave and he wrote a poem, ranked among
his best, which shows the tenderness there was in him.

Over many lands and many seas I have travelled,
   only to stand by a tomb, brother, to weep what is lost.
Give you death's last gift, tears, words of sorrowful
   parting,

tears to the careless earth, words to the silent dead.
But since fate has taken you, you, your very self, from
   me,
brother, pitied, beloved, gone from me in your youth,
these rites now I pay, from olden time taught our
   fathers,
weeping pay to the dead what to the dead is due.
Wet with a brother's tears, receive from my hand the
   last tribute.
And forever, my dear, greeting—forever goodbye.

But his love story was not yet ended. Lesbia called
him back. Probably he went to Rome of himself, moved
in part by the terrible need to see her. And then—did
she meet him one day in a crowd, see him avoid her
with visible hatred and scorn, and suddenly feel an
amused determination to show him her power—show
herself, too, perhaps, for she was nearing forty and
needed reassurance. So she lifted a white hand and
beckoned to him and he fell at her feet:

When, past hope, there comes to the starving heart its
   desire,
comes after long despair, that—that—is the heart's best
   joy.
So joy best of best and richer than wealth has come to
   me,
  given to my desire, Lesbia, you yourself.
Back to my hopeless desire you came, you gave yourself to me,
Oh, a day of light, marked with splendor for me.
Where is the man who lives more blessed than I am—
   I only?
Who could ask of gods more that life can give?

The reunion could not have lasted long. The house
on the Palatine was changed. The good, stupid Metellus
was dead and strange stories about his death were
abroad. People capable of being shocked visited it no
more and they were not missed. It was a house of
excesses; each latest experience must outdo the one

before. What he suffered there Catullus never put into
verse. Caelius Rufus was his close friend. When she
took him and brought him into her house to live,
Catullus at last saw the end. He broke off, this time for
always:

Hard—it is hard of a sudden to break with a love
  years-long cherished.
Yes, it is hard, but you must. This way or that, end it
  now.
Here only is your salvation. This fight you must win—
  here be victor.
    This you shall do. If you can or if you cannot.
    You must.
O Gods, if ever you pity, if ever you bring to the
  stricken,
    help in the anguish of death, in life's extremity,
look on my misery, save him who vows he has lived
  free from evil.
    Purge this plague from my blood, make me clean
    of this taint,
creeping like slow corruption within me, body, bone,
  sinew.
    Not in all my heart space where joy may come.
No more now I pray she might love me again as I love
  her,
not for what cannot be, that she should wish to be true.
I would be healed, rise up from this torment of sickness
  that fouls me.
    O Gods, give only this—this to your worshipper.

He had but a year or two left to live. In his life as in
his love he was the quintessential lover, he died young.
We hear in his writings of a cough that racked him, the
fitting accompaniment to a broken heart. Shortly before
his death and after the trial and Clodia's increased
recklessness that followed it, he wrote to Caelius:

Caelius, Lesbia—she, our Lesbia—Oh, that
only Lesbia, whom Catullus only

loved as never himself and all his dearest,
now on highways and byways seeks her lovers,
strips all Rome's noble great-souled sons of their
money.

These bitter and poignant words are the last we know
of Clodia and her poet.

# CHAPTER VIII

## HORACE

THERE are people to whom any sense of fitness would assign a short life. Catullus is one of them. Indeed one can hardly conceieve of him as living on to old age and the hardest heart could not wish that he had. In his space of thirty- odd years he had felt more than most octogenarians, even octogenarian poets. All things were always final with him and moderation in any shape or form impossible. One cannot think without profound weariness of his going on like that. To live perpetually at such an altitude is not for humanity and Catullus would have been worn out long before old age overtook him. Fate at the end was kind to him.

But there are other people whom anyone would like to have live forever, and in that number Horace stands foremost. He would have liked it, too. He had that most delightful gift of enjoying keenly all life's simplest pleasures, a grassy bank by a river, a glowing fire on a cold night, a handful of ripe olives, the sky, the sunshine, the cooling wind. And it is not a doubtful assumption that of those people we would choose out to be immortal nine-tenths would have that very gift. There is none other that helps life along as much, for others as well as for the possessor.

Who would not like to see Horace walk in through

his door any day in the year? Immediately everything
would seem more agreeable, the cocktails better flavored,
the armchairs softer, even the comfort of the warm
sheltered room would take on the proportions of an
active delight. And the talk would never centre round
himself. Every attempt to make it do so would be
warded off deprecatingly with a touch of gay humor.
Sitting in your armchair he would be the most stimulat-
ing of listeners—but any balloon you launched would be
in danger of a puncture from a sly dart of irony, which
yet, with all its cutting edge, would fail to wound.

And if you were in difficulties, if you had spent too
freely, or quarrelled with an important neighbor or
offended your employer or tried to be on with the new
love before you were fairly off the old, you would have
in him the most understanding and the shrewdest, most
worldly-wise of advisers.

Horace is the complete man of the world, with
tolerance for all and partisanship for none; able to get
on with everyone and at home everywhere; ready for
any pleasure, averse to all the disturbing passions, viewing this earthly scene with some detachment—and almost never in a state of mind where a laugh comes
hard. The description does not suggest a poet, and indeed no one could be further from a lunatic or your
veritable true lover either than Horace is. Not a touch
of madness in that clear, cool, balanced head. He is
Benjamin Franklin turned poet, or rather, for he never
borders upon the provincial, a poetical Montaigne. He
is a poet whose distinguishing characteristic is common
sense, a combination never known before or since.

He was just turned twenty-one when Cicero died and
Rome entered upon one of her worst periods of civil
war. He took sides with Brutus and fought with him
through the campaign that resulted in the final defeat
of the republican cause and the establishment of Augustus and Antony as masters of the world. He came back
to Rome heartsick, hardly more than a boy even then,
to find that his little estate had been confiscated and

that he was penniless. A bad beginning, which would have turned many a man with his great ability and great sensibility into an irreconcilable or a misanthrope, and his earliest writing has a bitterness, even a brutality sometimes, which show how close he had come to the danger of being permanently warped or stunted. But this temper of mind soon passed. What Horace did was to face the fact that the Republic was dead and Augustus completely alive, and to get himself a small governmental post as a clerk. He never appeared thereafter in any of his writings as the champion of republican ideas. Quite the contrary. He extolled Augustus to the skies with praise which in any other period except the Roman Empire would have been fulsome almost beyond belief. And yet his reader notes these facts with no sense of condemnation. No one who knows Horace despises him for a time-server. He was not that. He was a man of supreme good sense who saw that the Republic was gone irrevocably and the Empire had arrived to stay, and who chose not to spend his life in a futile effort to turn back the hands of the clock. The result was that he emerged from an experience of early pain and defeat that would have embittered most men, and from a shifting of allegiance that might well have resulted in a cowed and servile spirit, a man of mellow serenity and unshaken independence. These are the triumphs which can be achieved by an evenly poised spirit, by what is one of the rarest of qualities, wisdom.

After dealing him blows so hard and so many, fate turned kind. Augustus' all powerful minister, Maecenas, met him and took a fancy to him, although Horace says of himself he was so shy at the first meeting, he could not get out a sentence without stammering. A great friendship resulted which lasted for thirty years. Maecenas, dying a few weeks before Horace, on his death-bed bade the emperor, "Be mindful of Horatius Flaccus as of myself." Horace's troubles were ended. Maecenas' circle, the best men of the day, was opened to him; Maecenas' purse, too, enough that is for Horace's very simple needs, and he was free. The world was his to do exactly what he pleased.

There was never any question in his mind what that was. In one of his earlier pieces he makes himself go for advice to a famous lawyer, Trebatius, one of Cicero's correspondents: "Direct me, Trebatius. What shall I do? *Trebatius:* Keep still. *Horace:* You mean not write any more verses—not at all? *Trebatius:* That's what I say. *Horace:* I'll be hanged if that wouldn't be best. But I can't sleep all the time—No, it won't do. Everyone has his own way of enjoying himself. Mine is to put words into metre. No use talking about it. Whether peaceful old age awaits me or even now black-pinioned death flies round me, rich, poor, in Rome or, if chance so bids, in exile, whatever my life shall be, bright or dark, I will write."

So he felt through thirty years. All that time he "played with words on paper," as he called his writing, and he never had any other pursuit. Yet the result is only one slender volume. There was one great advantage in the way they did it in Rome, nothing urged quantity upon Horace. The idea could never occur to him that the more pages he filled the better it would be for his purse. In the Roman system the pursuit of literature and the pursuit of money were in large measure separated. In this particular case that was very well for the world, because Horace had by nature, as no one more, the gift of brevity. The result of his freedom to write as he pleased was poetry which belongs to that rare order of verse which is distilled; only the essence left. He gave a good deal of advice, first and last, to would-be writers, and of it all "Be brief" comes first: "So that the thought does not stand in its own way, hindered by words that weigh down the tired ears." And remember always, "More ought to be scratched out than left."

What he taught he practised, even in his verses which were not poetry, but only prose done metrically. These, his *Satires* and *Epistles* as they are called—he called

them *Talks* and *Letters,* better suited to their informality—make up full half of his writing, and they prove
beyond all question that what he said of himself was
true, he loved "to put words into metre." No other
reason can be found for his not having written them
in prose. They are little rambling treatises about everything in the world, a great deal of excellent literary
criticism and some not so good, a great deal of tiresome
copy-book morality and some that is arrestingly true,
many wise observations on education, and no less on
cooking. He discusses the Epicurean and Stoic philosophies, gives in great detail the mishaps of a journey,
makes fun of the way a boring person talks, applies
common sense to Greek poetry, and so on and so on,
all along the dead level of prose, and saved from being
dull only by that admirable brevity. Why he did not
use the magnificent medium Cicero had left to Roman
literature and write them as little prose essays, would be
inexplicable if it were not for his own words.

He loved to produce a smooth-flowing metrical line,
and the more complicated the measure the greater his
enjoyment. It was a delight to him to try his hand at
turning the many varied metres of the Greek lyric poets
into Latin, a veritable *tour-de-force.* The first eleven
poems of his odes are written in ten different measures,
completely unlike each other. His polish and perfection
of technique in using these intricate rhythms, his accomplished method, are his alone. No one has ever
rivalled him. But the singing gift, the power of "song
that wells up as from the bird's throat," which is our
idea, more or less, of the lyric poet's endowment, was
never Horace's at all. He utterly disclaimed it for himself. Poetical spontaneity, he tells us, was not for him.
"Toiling hard" he made his songs.

He was one of the most skilled technicians that ever
put pen to paper. Words and phrases were his passion.
"Sometimes," he says in discussing composition, "a
beautiful word leaps out." So they do continually in his
own writing. "A cunning combination can make a

familiar word seem brand-new," he writes and he knows
well what he is praising. He is the poet of the exquisite
phrase, the consummately perfect word. What he says
may be negligible, but the way he says it is entrancing.
When Hamlet bids Horatio

> Absent thee from felicity a while—

there is perfect beauty of poetry in the words, but precisely in those words and no others, in the expression,
not the thought. Put that into different words and the
poetry has gone: "Refrain from happiness for a time,"
"Withdraw temporarily from delight"—there is not a
particle of significance in either statement. But in

> Men must endure
> Their going hence, even as their coming hither;
> Ripeness is all:

there is something which could not be completely lost,
however worded.

A slight alteration would reduce to prose the loveliest
phrases in poetry: "In cradle of the rude, imperious
surge"; "Through verdurous glooms and winding, mossy
ways"; "Under the glassy, cool, translucent wave." But
just as Catullus' burning intensity comes through even
poor translations, so no verbal change could nullify the
passion of

> —for I love you so
> That I in your sweet thoughts would be forgot
> If thinking on me then should make you woe.

"Hitherto shalt thou come, but no further, and here
shall thy proud waves be stayed" might be turned into
a simple geographical statement, but truth of poetry
independent of the particular expression is in, "Though
I speak with the tongues of men and of angels, and
have not love, I am become as sounding brass, or a
tinkling cymbal."

That order of poetry is nowhere in Horace. His thought is hardly more than sagacious at its best and is far oftener commonplace than not. He says of his satires, "Change the order of my words and the poetry is gone," and in a sense it is true of everything he wrote. It is never what he says that is important but always how he says it. For this reason he is the most difficult of Latin writers to give an account of to those who do not read Latin. His poetry is completely untranslatable and all of his admirers who have tried to turn him into English, very distinguished personages some of them, have only, each in his turn, produced one more illustration of the fact.

The following examples, perhaps it is necessary to state, are all translations of the same lines, and, what could certainly not be deduced without the statement, of lines which rank among the most famous in Horace.

Addison turned them into:

The man resolved and steady to his trust,
Inflexible to ill and obstinately just,
May the rude rabble's insolence despise,
Their senseless clamours and tumultuous cries.
The tyrant's fierceness he beguiles,
And with superior greatness smiles.

Byron made out of them:

The man of firm and noble soul
No factious clamours can control.
No threat'ning tyrant's darkling brow
Can swerve him from his just intent.
Gales to curbe the Adriatic main,
Would awe his fixed, determined mind in vain.

And as Gladstone tried his hand on them, they became:

The just man in his purpose strong
No madding crowd can bend to wrong.
The forceful tyrant's brow and word,

Rude Auster, fickle Adria's lord,
His firm-set spirit cannot move,
Nor the great hand of thund'ring Jove.

Present indications are, therefore, that he will remain
a closed book except to the Latinists. What one of his
admirers soon after his death called his "curious felicity"
can never be transferred to another tongue, and he had
no glimpse of new truth to show, no revelation of what
lies hidden in men's hearts until the poet speaks it for
them.

The idea of the poet as an impassioned, inspired
creature, compact of emotion and imagination, must be
revised. Horace cannot be fitted into the category. Passion and common sense are not compatible. Passion
stands higher—or lower; the two do not operate on the
same level. The lover, no matter how averse by nature
to follies, is allied to the lunatic for the time being.
Horace is a passionless poet always. It is true that his
poems are continually decorated with the pretty names
of ladies he declares he has succumbed to: Phyllis and
Lyce and Cinara, Leuconoe and Pyrrha and Chloe,
Glycera and Neaera and Lalage, and many another—of
whom some, the number drives one to conclude, had
existence only in his verse—but it is more than doubtful
whether any woman ever cost him a pang. All the
indications are that he was never what we call in love.
To our notions a lover, and certainly a poet-lover, must
waste, at least a little, in despair and Horace never did,
not even a very, very little. He had an exceedingly
pleasant time with all of them. His idea of love was
that it should add to life's enjoyment and nothing is
clearer than that he made it do so. He must have had
a wonderful skill in detaching himself from one lovely
lady to pass on to another, for there is never a hint at
any of the usual accompaniments of such behavior,
tears, reproaches, a broken heart or two. In fact they
are incredible face to face with Horace. In his presence
they would instantly have seemed quite absurd and

rather ill-mannered. The anguished maiden would have found herself laughing long before the moment of parting came and she would be left in the end with some excellent advice about her next move. And Horace would lie on a grassy bank by a murmuring river with another fair creature to weave rosy garlands for him and fill his cup with golden wine.

The present writer, warned by the sad results of eminent men's efforts, does not venture to turn into English even a single one of the odes to illustrate this attitude toward the great passion, but a very fair idea of the spirit of Horace's love poetry can be had from the sixteenth century lover-poets of England. Those of the seventeenth century are apt to mingle religion with love, than which nothing could be more foreign to Horace, but those of a hundred years earlier reproduce his attitude and often consciously. He influenced them enormously and the reason was that fundamentally they looked at life and love as he did. To be sure, the comparison holds good only within strict limits. The grace and charm of Horace's verse cannot be matched by the best of them, but they felt above love the way he did and what they produced is far more like him than any translation. He might indeed have written every word of Lyly's *Cupid and my Campaspe played*. Marlowe's *Passionate Shepherd to his Love* is precisely passion as Horace saw it:

> Come live with me and be my Love,
> And we will all the pleasures prove
> That hills and valleys, dales and fields
> Or woods or steepy mountain yields.

Drayton often follows him:

> But see how patient I am grown
> In all this coil about thee;
> Come, nice thing, let my heart alone,
> I cannot live without thee.

Daniel is only Horace's echo when he writes:

> And sport, Sweet Maid, in season of these years,
> And learn to gather flowers before they wither—

But indeed if Shakespeare's sonnets are excepted and a very few other poems, all sixteenth century love poetry is made after Horace's receipt:

> Let now the chimneys blaze
> And cups o'erflow with wine;
> Let well-tuned words amaze
> With harmony divine.
> Now yellow waxen lights
> Shall wait on honey love—

That is Horace's lover's paradise and he himself could have described it no more exactly.

Common sense is perhaps not necessarily destructive to the imagination, but on most of the soaring flights your truly inspired poet essays it would prove a dragging weight. Horace never soared at all. He was the least inspired of poets and he was contentedly aware that he was. He admired Virgil exceedingly and other lofty epic and tragic poets of the day whose names alone have come down to us, but for himself he wanted only the pleasant ways of earth. He esteemed—more, one feels sure, than he loved—the mighty Greek masters, and he bade young writers turn their pages all the day long and the night, but he never swerved from what his cool head showed him was his own little path, serenely sure those heights were not for him: "Like a river rushing from the mountain, on sweeps Pindar, deep-mouthed, tremendous . . . [or] a mighty wind lifts him aloft into the region of the clouds. I am like the bee that busy works in the sweet wild thyme around the groves and banks of wide-watered Tibur. Even so small and toiling hard like her I build my songs."

This attitude toward his work is typical of him. Never was there a poet of fewer pretensions, and yet with all his gay self-depreciation he knew his powers and that he had "raised a monument more lasting than brass and higher than the crumbling magnificence of pyramids," and that he would be read—the words in their unintentional understatement are almost ironical—"as long as pontifex and vestal virgin climbed to the Capitol."

A few times this consciousness of his genius overcomes the habit of his genuine modesty, but only once or twice. With more pretentiousness and greater self-assurance he would not have been the completely delightful person he was. His genius must be taken on faith by all who cannot read him in the original, but anyone who cares to run through the poorest translation will perceive something of his delightfulness. No misdirected efforts on the part of a translator can quite prevent that from coming through.

To begin with, he was that charming contradiction, a man who enjoyed luxury and yet was completely independent of it. The choice bouquet of an old wine was never wasted upon his palate nor the extraordinary recherché dishes of the day which would seem to have been an epicure's paradise. Horace knew all about the superiority of a chicken drowned in wine to one killed in the usual way, of game caught in mild weather rather than cold, of fruit plucked while the moon was on the wane, and precisely when in the composition of a fish sauce Greek wine should be used. But this exquisiteness amused him far more than it pleased him and he liked best "My own pot of leeks and pease with a thin bit of bread and only three slaves [!] to serve me. A white stone table where two bowls stand with the mixing vessel [the wine was mixed with water, often sea water, to give a tang like Apollinaris], a pitcher and a platter of common earthenware. Thence care-free to sleep and lie abed till ten, with no business to send me early abroad. . . . So I live more sweetly than the greatest of the earth."

This sort of thing, repeated again and again, has not a touch of affectation. It is not the luxury-sated, blasé man about town, sentimentalizing over what nothing would induce him to try. It is the very reverse of this, the freedom given by a mind which can find securely the source of pleasure within and needs no outside stimulus—except, to be sure, a cup of wine or, rather, many cups. On this point Horace would have admitted no opposition. He had the most positive convictions on wine's virtue as well as its delights. "No songs can please nor yet live long which are written by those who drink water"; "Plant no tree before the sacred vine, O Varus. To the dry all things are hard by God's ordainment"; "O jar of wine born when I was born, worthy to be brought forth on a glad day, come out now to us, O gentle spur of the spirit, without you harsh and hard to move." It is the subject of his most impassioned verse.

Still, any *vino del paese* was good enough for him, so he always protested, and when Maecenas gave him a country place—Horace's Sabine Farm, the most famous farm in literature, his more than pleasure, his unalloyed delight, in plainest country living overflows in poem after poem: "This was among my prayers: a portion of land, not so big, a garden and near the house a spring of never-failing water, and a little wood beyond. The gods have done more and better. It is well. I ask no more." But he can never have done writing about it: "Not ivory nor gold in fretted ceilings shine in my house, not marble from Hymettus. . . . Nothing beyond what I have do I ask, blessed in my one, my only Sabine farm." It was his "corner of earth that smiled at him before all others." He prays to "the lord of the curved lyre": "What does his poet ask of Apollo enshrined? Not rich grain lands in fertile Sardinia, not gold nor ivory of India. Olives are my fare and tender herbs from field and garden. O Son of Latona, give me to enjoy what is mine—and with unweakened mind an old age not uncomely or deprived of poetry." "There are those who have not," he wrote. "There is one who does not care to have."

This attitude of moderation was his by nature; it was

also in accordance with his reasoned convictions. He was not a man who lived carelessly on the surface. That was his way only in his love affairs. He was a serious observer of life. Temperamentally he was inclined to be happy and he wanted happiness intensely, but by a necessity of his nature he could find it only if he thought things through. He had to have some secure basis to build upon; he could not and would not feel himself the sport of a blind chance he had no defense against. That way lay unreasoning misery for him and he refused to acquiesce miserably in an existence that was not reasonable. He insisted upon finding sense in the way things are, and so a possibility of living serenely through life's cares and troubles, difficulties and dangers. It was the impulse which plays a great part in religion. It is true that Horace was far from what we think of as a religious nature. Strange thoughts that transcend our wonted themes and into glory peep were never for a moment his. He knew nothing about mystic heights as a man any more than he did as a poet, but he had a religion, although it was constructed by common sense alone and adapted to satisfy only its sober demands.

Of formal religion in Rome at that time there was little left, and nothing at all that could make a rational appeal. The emperor was almost at the point of being the one true effective god. But Greek thought had found its way to Rome. There had come seekers for truth in the Platonic fashion, not from lovely visions of deities incarnate in woodland, river and sea, but from what men found within themselves. Out of these philosophies Horace took what suited him and he laid a foundation he could build his life upon.

Happiness and misery, he said to himself, are inside emotions, not outside facts; essentially, then, they are under my control. I can do nothing about what fate sends me, but I can do everything about the way I take what is sent. I can so order my own spirit that no matter how outrageous fortune is I can keep my balance within unmoved. "Do you know, friend, what I feel, for what I pray? Not to waver to and fro, hanging upon the hope of the dubious hour. God may give this or that—life—wealth. I will my own self make my spirit undisturbed."

There lies the whole secret of life. The only important matter is what we are. "The fool," he writes, "finds fault with a place. The fault is not there but in the mind, and that can never escape from itself." It is his underlying thought, expressed in countless ways; "They change their sky, but not their mind, who run across the sea. The thing you seek is here, in every meanest village, if a balanced and serene temper does not fail you." Always he urges, "Prepare what will make you a friend to your own self."

And the receipt to secure this even balance, this equanimity—a word made up from the two Latin words Horace uses to express the idea—is to live within carefu' limits, to contract one's desires, to forego mountain tops and perilous ecstasies, and choose forever and always safety first. This is Horace's creed of "golden mediocrity," which he who practices will be secure alike from the envy threatening great palaces and—since he will never take a risk—from the danger of helpless, sordid poverty. For life's voyage shorten sail, no matter what the wind. "Even," he writes, "the wise man is a fool if he seeks virtue itself beyond what is enough."

So, in perfect poise, undistracted by hope or fear, a man can fully live where every one of us must, whether we will or not and no matter how hard we let the future press upon us, in this very present, passing moment. "He is master of himself and happy who as the day ends can say, I have lived—tomorrow come cloud, come sunshine. Not Jove himself can blot out one single deed that lies behind, nor can he ever bring to naught or make undone what once the flying hour has borne away." The only sure thing in life is death, "pale death, which knocks with equal hand at poor men's hovels and the towers of kings," and "life's brief space forbids

long hope." Then "Believe that each dawn brings your
last day to you," and "Why not beneath a tall plane
tree or this pine here recline at ease, roses to wreathe
the hair and perfumes of Araby to give sweet scents.
Boy, be swift to quench the fire of the wine-cup with
water from the stream gliding by, and fetch us Lyde.
Bid her make haste with her ivory lyre." Horace had
noted well Catullus' words to Lesbia and he could echo
them from his heart: "The swift moons can repair their
losses in the sky. We, when we are gone where the
great dead have passed, are dust and shadow. Who
knows if the gods will add tomorrow to today."

That is Horace's philosophy and, in general, the
religion of the man of the world. It is a sad religion,
for all its emphasis upon Lyde and her lyre and the
pleasant river bank. He who embraces it sincerely will
always be able to command a merry spirit for others,
but his own self melancholy will claim. There is no
combination more attractive. The underlying sadness
tempers the gaiety to something gentle and infinitely
endearing. It is genuinely gay; any appeal for pity, however subtle, would be ruinous, but always it suggests
a spirit that is gallant to look at darkness undismayed,
but deeply, sorrowfully regretful that fate has so or-
dained. This is the innermost secret of Horace's never-
failing charm, the reason, more than all his felicities of
words and measures, why the generations since have
loved him as his own did. One of his devoted admirers
wrote soon after his death: "Admit him and he plays
around your heart"—plays always, but always close
to the heart.

And yet, deplorable contradiction, never was poet
such an inveterate preacher. Poetry and preaching do
not go well together; when the preacher mounts the pulpit the poet usually goes away. Horace was not aware of
this fact; no Roman was. The Roman idea was that the
more a man preached, provided he did it with due regard
to metrical considerations, the greater poet he was. Morality in rolling hexameters was poetry's highest achieve-

ment, along with patriotism, of course. How far preaching came natural to Horace, how far Rome thrust it
upon him, no one now can know. As a Roman who was
a poet he must press his poetry into the service of the
state and urge citizens on to their duty. One does not
really resent his doing so in the *Satires* and *Epistles*.
He writes them avowedly as a teacher and often he
teaches very pleasantly and wisely. But in his odes it
is enraging in the midst of lovely poetry to come upon
this sort of thing: "The centuries, fertile in vice, have
debased marriage and the race and the home. Derived
from this source ruin has overflowed country and
people. The grown girl delights to be taught the move-
ments of the voluptuous dance." Or, "Now few acres
are left for the plough by the great mass of regal buildings. . . . Not thus was it ordered when Romulus ruled
or unshaven Cato or by the maxims of the ancients.
Their private list of possessions was short, the common
wealth was great." Or, "Force devoid of intelligence falls
by its own weight," and so on, with all the excellent
results force under wise control can produce. A great
deal about how the world is running down until by now
there is little hope left for it: "Our parents, worse than
our grandparents, gave birth to us who are worse than
they, and we shall in our turn bear offspring still more
evil."

It would be hard to find in the whole of Greek
literature as much preaching as Horace does all by
himself. Euripides saw war as completely evil and he
wrote the greatest anti-war piece of literature there is,
the *Trojan Women*, but from first to last he never
mounts the pulpit. He never denounces war at all; he
only shows what it is. The preacher, full-fledged, arrived
in literature with the Romans. Even Plautus, so averse
to it by nature, had now and then to assume the office.
Terence took eagerly to it and so did Cicero. But
Horace, in proportion to the rest of his writing, more
than they all. There was a mighty moulding force at
work to make this singer of lovely songs, this gay and

humorous spirit, this mind of serene detachment, into the earnest denouncer of vice and exhorter to virtue. Rome was back of Horace. And yet, though one may wish a kinder fate had placed him in Athens in her prime, there is a warm and winning quality in his eagerness to do his bit in helping Augustus turn the empire back to the good old ways and create again a plain-living, high-acting Rome. We look with awe upon the great Greek tragedians who seem hardly aware of mere mortality. Horace plays around our heart. The Greek poets are our masters; the Latin poets are our own familiar friends.

# CHAPTER IX

## THE ROME OF AUGUSTUS AS
## HORACE SAW IT

THROUGH the streets of the great city Horace strolled, cocking an amused eye at a fashionable lady's short dress, at a perfumed young elegant's latest thing in the way of togas, at the bearers of a great personage's litter —no carriages were allowed in the streets during the day—at his own slave on tip-toe to scan eagerly a poster of a gladiatorial show, at a grand funeral procession preceded by blaring brass horns and trumpets, and with especial delight at a fastidious poet's latest effusion hung outside the book shop where it was being pawed over by the sweaty hands of the vulgar. He stopped before a famous painter's work in a portico—there were miles of these roofed colonnades—had a look at a merchant's stock of "pearls from farthest Arabia and India, giver of wealth"; at other shops where could be bought "silver and antique marble and bronze and works of art, jewels and Tyrian purple," rare and beautiful things from everywhere in the world. "The Tiber," a writer in the next generation wrote, "is the most placid merchant of all that is produced over the whole earth."

But the splendor was only part of the spectacle. The crowd—Horace's abhorrence, "I hate the common herd and keep them off"—is so dense, he must "push and

392

struggle and knock aside the slow," while they shout
after him with jeering impudence, "what are you after,
you crazy fellow, thinking you must knock down whatever stands in your way if you're hurrying to Maecenas."
The description, brief as it is, is full of significance.
Rome was a very big city by then, but the words leave
no doubt that poets were highly interesting objects there.
Even the vulgar recognized Horace as he passed on his
way and knew perfectly where he was probably going.
It is clear, too, that if the crowd was not mannerly and
good tempered, it was not submissive and servile either.
Never in Rome did the rank and file—those above the
slave-class, of course—reach the condition of helpless
insignificance to which Europe again and again saw
the common people reduced. The city crowd was something the most magnificent emperor must bear in mind.
Romans, penniless, in rags, however reduced, were a
force to be reckoned with. No other proletariat in all
history ever got free food for themselves and free shows
too.

In the satire quoted, Horace has been to call on a
man who lives on the Aventine and now must make his
way to the Quirinal: "You see how convenient the
distance is for a mere mortal." (It meant a four-mile
walk up and down hill.) "Every one is abroad. A canny
contractor hurries by with his mules and porters; here
a derrick is hoisting now a rock, now a huge beam; sad
funerals struggle to pass on; there a mad dog is running
away; next comes a muddy pig." The words are a clear
little vignette of a street-scene in that city which is so
familiar to us and yet really so little known. They put
Rome before us, her very self, as she would look if a
view of her could be flashed for a moment upon the
silver screen.

All over the world and in every age a great city is
a place of contrasts, but Rome was so, as even an
Oriental city could hardly be today. The inner balance
of the spirit was precious to Horace because all outside
was unbalanced. During the empire the pendulum swung

in ever wider and wider sweeps, but even in his day
extremes had become the rule of life. On top absolute
despotism, at bottom well-nigh hopeless slavery; splendid
luxury and unspeakable squalor; monstrous forms of
irresponsible pleasure and fearful misery—everywhere
violent oppositions. Harmony had been the Greek ideal,
life within and without in equilibrium; the world seen
as beautiful and the spirit at home in it. To the Roman
this idea was forever incomprehensible. Horace, akin
in many ways to the Greek, never imagined such a
condition even to the degree of longing for it. His
search was not to adjust himself to life—nor life to
himself, but to find within himself the good, which was
in direct contradiction to life. The sharp division between facts, things, all that the Roman called reality
exactly as we do today, and the ideas and ideals within
a man was never sharper than during the Roman Empire. To Horace and his kind there were two distinct
worlds, one without and one within; they were not seen
as related.

Horace's Rome is first of all a place where money
rules—"Queen Money" is his phrase. He who cared
little for it by nature, lived in an atmosphere so permeated by it, that it is perpetually on his lips; the age,
as it were, superinduced an attitude alien to Horace himself. Here is a notable change from the age of Cicero,
distant by so short a space of actual time. Horace as
a boy must often have had the great orator pointed out
to him. But in Cicero money is completely in the background; it is almost never mentioned. Cicero was a
lover of the good things of life it can buy as Horace
was not; money was actually far more important to
him. The different part it plays in the writings of each
is due only to the difference between the aristocrat and
the self-made man. Cicero, not by birth, nor indeed by
nature, but perfectly by acquisition, had the tone of the
old republican aristocracy where money was taken for
granted and never talked about. Why should it be? It
was always there and no more interesting as a subject

of conversation than the tides of the sea or any other fixed phenomenon of nature. But all that was changed with the coming of Augustus. No intelligent despot allows an old aristocracy to continue. Very skillfully, very swiftly and with complete finality the great families of Rome were removed to the far background. In the society Horace was familiar with there was no settled class of any sort. The man who got rich got all the other prizes, too; he was the one to be admired and emulated and chosen for office. His birth mattered not at all. He might be a freedman, born a slave, with no tradition behind him and no education to fit him for high responsibilities. Horace delights in holding up to scorn the vulgar new-made millionaire to whose equisite dinners men of fashion and men of letters will flock and as they enjoy his chef's triumphs, make use of their napkins to conceal irrepressible amusement at their host's ostentatious display.

There are two curious little letters among his *Epistles* which illustrate better than anything else he wrote how all-important money had become. In each of them he tells a young man how to better his fortunes, and the advice he gives is to make friends with the rich. A morose Greek philosopher, Horace observes, may say, "If I can live contentedly on poor fare, I can dispense with people who have money," but a wiser view of life is that of the man who says, "If I can make use of people who have money, I can dispense with poor fare." In point of fact, he declares, the latter is really the one to be respected, the man of energy and enterprise, who is determined to get on and will not sit down lazily, contented with a little. He ends his letter with a warning to be tactful: Those who are silent about their poverty in the presence of the rich get more than he who keeps asking. Remember to take modestly and not be greedy, even though the end and aim of your friendship is to be enriched. In the second letter which is addressed, seriously, without a touch of irony, to "Lollius, most independent of men," he writes that the inexperienced are apt to think it will be a simple matter to cultivate a powerful friend, but the man who has tried it knows there are many hazards. Lollius must above all guard against that independence of his. If the great man wants to go a-hunting, up with you; leave your bed; put by your books; yield always to his wishes. As he is grave or gay so do you be, nor for heaven's sake when he feels like doing something else, try to read his poetry. The concluding exhortation, that while the young man is making himself agreeable, he must not forget to cultivate his higher powers by the study of philosophy, is also spoken in all seriousness and with no idea of irony.

They are illuminating letters. One can see the young men, faced with the problem of what they are to do, asking advice from a conspicuously successful older friend to whose career they are inclining. Horace's father had been born a slave; he himself was ranked with the great, and the reason was that he had made himself acceptable to a rich and powerful man. No one who reads him can doubt that he had a deep affection for Maecenas. It appears, indeed, to have been the great affection of his life, but to his worldly common sense friendship with the rich as a career had nothing to do with the emotions. He would never have been guilty of the sentimentality of urging the young men to love those whose dependents they became. There was no hypocrisy in him ever. The methods he recommended to them were undoubtedly those he had himself practiced toward Maecenas; what he had felt while doing so, his genuine devotion, seemed to him quite beside the point. It was all a clear matter of business. It never entered his mind that there was anything objectionable in a show of devotion for the purpose of getting money from a man. Nature did not originally incline the Roman character to servility. Horace and his young friends were the product of an age where it was important so far beyond everything else to have a good deal of money, and where it had become so difficult to get it, that the sense of

honor in its pursuit had been lost even to a man like
Horace, in other ways highly honorable.

Money under one guise or another appears perpetually
in his writing. The miser, now almost dropped from
literature, plays a large part. He was evidently a most
familiar figure in Augustan days and Horace knows his
readers will not blame him for exaggeration when he
shows him hardly willing to spend a few pennies from
his great hoard on medicine necessary to save his life.
And, of course, side by side with him is his invariable
foil, the spendthrift and the gambler. Money always,
well to the fore. "Everything," is Horace's ironical
summary, "virtue, honor, fame, everything human and
divine, obey beautiful riches. He who has heaped them
up is renowned, brave, just. A wise man, too? Yes, and
a king."

Throughout the poems, too, keep recurring the things
money can buy, all manner of expensiveness; ivory
couches, mosaic floors, hangings of Tyrian purple, embroideries, inlay, rare antiques, jewels, silver dishes,
golden vases, in complete contrast to Greek literature
where furniture and furnishings play no part at all. It
is as impossible to conceive of Pindar's describing the
menu and the dining table of Hieron of Sicily, his
familiar host and, no doubt, a sovereign surrounded by
magnificence, or of Plato in the *Symposium* moved
either to admiration or disapproval by Agathon's table
cloth, as it is to think of Horace apart from his keen
interest in the way people did their houses and served
their dinner parties. It is true that he never praised
luxury or enjoyed it much, but he was always keenly
aware of it. Agathon and his guests no doubt ate carelessly what was set before them and took all the details
incidental to the meal with complete indifference as a
matter of course. But who could take it as a matter of
course if he saw as Horace did, a slave enter the dining
room bearing a peacock roasted in its feathers, the
gorgeous tail outspread, so that the glowing creature
looked as if it had but alighted for a moment on the

silver dish? Or when a whole boar, bending the great platter with its weight, was presented to the company? In the eyes of Plato's Athenian gentlemen a dinner party was chiefly an occasion for conversation; to Horace's friends it was a matter of spectacular display and extraordinarily elaborate and overwhelmingly abundant food.

Cooking and serving and bills of fare occupy a great deal of Horace's attention. No less than the whole of two poems, and long ones at that, and the half of another are about nothing else: *Horace:* "How did you fare at the grand dinner party?" *Friend:* "Never better in my life." *Horace:* "Do tell me if it won't bore you, what were the hors d'oeuvres?" And a hundred lines follow which make fun of the menu, indeed, but give it nevertheless in greatest detail, together with a number of receipts for cooking the especially delicious dishes. On that occasion those Roman gentlemen ate: cold wild boar with all sorts of pickled vegetables; oysters and shell fish with a marvelous sauce; two varieties of turbot; a wonderful dish where a great fish seemed to be swimming among shrimp, with a relish made of fish from Spain, wine from Greece, vinegar from Lesbos and white pepper; then wild fowl served with corn; the liver of a white goose fattened on ripe figs; shoulder of hare ("so much more succulent than the lower part"); broiled black birds and wood pigeons. Sweets are not mentioned and of fruit only bright red apples, but elsewhere Horace speaks of dainties for dessert as beneath the attention of a true epicure and advises a final course of black mulberries—but they must be gathered before the sun is high.

"We rise from table," he remarks, "pale from overeating," and the modern reader understands why the early Christians put gluttony among the seven deadly sins. The practice of using emetics to make more and more eating possible seems to have become the fashion only at a later date. Horace does not mention it and it is so exactly the sort of thing he most enjoyed holding up to scorn, he would never have passed it over. But to those who desire to understand the quality of Rome it offers a profitable subject for meditation.

Indeed, along with the elegance and even magnificence of Horace's dinner parties there might be on occasion a lack of the most ordinary decency. Horace was so aware of tablecloths because they were so often dirty, exceedingly dirty. He sends an invitation to a friend with the promise that if he will come and dine with him neither cloth nor napkins will be in such a condition as to make him wrinkle his nose in disgust. Why should such things be, he laments, when cleanliness is so easy and so cheap. All the same, he ends the letter with the simple statement that his guest may count on plenty of room at table and not fear objectionable odors, as happens when people are seated too close to one another. And this is Rome of the stupendous Roman baths.

With those urbane gentlemen of the great Augustan age coarseness lay just beneath the polished surface and often it came out on top. If a friend reclining next him at table, Horace writes, drinks rather too much, lets fall the precious old china, then does unprintable—in English—things, and lastly leans across him and snatches away his piece of chicken, will he hold him less dear or less agreeable on that account? No, indeed, the reader is swift to conclude. Horace and the people he was writing for were perfectly accustomed to these little *faux pas* and had only a tolerant smile for them.

Horace went on a journey once with some very great personages. Maecenas was one of them and "the most learned of Greeks" another, two prominent diplomats also, of whom Horace describes one as "an exquisite finished to a hair," and three well-known men of letters, Virgil among them. It was a distinguished company such as the world has not often seen. Three of them after nineteen hundred years are still familiar household names. On their way a night is spent at a friend's villa where they are entertained while at dinner by a little play, a dialogue between "Sarmentus, a buffoon, and Messius, nicknamed the Cock," the former, as appears, a thin little man and the latter a huge, phenomenally ugly peasant. This was the diversion they offered that gathering: *Sarmentus:* "I say, you're like a wild horse" (laughter from the audience). *Messius* (shaking his head ferociously): "So I am—Look out." *Sarmentus* (eyes fixed on a hideous great hairy scar that marks Messius' forehead): "Aha, if your horn hadn't been cut out from your head, what wouldn't you do, if you threaten like that, all mutilated." He goes on to press the point still nearer home by jokes on the kind of diseases that leave such disfigurements and on Messius' pleasant vices, and the big man is urged to "dance the Cyclops" for the company, as he looks just like one. But he on his side scores as well: "Oh, you—you're just a slave. Whatever made you run away from your mistress? It couldn't be because she starved you—why, you're tiny enough to grow fat on next to nothing." It *was* a delightful entertainment, Horace concludes. And the grave and witty gentlemen of the *Symposium* come to mind, who dismiss the flute girl and her "noise" so that they may have no disturbance in the entertainment they want for their dinner of high discourse.

Of course the comparison is not quite fair: Horace is apparently recounting what really did happen, Plato probably only imagining what might have; all the same, it holds good fundamentally as regards the quality of the Greek and the Roman. "Tell me how you amuse yourself and I will tell you what you are." The very élite of Rome made up that little gathering who were so diverted by the clowning and the diseases and the big hairy scar. They were for the Augustan age what Socrates and Aristophanes and the others in the *Symposium* were for the age of Pericles, and it is difficult to think of any of the Athenians transferred to the Roman table finding much amusement there. Ugliness and deformity and disease were not the subjects Aristophanes chose for his jokes, nor was he given to dialogue of the "you're another and worse too" variety. And Horace and Virgil at the Greek supper would very soon have been bored by the long speeches about nothing real in all the world. That kind of fine-spun theorizing would have seemed to them a pure waste of time, neither pleasureable nor profitable. Horace has given us his ideal of first-rate talk: "Let us discuss what is important to us, not other people's houses or villas or whether Lepos dances badly or not, but whether riches or virtue make men happy, and whether motives of right or utility should influence us in seeking friends." Conversation of that kind, a Roman thought, got people somewhere. It helped them to be good citizens. If they wanted to be amused, there were the fools and the clowns and the gladiators too.

None of the dinners Horace describes were enlivened by the spectacle of a pair of men or several pairs, fighting to kill each other, with the divertissement a failure if neither of them did. These were the invention of a later day, but to public gladiatorial contests Rome had been accustomed for two hundred years and more before Horace's time, and it is hardly surprising that he found nothing to object to in them. He was in good company: Cicero took them as complacently. Horace never indeed describes a fight or speaks of having been present at one, but gladiators he mentions more than once and always in as matter-of-fact a way as he would an actor or a singer. In one of his Satires he reports a little talk with Maecenas, where in between a question as to what o'clock it is and a remark about the weather, they discuss the chances of two favorites billed to fight each other: "Is the Chicken with Thracian armour (a very small shield) a match for Syrus?"

It goes without saying that he never took note of slaves, but it is worthy of remark that a man sensitive and quick of feeling as he was should write of their terrible punishments with complete unconcern. He does say mildly that a man who has a slave crucified because he stole a bit of food must be out of his mind, but he speaks of slaves being beaten as a matter of course, of "the horrible scourge," with pieces of metal attached to the lashes, and of others of the methods of torture devised to keep in order a class grown dangerous because of its enormous size. A man of position, says Horace, is mean if he walks out with only five slaves attending him; on the other hand, one who can be seen with two hundred has passed the limit of good sense. And yet in spite of their great numbers they were so completely without any human significance, so casually mistreated and murdered in that city accustomed by all the favorite forms of amusement to mortal agony and violent death, that their condition never drew a passing thought from even the very best, a man like Horace, a thinker, gentle, kindly, dutiful. His bewilderment, if he could be recalled to life and confronted with our point of view, would be pitiful. He was wise and good, yet he lived with a monstrous evil and never caught a glimpse of it. So does custom keep men blinded.

In certain other respects, however, important too, our way would seem quite familiar to the Romans, more by far than the Greek way. Socrates in the *Symposium*, when Alcibiades challenged him to drink two quarts of wine, could have done so or not as he chose, but the diners-out of Horace's day had no such freedom. He speaks often of the master of the drinking, who was always appointed to dictate how much each man was to drink. Very many unseemly dinner parties must have paved the way for that regulation. A Roman in his cups would have been hard to handle, surly, quarrelsome, dangerous. No doubt there had been banquets without number which had ended in fights, broken furniture, injuries, deaths. Pass a law then, the invariable Roman remedy, to keep drunkenness within bounds. Of course it worked both ways: everybody was obliged to empty the same number of glasses and the temperate man had to drink a great deal more than he wanted, but whenever laws are brought in to regulate the majority who have not abused their liberty for the sake of the minority who have, just such unexpected results come to pass. Indeed, any attempt to establish a uniform average in that stubbornly individual phenomenon, human nature, will have only one result that can be foretold with certainty: it will press hardest upon the best, as everyone knows who is driven by large numbers to use mass methods.

The Athenian idea was that a gentleman could be left free and trusted not to get obnoxious to others over his wine. The Roman idea was that he assuredly could not be, but that he could and should be kept in order. Harmony, said the Athenian. Freedom, because the good life was in conformity with a man's innermost desires. Discipline, said the Roman. Careful regulation, because the good life must be imposed upon human nature that desired evil.

Horace deplored the drinking laws: "O country, when shall I see you. O nights and feasts of the gods where each, free from absurd rules, may drink as he pleases." And it did not escape his keen vision that all law was an empty form unless the moral feeling of the people was back of it. Nevertheless through his poems as through Roman literature there is discernible always, expressed or implicit, the sense of life controlled and ordered by stern outside forces, along with the law "the adamantine nails of dire Necessity," the inexorable decrees of Jove, Fate that spins and cuts the thread at will. "Must" is constantly on Horace's lips. "This you must do—must submit to—must face—must endure." So Romans saw life, and with all Horace's search for freedom within, he was not able ever to feel that he was free.

Catullus is the notable exception. "The dread goddess, Necessity" had no place among his deities. He saw his life in his own hands—and Lesbia's, but then high passion is never aware of any necessity other than its own, and except for Catullus, high passion is the rarest of visitants in Roman literature.

Such are the outstanding features in Horace's minia·
ture of Rome, but what he leaves out of it has significance too. The political game which took up all the
foreground for Cicero is not there at all. The result
foreshadowed by the condition in Cicero's day came
to pass: the citizen body could not cope with its own
corruption; the frightful evils that followed had to be
terminated; hence a dictator, with all the responsibility
and all power to regulate everything in the state. And
the many brilliant and able men of the great Augustan
age drew deep breaths of relief at seeing themselves
freed from trouble and concern about public matters
to devote themselves to their own business. They had
been angrily impatient of the dishonesty and stupidity
and inefficiency of the Republic's officials. They were
sick to death of the wars and the mismanagement of
home affairs, foreign affairs, and miscarriages of justice.
That was ended now. A strong and sagacious man was
emperor, whose will was the only law that counted, and
Romans rejoiced. What lay before their country in the
future, the most irresponsible despotism the western
world has ever seen, they could not know; nor were
they interested to build for the future. That kind of
disinterested patriotism was dead in Rome and would
not rise again except here and there in a few men, so
few they never mattered at all.

In one of Horace's *Epistles* there is a little description
of the theatre as he knew it, which seems to stand in
brief, not indeed for him or his group, but for the
general spirit of the day, as the popular theatre does
stand always and everywhere: "The people, even while
the actors are speaking the verses, call for a bear show
or a wrestling match. Pleasure has moved away from
the ear to the restless eye and entertainment with no
meaning. For four hours or more the curtain is up,
while troops of horsemen fly past and hordes of foot-
men. Kings of fallen fortune are dragged in with hands
bound behind the back. War chariots hasten by, carts,
carriages, ships, ivory is borne along and all the spoils

of Corinth. That hybrid creature, the giraffe, then catches the crowd's attention or, it may be, a white elephant. And what actors' voices are strong enough to rise above the din? The spectators ask each other, 'Has the actor said anything yet?' 'I don't think so.' 'What are you so pleased with then?' 'Oh, that beautiful purple dress of his.' "

The spectacle, ever growing more and more varied and more and more gorgeous, was what Rome by now wanted. Not what satisfied the mind nor yet the spirit, but what satisfied the restless eye. Rome's importance was her size and her wealth and her power. Roman citizens' lives consisted in the abundance of the things that they possessed. To Pericles, Athens' glory was not the Parthenon, not the Acropolis, but that Athens had become the school of Greece in all ways of wisdom. Augustus' title to glory, repeated over and over again, was that he had found Rome a city of brick and left her a city of marble.

# CHAPTER X

### THE ROMAN WAY

"To the people of Romulus I set no fixed goal to achievement," Virgil makes Jupiter in the *Æneid* say of Rome's future glory, "no end to empire. I have given them authority without limit." Unlimited is what the Romans were, in desires, in ambitions, in appetites, as well as in power and extent of empire. There is a note of exaggeration in Rome, contradicting on first sight the outstanding national quality of practical sagacity which made them great empire builders. But upon closer view it ceases to be a contradiction. The Romans were pre-eminently men of war. The only choice they had for centuries was to conquer or be conquered. Possibly war was their most natural expression; certainly it was the price they must pay for being a nation. Under the spur of its desperate necessities in eight hundred years of fighting, as Livy reckons them, from the founding of the city to his own day, they developed extraordinarily one side of their genius, a sure, keen-sighted, steady common sense, but war, with its alternations of stern repression and orgies of rapine and plunder, was not a training to modify violent desires. Always rude, primitive, physical appetites were well to the fore.

What constitutes Rome's greatness, in the last analy-

406

sis, is that powerful as these were in her people there was something still more powerful; ingrained in them was the idea of discipline, the soldier's fundamental idea. However fierce the urge of their nature was, the feeling for law and order was deeper, the deepest thing in them. Their outbreaks were terrible; civil wars such as our world has not seen again; dealings with conquered enemies which are a fearful page in history. Nevertheless, the outstanding fact about Rome is her unwavering adherence to the idea of a controlled life, subject not to this or that individual, but to a system embodying the principles of justice and fair dealing.

How savage the Roman nature was which the Roman laws controlled is seen written large in Rome's favorite amusements, too familiar to need more than a cursory mention: wild beast hunts—so-called, the hunting place was the arena; naval battles for which the circus was flooded by means of hidden canals; and, most usual and best loved by the people, the gladiators, when the great amphitheatre was packed close tier upon tier, all Rome there to see human beings by the tens and hundreds killing each other, to give the victor in a contest the signal for death and eagerly watch the upraised dagger plunge into the helpless body and the blood spurt forth.

That was Rome's dearest delight and her unique contribution to the sport of the world. None of these spectacles were Greek. They entered Greece only under Roman leadership and Athens, it is claimed, never allowed gladiators. Twice, we are told, the citizens stopped a fight as it was about to begin, both times aroused by the protest of a great man. "Athenians," cried one of them, "before you admit the gladiators, come with me and destroy the altar to Pity," and the people with one voice declared that their theatre should never be so defiled. The second time, a revered and beloved philosopher denounced the brutality they were about to witness, and the result was the same. But everywhere else Rome went the bloody games followed, and all the time they grew more bloody and more extravagant. On one occasion we read of a hundred lions perishing and as many lionesses. On another, five thousand animals were killed, bulls, tigers, panthers, elephants. The poet Martial, who wrote endless epigrams to flatter the great Vespasian's son, the Emperor Domitian, some seventy-five years after Augustus, says: "The hunter by the Ganges has not to fear in the countries of the Orient as many tigers as Rome has seen. This city can no longer count her joys. Caesar, your arena surpasses the triumph and splendor of Bacchus whose car only two tigers draw."

Of how many human beings met their death in these ways no estimate at all can be made. The supply of prisoners of war could not begin to meet the demand and men condemned to die were sent to help fill the gladiatorial schools, as they were called; masters, too, often sold their slaves to them; there were even volunters. Cicero speaks of these more than once. As the games went on, the exaggeration in every direction resulted in what seems to the modern reader incredible, the creations of a monstrous fantasy. We hear of the arena being sprinkled with gold dust; of dwarfs matched against each other and against wild beasts; women, too. Martial tells of having seen a woman kill a lion. Emperors fought, in carefully arranged contests, of course. The son of Rome's best ruler, Marcus Aurelius, boasted that he had killed or conquered two thousand gladiators, using his left hand only. The account ends by growing monotonous. Human ingenuity in devising new and more diverting ways of slaughter was finally exhausted and all that could be done to satisfy the impatient spectators was to increase the number engaged. In one naval battle when the arena was flooded, it is recorded that twenty-four ships took part, large enough to hold in all nineteen thousand men.

It is impossible to escape the suspicion, as one reads description after description, that journalese was not unknown in Rome. Surely, the reader is driven to reason, a people with a tendency to exaggeration would not always successfully repress it on a subject that almost irresistibly invited it, even though they claimed to be writing accurate historical records. When finally one is told of an emperor in the later days of the empire who "would never dine without human blood," without, that is, watching men kill each other, suspicion becomes a certainty. It is too perfectly the tabloid newspaper headline. How could such a fact be known? The gossip of palace slaves? Or even the assertion of the imperial brute himself, wanting, as a Roman would, to appear to out-Nero Nero? Especially monstrous events in the games and especially enormous numbers of those killed in them are hardly to be accepted as plain history, but they do show what Aristotle called the truth which is truer than history. Romans wrote them for Romans, and Romans enjoyed reading and believing them.

To pass from this contemplation, from the way Rome was pleased to amuse herself, to the consideration of what she really did in the world, is to make a startling transition. The Romans did not trample all nations down before them in ruthless brutality and kill and kill in a savage lust for blood. They created a great civilization. Rome's monumental achievement, never effaced from the world, was law. A people violent by nature, of enormous appetites and brutal force, produced the great Law of Nations which sustained with equal justice the rights of free-born men everywhere. The fact with all its familiarity has the power to astonish whenever it comes to mind, but the reasons are easily to be seen. The little town on the seven hills conquered the other little towns around her, because her citizens could obey orders. No one who knows Rome at all will feel this a mere conjecture. The father who condemned his son to death for winning a victory against orders is a legendary figure of deep significance. The orgy of the arena was a relaxation, in the same way as destroying a captured city was or a murderous civil outbreak. They were incidental merely. The conception of a power outside themselves to which they must and would submit was enduring. Over the lawless earth where petty tribes were forever fighting other petty tribes for the right to live, where there was nothing more enlightened than tribal customs untold ages old, marched the Roman, bringing with him as certainly as his sword and his lance his idea of an ordered life in which no man and no tribe was free, but all bound to obey an impersonal, absolute authority which imposed the necessity of self-controlled action. Along with the tremendous Roman roads and aqueducts went the ideal of which they were the symbol, civilization, founded and upheld by law.

The conception was magnificent, grandiose. It was Rome who spread wherever she went the great idea that a man must be assumed to be innocent until he was proved to be guilty; who pronounced it the height of injustice to carry any law out logically without regard to the practical good or ill which resulted; who never in her law-making quite lost sight of the conception that all, men or women, free or slaves, were "by nature" equal.

The civilization that resulted showed again and again the strength which no mere external force, however powerful, ever possesses. The Gauls were fierce fighters, people of high spirit, undisciplined too, but when once they had experienced what Roman civilization meant, its superiority was so evident, they never after Caesar's conquest had any general uprising against the Roman rule. The Acts of the Apostles gives a wonderful picture of what it meant to belong to Rome. St. Paul, though a Jew of Tarsus, was yet a Roman, so the record states, the little Asia Minor city having been admitted to the Roman federation. In a town where he was preaching, the magistrates, induced by the Jews, seized him and ordered him to be scourged, but just before they did so Paul cried out that he was a Roman citizen, and they sent word to their officer, "Take heed what thou doest, for he is a Roman." Then "the chief captain came and asked him, Art thou a Roman? He said, Yea.

And the chief captain answered, With a great sum obtained I this freedom. And Paul said, But I was born free." The proud words received their due: St. Paul under strong escort was sent away from the town where his enemies were determined to kill him, to the Roman governor of the province, and in his presence uttered the words which had the power to remove him from local prejudice and personal spite into an atmosphere of impersonal justice: "I appeal unto Caesar." The governor gave the required answer, the only one that could be made: "Thou hast appealed unto Caesar, unto Caesar shalt thou go." And Paul, conducted by Roman soldiers, went to Rome.

When early in the third century all free-born citizens of every city in the empire were given the Roman citizenship, the conception of a universal community, over-riding narrow national bounds, and of a world-peace, the ideal men have always yearned for, seemed on the point of accomplishment.

Undoubtedly the idea was of Greek not Roman origin. It came to Rome by way of Greek philosophy and Alexander the Great, but the Romans alone brought it down to earth and made it work. Law, which is the practical realization of the ideal of justice, was naturally and inevitably first and foremost a Roman product. The Greeks theorized; the Romans translated their theories into action. And it must always be remembered, too, that they and no other nation were the inheritors of the great Greek thought. The town that fought its way to the position of mistress of the western world and a considerable portion of the eastern and southern, too, did not surpass the other peoples of the earth solely in the power to obey better, to fight more intelligently, and to bear hardship with stiffer-backed endurance. Only the Romans really perceived what Greece had been. They admired her often to their own harm; they copied her instead of developing their own natural bent, but they recognized her greatness and they showed thereby their own.

Another certain indication of a nobility in the Roman strain and a lofty ideality, too, which seems strangely remote from the Rome of Cicero and Horace, is given by their golden-deed stories. The stories a nation repeats about its great men show, as nothing does more, the national ideal. Did Nelson really say, "England expects every man to do his duty"? Did Francis I exclaim, *"Tout est perdu fors l'honneur"?* Perhaps they did, but certainly if they had not, some other Englishman, some other Frenchman, would have been found to hang the words upon, so completely do they express the English and the French ideas of the thing to say when a man is up against it. And whether Regulus did in actual truth go back to Carthage to die under torture because he had promised, or not, is unimportant in revealing the Roman character compared with the fact that the story was repeated through the centuries as showing how Romans thought a man should keep his word.

No other nation has tales of heroism and patriotic devotion and disinterested virtue to compare with the Roman: Horatius at the bridge, Curtius leaping into the gulf, the boy threatened with torture to make him reveal the Roman plans, who thrusts his hand into the fire and holds it there—numbers of them have come down, splendid stories, unsurpassed by those of any other people and very rarely equalled. Even if not one of them ever happened they are true, exactly as the accounts of the games are true. They were Roman conceptions and they embodied what Romans believed human beings should and could achieve. The national ideal is an important factor in understanding a nation. High honor and love of country that made nothing of torture and death was what the Romans set first as the greatest thing of all.

As regards Roman literature and art, in the one as in the other all the Romans did for a long time was to try to follow the Greek way, in spite of the fact that it pointed in a direction where their own genius would not naturally have led them. Greek art and Greek letters have little in common with the Roman, although Cicero would have disputed the assertion, and with reason. He had been carefully trained and cultivated in the Greek tradition. Greek art was the whole of art to him; he was not aware of any other. No doubt that lovely ivy-embowered villa of his was done in strict conformity with Greek canons of taste and transplanted to Athens would have seemed perfectly in keeping there. All Roman culture came from Greece, and respectful copies and adaptations of Greek statues and temples and houses were all that Rome wanted. Horace, too, might have disputed the assertion. A Greek could hardly have been more aware than he was of the loveliness of his bit of land, his elms and poplars and smooth lawn sloping to the river. But he, like Cicero, was the foster-child of Greece. The Greek lyric poets were his models and his eye had been trained by them. He saw beauty where they pointed to it, in the ordinary surroundings of life.

That was the peculiar gift of the Greeks, to perceive the beauty of familiar, every-day things, and their art and literature which was concerned to reveal this beauty, is the great example of classic art and literature as distinguished from romantic. The Greeks were the classicists of antiquity and they are still today the pre-eminent classicists. What marked all they did, the classic stamp, is a direct simplicity in expressing the significance of actual life. It was there the Greek artists and poets found what they wanted. The unfamiliar and the extraordinary were on the whole repellent to them and they detested every form of exaggeration. Their desire was to express truthfully what lay at hand, which they saw as beautiful and full of meaning.

But that was not the Roman way. When not directly under Greek guidance the Roman did not perceive beauty in every-day matters, or indeed care to do so. Beauty was unimportant to him. Life in his eyes was a very serious and a very arduous business, and he had no time for what he would have thought of as a mere decoration of it. Before money and leisure had corrupted the nation, as all Romans thought they had, the natural Roman attitude toward art, even the attitude of the best and greatest spirits, was very like what that of the commander of a beleaguered fort would be if he saw one of his men busily carving into a pleasing shape the handle of his weapon. There were imperative tasks to summon men for all that was in them. Painting, sculpture, such-like trifles, were to be left to what a Roman writer called "the hungry Greekling."

Still, as Rome grew rich and strong and proud, she felt, of course, the need to display her power by a visible magnificence, and she built splendid temples and palaces and triumphal arches, but they were all Greekish—Greek seen through Roman eyes, bigger and better Greek. To the Roman the big was in itself admirable. The biggest temple in the world was as such better than the rest. If a Corinthian capital was lovely, two, one on top of the other, would be twice as lovely. But at bottom none of all that decorative splendor was Roman, the stately temples that housed Grecian gods, the processions of white-clad priests and vestals winding up the Capitoline with youths and maidens singing a hymn to deities whose home was a Greek island in the Ægean. Such things were all very right and proper to mark the correct grandeur of official Rome, but they had nothing to do with the real religion of a Roman. The worship dear to his heart was given to the little household gods, tiny, rude figures, to which were offered no frankincense, no choice yearling from the flock, nothing rare or precious, but only a bit of the every-day food. We do not hear of any beauty or dignity connected with their worship. That would have estranged the Roman and put him off. Beauty and dignity were appropriate in the imposing temple of Jupiter, Greatest and Best, but for daily use give him comfortable homeliness. The Greeks would have found rude homeliness uncomfortable. They had to have their very pots and pans agreeable to look at.

But when the Romans stopped thinking about culture and the Greeks and devoted themselves to the things they really wanted to do, then they showed that they, too, could create beauty, beauty on a great scale, but always as a by-product, not deliberately sought. "In Rome the true artist is the engineer." Roman genius was called into action by the enormous practical needs of a world empire. Rome met them magnificently. Buildings tremendous, indomitable, amphitheatres where eighty thousand could watch a spectacle, baths where three thousand could bathe at the same time, which nearly two thousand years have left practically intact. Bridges and aqueducts that spanned wide rivers and traversed great spaces with a beautiful, sure precision of soaring arches and massive piers. And always along with them the mighty Roman road, a monument of dogged, unconquerable human effort, huge stone joined to huge stone, marching on and on irresistibly, through unknown hostile forests, over ramparts of mountains, across sun-baked deserts, to the very edges of the habitable world.

That is the true art of Rome, the spontaneous expression of the Roman spirit, its keen realization of the adaptation of practical means to practical ends, its willpower and enduring effort, its tremendous energy and audacity and pride. Beauty was a purely incidental result, not consciously brought about by any thought of it in engineers and builders faced with problems of terrific difficulty, but only by the curious agreement there exists in the nature of things between an admirably utilitarian creation and non-utilitarian beauty.

The conscious art of such a people would be, so any one would reason, sternly realistic, revealing life as pitiless fact, with no desire to express anything except implacable truth. And such is the case with the peculiarly Roman achievement in sculpture, the portrait-bust. These heads are all implacably true with the external truth of accuracy. An exact likeness was all the sculptor sought. He reproduced in his marble every detail of the heads of the hard-faced, tired old men who were

to be immortalized, not one unhappy line spared us in
the deeply corrugated brow or one fold in the heavy
hanging flesh beneath the chin, no least softening of
the stupid brutality or the peevish ill-humor which so
often dominates the whole. A Roman did not ask to be
flattered. He was content with what he was. The more
faithful the portrait, the greater the artist's success in the
eyes of his patron. This is as true of the women as of
the men. An empress did not want her hard mouth
softened or the long lobes of her big ears curtailed. A
great courtesan complacently allowed the ugly lines of
her head and brow to be set down without extenuation.
It is impossible to avoid the conviction that they either
did not see ugliness, or were indifferent to it. How
far removed this photography in marble is from the
realism of the Greeks becomes instantly clear if one
calls to mind the statue of the Greek girl bending over
the basin to wash her hands. Classic art is embodied in
her; a commonplace act is invested with perfect beauty.

Now and again among the Roman statues there is
one like that of the Chief Vestal, which rises above
the exact reproduction of an individual face into a kind
of grandeur through the very faithfulness of the
transcriber who put with precision into marble the
virile force, the profound gravity, the strength without
a shadow of human weakness, which made that face a
type of what Rome believed herself to be. But these
are the rare exceptions.

For the rest, when the Roman sculptors were not
copying Greece—and making the copies heavy and ill-
proportioned—they took with enthusiasm to allegorical
bas-reliefs, the counterpart of Horace's sermons, where
the artist sermonized and admiring Rome was edified,
*l'art pour la moralité* never more consciously pursued
and the art completely over-weighted by the morality.
Only in one small department Rome achieved a rich
beauty of her own, in those familiar, often-copied
panels of the teeming gifts of earth—fruits and flowers
and chubby boys gathering great bunches of grapes

from weighted vines, shocks of full-eared grain, and cows and sheep, one crowding upon the other almost without design, all the luxuriant abundance poured forth by the copious fertility of the south. They are truly Roman; they have nothing in common with the sparing use in Greek decoration of the flower-pattern. The Greek soil did not lavish her gifts from a never-emptied horn of plenty. Fruits, flowers, like everything else in Greece, were to be used by the artist "with economy."

One of the great Victorians has said that if classicism is the love of the usual in beauty, romanticism is the love of the strange in beauty, and the statement gives to admiration the essence of the difference between the two. The very words romance, romantic, call up a vision, vague yet bright, that banishes the drabness and monotony of every-day life with a sense of possible excitements and adventures. Of course, if every-day life did not look drab and monotonous there would be no reason to turn to romance. That is primarily why the Greeks were not romantic. Facts were full of interest to them. They found enough beauty and delight in them to have no desire to go beyond.

But to the Romans facts were not beautiful nor, in themselves, interesting. The eagerness for inquiry into everything in the universe which had stamped Greece never reached Rome. Cicero's remark that the investigation of nature seeks to find out either things which nobody can know or things which nobody needs to know, expresses perfectly the Roman attitude. They were not an intellectual people. Their place was the world of practical affairs, not of thought. Science ended as Greece went down and Rome came up. Romans travelled all over the earth, but they did not become geographers; they solved the problems of the arch as it had never been done before, but they were not physicists. They were persistently indifferent to theory. It was enough for them to know that such a thing could be accomplished in such a way; the reason was unimportant. They were not interested in why, only in how.

Beauty was still less interesting. It was never quite real to them. Reality, facts, they saw as we do, chiefly as ugly and unpleasant. "Face the facts," "Come down to reality"—the phrases would have had the same meaning to the Romans that they have to us. How hideous and grim reality can be was forced upon their attention as it is not upon ours. We have learned to protect ourselves by shutting away within stone walls shocking sights, but in Rome after the great slave insurrection the main road to the city was lined for more than a mile with the crosses of crucified slaves. Even the horrors of war we disguise in part, but when a friend of Plutarch's visited a battlefield which had established an emperor on the throne, he found bodies piled up sometimes as high as the eaves of a little temple there. In plain, cold fact, reality, as they saw it was more often hateful than not. Their very amusements were perpetually showing them the horrible forms human agony and death can take.

When a people see chiefly ugliness in the world, they will find a refuge from it. Roman literature took the turn which literature has again and again taken when reality is perceived as nothing from which men can get spiritual delight. The writers of Rome's golden age of letters turned to romance.

What we today call realism, the view that life is devoid of beauty and meaning, always has romance for a companion. They do not go hand in hand, but one follows close behind the other, to catch up ever and again and outstrip it for a while and then fall back. The human spirit will not live long at a time in the prison of senseless ugliness. Invariably a romantic reaction comes. The Greeks, who would have nothing to do with extremes, knew neither the one nor the other. They were realists to whom the real was beautiful and the direct expression of that spirit is classic art.

But the Romans, to whom the real was the reverse of beautiful, ended inevitably by turning away from it to romance. Catullus is one of the rare examples of both points of view in one man. He is himself representative of the Roman spirit complete. He sighs to Lesbia from the very height of romantic love; he writes enchanting fairy tales of strange mythological creatures and soars away from everything on earth; then he comes down, to find only filthy mire and to write verses about his factual surroundings which are uglier by far even than the portrait-busts. Reality was in general hideous to him. He had perpetually to escape from it, only to return and then again reject it.

In the Augustan age, the result of a cruel and bitter war which had not brought even to the victors the high exultation of a great enterprise achieved, Roman literature came to its full stature of growth, and the greatest writers of the period turned away from reality and their own world where peace had been bought at the price of republican liberty, to the world of romance and the wonderful regions open to the imagination. The golden age of Roman literature is not classic, but romantic.

# CHAPTER XI

## ENTER THE ROMANTIC ROMAN:
## VIRGIL, LIVY, SENECA

A GREAT literary gossip of the second century A.D. whose work has come down to us in many volumes and whose name was Aulus Gellius has recorded a comparison he once heard a literary friend of his make between Pindar's and Virgil's description of Ætna in eruption. The Greek poet writes: "In the darkness of the night the red flame whirls rocks with a roar far down to the sea. And high aloft are sent fearful fountains of fire." Virgil says: "Skyward are sent balls of flame that lick the stars and ever and again rocks are spewed forth, the torn entrails of the mountains, and molten crags are hurled groaning to heaven." "Pindar," the critic pointed out to his friend, "describes what actually happened and what he saw with his own eyes, but Virgil's 'balls of flame that lick the stars' is a useless and foolish elaboration, and when he says crags are molten and groan and are hurled to heaven, this is such an account as Pindar never wrote and is monstrous." That is a comparison between a classic and a romantic description. Pindar was using his eyes, Virgil his imagination. The man who compared them was a classicist who, of course, detested romantic exaggeration, and could not see the grandeur that we see in Virgil's "flame that licks the stars."

420

The romantic artist must not be judged by the canon of strict accuracy. He will not be bound by fact, "the world being inferior to the soul," as Bacon says, "by reason whereof there is a more ample greatness, a more exact goodness, and a more absolute variety, than can be found in the nature of things." To the classicist the nature of things is the truth and he desires only to see clearly what it is. The romanticist is the adventurer drawn on by the new and the strange where to him truth is to be found. The classic writer depends upon reason no less than upon imagination. To the romantic writer imagination can transcend the narrow limits of experience and move on unhampered by it to what eye hath not seen nor ear heard.

The *Æneid* from first to last is pure romance and Virgil, Rome's greatest poet, is one of the world's greatest romanticists.

He was a few years older than Horace who loved him and wrote of him with tender admiration. Everyone seems to have felt like that about him. The allusions to him in Latin literature show a feeling far beyond that for any other man of letters, and in later days it is safe to say that of all poets, of all writers, indeed, he has been the most loved and praised. He was the only ancient author, either Greek or Roman, to make his way into the Christian church. There was a legend, often repeated and embodied in a hymn, that St. Paul had visited his grave and dropped a tear upon it. Again and again his name was introduced into a ritual of the church as one of the prophets, because in an early poem he wrote of a child about to be born who would bring back the golden age and the reign of peace, interpreted by the Christians as meaning the birth of Christ. So all his poems became in some sort sanctified. The monasteries most hostile to pagan learning could allow copies of them, and pious Christians felt it no sin to use him for looking into the future by opening the *Æneid* and reading the first line their eyes happened to light upon. His transformation into a magician was the next step, and as such the polished, suave man of letters figured strangely during the Middle Ages. To Dante he was "the poet," the one to conduct him through Hell and Purgatory, and "my master and my author, he who taught me the good style that did me honor." And from his death on. to the present, from Juvenal who—early in the second century—deplored the schoolmaster's hardships in having to listen to "the same daily fare always repeated from the soot-blackened Virgil," up to the last June before the College Board examinations, the generations of school children have owed part of their training to him. In our western world the Bible alone has had a wider influence. From this point of view he is more important than the poets of Greece. For seventeen or eighteen hundred years, he was the master of literature to all the western nations.

The romantic spirit took root and spread through Europe; the classic spirit departed. So much is fact. How far the great Latin romantics were responsible for the change is one of the matters not susceptible of proof. It is impossible to say what would have happened if Virgil and Livy and their greatly inferior, but very influential follower, Seneca, had not lived. In the immense German forests, in the soft sea-airs of Ireland, there were no sharp, clear outlines as in Greece. Luminous mists made dim distances where the imagination was free to see what it chose. Also as the church grew in power, side by side with the intellectualizing effort of dogmatic theology, eastern mysticism worked, with its absolute conviction of "a more ample greatness, a more exact goodness than can be found in the nature of things." There was much apart from Roman literature that pointed to romanticism. But, at the least, it may be said with certainty that Virgil and Livy inaugurated the new movement of the spirit the world was ready for. Classicism had grown thinner and dryer from the beginning of the fourth century B.C. on. It became precious, pedantic, all polished surface. Learning and style were the combination out of which to make poetry. This tendency is the evil genius of the classic spirit and has killed it many a time since the polite and erudite and cultivated society of Alexandria dealt it the blow which by the time Virgil appeared had been fatal to it.

"A talent is formed in stillness," said Goethe, "a character in the stream of the world." That is the romantic view; the Greeks of the great age would have violently disagreed. The stream of the world was to them precisely the place to develop the artist, the classical artist, whose eyes are ever turned upon life. But it is not the place to develop the imagination. The romantic artist withdraws from the busy haunts of men to some fair and tranquil retreat, in Sicilian meadows, or by the deep blue sea of the south, or on the hillslope of an English lake, where he may see and tell of things invisible to mortal sight. Alone of the Augustan poets Virgil had no love for life in Rome. During all the years that he wrote he lived in the country, near the Bay of Naples. Even Augustus, who cared much for him and recognized early his genius, was unable to persuade him to do more than make brief visits to the capital.

Very little is known about him. His home was near Mantua and he lost it as Horace did his after the republican cause was defeated. In Naples they called him "the maiden," for his purity of life, some said, others, for his gentleness, and it may be both had a share in the nickname. He went once to Greece and Horace wrote a poem to the ship that carried so precious a burden. One account is that he died on the way home, another, that this happened after a second voyage. Our gossip, Aulus Gellius, tells at length how on his death bed he begged his friends to burn the *Æneid*, "because," Gellius says, "those parts which he left perfected and polished enjoy the highest praise for poetical beauty, but those which he was unable to revise because he was overtaken by death are not worthy of the taste of the most elegant of poets." Augustus is said to have prevented this last wish from being fulfilled. The point

of the story is, of course, the intense desire it shows on
Virgil's part for perfected finish, and this is borne out
by the length of time he spent on each piece of writing—
eleven years given to the *Æneid* alone.

Before he began it he had written two poems or sets
of poems: the earlier his *Eclogues*—in English, Selec-
tions—which were an imitation of a Sicilian poet's
pastoral verse, but oddly Romanized, so that the shepherds every now and then stop singing of flocks and
herds and flowery meadows and the lovely Galatea, to
discuss political doings and burst forth into Caesar's
praises; the later, his *Georgics*—a Greek word meaning
the tillage of the land—a unique and very beautiful
poem, the literary equivalent of the lovely fruit and
flower panel. "What makes a cornfield smile; under
what star the soil should be upturned and when it suits
best for wedding the vine to the elm; what care oxen
need; what is the method of breeding cattle; and what
is the weight of men's experience in preserving the
frugal commonwealth of bees; such is the song I now
essay." So the poem begins. It is practical husbandry
done in lovely verse, an achievement which would off-
hand appear impossible, and has certainly never been
repeated since. There are careful descriptions of the
soil each crop needs, the time for planting and watering
and weeding; a long description of how to breed the
farm animals, together with a detailed account of the
diseases they are liable to and their remedies; and lastly,
everything conceivable about bee-culture, including the
fact, even to Virgil mildly surprising, that they do not
bring forth their young as do all other creatures, but
"pick them up in their mouths from leaves and grateful
herbage."

The good, common-sense directions are exquisitely
decorated: "The best planting season for vines is the
bloom of spring, spring that does good to woodland
foliage and forestry. It is then that the pathless brakes
are musical with singing birds and the cattle pair in
their season. The fostering soil brings forth, and the

warm western winds unseal the womb of the fields. A
gentle moisture rises over all and the young vine branch
puts out its buds and unfolds all its leaves. I do not
believe the days were fairer or their course more
blissful when the young world first came into being; it
was spring then—it was spring-tide that the great globe
was keeping, when an iron race of men rose from the
hard soil and beasts were turned into the woods and
stars into the sky."

But a quotation here and there can show nothing
really of what the poem is. The slow course of the
narrative, the piling up of detail after detail in the life
of the farm, the deep feeling for earth and her produce,
the sense of the primal value of the labor that causes
earth to produce, end by making a powerful impression
of the beauty and the meaning in these fundamentals of
human life.

It is the poem in which Virgil and Latin poetry come
nearest to the classic.

Now and again, however, the Roman gets the better
of the artist. Virgil sees no reason why cattle disease
is not a subject for a poet, and he tells at length about
"the noisome scab" on sheep, and how to open with
a knife "the mouth of the swollen sore," and about "the
panting cough that shakes disease swine," when "black
blood trickles from their nostrils," and the dying agonies
of a bull stricken with distemper, "convulsed and vomit-
ing bloody foam"—a veterinary's pamphlet sonorously
versified.

The note of exaggeration, too, foreign to classic art
and always at home in romantic art, is never far away:
"The bull comes upon his foe like a billow that begins
to grow white out in midsea, curving up like a bellying
sail—like it also when it rolls to shore and roars terrific
among the rocks, breaking high as the towering cliff."
And at the very end the poem lapses into wild romanticism; the poet wanders away from his bees to the
bottom of the ocean and all manner of fantastic creatures of the sea with "grass-green glare of fiery eyes."

Virgil was at last trying his hand at mythology. From this ending to the subject of the *Æneid* there was but a short step.

A romantic subject may be treated classically and a classic subject romantically. The beauty of a Greek god is human, realized by the artist from the living men he had seen; it is what a romantic subject will become under classic treatment. The romance has suffered: the statue is a god merely because it is so labelled. The strange beauty of a Hindoo god, like nothing ever seen on earth, is completely romantic. The Hindoo artist's imagination has conceived something beyond or, at the least, apart from, humanity. The same distinction emerges from a comparison between the romantic *Æneid* and the classic *Iliad*. The *Iliad* has as romantic a subject as the *Æneid*, as romantic, indeed, as there could be: battles where heroes and gods fight for a marvelously beautiful woman, and conclaves held in silver Olympus where deities watch the contest and give victory to this side or that. But when Homer's method of treatment is compared with Virgil's the difference between classic romanticism and the purely romantic is instantly perceived.

In the *Iliad*, Achilles has lost his armor, and his goddess-mother goes to the fire-god to beg a new set from him. She finds him "in his halls wrought of brass by his own hand, sweating and toiling and with busy hand plying the bellows. He was fashioning a score of tripods, all placed on wheels of gold that they might roll in and back, a marvel to behold. Not yet was added the neat handles, for which the god was forging rivets busily." This description of a god, like the Greek statue, is a classic treatment of a romantic theme which does damage to the romance. The classic artist's home is the earth; if he ascends to heaven, heaven takes on the look of earth. But when Æneas loses his armor and his mother goes to Vulcan for the same purpose there is nothing of earth in the scene: "An island towering with fiery mountains; beneath thunders a cavern blasted out by the Cyclops' forges; the sound of mighty blows echo on anvils; molten metal hisses; fires dart from the great jaws of the furnace. Hither the lord of fire descends from heaven's height. There in the mighty cave the Cyclops were forging"—not smoothly rolling tripods fitted with neat handles, but "the thunderbolt, one of those many which the great Father showers down on earth. Three spokes of frozen rain, three of watery cloud, had they put together, three of ruddy flame and the winged wind of the south; and now they blend the awful flash and the noise and the terror and the fury of the untiring lightning flame." That is what your true romantic can do with the fearful fire-god and the forges of the Cyclops. Thunderbolts, every reader must feel, are what ought to be produced by such means.

If it is objected that the pictures of the supernatural in the *Iliad* are not classic, but only primitive, the truth is that the realism so strikingly marked in Homer is essentially the same as that which stamps the whole of Greek art. It is not a mere matter of childish details. His Olympians are human just as the Hermes and the Venus of Milo are.

When the Old Testament writer says that the Lord God was walking in the garden in the cool of the evening, he too, like Homer, is doing all that a classicist can do with such a subject: he makes it delightful, quaint and charming. But the description in the Book of Revelation, "And I saw a great white throne and him that sat on it, from whose face the earth and the heaven fled away and there was found no place for them," is the work of a lofty romantic imagination.

To us romance means chiefly the passion of love. The Greeks, Plato excepted, did not think much of that as a subject for literature. They practically ignored it. Even Greek tragedy has very little to do with it. The romantic lover, we know, is allied to the lunatic, and the Greeks had a complete prepossession in favor of sanity. To be sure, the *Iliad* centres in Helen, but Homer's treatment of the loveliest woman of the world is soberly matter-of-fact. When Paris is about to be killed by Menelaus, Aphrodite saves him and carries him away to Troy and his own house. Then she goes to find Helen and bring her to him. Helen is sullen and unwilling. She bids the goddess if she loves him so much, to serve him herself, "and he may take thee for his wife—or his handmaid. I will never go to share his couch." But under Aphrodite's threats she does go and speaks to Paris scornfully, with averted eyes: "Thou hast left the battle. Would thou hadst perished by the mighty hand of him who was my husband. Once thou didst boast to be his peer. Then up—defy him. Yet I counsel thee not—for fear he smite thee and thou be slain." Paris takes all this with the serenity of a man who knows he is going to have what he wants no matter how his wife talks. Menelaus is victor at the moment, he tells her, but he may yet vanquish him in turn. "But now is the time for love. Never before have I felt such sweetness of desire. He spake and went to his fair couch and the lady followed him." There could be nothing less romantic. Angry, scolding, reluctant Helen, and Paris completely indifferent to all save one thing.

Virgil could do a great love story. Æneas and Dido are not only the hero and heroine of our very first romance, they are great lovers, too, the woman the greater, as through the ages the poets have loved to portray her. She "is pierced by love's cruel shaft, feeding the wound with her life-blood and wasting under a hidden fire"; if she is with him "she begins to speak and stops midway in the utterance"; he speaks and "she hangs upon his lips." When the night comes and the banquet hall is empty, she steals there from her bed to find the couch he had lain on and stretch herself upon it. "Him far away she sees and hears, herself far away."

The episode of the hunting party is ushered in with all the trappings of romance. Before the palace door "Dido's charger splendid in purple and gold champs his foaming bit." The queen "comes forth with a great company attending her. Her cloak was purple bordered with embroidery; her quiver of gold, her hair knotted up with gold, her purple dress was fastened with a golden clasp." A hero's beauty in romance is quite as important as a heroine's, and when Æneas joins her he is "like Apollo as he leaves his wintry Lycia and visits Delos, his mother-isle; his flowing hair restrained by a wreath of soft leaves and entwined with gold; his arrows ring upon his shoulders. Even so swift came Æneas, such the beauty that shone forth from his peerless look and mien." Their union, when the hunt is broken up by the storm, takes place in surroundings perfectly fitted to two such personages, a Gustave Doré cavern lit by lightning flashes and echoing the roll of thunder and the cry of the mountain nymphs.

Virgil's attitude at this point in the story, the Roman attitude, was to have a far-reaching influence. Dido has made the fatal slip; her good name is lost; she has fallen from her high estate. Not so Æneas; the matter is merely incidental to him. His good name is not affected at all. Jupiter sends down the messenger god to bid him remember his high charge to found the Roman race, and he makes ready to sail with little more distress than at the difficulty of how to break the news to her: "What first beginning can he make?" But for her, of course, everything is over. She pleads with him for a moment in beautiful, tender words: "Flying, and from me? By these tears and by your plighted hand—since I myself have left my wretched self nothing else to plead—by our union, by marriage-rites yet unfulfilled, if in anything I have deserved well of you, if anything of mine was ever sweet to you"—but the gods have spoken and Æneas must go, and all that is left for Dido and her tarnished fair fame is death, the only refuge in such straits for the romantic heroine through all the centuries since.

Here is a great change from Homer and his treatment of Helen. A long way has been travelled on the long road of woman's destiny. In the *Iliad*, Helen is not blamed at all. What could a woman do but go with

whatever man was at hand to carry her off? All the
blame is put upon Paris. In the *Odyssey*, when Tele-
machus goes to Menelaus' palace to ask news of his
father, Helen comes down into the great hall, lovely
and serene. A handmaid places a well-wrought chair for
her; another brings her silver work-basket, and Helen
sits and works and talks tranquilly of ruined Troy and
the men gaze adoringly. Homer is logical: a woman was
helpless in those days; the fault could not be hers. But
Roman women were not like that ever; they were responsible human beings, a force to be reckoned with;
Dido clearly did not have to yield to Æneas. Then, by
a curious shifting of the balance, all the blame was put
upon her. Æneas got none of it. This was the Roman
point of view, in line with all the early stories of Lucretia
and Virginia and the like, and embodied in Virgil's poem
it went over the whole western world, never even challenged until almost the end of the nineteenth century.
Trollope held it as firmly as Virgil. When lovely woman
stooped to folly, her only refuge was to die, while the
man in the case did just as Æneas did, married somebody else.

The completely romantic view of woman, as what
Havelock Ellis called "a silly angel," is only dimly
foreshadowed by Virgil. It could never have found a
real footing in Rome. Dido is the Roman matron, remembering for her consolation as she dies that she has
built a splendid city and avenged a brother's death. But
the foundation for the later development was laid, and
the long line of lovely, innocent, trusting women, betrayed to their undoing, who for hundreds of years took
possession of romance, goes directly back to the *Æneid*.

There is nothing more romantic than heroism and
great deeds in battle and a glorious death. They are all
ideas Greek literature fights shy of. The *Iliad* is a poem
of battles but there is very little talk about glory of
any kind, and none at all about the glory of a noble
death. Homer's heroes all know that there is a time for
heroism and a time not. When a mightier warrior faces

them they retreat, even if unwillingly, "for this sore grief enters my heart, Hector some day shall boast that I fled before his face," but they never lose the common-sense point of view that "there is no shame in fleeing from ruin, yea, even in the night. Better he fares who flees from trouble than he that is overtaken." A matter-of-fact atmosphere pervades the ringing plains of windy Troy. When Ajax dares to fight with Hector and withstand him, his reward at close of day is substantial: "And wide-ruling Agamemnon gave to Ajax slices of the full length of the [roasted] ox's back for his honor." Homeric heroes do a great deal of eating and drinking and cooking, too; there are receipts given, how to make a pleasant drink from grated cheese and wine and barley, what relishes go best with wine, and so on. The things of daily life play quite as prominent a part as valorous deeds do and "the joy of battle."

All this is completely unlike the *Æneid*. The heroes there are not human beings, but bigger, stronger, grander. Hector in the *Iliad* advancing to battle is "like a stalled horse, full fed at the manger, when he breaks his tether and speeds exultingly over the plain," or—the extreme of romantic description in the poem—"all in bronze shone Hector even as the lightning of Father Zeus." But Æneas in the same case is "vast as Mount Athos or Mount Eryx, vast as Father Apennine himself when he shakes his mighty oaks and lifts his snow-topped peak to the sky," or "like Ægaeon who, fable tells, had a hundred arms and a hundred hands and flashed fire through fifty mouths from the depths of fifty bosoms, thundering on fifty strong shields and drawing fifty sharp swords—even so Æneas slakes his victorious fury the whole field over."

No one in the *Æneid*, except Dido alone, ever comes down to earth. The heroes never are afraid. They fight for glory only and in its pursuit they are as disdainful of death as the knights of the Round Table or Charlemagne's paladins. "The combatants rush on glorious death through a storm of wounds" over and over again.

They pray for death and they go willingly to meet it. "Death I fear not," a wounded warrior cries advancing upon Æneas, "I come to die." "Have compassion upon me," another hero, defeated, prays. "Dash me on reef, on rock, that none may know my shame." Æneas bitterly regrets that he did not die when Troy fell:

> Ye Troyan ashes and dear shades of mine,
> I call you witness, that at your last fall
> I fled no stroke of any Greekish sword,
> And if the fates would I had fallen in fight,
> That by my hand I did deserve it well.

But Homer's heroes never want to die. Death is the worst of ills. "Then Hector knew the truth in his heart and he spoke and said, Aye, now verily is evil death come very nigh me nor is there way of escape. He ended and the dark shadow of death came down and his soul flew forth and was gone to the house of Hades, wailing his fate, leaving fair youth and vigor."

Nowhere, indeed, is the distinction between the classicist and the romanticist seen more clearly than in the way they regard death. On the whole, in Latin literature death is desirable. Even to Horace, the most classic in spirit of all Roman writers, it is "sweet and seemly to die for one's country." English poetry has the same tendency in a notable degree, "Eloquent, just and mighty death," "Dear, beauteous death, the jewel of the just"—there are endless examples. It is the romantic view: the lure to the spirit of the mystery life cannot solve, the sense of all that the unknown may hold, the thrill of the final great adventure. But to the classicist death is always evil unalloyed. Homer's heroes speak in that respect for all Greece. His familiar line that it is better to be a serf on earth than to rule over the dead gives the Greek point of view.

Quotations to decorate soldiers' monuments are found by the score in Latin, but not in Greek. Greek heroism wears an air of soberness always. It is never exultant.

The epitaphs the Greeks set on their old soldiers' monuments do not praise heroic death or speak of glory. In all their literature they talk very little of either. They saw too clearly the agony they are rooted in. The Roman boy's thrusting his hand into the fire was beyond question magnificent, a superb gesture of defiance, but I believe a Greek would have been hard put to it to understand it. The Greeks had no gestures. Æneas, when the great storm comes upon him, lifts his hands to heaven and cries aloud, "Oh, thrice and four times blessed, those who died beneath the walls of Troy." The words are taken from the *Odyssey*, but spoken so differently. Odysseus huddled in the bottom of the boat says them wretchedly to himself. It is impossible to imagine the Greek hero declaiming them to the winds and waves, but it is completely in keeping with the Latin. All the talk in the *Æneid* is grand. To Virgil, the romantic, the ordinary had no place in an epic. But the classic Homer thought otherwise.

The real subject of the *Æneid* is not Æneas, as the real subject of the *Iliad* is the wrath of Achilles; it is Rome and the glories of her empire, seen as the romanticist sees the great past. The first title given it was *The Deeds of the Roman People.* Æneas is important because he carries Rome's destiny; he is to be her founder by the high decrees of fate. Repeatedly in the poem the names of the men who made Rome are rehearsed, glowing history in noble poetry: "Love of country shall conquer and the unmeasured thirst for glory. Look—the Decii and the Drusi and Torquatus with his pitiless ax, and Camillus bringing home the standards saved. What tongue would leave you unpraised, great Cato, or you, great Cossus, or pass over in silence the race of the Gracchi or the two Scipios, twin thunderbolts of war, Africa's ruin, or Fabricius mighty in his poverty, or you, Serranus, sowing your own ploughed field? Others, I doubt not, will mold better the breathing bronze to lifelike softness and from marble draw forth living faces. They will plead better at the bar, and mark out the courses of the sky with their rod and tell of the rising stars. Do you, Roman, remember to rule nations with power supreme. Your art shall be this, to impose the custom of peace, to spare the humbled and war down the proud."

The words are a poetical condensation of Livy's history. No connection or acquaintance, even, between the two men is mentioned anywhere, but the connection between their work is close. Livy was considerably the younger, but he had been engaged upon his history for some ten or twelve years before Virgil died. The two must have known each other's work. Livy's idea of "the founding of this great city and the establishment of an empire which is now in power next to the immortal gods" is precisely Virgil's. Both men took the same theme and the prose writer saw it almost as romantically as the poet: Rome was built up by men of grand character, who were the instruments of divine providence and who were governed by a standard of simple goodness unknown to the corruptions of civilization.

Through Livy's pages moves a solemn pageant of stately figures, all the heroes, the soldiers, statesmen, patriots, who for Rome's sake endured to die and are immortal for ever. That classic sense for fact which so drove on Polybius, Terence's friend, the Greek historian, that he must travel over the Alps, a terrific journey then, to test the accounts of Hannibal's passage before writing about it, that sent him hurrying here and there to read an old inscription or an ancient book, never troubled Livy at all. He was sure of the only ground he really cared about, that "Romans never were worsted in an open fight or upon equal terms," that every war Rome fought was "just and pious," and that all of Rome's enemies were base and treacherous. His simple course when authorities differed was to choose the account most favorable to Rome. As a historian he must yield to the Greek, but he has been a living influence through the centuries since he wrote, while Polybius, so accurate and so dull, has not lived at all outside the scholar's library. Polybius' account of Hannibal is painstakingly careful and completely unimpressive. The Hannibal we know, the brilliant genius of war, the indomitable master of the Alps, the scourge of Italy, is Livy's creation, as is too the picture of the magnificent tenacity and endurance which finally defeated him.

Livy is a great writer, endowed with the fire and the power of a great imagination. It must not be supposed that he let himself be carried away to invent on occasion. He was a conscientious man who wanted to write only what was true. In his preface he says: "Such things as are reported either before or at the founding of the city, set out more by poet's fables than grounded upon pure and faithful records, I mean neither to assert nor disprove." There was no defect in his honesty, but only in his criticism, and artists are seldom critics.

Goethe's sweeping statement about English writers, that inspiration is everything to them, reflection nothing, is exactly applicable to Livy. He saw only the actors on history's stage; the causes responsible for the drama and what went on behind the scenes meant nothing to him. His real interest was in the good and the great of mankind—of Roman mankind. He had that delightful characteristic, so often a companion to the romantic temperament, enthusiasm. The characters in his history live because he was himself so fired by what they did and suffered. Yet he never lost his grasp on the essential truths of human nature; he had in a high degree imaginative insight. And just as he was able to put himself in the place of one of his great Romans and understand him with an unerring perception, in the same way, through his passionate love for what he saw in that early Rome of republican simplicity and hardihood and self-sacrificing patriotism, and through his sure grasp of the combination of great qualities that was truly Roman, unlike any before or since, he was able to produce a characterization of a nation which lives as much as any of literature's foremost characters live. Rome to us is Livy's Rome.

His place is hardly among historians, as we understand the term. He was more than that. What he wrote has an interest altogether independent of its accuracy. He was a great romantic historian—if the term may be allowed. Like Virgil he showed romance at its best, presenting an ideal which is not supernatural or superhuman, but felt instantly to be realizable, although never yet realized, and which has aroused in unnumbered readers the longing to bring it to pass.

But just as there always follows close upon classicism the danger of an arid superficiality, a pedantry that seeks only correctness and dispenses with life, losing the spirit in the passion for the fact, so romanticism has an evil attending genius, sentimentality. The boundary between the two is so tenuous, so easily overpassed. Virgil transgressed it more than once. The romantic is imaginative, the sentimental is unreal; the romantic is idealistic, the sentimental is false. The mark of insincerity is upon all the sentimental: sentimentality is unconscious insincerity. The romanticist, as such, is as sincere as the classicist; it is only that his idea of truth is different. But the sentimentalist does not care about truth. He is always able to believe what he wants to believe.

Sentimental romance came to Rome very shortly after Livy and Virgil died, and took possession of a field which has ever since been peculiarly open to it, the drama. It was almost inevitable that the sentimental play should be a Roman product. There is a kinship between exaggeration and sentimentality. The sentimental always inclines to the exaggerated, and the Romans with their strong natural leaning toward exaggeration were peculiarly liable to it. In sentimental romance anything is admissible. The writer's only object is to say what his audience want to hear in a way that will hold their interest. And as regards the latter, his field of choice is wide: bent as he is only on what is agreeable, he has no need to trouble himself with considerations of what is natural and probable. Forms of sentimentality vary in different ages and in different countries, but their common source is always easy to see. The Roman variety, of course, insisted upon human nature's being grand and heroic; dauntless courage and unshaken fortitude were the qualities all the sympathetic characters in their romance must possess. It is safe to say that the notion of lovely helplessness would never have had a real development in ancient Rome even if she had lasted centuries longer than she did. But on the whole the general range of sentimental ideas was much what it is today. The popular hero and heroine everywhere show their Roman descent by always regarding death as a negligible matter. To the Roman sentimentalist, exactly as to the modern, every man went joyfully to die for his country and every mother wanted to send her son for the same purpose. The poor and lowly were happier than the rich and powerful; the old farm of boyhood's days to be preferred to marble halls; a mother always a mother, and so on.

All this is completely opposed to what the Greeks wanted. A Greek tragic drama has always, indeed, a romantic subject. The central idea of tragedy is rooted in strangeness, great souls suffering extraordinary calamities, but to the Greek it must be presented classically, which is to say, in the way most opposed to the sentimental, nothing exaggerated, nothing distorted away from nature. A Greek tragedy has no popular appeal, as we understand the words. It is the product of an art austere, reserved, precise to the verge of hardness; tragedy achieved in the manner most difficult for that achievement, with strict economy of adjective, description, detail. It had no popular appeal, as the Romans understood the words, either. The idea of rewriting it to suit modern Roman taste occurred to a very able man shortly after Virgil died and he became thereby the father of the sentimental drama.

His name was Seneca and he is best known as a statesman who for a few years held the reins in Rome, and as a devoted preacher of the Stoic doctrine. But his influence upon the theatre is his most enduring title to fame. Along with his Stoicism he had an ardent romanticism. He set himself to make Greek plays over into romantic dramas that should give Roman audiences what they wanted, and to read him is like turning a magnifying glass on romance and on Rome.

Perhaps the most striking example of what resulted is his *Trojan Women*, based on Euripides' tragedy. A comparison between the two illustrates clearly the methods of the sentimental romantic.

In both plays the curtain rises upon the battlefield some days after Troy has fallen. Euripides shows an old woman asleep on the ground in front. As the day brightens she wakes slowly and lifts herself up painfully. She talks to herself in words that could be spoken only quietly, almost dully, as an old woman brought to the utmost of misery would speak:

> Up from the earth, O weary head.
> This is not Troy, about, above—
> Not Troy, nor we the lords thereof.
> Thou breaking neck, be strengthened.
> . . . . . . . . . . . . . .
> Who am I that I sit
> Here at a Greek king's door—
> A woman that hath no home,
> Weeping alone for her dead—

The whole speech is purely human; there is nothing in it of what we call a queenly spirit. To Seneca it seemed very poor, unworthy of royalty and sure to put a Roman audience completely off. His Hecuba is discovered erect with flashing eyes; her queenly spirit is visible in every inch of her, and her speech is delivered to the universe:

Whoever puts his faith in royal power,
Who rules in a great hall and trusts to riches,
Let him behold you, Troy, and look on me.

Never has fortune shown a greater proof
How frail is the dependence of the proud.
Now breaks and falls the lofty pillar—Mighty Asia falls.
Divinities, hostile to me and mine,
I call you witness, and I call you too,
Great sons, my children: bear me witness that
I, Hecuba, saw all the woe to come.
I saw it first nor did I fear to speak.
I told you—

The speech is all like that, with never a touch of pitifulness or human weakness. This Hecuba is not a suffering
woman; she is the great queen whose courage no calamity can break. She is also the authoritative and
weighty Roman matron as she was popularly conceived,
ready to speak her mind on any subject and always able
to say, I told you so. Of course she is completely
disdainful of death. "Mourn not that Priam has died,"
she and the Trojan women tell each other. "Dead he is
happy, as are all who die in battle." Euripides' Hecuba
says:

> Death cannot be what life is, Child. The cup
> Of death is empty and life hath always hope.

She is not heroic. When she hears that the Greek chiefs
have drawn lots for her and her companions, and that
she has fallen to one of Troy's bitterest foes, she only
mourns:

> Weep for me.
> Mine is the crown of misery.

But Seneca's Hecuba hear exultingly that not a man
in the host is willing to draw for her—a disposition
quite comprehensible to the reader—and cries:

> They fear me! I alone make Greeks afraid.

The climax of each play is the death of Andromache's
little son who must be killed in order that Hector's race

shall end. In Euripides a very human herald comes to get the boy, who speaks gently to the mother in her agony:

> 'Tis ordered that this child—Oh,
> How can I tell her of it? 'Tis their will
> Thy son shall die. . . . Nay, let the thing
> Be done. Thou shalt be wiser so. Nor cling
> So fiercely to him—

Such a herald of the host would not have impressed a Roman audience, and Seneca himself no doubt thought the speech a very tame prelude to the death of mighty Hector's son. His herald enters, as he declares with his first words, terrified to the depths of his being, a horrid tremor shaking his limbs. As well it might, for he has seen—"I saw it, I myself"—the sun eclipsed and a fearful earthquake that convulsed the sea and sent cliffs crashing down and laid forests low and tore the land apart and opened a fearful cavern from which there breathed a breath as from the dead—to usher forth the ghost of Achilles.

Euripides uses Andromache's farewell to the child to give a picture of suffering as moving as any ever painted:

> Go, die, my best beloved, my cherished one,
> In fierce men's hands, leaving me here alone. . . .
> Weepest thou?
> Nay, why, my little one? Thou canst not know. . . .
> Thou little thing
> That curlest in my arms, what sweet scents cling
> All round thy neck. . . . Kiss me. This one time.
> Not ever again—

Seneca did not like that. The Greek poet brought the great mythical figure of the Trojan princess down to earth and made her feel only what any woman in agony might feel. A Roman audience expected something better from Hector's wife. Seneca's Andromache is the Mother, in the grandest aspect of that character known to the stage. She tells the Trojan women that she would of course have killed herself as soon as Hector died except for her child:

> He held me back. 'Tis he who masters me.
> 'Tis he forbids me to seek death.
> ... Ah, he has taken from me
> The great reward that greatest evils bring,
> To be afraid of nothing.

She then decides to hide him and tell the Greeks that he is dead, but he, in accordance with the best traditions of the Roman boy, refuses with a proud gesture to stoop to such an act. She is joyful at this proof of proper spirit: "You scorn a safe hiding place," she cries, "I know your noble nature." His reluctance is but just overcome and he hidden, when Ulysses comes to get him and instantly suspects a trick. He threatens Andromache with torture, described in detail, if she will not give him up. She, of course, is utterly unmoved. Mothers, she tells him, are never afraid for themselves. Even when the child is finally discovered she keeps her haughty composure; she bids her son be glad, because their reason for killing him is that they are afraid of him: "You are a little boy, indeed, but already one to be feared."

In Euripides' play, when the herald returns he is bringing back the dead child to his mother, but she has gone, a captive in a Greek ship to her son's murderers. The grandmother receives the little dead body and speaks quietly to it:

> Poor little child.
> Was it our ancient wall so savagely hath rent
> Thy curls ... here where thy mother laid.
> Her kisses. Where the bone-edge frayed
> Grins white above—ah, heaven, I will not see. . . .
> Oh, dear proud lips, so full of hope,
> And closed forever—

Then she and the women wrap the body "in linen white," and it is borne off to be buried "in his low sepulchre." The horrors of the death are not mentioned except for that brief speech of Hecuba's.

Seneca's messenger does not bring the dead body back, because as he explains in detail, the height from which the boy was thrown was so great, there was really nothing left except bits ground deep into the earth. However, he tells the mother she must be proud, for the boy endured to die with a great spirit. He walked to his place of death with steps that never faltered. When he reached the summit he looked upon the Greek host fearlessly and they all wept, Ulysses, too. Not an eye dry except the noble boy's. Then pushing away the hands that held him he leaped of his own accord and died, dashed into pieces. "Just like his father," says Andromache, and Hecuba ends the play with the conclusion that death alone is to be desired.

If literature is made up of the best, Seneca is unimportant for Latin literature, but the kind of drama he was the first to write has kept its popularity unimpaired down to today, and if great influence makes a great literary figure, he stands close to the first rank. In his plays the tendencies of Roman thought and feeling stand out in a form so heightened that they are unmistakable. He marks without the possibility of confusion the broad outlines of the Roman way as distinguished from the Greek way, and he is another proof that we are the inheritors not of Greece, but of Rome.

# CHAPTER XII

## JUVENAL'S ROME AND THE STOICS

A STRANGE page of history opens with the death of Augustus, strange and difficult to understand. In less than two centuries after he died Latin literature was practically over and the empire was beginning to fall. The Augustan age, when men of genius wrote books which nearly two thousand years of life assure us are immortal, was the prelude to a swift deterioration and the complete extinction of Roman letters. Four great and good emperors succeeded each other in the second century, giving Europe, the historians declare, a peace and prosperity she was not to see again, and yet during that century the mighty structure of the empire began to collapse. The last of the four, Marcus Aurelius, was a devoted follower of Rome's noble philosophy, Stoicism. He raised it to the throne and through his virtues it acquired a new greatness and a fresh lustre, but with his death it ended. From then on, in the literature that has come down to us, Stoicism is never spoken of as an influence. The history of the first two centuries of the empire is a record of a great literature that ushers in its own destruction, great rulers that leave the Roman state tottering, a great spiritual movement that dies with its highest expression.

No one can doubt that the three are connected. The

same causes must lie back of them all, and the final cause must be the weakening and the failure of what the whole world in the last analysis depends on: men's energy and fortitude, their morality and vision. That was certainly taking place during these disastrous years, but the accounts given by contemporary writers show such an extraordinary divergence, it is impossible to bring what they say into a coherent whole or to see cause and effect in any clear detail.

During the two centuries when ancient Rome was dying and Latin literature almost dead, three names stand out: Tacitus the historian, a man of genius hardly surpassed by earlier writers; Juvenal the brilliant and bitter satirist; and Seneca of the sentimental plays, who has left us the best exposition there is in Latin of the Stoic doctrine. His two great successors, Epictetus and Marcus Aurelius, chose to express themselves in Greek and so are technically outside of Roman letters, but they are equally important with Seneca in showing what Stoicism became when it passed from Greece to Rome. The clear picture given by these three last and most famous Stoics of what resulted when a second-rate Greek philosophy had developed into a first-rate Roman religion, together with the history of Tacitus and the satires of Juvenal, are our best sources of knowledge for the momentous years that brought classical antiquity to an end.

But they are not sources consistent with each other. Juvenal's and Tacitus' Rome is so different from that of the Stoics, there is no way to make one city out of the two. Roman life as the historian and the satirist see it is evil without a single mitigating feature. As the Stoics show it, it is lived on loftiest heights with never a descent from them. To Juvenal, private life in Rome was given over to abominable vice; to Tacitus, public life was a mad reign of terror. In Seneca's letters, in the discourses of Epictetus, in Marcus Aurelius' diary, there is an atmosphere of purity, goodness, noble strength, such as pervades few books in all the literature of the

world. In this last age of ancient Rome, the most acute
extremes existed side by side. No reaction from the
one ushered in the other: the spirit of black hopelessness
for mankind as sunk irretrievably in the abyss of
degradation, stood face to face with the spirit of unshakable confidence in man's divinity.

The picture Tacitus and Juvenal drew is the one the
world has accepted. It is so vividly and so powerfully
done, the detail so convincing, the colors so sombre and
yet so arresting, the impression it makes is overwhelming. All records of infamy seem to pale by comparison.
And, at the same time, the sincerity of both writers is
instantly apparent; monstrous as the deeds are they
relate, the reader never doubts that they took place
essentially as they are described. For truth, however,
more is needed than sincerity joined to accuracy. Before
either comes disinterestedness. The power to disengage
oneself from one's subject and put personal bias aside
is the first requisite, and this neither the historian nor
the satirist, great as they were, possessed. The tasks
they set themselves, Juvenal to denounce the age he
lived in, Tacitus to write the history of it, were those
that need especially a balanced judgment, and both
men had come too close personally to the evils of their
times to be able to keep the balance. Each was unfortunate in his life, although for completely different
reasons, and suffering had warped their point of view
before ever they began to write.

Of Juvenal's life nothing is directly known except
that it fell during the last part of the first and the early
part of the second century. He never writes about himself. Nevertheless no one who reads the satires can
doubt that he was a very poor and a very proud man,
wretched at living in a city where to be poor was to be
perpetually affronted and treated with insolence, often
by inferiors, even by slaves. Juvenal's patron was no
Maecenas. All he did for his dependents was to ask
them occasionally to dinner where they were served
different food from that placed before him. He feasted

on lobster and asparagus, a mullet from Corsica, a lamprey from Sicily, a fattened goose's liver, a huge capon, a boar with truffles, a peacock—"Gods! a whole boar! entire!—Go, gorged with peacock." The hungry clients got a tiny crab, an eel caught in the sewers, a dubious kind of fungus. "Surely," they whisper, "he will give us what is left of the hare—some scraps of the boar's haunch." But no. "If you can endure this," Juvenal storms, "you deserve it. You will submit to being whipped." And one sees the man of genius stalking home to his attic, his heart burning within him, to stay there until actual starvation drives him to the rich man's door again.

In one passage he describes a school-master's lot in such a way, one cannot but suspect that personal experience is behind the words. "Do you teach? Bowels of iron is what a teacher needs when each pupil stands up in turn and recites the self-same things in the self-same way. The same daily fare again and again—it's death to the wretched master. 'What would I not give,' cries he, 'that the boy's father might listen to him as often as I do.' And you live in a hole no blacksmith would put up with—and the lamps stink—and the boys thumb their begrimed Horace and their smoke-blackened Virgil—Be sure, O parents, to require the teacher to mould the young minds as a man moulds wax—and when the year ends reward him with a jockey's wage."

Such a man condemned to such a life, a genius, acutely sensitive, feeling his degradation at every turn, despising himself for accepting scraps flung him by men he despised, could hardly have failed to see life as a black and desperate business. "If nature denies me talent," he cries, "my indignation will write my verses for me."

Taken by himself alone, if his authority were accepted without question, he would explain clearly, completely, and convincingly why Rome fell. His Rome is inhabited by a vile, degenerate people; it is a place where virtue has all but perished and what little is left exists only

to suffer. It is a nightmare city where men must "dread
poison when wine sparkles in a golden cup," and wives
"learned in the arch-poisoner's arts carry to burial their
husbands' blackened corpses," and every day in the
year you meet a man who "has given aconite to a half-
dozen relatives." Where "no one can sleep for thinking
of a money-loving daughter-in-law seduced, of brides
that have lost their virtue, of adulterers not out of their
'teens"; where "every street is thronged with gloomy-
faced debauchees," and banquets celebrate unnatural
and incestuous vice; where spies abound "whose gentle
whisper cuts men's throats"; where no women is decent
and no man to be trusted and all wealth dishonestly got
and all position attained by abominable means: "The
way to be somebody today is to dare some crime."

This is a picture of a very different place from the
one through which, a century before, Horace used to
make his way to Maecenas. In a hundred years much,
no doubt, may happen, and yet the change here is so
great one must question if the difference lay wholly
in the two Romes and not partly in the two reporters.
When Horace wrote he did not have a case to make
out—except, of course, on those occasions when his
duty as a Roman patriot pressed upon him. But by
nature he had no prepossessions which impelled him
to emphasize either the bright or the dark, and he looked
at human nature very tolerantly. He held up many a
one to ridicule and even to scorn; he saw people very
seldom as great and good and sometimes as intolerable;
he was in no sense an optimist and he knew his Rome
through and through. Nevertheless one never closes
the book of his satires with a sense that the world of
men is detestable. Horace did not find it so. His eyes
were as keen to detect the good as the bad, and with
all its follies and frailties he liked mankind.

This is the temper of mind which enables a man to
estimate truthfully the world around him. It was not
Juvenal's. His satires leave one wondering if he ever
liked anything, so black and evil as he saw it, was the

world he lived in. Whenever he writes, a flood of hate and furious anger fills him and sweeps him away to include everything in his denunciations. He cannot discriminate; all everywhere are abominable and all equally abominable.

His attitude and his method may be seen excellently well in the same satire by which his trustworthiness as a reporter of his own times may be most easily judged, the famous sixth satire. It has been called his "Ballad of Bad Women," but a juster title would be "The Way of All Women," for all women are bad, hateful alike when they chatter Greek and insist on discussing the poets as when they poison their stepsons.

It is far too long an indictment to be given here, but the manner and matter is clear from a mere résumé of the main heads of the first half: What! You who once had your wits are taking a wife—a she-tyrant, when there is rope to be had for a noose? But, says he, he wants a son! And a virtuous woman! O doctors, come and bleed him. Think of that woman who left her husband for a gladiator—of the Empress Messalina's vices. But there—women's lust is the least of their sins. Here's one who brought her husband a fortune—and bought her liberty with her dowry. She can write her love letters under his very nose. This man or that burns with love for his wife. Why! If you shake out the truth, it's her face he loves, not her. Let three wrinkles appear and it's 'Be off. There's another wife coming.' But until then she rules the roost—and her extravagances! Still, suppose a woman could be found, charming, rich, virtuous—could anyone endure to be married to all the perfections? Any wench for my wife rather than you, O mother of the Gracchi. What man was ever so much in love with a woman as not to hate her seven hours out of twelve? Perhaps some faults *are* small, but they are intolerable to husbands—a woman forever showing off her Greek, for instance. Of course, if you really love your wife, you are lost beyond hope; no woman ever spares the man who loves her. She will

arrange your friendships—turn your old friend from
your door. 'Crucify that slave,' she cries. 'Why? Give
the man a hearing when. his life is at stake.' 'Idiot—
calling a slave a man. Why? It is my will.' So she
lords it—then gets tired of him and finds another husband—eight in five years. Give up all hope of peace,
of course, as long. as your mother-in-law `lives. But in
any trouble *cherchez la femme*. Never a case in court
in which a woman was not at the bottom of the business. But what can you expect now they've taken to
wrestling and fencing? Modesty in a woman like that?
Actually panting as she goes through her exercises!
Suppose you find her `with a lover. Is she ashamed?
Listen to the lady: 'We agreed long ago that you were
to go your way and I mine.' Now-a-days a woman eats
great oysters at midnight and drinks until the roof spins
round. My old friends advise—keep your women at
home, under lock and key. Yes—and who will guard the
guards? So many varieties and all intolerable: the musical woman ever at an instrument; the one who talks to
generals in uniform and can tell you what the Chinese
are after; and, worst of all, she who will discuss Virgil
and Homer. For heaven's sake, get a wife who doesn't
understand all she reads. How I hate a woman who
quotes ancient poets to me I never heard of. And all of
them plaster their faces with dough and ointments. They
will wash them off for company, but when do they
want to look nice at home?"

And so on and so on for some hundreds of lines
more, which include a warning to stepsons in general
that "those hot cakes are black with poison of a mother's
baking," and end with the statement that you will meet
every morning a woman who has murdered her husband
—"no street but has its Clytemnestra."

This is a fair sample of the way Juvenal looked at
life. The trustworthiness of his entire picture of Rome
can be estimated by the trustworthiness of this picture
of the women. He hates them so intensely that he loses
all sense of perspective, or, more truly, he never had

any. Horrible crimes and silly habits are alike damned
eternally and whatever happens is the woman's fault.
The lady divorced for three wrinkles is a villain, not a
victim.

His honesty cannot be questioned. It comes through
everything he writes. He is terrifically in earnest, desperately sincere. Certainly he saw all the abominations
he says he did, but he was unable, both temperamentally
and by reason of his misfortunes, to see anything that
was not abominable. His rooted conviction was that the
present was *per se* evil and the past good—and the
farther off the better. In the last satires, written, he tells
us, when that drastic teacher, old age, had taken him in
hand, and when the fame of his writings must have
softened life's rigors for him, his indignation declines
into a milder temper. "How can sad Poverty sing songs?"
he wrote in an early satire. "Horace's stomach was well-
filled." And certainly in considering the different accounts the two men give of their own times the explanation must have weight. Wrath against one's own wrongs
is so easily confused with wrath against the wrongs of
the world.

Tacitus, Juvenal's contemporary and a greater writer
by far, one of Rome's greatest, also suffered and also
saw life as evil chiefly, almost unrelieved. He was not
poor like Juvenal; he came of a rich and highly placed
family, but the first part of his youth was passed during
a time when the condition of the Roman state was as
bad as it could well be. He was probably in his early
'teens when Nero was killed, and the atrocities of Nero's
last years must have been familiar topics of talk throughout his boyhood. He was grown to manhood when Domitian came to the throne and his best years were
over when that monster died. They were years of silence
for all except debased flatterers. "Ancient times," wrote
Tacitus, "saw the utmost of freedom, we of servitude.
Robbed by an inquisition of the common use of speech
and hearing, we should have lost our very memory
with our voice, were it as much in our power to forget

as to be dumb. Now at last [with Domitian's death] our breath has come back, but genius and learning are more easily extinguished than recalled. Fifteen years have been subtracted from our lives, and we are the wretched survivors not only of those taken from us, but of our own selves." In the spirit of these sombre and moving words he writes his history.

The city he takes us into is essentially the same in its moral aspect as Juvenal's city, but it is peopled by politicians and courtiers. Tacitus' world is the great world of the court and the senate, the circles he himself moved in, remote from any Juvenal touched. It is the aristocratic Rome Cicero and Horace knew, but between them and Tacitus is a gulf so wide, it is astounding that they are separated by a mere century or less.

The history of the successors of Augustus, as related by Tacitus, is of men made mad by awful, limitless power. To be the absolute master of the civilized world, to be free in the complete sense of the word, able to indulge every wish the moment it entered the mind, to carry out each caprice no matter how extravagant, to have nothing stand in the way of any desire whatsoever, not a person in all the world, not law, not custom, not religion—the weight of that terrific responsibility was too much for the first men upon whom it fell. Indeed, the fact that during the following century rulers were found who were equal to it shows, better, perhaps, than anything else in Roman history, what the Roman character was capable of at its best. But during the earlier years Tacitus gives us an uninterrupted succession of abominable tyrants. "A black and shameful age," is his summary. "If the narrative in which I am engaged was a record of wars and of men who died in the service of their country, even then the continued disasters would make the reader turn with abhorrence from so many tragic events. How much more from the present subject where we have nothing but base servility and a deluge of blood spilt by a despot in the hour of peace." The base servility was most conspicuous in the case of mem-

bers of the senate, who, Tacitus says, "tried to see
which could be the most obsequious slave. The emperor
[Tiberius, in this case, Augustus' heir] was used to say
as often as he went from the senate-house, 'These men—
how ready they are for slavery.' " They descended to
incredible depths. At the end of an especially murderous
outbreak on the part of Nero, in which Seneca and the
poet Lucan lost their lives, when, writes Tacitus, "the
city presented a scene of blood, and funerals darkened
all the streets," those who had lost their dearest "adorned
the emperor's house with laurel and printed kisses on his
hand," and a consul-elect moved that "A temple should
be built to the Deified Nero, who had risen above the
condition of human nature and was entitled to religious
worship."

The special horror of the age was the body of in-
formers, Juvenal's spies, "whose gentle whisper cuts
men's throats," who, if successful in an accusation, were
rewarded with part of the estate of the condemned. So
fostered, they spread. "None could trust each other,"
Tacitus sums up, "not relatives, not friends. The very
walls were suspect." The success of this infamy was
made easy. People were found guilty on the most
frivolous charges, a man killed because he had dreamed
he saw the emperor wearing a withered wreath—taken
for a bad omen; a woman exiled because "she harbored
resentment" on account of a husband's fate; another
put to death for weeping over a son's execution.
"Natural affection was made a felony and a mother's
tear was treason." Many times the accusation was of
"secret practices in the magic arts," and with these
words classical antiquity and the spirit of enlightenment
seemed to end; the reader feels suddenly transported to
the Middle Ages. "The magic art" would have sounded
to Cicero precisely as it does to us.

Within the palace during those years of terror an
incredible state of things prevailed. All the emperors
died violent deaths, but only after each had murdered
those nearest to him. Often their crimes were fantastic,

as when Nero put his mother aboard a ship designed so that suddenly in the night it went to pieces, or when the Empress Messalina during the emperor's absence married publicly and with great pomp another man. "It will appear a fabulous tale," Tacitus comments on this last exploit, "but to amuse with fiction is not the design of this work."

Now and again, however, he does amuse, although, of course, without intention. The duel for the possession of Nero between his mother, that truly terrific woman, Agrippina, and the subtle, but even more to be dreaded Poppaea, who became his wife, is a lively narrative. The latter was so fascinating, even Tacitus' austerity softens in describing her: "Virtue excepted, she possessed all the qualities that adorn the female character —the graces of an elegant form, conversation decorated with every winning art, a refined wit. Her favors were bestowed where she saw her interest—a politician in her pleasures." Her methods in detaching Nero from his mother exemplified these traits: "She would make gentle fun of the emperor—call him a pupil under tuition, deprived of personal liberty." Then she would grow serious: "If Agrippina had determined that no one should be her daughter-in-law but a woman the emperor held in detestation, she would herself retire to some remote corner of the earth where she could not see his disgrace." And the words would end in tears. Agrippina with all her violence of character could not hold out against this combination of charm and policy; her death followed.

But before she was removed she had given the state much disquiet. Not because she served poisoned mushrooms to her imperial husband. That, after all, could be accounted a deed within woman's conceded field of action, the home. All that the senate did then was to set upon the throne the son for whom she had committed the murder. But when it came to her taking part in public life, the foundations of Rome rocked. Shortly after Nero's accession, as he was about to give audience to some foreign ambassadors, Agrippina entered and advanced to the tribunal, with the evident intention of taking her seat there and her share in the proceedings. "All who beheld the scene were struck with horror and amazement," says Tacitus. "Seneca alone in the universal confusion had the presence of mind to bid the emperor step forward to greet his mother [as though granting her also an audience]. So, under an appearance of filial respect, the honor of the state was saved."

Juvenal's sixth satire is not the only indication that the men of Rome were beginning to have to defend actively that masculine supremacy which had been, on the whole, so satisfactorily understood in the good days of old.

Side by side with the crimes of violence, and quite as conspicuous, were the crimes of vice. Rome had reached a condition when these did not have to be concealed. Poison still must be administered with some degree of privacy, but scenes of brutal lust were enacted publicly, not only at banquets and great entertainments, but at the spectacles of the games. Tacitus never descends to the arena, but another author of the time makes good this deficiency, Martial, the writer of epigrams. He describes in many a verse what the amphitheatre became under Domitian, when mythological tales of monstrous vice were enacted before the whole city, always, Martial is forever repeating, to the great glory of the one and only lord of all the earth.

To turn from these writers to the Stoics of the same day is like being lifted from a reeking slum or a battle-field heaped with dead to a mountain top or an untrodden shore of the open sea. While Nero was reigning, Seneca from that court red with blood and black with shame, was writing, "We do not need to beg the keeper of a temple to let us approach his idol, God is near you, with you, within you. A holy spirit dwells within us." A few years after Juvenal died, a Caesar of Rome in his soldier's tent on the wild bank of the Danube was solving for himself life's enigma in terms of unselfish duty unflinchingly pursued—"each task from hour to hour performed as though it were to be the last, free from passion, insincerity, self-love, discontent . . . offering to God who is within thee a manly being, a citizen, a soldier at his post, ready to depart from life as soon as the trumpet sounds." And, at the opposite end of the social scale, a man born to a terrible fate, a slave to one of Nero's creatures, had declared not long before that no evil could happen to him because nothing could happen save by the will of God. Then "Let us sing hymns to God and bless him and tell of his benefits."

This is the voice not of philosophy, but of religion. Stoicism from its earliest beginnings was religious. In the fourth century B.C., Zeno, its founder, was preaching in Athens the belief in one supreme God of boundless power and goodness, who was not to be worshipped in temples, unworthy of Deity, but who dwelt in every man, uniting all into one great commonwealth, where there was no distinction between rich or poor, man or woman, bond or free. Three hundred and fifty years later, St. Paul on the Areopagus told the Athenians: "God dwelleth not in temples made with hands. . . . He hath made of one blood all nations of men . . . that they should seek the Lord, if haply they might feel after him and find him, though he be not far from everyone of us: For in him we live and move and have our being." These words are a concise declaration of the Stoic creed, the fundamental tenets of the school.

It must not however be concluded that Stoicism was a religion only and not a philosophy. Zeno had been constrained by the necessity which has pressed upon most of the world's great religious leaders, to attach a rational account of the universe to the intuitive convictions of faith, but his explanation had both of the weaknesses always present when knowledge is sought, not for its own sake, but to prop up something else: it was not very good reason and it was asserted to be infallibly true. As a result, it did not greatly commend itself to the Athenians, intellectualists by nature and trained in the school of Socrates to believe in the dispassionate search for truth and in pursuing it with the Socratic spirit, always remembering that "This may be true, Cratylus. On the other hand, it may very well not be." To fourth-century Athens, belief and rational proof were inextricably connected and the rationality of the proof forever open to re-examination.

A dogmatic theology cannot take root in such soil. Stoicism crossed the Adriatic to find the conditions necessary for its growth.

The Romans were not philosophically minded. Theories of knowledge and of final causes were unimportant and could be accepted without much probing into the basis of truth they rested on. But when the question had to do with the guiding principles needed for life, they knew better than the Greeks what was important. They were men of practical vision: they perceived the struggle between good and evil as the Greeks never did. Pleasure and morality were not seen as opposed to each other in Greece. Socrates visiting a famous courtesan to discover if she was as beautiful as people said, carrying on an agreeable conversation with her, giving her advice how best to attach her lovers to her, leaving her with a charming compliment to her beauty, is representative of all Greece. But to the Romans the opposition between duty and pleasure was absolute. Men's natural inclinations were evil; their manifest obligation was sternly to control them. Socrates' idea, so characteristically Greek, that no one can know virtue without embracing and practising it—we needs must love the highest when we see it—was totally inadequate to life's hard demands, as Romans saw them.

To men so disposed came Stoicism with its final emphasis upon the will. The Stoic's eyes were fixed on life, not on intellectual truth. Right and wrong had to do not with the reason, but with the will. All virtue was vain that did not result in virtuous doing. It was a doctrine fitted to the deepest demands of the Roman nature. They wanted not philosophy, which is for understanding, but religion, which is for action. "We are the most religious of all nations," wrote Cicero, and when religion is seen as a force to make men better, not to explain the universe, his words are true. It was in Rome that the conquest of Christianity was most complete, and it was from Rome that the Christianizing of the world proceeded. The fact is easily comprehensible when the Roman genius for religion is perceived—religion as it is understood by the west, the power of the good to conquer the evil.

The Christian Church never proclaimed in stronger terms the all-sufficiency of this power than the Stoics did. Whoever recognized the divine light within him and strove to keep it bright, was removed from the possibility of evil. Pain, sorrow, death, could not enter that inner shrine. It was the impregnable citadel where peace reigned, no matter what was without. Epictetus, a slave who knew the horrors of Nero's court, felt himself free in his slavery and independent of all men could do to him. "Suppose the tyrant says he will throw me into prison—my spirit cannot be imprisoned. 'But I can put you to death.' 'No—You can only cut off my head.'" The only thing that matters is a will bent upon the good, and this is wholly within a man's own mastery. That alone is our concern. Our lot in life, slave or emperor, God assigns. All we have to do is to play well the part he gives us, as the actor does, whatever the rôle he is cast for. Outside success and failure are of no consequence. "Virtue consists in aiming at the mark, not hitting it." The man who tries hardest is thereby the most successful. The wise man of the Stoics' ideal is like the good athlete who strives to the utmost, but to play the game, not to win it.

The power there is in an ideal to bring about its own reality was exemplified many a time in those last days of Rome. In the city where Tacitus and Juvenal saw public exhibitions of unnamable vice, the Stoics lived lives of austere purity. To them all sexual relations outside of marriage were "disgraceful by reason of their lawlessness and foulness." They held—it is an instance of their astonishing modernity—the equality of man and woman, and conceded no more license to the one than to the other. "Do you allow to the master of the house an intrigue with his slave-woman?" they asked. "Then, of course, you allow the mistress to consort with her man-slave? No? Yet you hold a man superior to a woman? Less able, then, to restrain his desires? Your position, you see, is untenable. If men claim superiority to women they must show themselves superior in self-control."

In an age of cruelty, widespread as it never was to be again, the Stoics declared the cruel man to be possessed by "a dreadful disease of the mind" which reached "the extreme of insanity when pleasure was felt in watching a human being die." Alone in the Roman world their voice was heard denouncing the centuries-old gladiatorial games.

They were alone, too, in teaching that a slave was to be treated as a human being. This insistence was the logical result of their belief in "the true Light, which lighteth every man that cometh into the world." Master and slave, by virtue of this sharing in common, became each a brother to the other. Perhaps it was here that their attitude stood out in sharpest contrast to that of their age. Rome saw in those days four hundred slaves at once led forth to die, men and women, young and old, because their master had been killed by one of them. The murderer was known, and even the brutal crowd in the streets was softened to pity at the sight of so many innocent people about to suffer death. But the senate refused mercy; an illustrious member stated that "those we have in our service are the scum of humanity collected from all quarters of the globe," and that the only way to keep them subject was to keep them in terror.

Precisely at this time Seneca was writing: "They are slaves,' people declare. Nay, they are men. Slaves? No, comrades." Epictetus followed, declaring that a slave is "your brother, who is sprung from God . . . of the same heavenly descent as you." The principle which became fundamental in Roman law, that all men are by nature equal, was derived, the historians agree, from the Stoics, and if Stoicism had no other claim to admiration, that alone would set it high among the great beneficient activities of the world.

How widespread the Stoics were is not known, but it is generally agreed that their numbers were large. If so, the fact speaks volumes for the strength of the Roman character, for Stoicism was a religion for the strong. It did not teach the practice of virtue as a means to eternal bliss, still less as a means to escape eternal misery. Tales, Seneca says, which represent the other world as terrible, are fiction. "There is no black darkness awaiting the dead, no lake of fire, . . . no renewal of the reign of tyrants." The Stoics fixed their attention on this earthly life. Goodness, here and now, was enough. The good man was the happy man whatever befell him, in death as in life. It was Seneca who said, "Virtue is its own reward." The Stoic asked for no other.

But always, consoling and strengthening, there was the consciousness of a divine presence and a divine purpose. "When you have shut your door and darkened your room," says Epictetus, "say not that you are alone. God is in your room." And Seneca writes: "God does not leave a good man in prosperity. He tries him, he strengthens him, he prepares him for himself." Therefore, knowing there is a purpose behind all, "I do not obey God—I agree with him. I follow him heart and soul, not because I must." "Is it God's will," asks Epictetus, "that I shall have a fever? It is my will too." And, as regards death, "To have God for our maker, father, guardian, should not that free us from all sadness and from all fear?" "Serenely take your leave," Marcus Aurelius writes, "serene as he who gives you your discharge."

So in latter-day Rome religion at its noblest confronted the utmost of depravity. The two streams seem not to have intermingled. The debased were not raised to a higher level by the presence among them of the great and good, and in the midst of vilest evil the Stoics never lowered their standard. Rome was a divided city, separated by a final division which cut deeper still than the old opposition between millionaire and pauper, autocrat and slave. Absolute good and absolute evil were arrayed against each other, with no conception of a principle of mediation between them. Vice was content, virtue too. The Stoic's creed armed the good man invulnerably against evil; it did not enlist him for active warfare upon the evil. The final view of ancient Rome given by her last great writers is of a state that has come to an inevitable standstill; progress is not possible.

# *C H A P T E R   XIII*

## THE END OF ANTIQUITY

THROUGHOUT the great days of the early Republic as they have come down to us in Polybius, in Livy, in Plutarch, in many an allusion in other writers, Rome was a nation perpetually at war. By the time Plautus was born she was absolute mistress of Italy, but the achievement took some five hundred years of fighting. Terence had been dead only a short time when the last Punic War made the Mediterranean a Roman sea. The east called next to the ever-moving, ever-growing power, and Cicero, fighting in Cilicia, was one of its instruments in extending Roman dominion far into Asia. Julius Caesar conquered the west and made Northern Africa a province of the empire. Horace's Rome was mistress from the Sahara to the Rhine and the Danube, from the Euphrates to the Atlantic.

"Keep the empire within its bounds" was the maxim Augustus bequeathed to his successors. The eight-hundred-years war of conquest was ended. The pioneer work of advancing against constantly opposing physical forces cannot in the nature of things go on forever. That task Rome had now completed. She had accomplished marvels; she had made the framework for a new world. A mightier task by far remained: to keep pace intellectually and spiritually with the enormous material advance, so as to be able to plan and build the new construction

461

which the new framework demanded. A vision and an understanding not needed before were now imperatively called for.

Caesar, it is possible, had both requisites and could have rebuilt the state, but Rome did not see that the old world had passed away, and he died in consequence. Augustus, taught by what Caesar had begun, understood the immediate needs of the present and established a system which worked efficiently for some centuries. But these two were Rome's only great constructive statesmen in her latter years. No other men were able to go forward with the march of events and meet new conditions with new provisions. On the contrary, all turned unanimously for help to the days of old. Go back to the virtues of our forefathers, the patriots cried, from Cicero on to the last martyrs for liberty in Tacitus' pages. The longing voiced by the whole of Latin literature is for a return to the times when Rome was simple and pious and able to bear hardship. All that men were able to do when confronted with difficulties such as never had been known before, was to look to the past, which always seems so good, so comprehensible, and try to apply to the baffling present the solutions of a life that was outgrown.

The old virtues were completely inadequate for the new day. The abilities of the pioneer and the conqueror, which had made the empire, could not meet the conditions which resulted from their achievements. To overcome nature or nations calls for one set of qualities; to use the victory as a basis for a better state in human affairs calls for another. When men must turn from extending their possessions to making wise use of them, audacity, self-reliance, endurance, are not enough. Individualism, whether of the road-builder in the wilderness or of the self-determined general in the field, must give way. It is suited only to the wilderness and the battlefield. After Rome's great victories had been won, the fruits of them could be gathered only by men working together. She had reached a point in her development when the good of the whole was bound up with the good of each man and the good of each man was bound up with the good of the whole, and the problem of achieving it was complicated far beyond the simple virtues of the simple man. Her first necessity was for intellectual and spiritual insight, for wisdom and disinterestedness.

What Rome was capable of, the achievement of her empire shows. The Roman character had great qualities, great potential strength. If the people had held together, realizing their interdependence and working for a common good, their problems, completely strange and enormously difficult though they were, would not, it may well be believed, have proved too much for them. But they were split into sharpest oppositions, extremes that ever grew more extreme and so more irresponsible. A narrow selfishness kept men blind when their own self-preservation demanded a world-wide outlook.

History repeats itself. The fact is a testimony to human stupidity. The saying has become a truism; nevertheless, the study of the past is relegated to the scholar and the school-boy. And yet it is really a chart for our guidance—no less than that. Where we now are going astray and losing ourselves, other men once did the same, and they left a record of the blind alleys they went down. We are like youth that can never learn from age—but youth is young, and wisdom is for the mature. We that are grown should not find it impossible to learn from the ages-old recorded experience of the past.

Our mechanical and industrial age is the only material achievement that can be compared with Rome's during the two thousand years in between. It is worth our while to perceive that the final reason for Rome's defeat was the failure of mind and spirit to rise to a new and great opportunity, to meet the challenge of new and great events. Material development outstripped human development; the Dark Ages took possession of Europe, and classical antiquity ended.

# CHRONOLOGY

753 B.C. Traditional date of founding of Rome.
266     Conquest of Italy to the Rubicon completed.
264–241 First Punic War.
218–201 Second Punic War.
184     Plautus died.
185–159 Traditional dates for Terence's birth and death.
167     Polybius brought to Rome.
149–146 Third Punic War and destruction of Carthage.
133–121 Tiberius and Caius Gracchus agitate reforms.
106     Cicero born.
102 or 100   Caesar born.
87      Catullus said to have been born; date uncertain.
82      Sulla dictator.
78      Sulla's death.
70      Virgil born.
65      Horace born.
63      Conspiracy of Catiline.
60      First Triumvirate—Caesar, Pompey, Crassus.
59      Livy born.
58–51   Conquest of Gaul by Caesar.
57      Catullus died. Again date conjectural.
49      War between Caesar and Pompey.
48      Pompey defeated at Pharsalus, flees to Egypt
        and there murdered.

| | |
|---|---|
| 44 | Assassination of Caesar. |
| 43 | Second Triumvirate—Octavius (Augustus), Antony, Lepidus. Cicero killed. |
| 42 | Battle of Philippi. Death of Brutus and Cassius. |
| 31 | Defeat of Antony in battle of Actium. Augustus sole ruler of empire. |
| 30 | Death of Antony and Cleopatra. |
| 19 | Virgil's death. |
| 8 | Horace's death. |
| 3(?) | Seneca born. |
| 14 A.D. | Death of Augustus |
| 17 | Livy's death. |
| 14–37 | Reign of Tiberius—extended law against high treason to include most trivial matters. Rewards given to informers. Suffocated when near death. |
| 37–41 | Caius (Caligula). At least half crazy. Murdered by soldiers. |
| 41–54 | Claudius, married Messalina, then Agrippina, who poisoned him after he had adopted her son, Nero. Tacitus probably born toward end of his reign. |
| 54–68 | Nero. Fled from uprising against him and killed himself just as soldiers arrived to execute him. End of the house of Caesar. |
| 65 | Seneca died by order of Nero. |
| 69 | The "Year of Three Emperors": Galba, killed by uprising of soldiers; Otho, killed himself after being defeated by Vitellius, who was in his turn killed by uprising of soldiers. |
| 69–79 | Vespasian. Good administrator. Capture of Jerusalem. Coliseum built. Vespasian succeeded by son. |
| 79–81 | Titus. Destruction of Herculaneum and Pompeii. Succeeded by his brother. |
| 81–96 | Domitian. Murdered by his freedman and his wife. |

96–180 The "Five Good Emperors": Nerva, Trajan, Hadrian, Antoninus Pius, Marcus Aurelius, each, from Nerva on, adopted by his predecessor.

Tacitus probably died during Trajan's reign, around 117. Juvenal known to be writing during Domitian's reign and probably died in Hadrian's reign, around 135. Epictetus born probably around 50 and died probably early in second century.

# REFERENCES

PAGE LINE

316   20   *Ad Att.* IV, 17. All quotations from Cicero's letters are taken from the admirable translation in the Loeb Classical Library.

317   17   Plutarch, *Caes.* According to Plutarch, Clodius was discovered, but Cicero says not.

319   16   *Ad Att.* I, 16.

321   17   *Q. Fr.* III, 9.

321   28   *Ad Att.* II, 95.

325   1   *Ad Att.* II, 15.

325   11   *Ad Att.* XII, 9.

326   26   Ib., VII, 8.

326   32   Ib., II, 25.

327   3   Ib., I, 14.

327   13   *Ad Fam.* IX, 16.

327   21   *Ad Att.* II, 25.

327   26   Ib., II, 19.

328   2   Ib., XIV, 18.

328   16   Ib., XIV, 13.

328   25   Ib., XIV, 9.

329   17   Ib., VI, 9.

| PAGE | LINE | |
|------|------|---|
| 330 | 2 | Ib., I, 8. |
| 330 | 8 | *Q. Fr.* III, 1. |
| 330 | 30 | *Ad Att.* IV, 4a. |
| 331 | 1 | *Ad Fam.* VII, 1. |
| 331 | 29 | Ib., VIII, 14. |
| 332 | 3 | *Ad Att.* VI, 1. |
| 332 | 13 | *Ad Fam.* IX, 22. |
| 332 | 23 | Ib., IX, 26. |
| 332 | 26 | Ib., IX, 20. |
| 333 | 4 | Ib., XIV, 1. |
| 333 | 12 | Ib., XIV, 20. |
| 333 | 20 | *Ad Att.* XII, 32. |
| 333 | 35 | *Ad Fam.* IV, 6. |
| 334 | 1 | *Ad Att.* XII, 15. |
| 334 | 11 | Ib., XVI, 15. |
| 334 | 12 | Ib., X, 10. |
| 334 | 23 | *Ad Fam.* VIII, 1. |
| 334 | 33 | *Ad Att.* III, 8. |
| 334 | 37 | Ib., VI, 2. |
| 334 | 39 | Ib., XV, 26. |
| 335 | 6 | Ib., XV, 11. |
| 335 | 23 | Ib., XV, 12. |
| 335 | 27 | Ib., XVI, 11. |
| 335 | 33 | *Ad Fam.* IX, 20. |
| 336 | 4 | *Ad Att.* XV, 15. |
| 337 | 20 | *Caes. B. G.* II end. |
| 338 | 10 | Ib., I, 38. |
| 339 | 22 | *Ad Fam.* VII, 15. |
| 339 | 28 | *De Am.* XXIII. |
| 339 | 34 | *Ad Fam.* XVI, 5, 6. |
| 340 | 14 | *Ad Att.* II, 9. |
| 340 | 19 | Ib., II, 18. |
| 341 | 4 | Ib., II, 20. |
| 341 | 22 | *Ad Att.* IX, 10. |

| PAGE | LINE | |
|------|------|---|
| 368 | 3 | Ib., XCII. |
| 368 | 12 | Ib., CIX. |
| 369 | 7 | Ib., LXVIII*b*. |
| 369 | 32 | Ib., LXXXV. |
| 370 | 1 | Ib., LXX. |
| 370 | 6 | Ib., LXXII. |
| 370 | 24 | Ib., LXXV. |
| 370 | 35 | Ib., VIII. |
| 371 | 35 | Ib., CI. |
| 372 | 20 | Ib., CVII. |
| 373 | 6 | Ib., LXXVI. |
| 373 | 37 | Ib., LVIII. |
| 378 | 6 | *Serm.* II, 1, 1. |
| 384 | 31 | *Carm.* IV, 2, 5, 25. |
| 385 | 2 | Ib., III, 30. |
| 385 | 29 | *Serm.* I, 6, 115. |
| 386 | 21 | Ib., II, 6, 1. |
| 386 | 26 | *Carm.* II, 18, 1. |
| 386 | 30 | Ib., I, 31. |
| 388 | 1 | *Ep.* I, 18, 106. |
| 390 | 10 | *Carm.* III, 6, 16. |
| 390 | 14 | Ib., III, 15, 1. |
| 390 | 19 | Ib., III, 4, 65. |
| 390 | 23 | Ib., III, 5, 46. |
| 392 | 14 | *Ep.* I, 6, 6. |
| 392 | 16 | Ib., II, 2, 180. |
| 392 | 24 | *Ser.* II, 6, 27. |
| 393 | 23 | *Ep.* II, 2, 72. |
| 394 | 22 | *Ep.* I, 6, 37. |
| 395 | 19 | Ib., I, 17 and 18. |
| 397 | 14 | *Serm.* II, 3, 151. |
| 397 | 12 | Ib., II, 3, 94. |
| 397 | 21 | But Aristophanes shows the fashion is beginning: *Wasps* 1212. |

PAGE  LINE

397   36   *Ser.* II, 2, 26.

398   11   Ib., II, 8 and 4.

398   33   *Ser.* II, 76.

399    7   *Ep.* I, 5, 22.

400    1   *Serm.* I, 5, 51.

401    7   Ib., II, 6, 73.

401   32   *Serm.* II, 6, 44.

401   38   Ib., I, 3, 81.

402    5   Ib., I, 3, 10.

403   18   Ib., II, 65.

404   27   *Ep.* II, 1, 185.

406    1   *Aen.* I, 278.

407   32   Lucian, Demonax 57 (quoted by Magnin, *Origines du Théatre*).

407   36   *Philostr. Apollon.* vit. IV, 22 (Magnin, *op. cit.*).

408    2   Xiph. LXIX, 8.

408    3   Suet. *Tit.* 7.

408    7   Mart. VIII, 26.

408   22   Xiph. LXVIII, 8.

408   25   Mart. I, 6.

408   27   Xiph. LXXII, 22.

408   34   Suet. *Claud.* 21.

409    6   Lactant. *De Mort. Pers.* 21 (quoted by Magnin, *op. cit.*).

420    6   *Noct. Att.* XVII, 8.

423   34   Ib., XVII, 7.

424   15   *Georg.* I, 1.

424   35   Ib., II, 323.

425   23   Ib., III, 440*ff.*

425   32   Ib., 235.

426   26   *Iliad*, XVIII, 370.

426   38   *Aen.* VIII, 415.

428    6   *Iliad*, III, 399.

PAGE LINE

428  27  *Aen.* IV, 1.

428  29  Ib., 75.

428  34  Ib., 80.

428  35  Ib., 129*ff*.

429  26  Ib., 314.

430  2  *Odys.* IV, 120.

433  8  Aen. I, 92.

433  12  *Odys.* V, 306.

433  28  *Aen.* VI, 823.

438  19  Eurip., *Troiad*, 98 (Gilbert Murray, *tr.*)

438  34  Sen. *Troad*, 1*ff*.

439  21  Eurip., *op. cit.*, 632.

439  27  Ib., 288.

439  32  Sen., *op. cit.*, 62.

440  4  Eurip., *op. cit.*, 725.

440  24  Eurip., *op. cit.*, 740.

441  5  Sen., *op. cit.*, 419.

441  32  Eurip., *op. cit.*, 1173.

445  31  There are only three personal references. Sat. III, 319; XI, 65; XV, 45.

445  39  Sat. V, 80.

446  16  Ib., VII, 150, 222.

447  1  Ib., X, 26.

447  3  Ib., I, 71.

447  5  Ib., 155.

447  6  Ib., 77.

447  9  Ib., II, 8.

447  10  Ib., II, 132.

447  11  Ib., IV, 110.

447  14  Ib., I, 73.

450  17  Ib., VII, 62.

450  35  Agric. VIII.

451  31  Ann. III, 65.

452  8  Ib., XV, 71.

**PAGE  LINE**

452    **12**   Ib., 74.

452    **20**   Ib., IV, 69.

453     **1**   Ib., XIV, 5.

453     **3**   Ib., XI, 26.

453    **14**   Ib., XIII, 71.

453    **20**   Ib., XIV, 1.

454     **4**   Ib., XIII, 5.

454    **33**   Sen. *Ep.* 41, 5.

454    **39**   *Marc. Aur.* II, 5.

455     **9**   Epict. *Disc.* I, 16.

458     **3**   Condensed from Stob III, 6, 23 (quoted by Arnold, *Roman Stoicism*).

458    **12**   Sen. *Clem.* I, 25, 3.

458    **24**   Tac. *Ann.* XIV, 42.

458    **34**   Sen. *Ep.* VI, 47.

459    **12**   Sen. *Dial.* VI, 19, 4.

459    **23**   Ib., I, 4, 7.

459    **26**   Sen. *Ep.* 96, 2.

459    **28**   Epict. *Disc.* IV, 1, 89 (quoted by Arnold, *op. cit.*).

459    **30**   *Arrian* Epict. I, 9.